Success in British History since 1914

Success in British History since 1914

Success Studybooks

Accounting and Costing
Accounting and Costing: Problems and Projects
Biology
British History 1760–1914
British History since 1914
Business Calculations
Chemistry
Commerce
Commerce: West African Edition
Economic Geography
Economics
Economics: West African Edition
Electronics
Elements of Banking
European History 1815–1941
Financial Accounting
Financial Accounting: Questions and Answers
Geography: Human and Regional
Geography: Physical and Mapwork
Investment
Law
Management: Personnel
Mathematics
Nutrition
Organic Chemistry
Principles of Accounting
Principles of Accounting: Answer Book
Statistics
Twentieth Century World Affairs

Success in
BRITISH HISTORY
SINCE 1914

Jack B. Watson, M.A.

John Murray

© Jack Watson 1983

First published 1983
by John Murray (Publishers) Ltd
50 Albemarle Street, London W1X 4BD

Typeset by Inforum Ltd, Portsmouth
Printed in Hong Kong
by Wing King Tong Co. Ltd.

British Library Cataloguing in Publication Data

Watson, Jack B.
    Success in British history since 1914.
    1. Great Britain—History—20th century
    I. Title
    941.082   DA566

ISBN 0-7195-3924-2

Foreword

This book aims primarily to achieve two things. The first is to trace the change and transformation which characterize British history since 1914, at the same time keeping hold of the essential continuity in the country's surviving traditions. The text covers not only the political and diplomatic developments but has much to say about the economy and about changes in society. Its treatment is therefore wide-ranging.

The second purpose is to assist the student of the period to some understanding of the events of the recent past, not least in considering causes and consequences, and to develop his abilities as a student of history. *Success in British History since 1914* is particularly appropriate for students at O level and equivalent examinations, and as introductory reading for A level, first-year degree courses and similar examinations in further and higher education. It contains numerous aids to study, from extensive cross-referencing and indexing to varied exercises and lists of further reading. The text is not meant to be seen merely as material to be learned, however. Almost all history is controversial and none more so than that of Britain in the twentieth century. While providing essential factual material, the book also suggests interpretations, but, above all, it encourages readers to arrive at their own conclusions. With practice, the student can become skilled in the use of cross references, tables, figures, the Glossary and Index, and can approach each new Unit with a growing appreciation of the important differences between evidence and assertion, generalization and example. The book continues to the present day and will therefore be useful to students of a variety of subjects where Britain's recent history may be illuminating, and to the general reader who seeks to be informed about the nation's affairs.

J.B.W.

Acknowledgments

That this book was not only begun but has been completed to the present day owes a great deal to the help and encouragement that I have had from colleagues and friends, and I am happy to record my debt to them. First and foremost I must thank Margaret Watson, my wife, for her innumerable contributions to the sections on Britain's economy, where she has offered lucid explanations of many tangled issues and has shown unflagging zeal in searching out statistical and other evidence. Ed Rayner has once again read my drafts with painstaking thoroughness, making constructive criticisms too many to detail. Bernard Seaman and Angela Kent have similarly given me the benefit of their expertise and advice, sparing no effort to make this book a better work than it would otherwise have been. I am also grateful to Carolyn Nichols for her careful editing of the text, and to Helen Syme of the Success Studybooks series for her work in preparing the book for publication, in particular in finding the illustrations. In the end, however, all historical writing involves selection and personal judgment and all those mentioned above must be exempted from blame for whatever faults remain in this book. The reader must judge how successfully the author has led him through the minefield that is British history since 1914.

J.B.W.

We are grateful to the following for their kind assistance in providing illustrations:

Associated Newspapers Group (Figs. 9.2(a), 11.2, 12.8, 15.1, 15.5), Associated Press (Fig. 20.3); BBC Hulton Picture Library (Figs. 2.1, 2.4, 4.3, 5.3, 5.4, 6.3, 6.6, 6.7, 7.1, 7.2, 7.3(a) and (b), 7.4, 8.1(a), 9.3, 10.1, 10.2, 10.3, 19.3); the British Library (Fig. 1.1); British Steel Corporation (Fig. 16.2); Camera Press London (Fig. 9.5(b)); Central Press Photos Ltd. (Figs. 5.2, 18.6); Conservative Research Department (Fig. 3.7); the *Daily Express* (Figs. 3.2, 3.6, 5.1, 6.1, 20.6); Fox Photos Ltd. (Fig. 7.6(a)); Freightliners Ltd. (Fig. 16.4); Greater London Council Photographic Library (Fig. 18.4); the *Guardian* (Table 21.2); Ian Berry, John Hillelson Agency Ltd. (Fig. 14.6); IBM United Kingdom Ltd. (Fig. 16.1); the *Illustrated London News* (Fig. 2.5); Imperial War Museum (Figs. 1.3, 1.5, 4.2, 12.2); John Frost Newspaper Library (Fig.

Contents

List of Maps

List of Tables

Unit One

The First World War

1.1 Into the Abyss

Britain and Germany went to war at 11 pm on 4 August 1914. The first shots had been fired a week earlier, on the continent of Europe, when Austria-Hungary declared war on Serbia, and the guns would not be silent now for more than four years. The First World War spread remorselessly, from Europe to the oceans, and to the overseas possessions of the belligerents. Few nations escaped it. Japan was involved from the outset, as an ally of Britain. In 1917 the USA too became involved. Before the war ended it had taken the lives of some eight-and-a-half million men, about 15 per cent of those mobilized in the belligerents' armed forces. Much of Europe was devastated, and much that had characterized it before the war had gone for ever when peace returned at last in November 1918.

At first sight it would seem that Britain went to war to honour an earlier promise to defend Belgium, which the Germans invaded on 3 August in their eagerness to strike at France. However, Britain's relations with Germany had been strained for some time. As the then industrial giants of Europe, Britain and Germany competed in various ways: for markets and economic pre-eminence; for naval superiority; for colonies; and for prestige. Since 1907 Britain had had *ententes* (friendly understandings) with France and Russia, thus drawing closer to Germany's continental rivals in opposition to the Dual Alliance of Germany and Austria-Hungary. British and German newspapers stirred feelings of mutual hostility, yet the British public was far from being united in enthusiasm for any military confrontation with the Germans – until the invasion of Belgium.

There had been no major international conflict in Europe for almost a hundred years before 1914 and, in spite of often fierce international competition, it seemed normal that crises would be defused by negotiations and compromise. Hopes ran high in 1914 that the latest crisis in the Balkans, between Austria-Hungary and Serbia, would end in similar compromise. Instead the Austrians issued an ultimatum, and then declared war. Germany clearly encouraged its partner in the Dual Alliance, Russia hastened to help Serbia and France honoured its obligations to Russia. The British hesitated, but opinion hardened when German troops entered Belgium. Almost over-night, war suddenly became 'necessary'. A flood of volunteers rushed to serve their King and Country, and the British government therefore had no need to conscript men into the forces until February 1916.

The war divided Europe fairly evenly. Britain fought alongside France, Belgium, Serbia and Russia – the Allies – and they were also later supported by Italy and Rumania. Against them were ranged Germany and Austria-Hungary – the Central Powers – who were joined by the Turkish Empire and Bulgaria. When the British government declared war, it did so on behalf of the entire British Empire, so that the Dominions (such as Canada) and dependencies (such as India and Jamaica) were also involved. Japan and, eventually, the USA and China, added further strength to the Allies, so that the Central Powers finally faced overwhelming opposition.

For millions in Britain, the aim of the war was to liberate Belgium. The expectation that this could be achieved in time for the troops to return home by Christmas 1914 was soon shattered. The liberation of Belgium remained a key objective, but the horrors of trench warfare and a growing hatred of the enemy demanded further and grander objectives. By January 1918 Lloyd George said the war must bring about:

> a great attempt . . . to establish by some international organization an alternative to war as a means of settling international disputes.

And he wanted, for Europe, 'genuine self-government on true democratic principles'. Woodrow Wilson, the President of the USA, had already told Congress that 'the world must be made safe for democracy'.

There were real ideological differences between the Allies and the Central Powers. Britain, France, Belgium and the USA had long practised parliamentary government and proclaimed the virtues of liberalism. The Central Powers, on the other hand, had remained more authoritarian in their government. They had more obviously influential high-born elites and deeper class divisions. In Germany the political and social structures appeared to go hand-in-hand with militarism. The Austro-Hungarian and Turkish Empires were also multinational: their governments ruled uneasily over peoples of differing nationalities. Britain, France and the states of western Europe were 'nation states', seemingly more modern. They too ruled multinational empires, but these empires were overseas and were thought somehow to be different. The Allies alleged that the Central Powers were out of date, politically, socially and in their mixtures of nationalities. The First World War thus became a war for democracy, for liberal values, for the freedom of subject peoples, for 'progress'; and it became, moreover, 'a war to end wars'.

For the soldiers in the blood-soaked trenches of the Western Front, the war seemed to mark only the end of civilization. Europe had plunged into the abyss, carrying with it the continent's young men. Wilfred Owen wrote of many when he described 'Jimmie', who had already 'seen some scrappin' ':

> But poor young Jim, 'e's livin' an' 'e's not:
> 'E reckoned 'e'd five chances, an' 'e 'ad;

'E's wounded, killed, and pris'ner, all the lot,
The bloody lot all rolled in one. Jim's mad.

Owen also wrote that he had enjoyed comradeship, exultation and laughter with his dead fellow-soldiers, but to those who survived them he had this to say:

You shall not hear their mirth:
You shall not come to think them well content
By any jest of mine. These men are worth
Your tears. You are not worth their merriment.

The conflict killed, maimed and scarred a whole generation. It would not be enough, when the war ended, if the statesmen merely uttered fine phrases and tried to redraw the map of Europe in the name of 'progress'. British society itself would have to be re-examined. On the day of the armistice in 1918 the Lord Mayor of Birmingham told his audience:

Today is the greatest day in the history of our country, and it marks the beginning of a new era in human development. . . . We must . . . use this great opportunity aright so that the world may be better and not worse by reason of the overthrow of the old order.

Two weeks later, seeking re-election as Britain's Prime Minister, Lloyd George found more memorable words:

What is our task? To make Britain a fit country for heroes to live in.

Their optimism seemed to be reasonably well founded. Britain had been the most prosperous country in Europe throughout the nineteenth century, and victory had now been achieved. The history of Britain after 1918, however, was to disappoint the hopes of millions.

1.2 Britain in 1914

(a) The Economy
Long before the end of the nineteenth century Britain had become an industrial nation, whose well-being depended heavily on the exporting of manufactured goods. The industrial revolution had given the country a head start in the mass-production of textiles, in the metal industries, in mining and in railway building. In 1840 Britain commanded some 32 per cent of total world trade, and it was already establishing a reputation as 'the world's workshop'. A generation later well over half the nation's foodstuffs were imported and, by the end of the century, agriculture contributed only 15 per cent to national wealth and employed only 10 per cent of the nation's population, the lowest percentage in Europe. It did, however, remain an important sector of the British economy.

Average incomes rose significantly in Britain in the century before 1914, in spite of temporary setbacks and periodic slumps in the trade cycle. Since wages generally kept ahead of rising prices, the rise in incomes represented a real improvement in the standard of living. The average income in 1914 was the highest in Europe at about £550 pa, just ahead of France (*c*. £530) and Germany (*c*. £500), but below the average in the USA (*c*. £750). But these statistics are misleading. The incomes of the vast majority were well below this 'average', since incomes were unevenly distributed. The 'average' was exaggerated because of the large incomes of a minority. Table 1.1, however, shows that Britain's economic lead was already being eroded by 1914. Its *share* of world trade was shrinking, although rapid increases in the volume of world trade meant that the *volume* of British trade was still growing. More worrying was the slowing down of Britain's *rate of growth*: the Gross Domestic Product (GDP) in Britain rose at only 1.1 per cent a year after 1899, whereas it had risen at some 2 per cent a year during the second half of the nineteenth century. It seemed that Britain was slowing down while rivals, such as Germany and the USA, were expanding steadily. Solid foundations for British prosperity had been laid during the industrial revolution, but there was now a danger that Britain might be left with old and uncompetitive machinery, when its rivals were busily equipping more up-to-date plant.

There were other reasons for disquiet. Before the end of the nineteenth century many of Britain's trading competitors had abandoned free trade in favour of protective tariffs, taxing imports and encouraging home manufacturers. British voters emphatically rejected such a policy in the general election

Table 1.1   Industry and trade before 1914

(*a*) *Manufacturing: Britain and Germany, 1911*

Country	Population (millions)	Cotton spindlage (millions)*	Railway track (miles)	Output (million metric tons)		
				Coal	Pig iron	Steel
Britain†	45	55.6	24 000	269	10	7.5
Germany	65	10.9	32 000	222	15	13

* 1913
† including Ireland

(*b*) *World trade*

	Total value	Percentage shares		
		Britain	Germany	USA
1900	£4 000 000 000	21	12	11
1913	£8 000 000 000	17	12	11

of 1906, and continued to believe they could enjoy untaxed imports from abroad and pay for them almost effortlessly with British goods and services. It became less easy, however, to sell British goods abroad. Even in the early nineteenth century the value of Britain's imports was almost always higher than that of its exports. In 1876 the gap between the two widened to more than £100 million and, in 1913, it stood at £146 million. Nevertheless, there was still an overall surplus on the balance of payments in the years before 1914, because Britain had a substantial income from 'invisible exports' (the earnings of the merchant navy, the interest on investments abroad and the profits of such activities as international banking and insurance). In 1913 invisible earnings enabled the nation to produce a surplus of some £200 million, in spite of the excess of imports over visible exports. But the pattern was already fixed: Britain would demand far more foreign imports than could be paid for merely by exported goods, and the policy of free trade did nothing to check this drain on the economy.

(b) Society

In 1914 almost half Britain's labour force was employed in industry and mining, with a further quarter working in trade and transport. Industrialization and the expansion of business had led to extensive urbanization. Millions already lived in large conurbations: the population of London was over four-and-a-half million, Glasgow had already reached one million, Birmingham, Liverpool and Manchester each had over 700 000 inhabitants, while Edinburgh, Leeds and Sheffield were each approaching half a million. The large number of people employed in domestic and personal service was one distinctive characteristic of British society at this time – more than 450 000 men and over two million women in 1914, the largest proportion of any work force in Europe – and even in the 1920s they continued to account for 13 per cent of the British labour force (see Table 1.2).

Unemployment was an all-too-familiar hazard for the British working classes. Average unemployment ran at about 5 per cent of the labour force in the half-century before 1914, but the percentage rose sharply in times of recession. It climbed twice to well above 5 per cent in the years 1900 to 1914, and the period 1908–9 was particularly bad: more than 12 per cent of the members of engineering and shipbuilding unions were without work, and more than 11 per cent of carpenters. Unemployment, ill health and old age were common causes of poverty among the lower classes, whose wages when in work permitted little saving. Charles Booth began in 1889 to publish his findings in a survey of *The Life and Labour of the People of London*. He found that a third of London's population lived in poverty on earnings of not more than £1 a week. Seebohm Rowntree made a study of York ten years later and found a similar situation. Bowley and Burnett-Hurst reported that conditions were no better in 1914, when they studied towns such as Warrington and Reading. What this meant for the millions of Britain's poor was summed up by one woman in York, who told Rowntree:

If there's anything extra to buy, such as a pair of boots for one of the children, me and the children goes without dinner.

Vast numbers of the poor lived in slum housing, mice-infested and with leaking roofs, and sometimes close to noisome cess-pits.

As yet the state interfered little in the lives of the people. The prevailing philosophy of nineteenth-century Britain was *laissez-faire*, or non-intervention. The nation's housing was provided by private landlords; its businesses were those of private enterprise. The upper and middle classes professed the ideals of liberalism, priding themselves on their freedom to advance themselves by initiative, thrift and self-help. For the poor, the price of this advancement often had to be paid in long hours, low wages and sub-standard housing. By 1914 the lower classes (often with middle-class leaders) had begun to organize themselves, both in trade unions and in parliament, where the Labour Party

Table 1.2 Some of the main occupations of British workers, 1911 and 1921 (thousands)

	1911	1921
Total labour force	18 340	19 355
Male workers	12 927	13 656
Female workers	5 413	5 699
Male occupations		
Metal manufacturing, engineering	1 795	2 125
Transport, communications	1 571	1 530
Agriculture, forestry	1 436	1 344
Mining, quarrying	1 202	1 240
Building, construction	1 140	894
Textiles, clothing	1 061	724
Food, drink, tobacco	806	228
Domestic, personal services	456	371
Female occupations		
Domestic, personal services	2 127	1 845
Textiles, clothing	1 014	822
Food, drink, tobacco	825	602
Professional occupations, services	383	441
Metal manufacturing, engineering	128	175

(based on the Census Reports)

Source: most of the statistics in this section are taken from Mitchell, B.R. and Deane, P.: *Abstract of British Historical Statistics*. Cambridge University Press (Cambridge, 1962).

already had some MPs. The Liberal government showed some awareness of existing social problems and working-class grievances. In the years 1908–11 means-tested old-age pensions were introduced at the age of seventy, labour exchanges were established and national insurance schemes were launched against ill health and, on a limited scale, against unemployment. But these were little more than beginnings in the long struggle to build a more equal and fairer society. For the masses, life in 1914 was still a life of toil for small rewards.

Inequality and injustice already threatened to bring disruption. Trade unions had gained important legal rights in the 1870s, including the right to strike and to picket, and their membership was growing steadily. In 1914 about three million workers belonged to some 1 200 unions, and numerous bitter confrontations had already occurred between unions and the authorities. The recession of 1908–9 was followed by increased union militancy. There were over 500 industrial disputes in 1910, more than 1 400 in 1913; forty million working days were lost through disputes in 1912, more than eleven million in 1913. A stoppage on the railways around Newcastle in 1910 was followed by confrontation in the Lancashire cotton industry, a fourteen-week stoppage in the shipyards and strife in the coalfields of South Wales, which led to violence at Tonypandy. Seamen, firemen, dockers, railwaymen and miners were among those involved in 1911, when two deaths occurred in Liverpool. Miners, dockers and transport workers were involved in 1912 and, a year later, the unions of miners, railwaymen and other transport workers combined to form the Triple Industrial Alliance to win concessions for the workers. The testing of this Alliance was postponed by the war; and the unions were already under criticism from those labour leaders who thought more could be achieved by pressure in parliament than by industrial conflict. The veteran socialist Keir Hardie, the Labour MP for Merthyr Tydfil, wrote in 1912:

> The effect of the transport workers' strike of this year has been disastrous, and has shown more than anything else could have done the futility of trying to fight the capitalists by what are known as Syndicalist methods (see Glossary).

Indeed, industrial action brought few gains to the workers in this period, but the labour movement was regularly to debate in the future whether strikes or the election of Labour MPs might do more to reshape society in the interests of the masses.

Militant suffragettes were another group who clamoured for the rights of the underprivileged in pre-1914 Britain, attacking a male-dominated society and demanding for women the right to vote. Like the protests of trade unionists, their campaigns were usually peaceful, but anger and frustration led to some violence. There was an attempt to blow up the Coronation Chair in Westminster Abbey. Some suffragettes set fire to churches, railway stations and Scottish castles. The government remained unmoved and, although progress had been made in local government, women were still debarred from national politics in 1914. It was obvious, however, that Britain's liberal and parliamentary state was failing to fulfil the aspirations of the masses and the under-privileged. By 1914 government was beginning, on a modest scale, to concern itself with the regulation of society – with the welfare of the masses, the grievances of organized labour and the redistribution of wealth – but winning the war became a higher priority, and the reshaping of British society had to wait for victory.

(c) The Constitution and Politics

Whatever its shortcomings, the British constitution in 1914 was one of the most liberal in the world. The majority of adult males, about eight million of them, elected the members of the House of Commons, voting by secret ballot in mainly single-member constituencies. The convention had long been accepted that the majority party in the Commons had the right to form the government. The Crown was little more than a figurehead, and authority rested chiefly with the Prime Minister and his Cabinet, based on their support in the House of Commons. Constitutional changes in 1911 had reduced the power of the unelected House of Lords to obstruct legislation which the Commons supported, depriving the Lords of control over 'money bills' and only allowing them to delay other bills for about two years. At the same time, the interval between general elections had been fixed at a maximum of five years and, in a separate act, members of the Commons gained a salary of £400 pa. This would allow men without private means to sit if they were elected. A crude but effective electoral system meant that the candidate with most votes in any constituency was automatically elected, even without an overall majority (see Glossary: Voting). This usually ensured that there was no need for a coalition government. Traditionally governments were formed by either the Conservatives or the Liberals.

   Table 1.3 shows the results of three twentieth-century general elections in the years before 1914. After the election of 1906 Britain had a Liberal government, led from 1908 by Asquith. The two elections in 1910 were the result of a constitutional crisis about the power of the House of Lords, which had recklessly rejected Lloyd George's People's Budget of the previous year; the constitutional changes of 1911 resulted from these elections. The Liberals had lost their overall majority, but they remained the governing party with the goodwill of Labour and Irish Nationalist MPs. It was the Liberal government, therefore, which led Britain into war in 1914.

   The election of 1906 had seen a substantial shift of support from the Conservatives to the Liberals. It was the result partly of a desire for change, after ten years of Conservative rule, and partly of the electorate's anxiety to continue with free trade, whereas a section of the Conservative Party was advocating protectionism under the name of Tariff Reform. The Conservatives were descended from the Tories, and traditionally associated with landowning, the Church of England, the preservation of the country's institutions and the protection of its overseas empire. Their Unionist allies were for maintaining the Union with Ireland, against the demand of the Irish Nationalists for a separate Irish parliament. The Conservatives liked to think that a natural

Fig. 1.1 Newspaper publicity for the suffragettes, 1908: the scene in court at Bow Street, London, when Christabel Pankhurst, from the dock, questioned Lloyd George, Chancellor of the Exchequer, during the resumed hearing of the charge against suffragette leaders of inciting to riot. Mrs Emmeline Pankhurst (extreme left) and her daughter Christabel founded the Women's Social and Political Union in 1903

Table 1.3 General elections pre-1914

Date	Conservatives and Unionists	Liberals	Labour	Irish Nationalists
1906	157	**377***	53†	83
January 1910	273	**275**	40	82
December 1910	272	**272**	42	84

* bold: the governing party
† includes 24 Lib-Labs, initially returned as Liberals

alliance existed between their Party and the labouring poor, continuing something of the medieval squire–tenant relationship, with its sense of mutual obligations and mutual respect.

The Liberals were descended from the Whigs. Broadly speaking, if the Conservatives wished to conserve, the Liberals wished to liberalize. Their traditional links were with religious nonconformism and free-thought, with the professional classes, small businessmen and private enterprise. They were passionately devoted to free trade and had a record of support for constitutional reform. But, like all British parties, the Liberals covered a wide range of opinions: their right wing differed little from the Conservatives, while their left wing embraced radicals like Lloyd George, aspiring to be a man of the people and disrespectful of such ancient institutions as the House of Lords. Radical Liberals were quick to rail against injustices, and the Liberals could sometimes appear as crusaders. Gladstone had crusaded for Irish Home Rule, for instance, but the weight of opposition had been too much for him. The Irish problem remained unsolved in 1914 and the bill to set up an Irish parliament, which was due to be implemented that year, having been delayed by the House of Lords, was postponed when war broke out (see Unit 4.4).

Before 1906 the Liberal Party was the virtually unchallenged alternative to the Conservative Party – in theory, the party of change as an alternative to the party of stability. What was new in the parliament elected in 1906 was the number of Labour members. In 1900 socialists in search of a more egalitarian society and trade unionists in search of better conditions for the workers had concluded that neither Liberals nor Conservatives properly represented the labouring poor. They set up the Labour Representation Committee, but were disappointed when only two of their fifteen candidates, Keir Hardie and Richard Bell, won election. Six years later, they fared better. Some LRC candidates were able to make local anti-Conservative pacts with the Liberals, and twenty-nine LRC men were elected to the Commons, under the leadership of Hardie. Almost at once the LRC label was simplified and the name 'Labour Party' was adopted. Soon afterwards, the Party won the affiliation of the Miners' Federation of Great Britain (the MFGB), and gained the support of the MFGB's Lib-Lab MPs to command, in all, fifty-three seats in the House of

Commons. By 1914 the Labour Party was an established minority group in British politics, but its support in the country was largely confined to parts of London, South Wales, Clydeside and the industrial north of England.

The aims of the Party were not entirely clear, although it demanded broad reform in the interests of the masses. Ramsay MacDonald, previously the Party Secretary, became the leader of the Parliamentary Labour Party in 1911. On the outbreak of war, which greatly troubled him, he surrendered the office to Arthur Henderson, but he returned as leader in 1922. The Party would certainly not be revolutionary in MacDonald's hands. He rejected Hardie's enthusiasm for a class war, and proclaimed his own belief in 'the growth of society'. He seemed to see the Labour Party as the reforming successor to the Liberal Party, for he had written in 1905:

> Socialism, the stage which follows Liberalism, retains everything of permanent value that was in Liberalism by virtue of its being the hereditary heir of Liberalism.

His assertion contained something of a forecast, since the decline of the Liberals and the upsurge of the Labour Party were to be features of postwar British politics. The Labour vote was to grow from half a million in January 1910 to well over two million in the general election of 1918.

1.3 Britain at War

(a) The Political Direction

Asquith recorded in his diary on 4 August 1914 that:

> the House (of Commons) took the fresh news today very calmly and with a good deal of dignity.

His government entered the war with a similar calmness and dignity: it blandly assumed that the civilian population would carry on as usual, and that the war would create little disturbance at home. Winston Churchill had been appointed to the Admiralty in 1911, and the navy was quickly made ready for action. An Expeditionary Force was ready too, created as one of Haldane's recent reforms at the War Office. It was speedily dispatched to the continent, and before the end of the month played a vital part in delaying the German advance at Mons. Haldane had left the War Office in 1912 and Kitchener, a veteran of earlier colonial wars, now took over. Otherwise the government changed hardly at all, and it was not until May 1915 that Asquith broadened it into a coalition, when he brought in Bonar Law, the leader of the Conservatives, and Balfour, a former leader; Arthur Henderson, the Labour leader, took charge of the Board of Education. The coalition took a rather more urgent view of the nation's war needs, and Lloyd George, as the Minister of Munitions, turned his considerable energies to the production of armaments.

On the Western Front, in Belgium and northern France, the war had already settled down to the stalemate of trench warfare. The death toll mounted. A search for new ideas resulted in an expedition to Gallipoli, to open a new front and to force a supply route through the Dardanelles to Britain's Russian ally. The attempt failed. It produced only new slaughter and led to a masterly evacuation at the end of 1915. In 1916 the Battle of Jutland failed to produce a victory for the British fleet, and on the Western Front a new offensive on the Somme brought heavy casualties and further disappointment in the summer and autumn of that year. Such frustration led to mounting dissatisfaction with Asquith's calm and dignified leadership and, encouraged by the press, the feeling grew that a more exciting figure was needed to lead the nation in its struggle.

Lloyd George seemed the most obvious man for the job. A fiery Welshman with a gift for mass oratory, the scourge of the House of Lords and author of Britain's national insurance schemes before 1914, he had distinguished himself in conjuring up munitions for the troops and, unlike Churchill, had cleverly avoided discredit for the Gallipoli campaign. In July 1916 he had become Secretary for War, after Kitchener was drowned on his way to visit Russia. The legend persisted that Lloyd George was 'a man of the people'. He had far more of a talent than Asquith for rousing popular enthusiasm, though he was also talented in making enemies. Baldwin was later to refer disparagingly to him as 'a dynamic force'; but given the continuing and unavailing slaughter, it seemed that Britain had need of such a force.

Matters came to a head in December 1916. Lloyd George proposed a small war council under his own leadership, to give new direction and inject energy into the war effort. Asquith and the Liberal leadership resented this attack on their authority. Most Conservatives sympathized with them in their dislike of the Welsh upstart, but Bonar Law was inclined to favour a change. Lloyd George resigned, and his cause might have been lost; but Asquith too resigned, confident that the King would have to recall him to lead the nation. Instead George V invited Bonar Law to form a government, but Bonar Law insisted that Asquith must serve in it, and Asquith insisted that he would serve in no government but his own. The King turned to Lloyd George, who promptly won the support of Henderson and almost the whole of the Parliamentary Labour Party. Bonar Law brought him the support of many of the Conservatives, and others followed, eventually. The Liberals, Lloyd George's own party, were seriously divided. Edward Grey, the Foreign Secretary for the past eleven years, and most of the leading Liberals stood by Asquith, implacably opposed to what they regarded as the Welshman's treachery, but Christopher Addison led a substantial number of lesser Liberals to desert them.

Lloyd George took office as Prime Minister on 7 December at the head of a tiny War Cabinet of five, which included Bonar Law and Henderson. For greater efficiency, the Prime Minister appointed a Secretary to the Cabinet for the first time. The supreme business of the new government was to win the war, and Balfour anticipated the almost dictatorial powers which Lloyd George now exercised:

If he wants to be a dictator, let him be. If he thinks he can win the war, let him try.

Victory in 1918 established Lloyd George's reputation as 'the man who won the war', but the Liberal Party had suffered grave damage. Its disarray was plain for all to see in the first postwar general election (see Unit 2.2).

(b) The Western Front and Other Battlefields

The First World War was actually several wars, linked together only loosely, between the western democracies and Germany, between Russia and the Central Powers, between Italy and Austria-Hungary, between states in the

DELIVERING THE GOODS.

Fig. 1.2 Lloyd George, Minister of Munitions, 1915, intent on harnessing both employees and employers to the war effort. This Punch *cartoon caught something of the energy and determination which made Lloyd George Prime Minister in 1916 – the obvious leader to win the war. (Compare Illingworth's representation of Churchill in 1940, Fig. 9.2(a), page 154)*

Balkans and between Arabs and Turks. There were many theatres of war but none was more bloody or more horrific than the Western Front, where the Allies grappled with Germany for four years in savage and almost immobile trench warfare.

The Central Powers were held together by the resources and military might of Germany, and German forces fought in almost every corner of war-torn Europe. British forces, and those of the British Empire, were even more widely scattered. They fought on the Western Front, at Gallipoli (see Unit 1.3(*a*)), in the Middle East against the Turks, and in Africa against Germany's overseas colonies; and they intervened elsewhere too when necessary, in Italy in 1917, for example, when Italian troops were routed at Caporetto.

A vitally important war, in which the British and Germans played the leading parts, also took place at sea. The great fleets, on which so much money had been lavished and in which so much pride was invested before 1914, met only once, at Jutland at the end of May 1916. The encounter proved indecisive, though the British suffered the greater casualties. Though far from being defeated, the German fleet nevertheless returned to port, and stayed there. But German submarines (U-boats) posed a greater threat to Britain, menacing the nation's vital supply lines. The loss of Britain's merchant shipping was alarming. In March–April 1917 alone, more than 600 vessels, amounting to some 1 200 000 tons of shipping, were sunk, and stocks of foodstuffs and raw materials fell perilously low. Counter-weapons were developed, among them hydrophones for detection, and depth charges for destruction. But above all (and mainly through Lloyd George's persistence), the convoy system was perfected, whereby clusters of Allied merchant ships were protected by naval escorts. The U-boat menace was contained, though never eliminated, and losses in early 1918 were reduced to about 300 000 tons a month. The indiscriminate activities of the U-boats helped to bring the USA into the war in support of the Allies in April 1917, so that in the end it was Germany which was strangled by naval blockade, when its enemies consolidated their control of the seas.

The war at sea and the land campaigns elsewhere, however, were always overshadowed in the eyes of the British public by the slaughter on the Western Front. By Christmas 1914 the two sides faced each other in lines of trenches stretching from the Channel coast, near the Franco-Belgian border, to Switzerland, near the Franco-German border. The German advance had been halted some seventy miles short of Paris, and the Germans now had to fight on two fronts. The German High Command had hoped to avoid this: the Schlieffen Plan had aimed to strike a quick and lethal blow at France, to free German troops for action against Russia on the Eastern Front. The Germans had deliberately advanced through Belgium to sweep into France more quickly, but they merely encountered ferocious Belgian, French and British resistance, and the attack ground to a halt.

The warfare on the Eastern Front was more fluid. By 1917 Russia trembled on the brink of defeat. Revolution occurred, and the Russians made peace with

Fig. 1.3 London buses pressed into service on the Western Front and shorn of their colourful civilian finery

the Germans at Brest-Litovsk in March 1918. The victory came too late for Germany to win similar success in the west, however, since four years of a war of attrition on the Western Front had sapped manpower, morale and resources.

From the autumn of 1914 to the spring of 1918 the armies on the Western Front counted their gains in yards and their dead in hundreds of thousands. It was a war of futile offensives, when the massive artillery pounded the enemy defences before the frantic and repeated charges of waves of infantrymen against barbed wire and machine-guns. Each passing year brought its catalogue of offensives and battles, later to be commemorated on countless war memorials with their melancholy lists of the dead: the Marne, Ypres 1914, Neuve Chapelle, Ypres 1915, Loos, Verdun, the Somme, Arras, Passchendaele. . . . Falkenhayn launched a massive German assault on Verdun in 1916 'to bleed the French white', aiming to measure his victory as much in Frenchmen slain as in territory won. Both French and Germans paid a terrible price but, like other offensives, the battle ended months later more or less where it began.

Later that year Douglas Haig launched his offensive on the Somme. Haig had been the British Commander-in-Chief in France since 1915. He stubbornly prolonged the Somme offensive for months, but it floundered in the mud. When it was abandoned at last, in November, the British had won only a handful of ruined hamlets for the loss of 420 000 lives. Overall, a million Allied and German lives were lost during Haig's campaign, and victory for either side seemed as far away as ever.

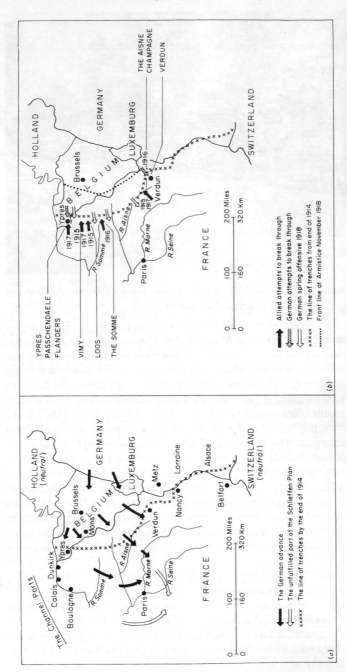

Fig. 1.4   The Western Front: (a) The failure of the Schlieffen Plan   (b) The war of attrition: some major engagements

In 1917 Nivelle drove his French troops to mutiny through his dogged persistence in throwing them against the enemy. The trenches had moved little by the beginning of 1918. Constantly topped up with new human sacrifices, the troops waited in their lice-infested dugouts, in a sea of mud, in a desolate and blasted landscape, for the next initiative of the politicians and generals. They had little to look forward to. In the words of Siegfried Sassoon:

> 'Good morning, good morning,' the General said,
> When we met him last week on our way to the line . . .
> 'He's a cheery old card,' grunted Harry to Jack,
> As they slogged up to Arras with rifle and pack
> – But he did for them both by his plan of attack.

Barbed wire and machine-guns prevented much movement, and the killing-power of weapons was steadily 'improved' – bayonets, refined with saw edges, rifles, mortars and howitzers. The authorities searched constantly for new weapons to end the stalemate. The Germans tried poison gas, which blinded and blistered, but produced no breakthrough. In 1916 the British invented the tank, but tanks were not effective until November 1917, when they were used at Cambrai. The warring nations took to the air in zeppelins and aeroplanes, but the latter were a foretaste of future warfare rather than a decisive contribution to the outcome of this war. Even so, the Royal Air Force was established in April 1918, when the Royal Flying Corps and the Royal Naval Air Service were merged.

The deadlock was broken in the end, as the generals always believed it would be, by the mass advance of infantrymen, climbing over the bodies of fallen comrades. The Germans broke through first. Reinforced by troops switched from the Eastern Front, they attacked desperately in the spring of 1918 in an effort to snatch victory before the full weight of United States manpower could be felt on the Western Front. They reached the Marne again, but their resources were inadequate for a further drive towards Paris: the Spring Offensive ran out of steam. The Allies hit back in August, under the now unified command of the French Marshal Foch. His counter-offensive gained added power from tanks and American reinforcements. Germany's allies were collapsing elsewhere in Europe, and Germany itself grew weak under the Allied naval blockade. Towards the end of September Ludendorff advised the German government that the enemy advance on the Western Front was unstoppable. The Germans surrendered at 11 am on the eleventh day of the eleventh month: 11 November 1918. It was a timely surrender, since the line of battle had still not reached German soil. Northern France had been liberated but the Germans were not yet out of Belgium, and the total evacuation of Belgium was one of the first conditions of the armistice.

(c) The People at War
DORA (the Defence of the Realm Acts, enacted in 1914 and thereafter extended), controls, censorship and conscription provided the firmest evidence

Fig. 1.5   Trench warfare: British soldiers on the Western Front attempt to relax in a lull between attacks. When it rained the trenches became waterlogged, soggy refuges in a sea of mud

that the civilian population of Britain was organized as never before during the First World War. As the war went on, whatever its first intentions, the government piled up regulations and shrouded the nation's domestic affairs in a veil of secrecy. War was waged against drunkenness, which hampered production, Lloyd George declaring in 1915 that the nation faced three enemies: Germany, Austria and Drink. The licensed opening hours of public houses were cut down. The Liberals were reluctant to make the government too much of a busybody while Asquith was in power, but Lloyd George had no such inhibitions. As Minister of Munitions he took steps to curtail labour disputes, while pressures from the labour movement pushed the government into efforts to peg rents and interest rates. When Lloyd George became Prime Minister he created new ministries for areas such as Labour, National Service and Food. The government took control of such key industries as the mines and the railways, and Lloyd George recruited businessmen in the hope of improving administrative efficiency. Conscription had already been introduced early in 1916, first for single and then for married men, and although conscientious objectors were allowed to opt out of military service, they were often treated harshly. Skilled men in vital industries were exempted from the forces, and some who had earlier volunteered were sent back to their workshops.

The war brought a major change in the lives of women. Many worked in the munitions factories and in a wide range of jobs previously done by men – on the railways and trams, on farms in a Land Army, as postal workers and general labourers. They joined the forces too, mainly to work behind the lines, though they often faced considerable dangers and performed invaluable duties as nurses and in auxiliary services. A further army of women, mainly from the middle classes, did voluntary work, organizing welfare services for the many casualties of a disrupted society. Some women performed a more sinister service too. It was an age of white feathers, to be sent to those men who seemed reluctant to join the armed forces, and the music halls rang to the blackmail of the ladies who sang:

> We don't want to lose you. But we think you ought to go!
> For your King and your Country both need you so.

Although the suffragettes had achieved little, it would now be difficult to deny women the vote when the First World War ended.

The unending casualty lists and the sad stream of wounded returning from the continent constantly reminded civilians, if they needed it, that the nation was at war. There were other reminders too. Early in the war, German naval raiders shelled Scarborough and the east coast. Zeppelin raids began in 1915, and there were also aeroplane raids later in the war. Aerial bombardment, though on a small scale compared with that in the Second World War, killed some 1 400 civilians, and there was damage to property, especially in London. Enemy naval activity played havoc with supplies. Prices soared, halving the value of money, and there was bitter resentment of the pay-gap between those in the forces and on low incomes and those in key industries with fast-rising wages. Taxation rose sharply as the government struggled to pay for the war. By 1917 there was concern about the nation's food supply. In the following year the government made a crude attempt to introduce rationing, though that was less the result of genuine shortages than of rumours about shortages, and of the public's insistence on queueing outside butchers' shops. Rather more effectively the government also imposed controls on the price of food, to curtail profiteering.

These government attempts to regulate many of the nation's affairs were sometimes referred to as 'war socialism'. But much of the planning was haphazard and even accidental. There was little enthusiasm, as yet, for co-ordinated and sustained intervention, and it would take another war in 1939 for government policy regularly to turn in that direction. In 1914–18 the aim was simply to win the war, and many ministers were surprised at the extent of the powers they found available to government. Nor did all the ministers know how to use their powers. Lloyd George commented on Neville Chamberlain, the Director of National Service: 'Not one of my successful selections' – and he dubbed Chamberlain a 'pinhead'.

1.4 Victory, at a Price

The true costs of victory in the First World War can never be measured precisely. The dead may be counted: over 900 000 subjects of Britain and the Empire lost their lives, three out of four of them from the United Kingdom. Government spending can be calculated: it reached some £7 800 million, and there was an outstanding debt of £850 million to the USA for supplies. Material damage may be measured: some eight million tons of merchant shipping were sunk, for example. But there had also been considerable disruption of the economy and society. The war distorted production patterns; overseas markets were lost; factories, machines and human beings were worked to capacity and, in some cases, worn out. 'Inessentials' were neglected, so that by 1918 there was a backlog in areas such as housing: it was calculated then that the nation was short of about 800 000 houses.

It hardly occurred to Lloyd George that he himself might be worn out. He had worked furiously for victory, and one of his ultimate successes was the appointment of Foch to unified command on the Western Front, which helped to bring about the final victory. Bonar Law bore witness to the Prime Minister's dedication:

> He thought of nothing and aimed at nothing, and hoped for nothing, except the successful end of the war . . . . We saw what courage meant.

In 1918 Lloyd George showed similar determination and courage in his new eagerness to win the peace.

He faced enormous problems, however. The troops had to be returned to civilian life; wartime controls and the economy as a whole had to be adjusted to peacetime conditions; shortages such as those in housing had to be made good. Treaties had to be made with the defeated powers. There were urgent problems in the Empire, not least those of settling the future of Ireland and defining the status of the Dominions and of India. It was also necessary to take account of Britain's changing mood. The First World War had unsettled old attitudes and left hidden scars. People seemed less likely to put up with inequalities and injustice. Industrial conflict threatened. Tens of thousands, many of them women, refused to return to domestic service. The old society had been shaken severely in a war which had seemed an assault on civilization itself.

Further Reading
Seaman, L.C.B.: *Post-Victorian Britain, 1902–1951*. Methuen (London, 1966), chapters 6–9.
Ferro, M.: *The Great War, 1914–1918*. Routledge (London, 1973).
Gibbons, S.R. and Morican, P.: *World War One*. Longman (Harlow, 1965).
Hawkins, F.: *From Ypres to Cambrai*. Elmfield Press (Leeds, 1973).
Taylor, A.J.P.: *The First World War*. Penguin (Harmondsworth, 1966).
Warner, O.: *The Battle of Jutland*. Lutterworth (London, 1972).

Documentary

The First World War. Macmillan Exploring History Kit (London, 1973).
Wilsher, L.: *Britain in World War I*. Holmes McDougall (Edinburgh, 1975).

Exercises

1. Explain what Table 1.1 shows of Britain's economy on the eve of the First World War, and what Table 1.2 shows of changes in Britain's society from 1911 to 1921.
2. Examine what this Unit shows of (*a*) unrest in British society before the outbreak of the First World War, (*b*) the effects of the war on British civilians and (*c*) the expectations of the British people for the postwar years.
3. What do you understand by *democracy*? (Refer to the Glossary on page 402 and to dictionary definitions.) In what ways was Britain in 1914 'a democracy'? Why was it claimed that the First World War was 'a war for democracy' (page 2)?
4. What evidence is there in this Unit and Unit 2.1 to support the claim that women in Britain achieved a new importance during the first twenty years of the twentieth century?
5. Why, and how, did Lloyd George become Prime Minister in 1916? How did he earn his reputation as 'the man who won the war' (page 13)?
6. 'A war of attrition' (page 15): explain the meaning of this description of the war on the Western Front, and illustrate its truth making use of Fig. 1.4.

Unit Two

Hope and Disillusionment, 1918–22

Thought was already being given to the country's political, economic and social reconstruction before the war ended. Committees examined the state of British society, and in 1917 Lloyd George appointed Christopher Addison as Minister of Reconstruction.

2.1   The Representation of the People

Inquiries into the electoral system resulted in the passing of the Representation of the People Act in June 1918, some months before the armistice. Before the war, MPs were elected by some 60 per cent of the adult male population. It was agreed that many more people, women among them, had now earned the right to vote. The Act of 1918 enfranchised all men at the age of twenty-one and, as a temporary measure, those of nineteen who had served in the war. Women's contribution to the war effort resulted in a limited victory for female emancipation. The vote was granted to 'responsible' women, which meant those aged at least thirty and ratepayers or householders, or married to ratepayers or householders. The electorate rose from eight million to over twenty-one million, the biggest step towards a democratic franchise ever taken in Britain. Frivolous young women – referred to as 'Flappers' in the 1920s – were nevertheless still discouraged from meddling in politics.

Frivolous candidates were discouraged too. A deposit of £150 was now required which would only be returned if the candidate won an eighth of the votes cast in his constituency. Elections were given a sharper focus: all the voting would now take place on a single day. (Previously the voting and the declaration of results had trickled on over several weeks.) The boundaries of constituencies were changed, to achieve greater equality of representation between the country's various regions, and to grant separate representation to boroughs with a population of more than 50 000. The new House of Commons would have 707 members of whom, for example, 66 were to be elected in Lancashire, where new borough constituencies were created in Blackpool and Southport (evidence of the recent growth of holiday resorts), and in Eccles and Nelson/Colne (evidence of the continuing spread of industry) (see Glossary: Constituencies). No change was made in the first-past-the-post system of determining the winning candidates (see Unit 1.2(c)), though the Labour Party complained of its unfairness. Many Conservatives and Liberals preferred such a system and those who wanted change could not agree on what form this

Fig. 2.1   Votes for Women – some of them – at last: 'responsible' nurses casting their votes in the general election of 1918

change should take. Plural voting also continued: some voters could vote in two constituencies, for example, graduates able to vote for a university MP, or businessmen able to vote as the occupiers of business premises, as well as voting in their home constituencies. The Act showed its wartime origins by taking away, for five years, the voting rights of conscientious objectors.

2.2   The General Election of 1918

A general election should have been held not later than 1915, under the terms of the Parliament Act of 1911, but the war prolonged the life of the old parliament. In 1918 there was general agreement that an election must be held as soon as there was peace, for, it was argued, the people's support was needed for a new government to tackle postwar problems. Labour members withdrew from Lloyd George's coalition within a few days of the armistice, preparing to offer a distinctive Labour programme of reform to the voters. Lloyd George himself saw the advantage to be gained by cashing in on his personal popularity as 'the man who won the war', and election day was arranged for 14 December, less than five weeks after the end of hostilities.

The central issue in the election was whether Lloyd George and a coalition government should continue in office. This was the Prime Minister's own ambition, and it was supported by the Conservatives under the guidance of their leader, Bonar Law. The Labour Party campaigned against them, urging the voters to return a Labour government. The Liberals were divided: a section of the party supported Lloyd George, but others (the Squiffites) clung to Asquith and bitterly denounced Lloyd George for his alleged treachery in 1916 (see Unit 1.3(*a*)). Lloyd George and Bonar Law agreed to express their joint approval of candidates who would support a coalition government, and Asquith claimed that such candidates were given a 'coupon' – the election in 1918 is sometimes referred to as the 'coupon election'. In fact, Lloyd George was generous enough to give the 'coupon' to some Liberals who were not his personal followers, and in some constituencies the candidates' attitudes towards a coalition were by no means clear-cut. In general, however, supporters of Lloyd George voted for 'coupon' candidates, while his opponents voted for a Squiffite Liberal or for a Labour candidate. In one sense the election was a popularity poll centring on the Prime Minister.

The timing of the election inevitably meant that the treatment of the defeated enemy powers was also a lively issue. The peace conference was to begin within weeks of the election (see Unit 4.1), and the mood of the British voters was vengeful. Wartime propaganda had been effective, and few candidates in any party were able to resist the talk of punishment, even those who wished to. Lloyd George had no great enthusiasm for vindictiveness, but Eric Geddes, one of his supporters, declared at Cambridge:

> We will get everything out of (Germany) that you can squeeze out of a lemon, and a bit more . . . squeeze her until you can hear the pips squeak.

Candidates competed in their demands for revenge and reparations. Slogan-mongering – 'Make Germany Pay' and 'Hang the Kaiser' – often took the place of argument and careful plans for the future. At Eccles the 'coupon' candidate, a Conservative, asserted his belief in the 'A1 British Empire with an A1 British People', catching the mood of the voters. The Squiffite Liberal was soundly defeated.

The specific policies which the new government would pursue were far from clear, but the Prime Minister promised that Britain would be 'a fit country for heroes to live in' and that, together with his wartime prestige and pre-war reputation as the champion of the underdog, was enough. The programme of the Labour Party included various social reforms, measures of nationalization, and independence for India and Ireland, but the Party suffered from fears caused by the recent Bolshevik revolution in Russia. Lloyd George suggested that the Labour Party was run by 'the extreme pacifist Bolshevist group', playing on the voters' contempt for pacifists who had opposed the war, and on their fears of Red revolutionaries.

Table 2.1 shows the great victory won by the 'coupon' candidates in the election of 1918, and the overwhelming defeat of their opponents. Asquith lost his seat in Fife, and many leading members of the Labour Party were defeated, among them MacDonald, Henderson and Snowden. Even so, the Labour Party won over two million votes, and gained more seats than in 1910. Lloyd George was clearly confirmed as the people's choice in the office of Prime Minister, but his position was not totally secure. Of his 'coupon' supporters, only 133 were Liberals, the overwhelming majority being Conservatives, who would expect him to pursue Conservative policies. Lloyd George had become almost the prisoner of the Conservatives, and there were few outlets now for the Welsh radicalism of his younger days.

Table 2.1   The general election of 1918

Supporters of the coalition (mainly 'coupon' candidates) 526		Opponents of the coalition 181	
Conservative and Unionist	389	Labour	59
Coalition Liberals	133	Asquith Liberals	28
Coalition Labour	4	Irish Nationalists	7
	—	Sinn Fein	73
	526	Others	14
			—
			181

There were obvious gaps among the members when the newly elected House of Commons met. Irish voters had elected seventy-three Sinn Fein MPs, whose first action was to assemble in Dublin and proclaim Ireland's independence. They refused to attend the 'English' parliament at Westminster. Among the

Fig. 2.2 An Irish stamp of 1968 commemorating the birth of Countess Markievicz, one of those who fought for Ireland's independence. The Countess was the first woman to be elected to the House of Commons but, as a Sinn Feiner, she refused to take her seat in London, insisting that Ireland's parliament must be in Dublin

Sinn Fein MPs was Countess Markievicz, the only woman elected in 1918. She would have been the first woman to sit in the House of Commons, but that distinction fell to Lady Astor in 1919, when she won a by-election at Plymouth. The boycott of the Commons by the Sinn Feiners served notice on the government that Ireland would be one of the most urgent postwar problems with which Lloyd George would have to deal (see Unit 4.4).

2.3   Reconstruction and Reform

(a) The Postwar Economy

An economic boom, following the armistice, suggested at first that the return to a peacetime economy would be quick and prosperous. Official plans had been made for the gradual and orderly return to civilian life of the armed forces, but these schemes collapsed even before the end of 1918. Many soldiers simply demobilized themselves, and went home. Most seemed to find work without much difficulty and in March 1919, the worst month, the trade unions estimated that unemployment was still less than 3 per cent of the labour force. Moreover, the average working week fell to about forty-eight hours without loss of earnings, suggesting that life might be easier than in pre-war years. Wartime shortages had created a demand for goods, and would-be buyers seemed to have money to pay for them. The output of British industry in 1920 seemed to be at least as high as in 1913. It was a false dawn, however, and the *Economist* was soon to comment sadly that, 'In April 1920 all was right with the world. In April 1921 all was wrong.'

The postwar boom only briefly masked Britain's economic difficulties. There had been strong competition in the selling of exports in 1914 (see Unit 1.2(*a*)), and it became fiercer in the 1920s. Many countries were deep in debt as a result of the First World War. Britain itself now had a National Debt which reached £7 000 million, some of this the debt to the USA. Like most countries, Britain desperately needed to sell its goods to earn foreign currency, to pay its debts and to buy only cheap essentials from abroad. But British goods no longer sold as readily as in the nineteenth century, and Britain's trading position had been further weakened during the war by the sale of about a quarter of its overseas investments, so that invisible earnings would now be less than before 1914. It was thus even more important for Britain to sell its goods overseas. But inflation pushed up costs – the pound lost more than half its buying power in the period 1914–20 – and with machinery which was often outdated, and industries designed to meet the needs of the nineteenth rather than the twentieth century, Britain was losing its competitive power. Lloyd George's government also raised the interest rate from 6 to 7 per cent during 1920 in an effort to check inflation, but this made it more expensive to borrow money for investment and modernization.

The boom ended quickly. Unsold goods led to reductions in output, and to unemployment. From this time until the Second World War there were never fewer than one million unemployed (in a population of about forty-five million), and there were sometimes considerably more.

Unemployment varied from one region to another. The basic industries were hit the hardest: coal, iron and steel, shipbuilding and textile-manufacturing had thrived in the nineteenth century, but they now faced formidable competition and the areas dependent on them suffered most from unemployment (see Fig. 2.3). New industries, such as electrical engineering, vehicle-building and chemicals, fared better. But by 1921 it was apparent that the land of 'light and beauty', which Lloyd George had hoped to create, was still a land of unemployment and inequality. Hope gave way to disillusionment and to anger.

The government of 1918 had been elected to uphold the traditional Liberal and Conservative beliefs in private enterprise and free trade; the voters had rejected the Labour programme of economic planning by the state and the public ownership of industry. The Labour Party and the trade unions were nevertheless angered by the government's refusal to make fundamental changes in the British economy. Lloyd George eagerly consulted experts and businessmen, but their advice was often confused and usually conservative. The coalition government did little to interfere with the economy. The McKenna Duties of 1915 had slightly modified free trade, by putting levies on certain imports such as motor-cars and clocks to reduce wartime imports, to save shipping space and raise revenue. These Duties remained, and the Safeguarding of Industries Act of 1921 added a levy of 33⅓ per cent on certain imports, such as electrical goods and chemicals from outside the Empire. But such measures were very limited, and the idea of more general protection for British industry by levies on foreign goods was not seriously considered.

Experts, businessmen and the press, on the other hand, focused attention on government spending. The idea grew that Lloyd George's government was extravagant and guilty of 'squandermania'. The government needed money for state services such as education and housing (see Unit 2.3(b)), and it was argued that this, on top of the huge war debts, led to too much taxation while adding to inflation and undermining foreign confidence in the pound. Some of the middle classes also thought the workers needed more discipline, fewer state services and even lower wages. Early in 1922 a committee of businessmen under Eric Geddes advised widespread reductions in the government's budget. Lloyd George himself vetoed some of the cuts which were to be made by Geddes' 'Axe', but education, housing, the armed forces and government spending generally all suffered. Teachers, for example, had to accept lower salaries. The cuts did nothing to tackle the fundamental problems of the British economy. J.M. Keynes later argued that government spending, far from being undesirable, could well aid a depressed economy by providing work, reducing unemployment and increasing purchasing power. But, as L.C.B. Seaman has commented, the outcry and cuts of 1922:

> set the tone of much average thinking in the inter-war period, firmly establishing the idea that any expenditure on social welfare of any sort or any kind of Government planning was certain to plunge the country into immediate bankruptcy.

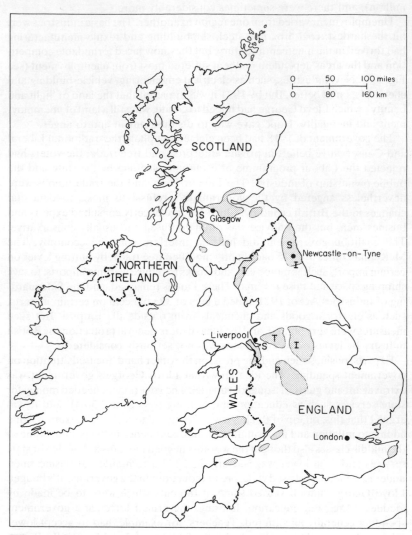

Main coalfields, where many of Britain's basic industries were located.
Areas of high unemployment in the inter-war years, for example in
S – Shipbuilding
I – Iron/Steel
T – Textiles
P – Pottery

Fig. 2.3 British coalfields and unemployment

(b) **Social Reform and Reorganization**
Although the coalition did almost nothing to manage the economy, it did introduce social and administrative reforms. Lloyd George bubbled with ideas, but the stuttering economy, overseas problems and the composition of the House of Commons after the 1918 election led to fewer major acts being passed than might have been expected after the Prime Minister's radical youth.

Like the Representation of the People Act, the Education Act of 1918 (the Fisher Act, named after H.A.L. Fisher, the President of the Board of Education) was passed before the general election. It raised the school leaving age from twelve to fourteen, ended all fees for elementary education, and made some provision for the continuing education of the mass of children who, at that time, did not go on to secondary schools. Local authorities were also given permission to open nursery schools for children under five. The results were disappointing. The extended education of elementary school children was one of the casualties of the government spending cuts, and few local authorities bothered to set up nursery schools.

Improvements in housing were badly needed in postwar Britain. Slums were widespread, and the war had held back renovation, causing many decent homes to fall into disrepair. A new Ministry of Health was set up and entrusted to Addison, who launched a housing programme in 1919. The Housing Acts offered local authorities government money to help them build 'council' houses for letting to the poor at rents they could afford. The principle was important: housing was now regarded as a social service, and taxpayers' money was used to help provide homes for the poor. The scheme was not popular with taxpayers. Mistakes were made, and money was wasted in paying inflated prices for many of the houses built; yet 200 000 new homes were provided during the lifetime of the coalition government. In 1923, however, it was estimated that the country was still short of more than 800 000 homes. Addison had been quickly dismissed for overspending, and the scheme was abandoned in 1922. The principle survived, however, and later Acts followed the lines marked out by Addison, the poor receiving much benefit in cities such as London, Manchester, Leeds and Bristol.

The Labour Party bitterly attacked Lloyd George for his failure to reduce unemployment. A Labour pamphlet complained in 1929:

> He did next to nothing to provide work; and, because he did next to nothing then, the problem that the country has to face today is far harder than it need have been if the right measures had been taken at the right time.

Instead, Lloyd George introduced a number of Unemployment Insurance Acts in the years 1920–2, to soften the effects of unemployment. The first extended the scheme he himself had introduced in 1911 (see Unit 1.2(b)). It was now to cover some twelve million lower-paid workers, namely those earning less than £250 a year, but excluding domestic servants and farm workers. When employed, a worker paid into the state insurance fund, with his employer and the government making similar payments. When unemployed, he received a weekly benefit, for not more than twenty-six weeks. In 1921, however, growing numbers were out of work for longer than this. When benefit ceased, they had to apply to the poor law authorities for relief, and thus became a drain on local rates.

The system soon began to break down. Local rates could not cope with the strain of a vast army of long-term unemployed. Another Act in 1921 therefore introduced the 'dole' (a popular term for 'uncovenanted' benefits, after the 'covenanted' twenty-six weeks). The dole was paid out of central government funds; the rate in 1921 was fifteen shillings (75p) a week. In November 1921 the government added five shillings (25p) for an unemployed man's wife and one shilling (5p) for each child. A man and wife could thus get one pound a week, and there was no shortage of critics to argue that this was too generous and a waste of the taxpayers' money. In the inter-war years the British showed a talent for losing sight of the central point and focusing on side-issues. Much more energy was devoted to arguing about the rate of unemployment benefit and the dole than to considering how to get rid of unemployment itself.

Other legislation in the years 1918–22 showed evidence of Lloyd George's earlier radical interests, and of his passion for administrative change such as had been introduced during the war. Many wartime controls and institutions were dismantled, though the Ministry of Labour survived. The Railways Act of 1921 returned the railways to a peacetime footing and created a rational system based on four regional private companies – the Southern, the Great Western, the LMS (London, Midland and Scottish) and the LNER (London and North-Eastern) – rather than the numerous smaller companies which had existed before 1914. This system lasted until the railways were nationalized in 1948. The government aimed to bring a similar order to the supply of electricity, setting up the Electricity Commission, a forerunner of the Central Electricity Board. Forests were brought under the Forestry Commission. Universities received government help through the new University Grants Committee, and state scholarships were introduced in 1920 to help gifted but poor students to reach university. Geddes' 'Axe' cut out the scholarships in 1922, but they were reintroduced two years later by Ramsay MacDonald's government. The Rent Act continued the wartime protection against rent increases for tenants of limited means. As a young Welshman, Lloyd George had had a fierce dislike of landlords and also of the Anglican Church in Wales. It gave him personal satisfaction when the latter was disestablished in 1919.

(c) Social Unrest

Lloyd George darted from one problem to another, so that his government sometimes seemed to have little sense of direction. Much of the Prime Minister's time was taken up with international peacemaking and with the problems of Ireland and the Empire (see Unit 4). But the government had to face the problem of persistent unrest, especially in industrial matters. There had been industrial conflict on the eve of the First World War (see

Unit 1.2(*b*)), and the trade unions, whose membership had doubled during the war, were militant. They attacked rising prices and profiteering. They suspected, with some justification, that the government lacked sympathy for the masses; and they grew more bitter as unemployment mounted. Early in 1919 confrontation occurred in Glasgow, and the government brought in troops and tanks to deal with the city's strikers, some of whom had Bolshevik ambitions. A wave of strikes was threatened, and unrest even extended to the police. Troops were again brought in when the police in Liverpool went on strike later in 1919.

Miners and railwaymen seemed to present the greatest problems to the government. The MFGB (Miners' Federation of Great Britain) demanded higher wages, a six-hour day and the public ownership of the pits. The government had taken wartime control of the coal industry, but hardly intended to continue it. Lloyd George bought time, however, by setting up an inquiry into the coal industry under the chairmanship of a judge, John Sankey. The Sankey Commission produced a variety of reports because of divisions between its members but, in general, it accepted the case for a small increase in wages, and also for a six-hour day underground 'subject to the economic position of the industry at the end of 1920'. The Commission was divided evenly on the question of public ownership, and Sankey himself gave public ownership his casting vote in June 1919:

> I recommend on the evidence before me that the principle of State ownership of the coal mines be accepted.

While the government considered what to do with the coal industry, it had to face a national rail strike, brought about by its own efforts to cut wages. The NUR (National Union of Railwaymen) resisted successfully, and the government had to back down. Small interim wage increases were also granted to the miners to end a two-week strike in October 1920, though the government did arm itself with the Emergency Powers Act, giving itself the right to rule by decree and to suspend trial by jury if the need arose.

'The economic position of the (coal) industry at the end of 1920' was not healthy. It faced foreign competition, and the slump was already reducing sales. Rejecting Sankey's recommendation, the government decided to hand the mines back to the private owners, who instantly looked for ways to save their profits by limiting wages and keeping up the hours worked. A massive coal strike began on 1 April 1921. The government busied itself with the movement of troops and the parading of its Emergency Powers. The MFGB demanded support for a general strike from the members of the Triple Industrial Alliance (see Unit 1.2(*b*)), only to find itself deserted by the NUR, whose leader Jimmy (J.H.) Thomas, refused to support a general strike on Black Friday, 15 April. The miners were forced to give in, though a subsidy from the government to the coal owners helped to soften the blow by keeping wages higher than they might otherwise have been. Even so, the miners had gained virtually nothing that the Sankey Commission had recommended, and had even failed in

Fig. 2.4 Miners on strike in Wigan, April 1921: their hopes ended in disappointment when workers in other industries refused to join them on Black Friday

their bid for national wage rates. Wages were now fixed, as before 1914, by district, so that some miners suffered greater hardships than others. And the miners were once more faced by the private coal owners, many of whom could think of making their pits more competitive only by cutting wages.

Black Friday marked the general defeat of trade unionists. Wages were cut in many industries, including the railways and, though inflation was curbed, workers generally were worse off. Some eighty-five million days were lost in strikes during 1921 and a further twenty million in 1922, but the government and the country had weathered the storm. The problems of industrial relations had not been solved, however, and the miners in particular were much embittered.

Some commentators asserted that communist conspiracy was at the root of the troubles. Without doubt, the Bolshevik revolution in Russia had encouraged communist ambitions. The British Communist Party was founded in 1920, and Willie Gallacher, one of its most active members, was among those arrested in Glasgow during the unrest of the previous year. Hotheads talked of 'planting the Red Flag on Buckingham Palace', and there was fierce criticism of the coalition government's meddling in the affairs of Russia, where British troops and equipment played a minor role in the efforts to overthrow the Bolsheviks during the Civil War of 1918–20, the 'Wars of Intervention' in the terminology of the Bolsheviks. Protest erupted in Britain in 1920, when London dockers stopped the sailing of the *Jolly George*, laden with military supplies for the Poles who had declared war on Russia; and the labour movement threatened a general strike should Lloyd George similarly declare war on Russia. But support for Marxism in Britain was limited, and the industrial unrest owed far more to the sufferings and disappointments of the workers than to revolutionary ideology. Unemployment reached two million in 1921, over 10 per cent of the labour force. At the same time, as part of the general disillusionment, the membership of trade unions fell, from over eight million in 1920 to less than six million in 1922. Meanwhile, the unions were reorganizing. Engineering unions drew together in 1920 in the AEU (Amalgamated Engineering Union), and two years later the TGWU (Transport and General Workers Union) was created from fourteen separate unions.

2.4   The Downfall of Lloyd George's Government

Lloyd George's reputation was fading. He was accused of selling honours to obtain money for the Liberal Party, and a variety of forms of trickery in conducting government business – accusations made especially by those who were jealous of the close circle of advisers with whom the Prime Minister surrounded himself. The achievements of the coalition government both at home and abroad were forgotten as attention focused on its obvious failures on the economic and industrial fronts. Lord Beaverbrook wrote of the sudden decline in Lloyd George's prestige:

> 1921 ushered in two cruel years which were to rip away all the gold brocade and the tinsel too. The illusions were being shattered and a great tragedy was being enacted for all to see.

Lloyd George's position in parliament had been vulnerable since the 1918 election: the Conservatives only supported him for as long as it suited the Conservative Party, and they grew increasingly restless during 1922. They were dismayed by the coalition government's Irish policy (see Unit 4.4), but it was the Chanak Crisis that helped to bring matters to a head. Lloyd George took his duties seriously as one of the chief peacemakers of the postwar world (see Unit 4). He believed it vital to uphold the peace against lawless action. British troops were stationed at Chanak in Turkey as part of the international supervision of the Dardanelles. When they were menaced by the nationalist forces of Mustapha Kemal, protesting at the alleged unfairness of the peace settlement to Turkey, the British government sent reinforcements and prepared, if necessary, to fight. The alarm in Britain was all the greater when Britain's allies refused to support Lloyd George's stand. In fact, the Crisis blew over, and the

British commander on the spot, General Harington, negotiated a settlement with Kemal. But the charge that he was a warmonger was now added to the list of Lloyd George's alleged faults. Since the government was losing its authority, the Cabinet decided to hold a general election to test popular feeling.

Austen Chamberlain (until recently Chancellor of the Exchequer, and elder brother of Neville Chamberlain, a later Prime Minister) called a meeting of Conservative MPs at the Carlton Club on 19 October 1922, to decide their attitude to coalition and Lloyd George. He hoped to rally support for continuing the coalition, but the meeting took a different view. Bonar Law advised ending the coalition, but perhaps the key speech was made by the hitherto little noticed Stanley Baldwin, the President of the Board of Trade. He would 'not beat about the bush', he said, and attacked Lloyd George:

> He is a dynamic force, and it is from that very fact that our troubles, in our opinion, arise. A dynamic force is a very terrible thing; it may crush you, but it is not necessarily right.

Baldwin went on to claim that Lloyd George had already 'smashed to pieces' the Liberal Party and that, if the coalition continued, 'the old Conservative Party' too would be 'smashed to atoms and lost in ruins' – and he instanced the division Lloyd George had brought about between Austen Chamberlain and himself. The meeting voted to leave the coalition by 187 to 87, and Lloyd George resigned as Prime Minister that same day. George V appointed Bonar Law in his place, and the parties prepared to fight the general election of November 1922.

2.5   The General Election of 1922

There was nothing very exciting about the election of 1922. Labour pitted the honest but uninspiring leadership of John (J.R.) Clynes against the unexciting Conservative leadership of Bonar Law. Both parties campaigned to form a single-party government, though some leading Conservatives continued to regret the desertion of Lloyd George. Austen Chamberlain refused to take office under Bonar Law, though Lord Curzon, the Foreign Secretary since 1919, swam with the tide, dropped his support of Lloyd George and clung to the Foreign Office. The Liberals were in far greater disarray, and the voters again had to choose between the Liberals who supported Lloyd George and those who supported Asquith.

Few great issues were put to the people and, like the election of 1918, that of 1922 had much to do with the image of Lloyd George. The magic had gone, however. Bonar Law rightly judged the temper of the British voters when he offered them quiet government, with the promise of 'the minimum of interference at home and of disturbance abroad'. The continuation of free trade was part of the general policy of non-interference, and problems like unemployment would be left, in the main, to take care of themselves. The other parties

Fig. 2.5 October 1922: newspapers on sale on Westminster Bridge carry the
story of the Prime Minister's resignation. It turned out that Lloyd George was
never again to hold national office

were hardly more enterprising. Clynes tried to reassure the voters that Labour
was not a class party, representing only workers and trade unions, no doubt
mindful of the fact that the Labour MPs elected in 1918 were almost all
sponsored by the unions. He also made broad appeals, asserting the greater
importance of 'the value of life as against property'. The middle classes were
not enthusiastic about Labour's leaders or about its programme. Asquith
Liberals mainly stressed their own record of opposition to Lloyd George, and
Lloyd George Liberals stoutly asserted their devotion to him.

Lloyd George kept his own seat at Caernarvon, but his supporters fared
badly and the election confirmed that he was no longer a popular hero. He was
never to hold office again. The verdict of the voters not only on the ex-Prime
Minister but on the parties was clear. The Conservatives won 347 seats, and the

Labour Party 142, to become, respectively, the government and the opposition; 117 Liberals were elected, 57 supporting Lloyd George and 60 supporting Asquith. In a House of Commons now smaller because of the removal of many Irish MPs, the Conservatives had a clear overall majority, and Bonar Law remained in office as Prime Minister.

The Labour MPs in the new House of Commons included more than sixty who were not trade union nominees and not themselves from the working classes. Such MPs often showed more interest in ideology than was common among the trade unionist MPs. They aimed not only to improve the conditions of the masses but to transform the structure of society, to abolish capitalism and to outlaw war. But the Labour Party firmly rejected links with the Communist Party, which now had two MPs but found it difficult to win further support from the voters. The Labour Party also changed its leadership after the election, making Ramsay MacDonald the Leader of His Majesty's Opposition in preference to Clynes. MacDonald now won respect from many members of the Party for his pacifism during the war of 1914–18. Henderson – 'Uncle Arthur' to many in the labour movement – might have been a rival candidate, since he had perhaps done most of all, as Secretary, to advance Labour's fortunes in recent years. But Henderson had been defeated at Widnes and had no seat in the Commons. MacDonald was an apparently safe choice, however. He was unlikely to strike terror into middle-class voters by expressing any extreme views; and his bearing was such that it was possible to think of him as a future Prime Minister.

The events of 1922 advanced the careers of both MacDonald and Stanley Baldwin. The latter was appointed Chancellor of the Exchequer by Bonar Law who, it proved, was already too ill to remain long as Prime Minister. Lloyd George was still in robust health but, for him, the election was a tragedy. He was to remain in parliament until 1945, but his days of glory were over. He looked back on an illustrious career, stretching back to his passionate opposition to the Boer War of 1899–1902. He had campaigned vigorously and effectively for social reform and for the reduction of the power of the House of Lords before 1914. He, more than anyone, was identified with victory in 1918. He won a huge vote of confidence from the voters when the war ended, and then presided over a government whose record was flawed but by no means insignificant; his work as a peacemaker both in international affairs, and in Ireland and the Empire will be considered in later Units. Lloyd George was a frequent subject of controversy during his lifetime, and remained so among historians after his retirement from public life and his death in 1945. A harsh critic has written:

> He had really no principles at all, only emotions. He excited admiration, but not respect.

One biographer, Kenneth Morgan, on the other hand, observed:

> His faults were many – his ruthlessness in personal relations, his unpredictability in

outlook and in policy. Yet surely his achievements make these seem trivial by comparison.

After 1922, Lloyd George might still have had much to offer the country had office been open to him, but it was not. He was later reconciled with the Liberals, but it was no longer possible for the man or his party to win enough popular support to enter office.

Further Reading
Seaman, L.C.B.: *Post-Victorian Britain, 1902–1951.* Methuen (London, 1966), chapters 9–10 and 14.
Ayling, S.E.: *Portraits of Power.* Harrap (London, 1965), Lloyd George.
Morgan, K.O.: *David Lloyd George, Welsh Radical to World Statesman.* University of Wales Press (Cardiff, 1963).
Morgan, K.O.: *The Age of Lloyd George – the Liberal Party and British Politics, 1890–1929.* George Allen and Unwin (London, 1971).
Mowat, C.L.: *Lloyd George.* Oxford University Press (Oxford, 1966).
Wilson, T.: *The Downfall of the Liberal Party, 1914–1935.* Collins (London, 1966).

Documentary
Gilbert, M.: *Lloyd George.* Prentice-Hall (Hemel Hempstead, 1968).
The Vote, 1832–1928. Jackdaw Wallet. Cape (London).

Exercises
1. Bearing in mind your definition in Question 3, Unit 1, how far do you consider it true that the Representation of the People Act (1918) was a giant stride towards democracy in Britain?
2. After reading Units 1.2(*c*), 1.3(*a*), 1.4, 2.1 and 2.2 state, with reasons, which of the groups listed in Table 2.1 you would have voted for in the general election of 1918.
3. Explain, and account for, the postwar connections between coalfields, basic industries and unemployment, suggested by Fig. 2.3.
4. What does Table 2.1 show of 'Lloyd George's position in parliament' (page 33) after the election of 1918? How does this help to explain (*a*) his limited freedom of action and (*b*) his downfall in 1922?
5. How far does the evidence support the author's references to the coalition government's 'obvious failures on the economic and industrial fronts' but other 'achievements' 'at home' (page 33). After reading Unit 4, consider also what were the government's 'achievements' 'abroad'.
6. List the examples you can find in Units 1 and 2 which help to explain why Lloyd George was a 'subject of controversy' (page 36).

Unit Three

Political Change and the British Economy, 1922–9

3.1 Vote and Vote Again

British voters elected new governments on three occasions in the years 1922 to 1924. Governments did not so much fall as commit suicide. Both Baldwin and MacDonald, whose stars had seemed to shine so brightly in 1922, threw away the office of Prime Minister almost as soon as they had gained it. Number 10 Downing Street, Lloyd George's home for almost six years, was now occupied in rapid succession by Bonar Law, Baldwin, MacDonald and then Baldwin again. Number 11 Downing Street, the official residence of the Chancellor of the Exchequer, saw similar quick changes, passing from Baldwin to Neville Chamberlain, Snowden and then to Winston Churchill. What seemed like a game of political musical chairs might have puzzled the public, but it is unlikely that they noticed many spectacular changes in policy in these years. Indeed, perhaps the most important political development was that MacDonald formed the country's first Labour government, which some middle-class voters were reassured to find remarkably like any other government. The unemployed drew little consolation from that fact, however.

Bonar Law's premiership lasted for only seven months. Gravely ill, he resigned in May 1923 and died soon afterwards of a cancer of the throat. Bonar Law had not had time to bring Austen Chamberlain back into the Conservative ranks and, in their choice of a new leader, the Conservatives were hardly embarrassed by a wealth of able candidates. Lord Curzon seemed to be the front runner but he was not well liked by his colleagues, who seized on the excuse that, as a member of the House of Lords, he could not become Prime Minister. Baldwin held the senior government office of Chancellor of the Exchequer and therefore seemed a logical choice to succeed Bonar Law, if not an exciting one. George V made Baldwin Prime Minister, the Conservatives confirmed him as the leader of their party, and the disappointed Curzon commented that Baldwin was 'a man of the utmost insignificance'.

Baldwin had first entered parliament in 1908 and held minor office in the later years of the war. He became President of the Board of Trade in 1921 and in 1922 denounced Lloyd George and gained the Exchequer. Here his main achievement was the settlement of Britain's debt to the USA, at that time £978 million, in a way which infuriated Bonar Law who thought Baldwin had given way to American pressures in agreeing to higher annual repayments than

Bonar Law wished to make. Now, almost overnight, Baldwin had secured the highest office, mainly because the Conservatives' more likely leader, Austen Chamberlain, had chosen to remain loyal to Lloyd George in 1922.

The most remarkable thing about Baldwin's government was that it provoked and lost an unnecessary election, and resigned, all within eight months. Baldwin had inherited a comfortable majority in the House of Commons, but he also inherited a very high level of unemployment, which he regarded as 'the gravest subject in the country today'. In October 1923 he spoke at Plymouth, declaring his new belief that the home market must be protected by tariffs – that free trade should be abandoned in order to provide jobs in British industry. At the same time, however, he referred to the Conservative pledge in the election of 1922 that free trade would continue:

> That pledge binds me, and in this Parliament there will be no fundamental change. I take those words strictly: I am not a man to play with a pledge.

The image of 'Honest Stan' was being fashioned, perhaps in a conscious effort to contrast Baldwin with the 'tricky' Lloyd George. But the government was now in the position of apparently believing that protection was needed to overcome unemployment, while rejecting it because of the previous year's election promise. The only way out of this dilemma seemed to be to put the issue of protection to the people in a general election. Baldwin later suggested another explanation for his sudden interest in protection: that he had reason to believe Lloyd George was about to declare support for it, and perhaps make a comeback with backing from men such as Austen Chamberlain, whose father, Joseph Chamberlain, had campaigned for protection twenty years earlier. If Baldwin became a protectionist first, it would steal the Welshman's thunder. But the price Baldwin paid was to cut short the life of his own government.

There was personal hostility between Baldwin and Lloyd George in the election campaign: Baldwin was bent on 'dishing the Goat' (Lloyd George), and Lloyd George hoped to have the opportunity to 'knife' the Prime Minister. At the same time, the Liberals hastily reunited their party. Lloyd George agreed to campaign under the leadership of Asquith and, whatever he might have intended earlier, he now expressed support for free trade and the other common policies of the 438 Liberal candidates. Liberal posters, reviving memories of the election of 1906, showed a large Liberal loaf of bread contrasted with a small Conservative one – the first resulting from free trade, the second from the protection Baldwin wanted.

The country voted in December 1923, but what the voters actually wanted was far from clear. There was not much change in the total votes cast for the three major parties between the elections of 1922 and 1923, but the first-past-the-post system produced extensive changes in the number of seats won. Table 3.1 shows that many voters lost confidence in the Conservatives, and that Baldwin's recklessness in calling the election cost his party more than eighty seats. On the whole the voters seemed not to want tariffs but, in spite of the improved showing of the Liberals, the electorate treated the former Liberal supporters of Lloyd George unkindly. Trade unionists again slipped back in comparison with the number of other Labour MPs elected. The combined anti-Conservative vote seemed to be a vote against protection, and the combined anti-Labour vote one against 'socialism', while the reunited Liberals, though advertising side-by-side photographs of Asquith and Lloyd George, seemed to many only to be masking a continuing rivalry between them.

No party had an outright majority in the House of Commons. Baldwin was the leader of the largest single party, and for a time he remained in office. But when parliament met in January 1924 the Conservatives could not win a vote of confidence, and Baldwin resigned. No two parties could agree on uniting in a coalition, and George V took the only course possible: as Labour was the second largest party in the Commons, he invited MacDonald to form a minority Labour government. It seemed likely that the Liberals would support him in some non-socialist policies, such as limited social reform, the continuing of free trade and the pursuit of goodwill abroad.

Perhaps no one was more surprised than MacDonald to find himself Prime Minister. Born poor and illegitimate at Lossiemouth in the north of Scotland, he had joined the Independent Labour Party in 1894 and led the Parliamentary Labour Party from 1911 to 1914. But his pacifism proved costly, and he could not win a parliamentary seat in the years 1918–22. Elected then at Aberavon, his rise to power was rapid. The office of Prime Minister, and that of Foreign Secretary which he also held in 1924, were his first positions in government.

3.2   The First Labour Government, 1924

Labour's success was due partly to changes in the party's organization in 1918, when it was agreed that the Labour Party would accept individual members, as was common practice in other political parties. In earlier years, Labour Party membership had been only by affiliation: members joined a body such as a trade union, or a society such as the Fabian Society, and it was the organization which was affiliated to the Labour Party. From its beginnings, the Labour Party had been an uneasy alliance of trade unionists and socialists (see Unit 1.2(c)). Many trade unionists wanted only to improve conditions for their members, whereas socialists aimed to transform society in the direction of greater equality. The Fabians, for example, were mainly middle-class intellectuals such as Sidney and Beatrice Webb and George Bernard Shaw, who worked for the gradual introduction of socialist principles in Britain. Individual membership tended to increase the pressures within the Labour Party for a socialist ideology. The changes of 1918 also included acceptance of what was known as Clause Four, defining the Party's aim:

> to secure for the producers by hand and brain the full fruits of their industry, and the most equitable distribution thereof that may be possible on the basis of the common ownership of the means of production . . ..

Table 3.1 General elections and governments in the 1920s

Date	ELECTION RESULTS						ELECTED GOVERNMENTS	
	Conservatives/ Unionists	Liberals		Labour	Other		Prime Minister	Chancellor of the Exchequer
		Lloyd George	Asquith	Re-united				
Nov. 1922	347*	57	60	—	142	9	Bonar Law Baldwin (May 1923)	Baldwin Neville Chamberlain (August 1923)
Dec. 1923	260	—	—	159	191	5	MacDonald	Snowden
Oct. 1924	419	—	—	40	151	5	Baldwin	Churchill
May 1929	260	—	—	59	288	8	MacDonald	Snowden

*bold: the party forming the next government

TO-MORROW-WHEN LABOUR RULES

Fig. 3.1 A Labour Party poster, with the hope of the better postwar world to which the British people looked forward in 1918

This was the policy of nationalization, by which enterprises (such as mines and factories) would be transferred from private owners to the state, supervised by parliament, and run for the public good rather than for private profit.

Individual membership also made possible the rapid growth of Labour Party branches in the constituencies. Before 1914 Labour had only 158 of these constituency parties. In 1923 it had over 500, enabling it to compete on more equal terms with the Conservatives and Liberals. But the Labour Party was still comparatively poor, in spite of financial support from the trade unions. Conservative candidates spent an average of £845 in the election of 1923, and Liberals (much helped by the funds Lloyd George had collected) an average of £789. Labour candidates, on the other hand, averaged only £464.

Trade unionists and socialists alike thrilled to the news of MacDonald's appointment as Prime Minister, and looked forward to the implementing of their programme for ending unemployment, a minimum wage for all workers, nationalization of important industries, and more equal sharing of wealth. They underestimated both the size of the country's problems and the weaknesses of the Labour government's position, since the latter was forced to rely on Liberal support in the Commons. Beatrice Webb, wife of Sidney Webb who was MacDonald's President of the Board of Trade, described how:

> on Wednesday the twenty Ministers designate, in their best suits . . . went to Buckingham Palace to be sworn in; having been previously drilled by Hankey [Secretary to the Cabinet]. Four of them came back to our weekly MPs' lunch . . .. They were all

laughing over Wheatley – the revolutionary – going down on both knees and actually kissing the King's hand.

MacDonald, in fact, chose his Ministers almost entirely from the least revolutionary Labour MPs; Wheatley was an exception. Beatrice Webb herself was far from being a revolutionary, but she thought there was too much mixing with 'smart society' and too much 'dressing up'. MacDonald wanted to disprove Churchill's taunt that Labour was 'not fit to govern', with the result that the members of his government were much more successful in being respectable than in being radical, and in the event they changed very little.

Wheatley, the Minister of Health, was the most energetic member of the Cabinet. He revived government help to local authorities for the building of council houses and half a million such homes were built under his Housing Act before it was replaced by new laws in 1933. The spending was never lavish, but the housing programme was effective. Snowden was not revolutionary in any way. He cautiously clung to free trade, and scrapped the McKenna Duties. There were modest increases in old age pensions and unemployment benefit, and state scholarships were brought back, but the programme for public works was on too small a scale to make much difference to the level of unemployment. The government, moreover, showed no special skill in curbing industrial unrest.

MacDonald himself aimed to improve international relations, helping to reconcile France and Germany, and exploring ways of strengthening the League of Nations (see Unit 4.2(c)). His government had too little time to achieve much, but it added to its opponents' suspicion that it was friendly towards communists. Britain at last gave official recognition to the Bolshevik government of the USSR, and the Labour government went on to sign a trade pact with the Russians and to discuss making them a loan, which caused fury among anti-communists.

The government's downfall came over a comparatively trivial matter concerning 'communism'. Conservatives in the Commons moved a vote of censure when a court case against Campbell, the acting editor of the *Workers' Weekly* and a communist, was suddenly dropped. Campbell had urged the armed forces to disobey orders if called on to shoot strikers, apparently an incitement to mutiny. When it was decided not to bring him to court, rumour circulated that Labour MPs were protecting him. The Liberals were not prepared to help bring down the government on such a minor issue and, in any case, they had no wish for another expensive general election. They put down an amendment demanding a commission of inquiry, thus offering MacDonald a way out of the problem. MacDonald had only to accept the inquiry to stay in office. But the Prime Minister had already been unsettled by rumours of scandals in the awarding of honours, afraid perhaps, like Baldwin in 1923, of being likened to Lloyd George. MacDonald insisted that his reputation was at stake, and that there should be no inquiry: his own word should be enough. To their own dismay, the Liberals found themselves outvoting the government with the help of gleeful Conservatives, who suddenly found an inquiry attractive.

MacDonald thus brought about another premature general election, in October 1924.

3.3   The General Election of 1924

Baldwin had changed his mind since 1923: he now preferred free trade to tariffs, since that was what the voters apparently preferred. As protection was no longer an issue, the Conservatives could fight the election as a crusade to save the country from the 'Red peril' – and one effect of this was likely to be the weakening of the Liberals, since they could be accused of supporting MacDonald during the early months of his government. Moreover, free-trade Liberals could now vote for the Conservatives without fear of tariffs. The Liberals were in difficulties: they were short of money, short of policies different from those of their rivals, and even short of candidates. Of course, not all the voters believed there was a Red peril, though the *Daily Mail* and other newspapers did their best to whip up a sense of crisis to help the Conservatives. The Labour Party's problem was to reassure the middle classes but, at the same time, to persuade their earlier supporters that they still stood for major reform.

A new storm broke on the Saturday before polling day. Ten days earlier, in Manchester, MacDonald had seen a copy of 'the Zinoviev Letter', supposed to have been written to the British Communist Party by Zinoviev, the Russian head of the Comintern (the Third International, a communist propaganda organization). The Letter urged the Communist Party to press for the British loan to the USSR, and gave general advice:

> From your last report it is evident that agitation propaganda in the (British) Army is weak, in the Navy a very little better . . . .. It would be desirable to have cells in all the units of troops . . . and also among factories working on munitions.

MacDonald drafted a reply but held it back until there was proof that the Letter was genuine. The *Daily Mail* and *The Times*, however, suddenly decided on the Saturday before polling that the Letter and MacDonald's reply must be printed, hoping no doubt that this would persuade more timid voters to rush to the Conservatives for protection against the Red bogey. MacDonald remained calm and apparently unconcerned. Even if it was genuine, the Letter said nothing new, and it was most unlikely to change anything. Four days after the 'revelations' in the press, the people voted.

The result of the election was a clear victory for the Conservatives (see Table 3.1). Labour lost forty seats, yet the total Labour vote was actually higher than in 1923. There is no way of measuring the effect on the voters of the affair of the Zinoviev Letter, but it may well have strengthened the resolve of Labour sympathizers not to be stampeded. The real casualties of the 1924 election were the Liberals, who lost over a million votes and over a hundred seats. Asquith himself was beaten at Paisley, where the mob hooted with joy at the old man's shipwreck, and his successful opponent wept genuine tears. Asquith went to the House of Lords, but resigned the Liberal leadership in favour of Lloyd George in 1926 and died two years later. The Liberal Party now had only

TOO MANY PRINCIPAL BOYS.

Fig. 3.2   Asquith resigned the leadership of the Liberal Party in 1926, two years after the disastrous election of 1924. He left the centre of the Liberal stage to Lloyd George, but this Daily Express cartoon (December 1926) suggested there were rivals for the leadership, including the father of Tony Wedgwood Benn who, fifty years later, aspired to lead the Labour Party

forty MPs; the voters had obviously decided that the struggle for power in Britain now lay between the Conservatives and Labour. If Baldwin's tactics had been mainly to woo Liberal voters, he seemed to have succeeded: the turnout in the election was high, and the Conservative vote increased by two-and-a-half million, many former Liberals no doubt backing Baldwin. On the other hand, Labour too got a million extra supporters.

3.4   Conflict and Stability, 1924-9: Baldwin's Government

(a) The Economy

The general election of 1924 led to five years of Conservative government, over which Stanley Baldwin presided unexcitingly. Austen Chamberlain rejoined his Conservative colleagues and was appointed Foreign Secretary. Winston Churchill became the Chancellor of the Exchequer, with no particular qualifications for the job. Joynson-Hicks ('Jix') was Home Secretary, eager to seek out communists, and Neville Chamberlain was the Minister of Health, ready enough to carry on Wheatley's housing programme. Except perhaps at the Foreign Office, where the elder Chamberlain served with distinction (see

Unit 4.2(*d*)), the government was not an outstanding one. Pledged to continue free trade, it left British industry to struggle as best it could for markets. Pledged not to squander the taxpayers' money, it introduced only modest social improvements, and had no obvious policy for reducing the level of unemployment which was still above a million. Even Austen Chamberlain began in a negative way by breaking the Labour government's links with the USSR.

Financial experts advised Churchill to return Britain to the gold standard, and this he did in 1925, thus pegging the pound sterling to the international price of gold, a practice which had ceased with the outbreak of war in 1914. The effect of the return to gold was to fix the value of the pound in relation to other currencies, such as the American dollar. In the opinion of most of the experts, this would help to bring stability to international finance and to trade, and several countries returned to the gold standard at about the same time. Unfortunately, the Conservatives felt that British prestige was involved in the issue. The pound had recently been buying about 4.40 American dollars, less than before 1914. Churchill wanted to return to the pre-war level, and the rate of exchange was fixed at around £1:4.80 dollars. This was all very well for those importing foreign goods, which would be cheaper, but was far from helpful for those trying to export British goods, which would be dearer to the foreign buyer. Other countries had taken the opportunity to reduce the value of their currencies to help their exports, so Britain's position was even weaker.

J.M. Keynes, the economist, having previously criticized the financial arrangements made in the peace settlement of 1919–20 in *The Economic Consequences of the Peace* (see Unit 4.1(*b*)), now criticized the Conservatives in *The Economic Consequences of Mr Churchill*. Difficulties in exporting had already helped to increase unemployment in Britain (see Unit 2.3(*a*)). The new exchange rate now limited Britain's ability to benefit from the reviving level of trade in the mid 1920s. It helped, in fact, to guarantee continuing unemployment, which stood at over 11 per cent in the spring of 1925. It also encouraged employers, such as the coalowners, to try to cut wages again in order to be competitive: the coalowners were inspired to attack wages within weeks of the return to gold. British governments, nevertheless, stuck stubbornly to the gold standard and the too-high exchange rate until 1931.

Invisible exports still kept the balance of payments in surplus in the 1920s, but the sale of British goods abroad remained disappointing. In 1913 Britain's percentage of total world trade was 17 per cent (see Table 1.1) and its percentage of world exports was about 14 per cent. By 1929 the first percentage was still over 15 per cent, but the share of exports had fallen to below 11 per cent. One important reason for this was that British exports were too expensive. In terms of volume, Britain exported only 86 per cent in 1929 of what it had exported in 1913, but it imported over 20 per cent more than in 1913. Coal, cotton textiles and certain engineering goods were among those which Britain found it especially hard to sell abroad, compared with earlier times. Private enterprise, meanwhile, provided jobs in newer industries, such as man-made fibres, vehicle-manufacturing and electrical goods, but these industries were seldom in the areas of highest unemployment. It was not the policy of Baldwin's government to interfere with private enterprise, with the free location of industry and with the fact that the new industries sold mainly on the home market rather than abroad.

The government did make some effort to reduce imports. The McKenna Duties were restored in 1925, but mainly to raise money for the government. The Safeguarding of Industries Act of 1921 was extended slightly to include silk, hops and sugar, but such changes were trivial, affecting the jobs of well below one per cent of the work force, and making no real movement away from free trade. Rather than trying to manage the economy and creating conditions for removing grievances about low pay and unemployment, Baldwin's government preferred a policy of standing aside and, when industrial conflict broke out, standing firm. During the election of 1924 Baldwin had made effective use of the radio to broadcast to the people and to project the image of a tranquil man who could safely be left to sort out the country's problems. He hardly claimed to be able to solve these problems, but his recipe for quietening disturbances was perhaps seen at its best during the General Strike.

(b) The Coal Industry and the General Strike
The miners and trade unionists in general had suffered setbacks after 1918 at the hands of the coalition government (see Unit 2.3(c)). But industrial unrest had occurred even during the Labour government of 1924, when the TGWU mounted a massive dock strike and then a transport strike in London, in both cases winning some improvements in pay. MacDonald's government avoided further open conflict in the coal industry, but that industry's problems remained grave. The coalowners did little to modernize the industry, and it faced increasing problems in competing with the Germans and Poles, whose mining technology advanced more rapidly. The market for coal was also damaged by the growing use of oil, especially as fuel for shipping. When Churchill returned the country to the gold standard in 1925, the outlook for British coal exports became even bleaker, yet the industry was much dependent on sales abroad. Unwilling to look for other ways of making coal production profitable, the coalowners demanded both wage cuts and a longer day, eight hours rather than seven.

Herbert Smith, the President of the Miners' Federation, summed up his members' reply: 'Nowt Doin' '. The Federation's Secretary, Arthur Cook, later expanded this into the slogan: 'Not a minute on the day. Not a penny off the pay.' The coalowners had set a deadline of 31 July 1925. This time, however, the transport workers seemed likely to support the miners, and they prepared to halt the movement of coal stocks. Baldwin hastily stepped in to buy peace. Like Lloyd George in 1921, he gave government money (£24 million) to keep up miners' wages for the time being, while appointing the Samuel Commission:

to inquire into and report upon the economic position of the Coal Industry and the conditions affecting it and to make any recommendations for the improvement thereof.

Samuel did not report until March 1926. In the meantime, the government began to prepare for a showdown, encouraging volunteers to set up the OMS (Organization for the Maintenance of Supplies) and to enrol would-be strike-breakers.

The Samuel Commission recommended that, although the mines should remain in private hands, reorganization was needed by amalgamating small collieries, updating their equipment and, in some cases, improving their management. Government subsidies to the coalowners were condemned, since they only made the owners more complacent. On the other hand, Samuel noted that:

> the dominant fact is that, in the last quarter of 1925, if the subsidy be excluded, 73 per cent of the coal was produced at a loss.

He also recommended that the government should play an active part in encouraging modernization. Since this would take time, the miners should take a temporary cut in their wages. Only this last recommendation appealed to the coalowners, and they demanded the cut take effect on 1 May 1926; they also demanded a longer day, although Samuel had shown the absurdity of that since they could not even sell the coal they already produced.

The MFGB rejected the owners' demands, and appealed to the Trades Union Congress for the support of the trade union movement generally. The TUC gave it, and threatened a General Strike for 3 May. The miners' strike (or lock-out, since the coalowners refused to employ those who would not accept their demands) began on 1 May, but the TUC desperately tried to get the government to intervene to prevent a General Strike. The government was not helpful. When printers at the *Daily Mail* refused to print an article claiming that a General Strike was 'a revolutionary movement', Baldwin made what he called an interference with the freedom of the press an excuse to break off talks with the TUC. The TUC had no alternative but to proceed with the strike, for which it had made almost no preparations.

The TUC view was that the strike was simply an industrial act to protect the living standards of the workers, and this view was expressed in the *Daily Herald* on 4 May:

> The miners are locked out to enforce reductions of wages and an increase in hours. The Government stands behind the mineowners. It has rebuffed the Trade Union Movement's every effort to pave the way to an honourable peace. . . . The unions are fighting to maintain the standard of life of the great mass of the people.

The Times expressed the official view, suggesting that the unions were trying to:

supersede Parliament and to override the will of the people . . . committing a high offence and a dangerous offence against the nation.

The *British Gazette*, a government newspaper edited by Churchill with a spirited hostility to the workers, developed the same theme, branding the General Strike 'a direct challenge to ordered government'. Baldwin himself was taking this line, and the *British Gazette* eagerly quoted him:

> This moment has been chosen to challenge the existing Constitution of the country and to substitute the reign of force for that which now exists . . . threatening the basis of ordered government and coming nearer to proclaiming civil war than we have been for centuries past.

The General Strike, therefore, was something of a war of words. The TUC launched the *British Worker* to put the unions' side of the question, and hotly denied that the strikers had any intention of attacking the constitution, parliament and the system of government. But the middle classes tended to see the strike as a threat, and old myths that the workers needed to be disciplined were revived. Moreover, some trade unionists were themselves cowed by the government's propaganda, and began to fear that they might be charged with acting illegally.

The government's determination to win was stronger than that of the TUC. Churchill in particular, ever ready for a confrontation, gloried in the fight. In fact, there was remarkably little violence. About three million workers took part in the strike, and the rest of the country did its best to carry on as usual, although communications were much disrupted. The OMS found no lack of volunteers to act as strike-breakers, many of them students and most of them middle-class, convinced they were patriotically saving the country from the 'Reds'. Many found it quite exciting to drive buses, some with a police escort, and to try to drive railway engines. They were much less keen on mining coal, however. The BBC, and such newspapers as were able to publish limited pages, showed little sympathy for the strikers, and the *British Worker* and *Daily Herald* won few converts to the workers' cause. The TUC quickly lost heart. The workers would need to be more ruthless to defeat the government, yet from the outset they tried to limit the effects of the strike. Health, food and sanitary services were not to be disrupted, according to the policy laid down by the General Council of the TUC. Hospitals, nursing homes, infant welfare centres and schools were to be protected against the interruption of supplies. Violence was to be avoided.

Since the government would not give way, the TUC looked for a way of saving face. The unions and workers had neither the money for a long strike, nor the ruthlessness for a bloody conflict. Herbert Samuel offered to mediate between the coalowners and the miners, and the TUC snatched at this straw to call off the General Strike on 12 May. Three members of the TUC General Council went to see Baldwin, among them Thomas, the Railwaymen's leader, eager for peace at any price, and Ernest Bevin of the TGWU, who tried in vain

THE

BRITISH WORKER

OFFICIAL STRIKE NEWS BULLETIN

Published by The General Council of the Trades Union Congress

No. 1.	WEDNESDAY EVENING, MAY 5, 1926.	PRICE ONE PENNY

IN LONDON AND THE SOUTH

Splendid Loyalty of Transport Workers

EVERY DOCKER OUT

" London dock workers are absolutely splendid," said an official of the Transport and General Workers' Union.

" So far as they are concerned, it is a 100 per cent. strike. There is no trouble and everything is going smoothly."

POLICE HELP REFUSED

At Swindon the railwaymen are obeying Mr. Cramp's injunction to remain steady and to preserve order. The Great Western works are, of course, closed, and no trains are running.

It was stated at a mass meeting of the N.U.R. that Mr. Collett (the

The General Council suggests that in all districts where large numbers of workers are id e sports should be organised and entertainments arranged.

This will both keep a number of people busy and provide amusement for many more.

chief mechanical engineer) had declined the oer of the police and the military to guard the railway works, saying he could rely on the strikers to preserve law and order. Railway workshops at Wolverton, Crewe, and elsewhere are closed.

CHANNEL SERVICES

At Dover the whole of the tramways staff are out. The cross-Channel boat service is greatly curtailed, and a large number of passengers are awaiting the opportunity to cross.

NOT ENOUGH!

From 2¼ to 3 million workers have ceased work.

The Government announced by yesterday's wireless that 30,000 volunteers had registered, expressing willingness to take the strikers' places. It doesn't seem enough!

Published for the General Council of the Trades Union Congress by Victoria House Printing Company, 2, Carmelite-street, London, E.C.4. Telephone (8 lines) : 8210 City.

WONDERFUL RESPONSE TO THE CALL

General Council's Message : Stand Firm and Keep Order

The workers' response has exceeded all expectations. The first day of the great General Strike is over. They have manifested their determination and unity to the whole world. They have resolved that the attempt of the mineowners to starve three million men, women and children into submission shall not succeed.

All the essential industries and all the transport services have been brought to a standstill. The only exception is that the distribution of milk and food has been permitted to continue. The Trades Union General Council is not making war on the people. It is anxious that the ordinary members of the public shall not be penalised for the unpatriotic conduct of the mineowners and the Government.

Never have the workers responded with greater enthusiasm to the call of their leaders. The only difficulty that the General Council is experiencing, in fact, is in persuading those workers in the second line of defence to continue at work until the withdrawal of their labour may be needed.

WORKERS' QUIET DIGNITY

The conduct of the trade unionists, too, constitutes a credit to the whole movement. Despite the presence of armed police and the military, the workers have preserved a quiet orderliness and dignity, which the General Council urges them to maintain, even in the face of the temptation and provocation which the Government is placing in their path.

To the unemployed, also, the General Council would address an earnest appeal. In the present fight there are two sides only—the workers on the one hand and those who are against them on the other.

Every unemployed man or woman who " blacklegs " on any job offered by employers or the authorities is merely helping to bring down the standard of living for the workers as a whole, and to create a resultant situation in which the number of unemployed must be greater than ever.

The General Council is confident that the unemployed will realise how closely their interests are involved in a successful issue to the greatest battle ever fought by the workers of the country in the defence of the right to live by work.

MESSAGE TO ALL WORKERS.

The General Council of the Trades Union Congress wishes to emphasise the fact that this is an industrial dispute. It expects every member taking part to be exemplary in his conduct and not to give any opportunity for police interference. The outbreak of any disturbances would be very damaging to the prospects of a successful termination to the dispute.

The Council sks pickets especially to avoid obstruction and to confine themselves strictly to their legitimate duties.

SOUTH WALES IS SOLID !

Not a Wheel Turning in Allied Industries

' MEN ARE SPLENDID !'

Throughout South Wales the stoppage is complete, and everywhere the men are loyally observing the orders of the T.U.C. to refrain from any conduct likely to lead to disturbance.

So unanimous has been the response to the call of the leaders, that not a wheel is turning in the industries affiliated to the T.U.C.

MONMOUTHSHIRE

Complete standstill of industries in the eastern valleys. Absolute unanimity prevails among the rank and file of the affiliated unions, and not a single wheel is turning in the allied industries.

Monmouth Education Authority—which has a majority of Labour representatives—has arranged to feed the school-children where required.

ABERDARE VALLEY

All railway and bus services are at a standstill. The miners' attitude indicates that they are absolutely loyal to the advice of their leaders to refrain from anything in the nature of riotous behaviour.

NEATH

The workers' have unanimously responded to the call in support of the miners, and the stoppage is complete.

With one exception, safety men are remaining at their posts. The behaviour of the men is splendid.

AMMAN VALLEY

Every industry and almost the entire transport services are at a standstill at Ammanford and throughout the populous Amman Valley.

GLAMORGANSHIRE

The men are obeying implicitly the instructions of their leaders not to create any disturbance. Crowded meetings of miners have registered their unanimous intention to stand by the T.U.C.

ABERTRIDWR

At the Windsor Colliery, Abertridwr, a deputation of the men and the management met and agreed to safety men being allowed to work.

A Trades Council, composed solely of branches affiliated to the T.U.C., has been formed to act as a Lock-out Committee for Abertridwr and Senghenydd.

PORT TALBOT

Perfect order is being maintained at Port Talbot, where all the industries are shut down.

Fig. 3.3 *The first issue of* The British Worker, *5 May 1926. The 'Message to All Workers' emphasized that they were engaged in 'an industrial dispute' and not in a strike aimed to overturn the constitution*

to get some promise that the Prime Minister would see justice done to the miners. Baldwin would promise nothing.

It took some time for all the strikers to return to work. Many felt betrayed and bitter, especially as there was nothing to protect them against victimization by vengeful employers, and they faced sackings and wage cuts. By 15 May there were actually more people on strike than before the General Strike had been called off. But Baldwin made soothing noises and condemned victimization, and the workers drifted back to their jobs – except the miners. The Miners' Federation still rejected lower wages and longer hours, and the Federation's leaders were not men to be bullied. Samuel could do little to persuade the coalowners to be sensible and, in spite of terrible suffering and starvation, the miners and their families held out. The public had always had some sympathy for the miners, and many subscriptions were raised to help them. Even so, the mining communities suffered. A miner's wife wrote:

> This is my fifth baby . . .. I have nothing for it and cannot get anything. The poverty among miners is pitiful and we cannot make ends meet when they are working, so how can we do now?

A visitor to the Leicestershire coalfield recorded:

> I visited one home where there were fourteen, including the parents, to be fed. Their bread bill is 11s 8d [about 58p], leaving 10d for all necessities beyond bread for fourteen people. [This income was from strike pay, poor relief and charity.]

Beatrice Webb took a different view. She thought the mining villages were healthier, on the whole, owing to the absence of dirty mining work. But even the miners, used as they were to suffering, were beaten in the end. By November 1926 the strike had collapsed in many coalfields, and at the end of the month it also collapsed in Yorkshire, South Wales and Durham. The owners got their eight-hour day and cuts in wages.

The miners' strike lost some markets for British coal exports, but the General Strike did little lasting damage to the economy as a whole. In 1927 the miners dug as much coal as in 1925, and industries which had laid off workers during 1926 because of coal shortages soon resumed normal output. Moreover, as a result of the events of 1926, there were fewer strikes in the late 1920s than in earlier years. The trade unions lost members, and male membership was below five million by 1930, in spite of the hard work of Walter Citrine, the General Secretary of the TUC, and Bevin in restoring the TUC's reputation. The Labour Party played little part in the events of 1926, though individual MPs spoke up for the workers in the Commons. The Labour Party actually benefited from the General Strike, since there was now increased interest in political action rather than industrial action – that is, in seeking change by electing Labour MPs rather than by strikes. The Labour Party won a number of by-elections and more seats in the following general election, in 1929.

THE MAN IN CONTROL.

JOHN BULL (*to the Pilot*). "YOU'VE GOT US THROUGH THAT FOG SPLENDIDLY."
MR. BALDWIN (*sticking quietly to his job*). "TELL ME ALL ABOUT THAT WHEN WE'RE PAST THESE ROCKS."

Fig. 3.4

Baldwin emerged from the General Strike as the man who had stood firm: a *Punch* cartoon showed him as the pilot, guiding the British ship through the crisis (see Fig. 3.4). But Baldwin's government could not resist its moment of spitefulness, and the Trade Disputes Act was passed in 1927, making a general strike or any strike in sympathy with workers in another industry illegal. The Act tightened the laws on picketing, to make it harder to organize an effective strike, and forbade civil servants' unions to be linked with the TUC. It also laid down that unions wishing to collect a levy on behalf of the Labour Party from

Fig. 3.5 A demonstration by trade unionists on the Thames Embankment, London, May 1927. The Trade Disputes Act was passed in spite of such protests

their members could do so only from members who 'contracted in' in writing. This reversed an Act of 1913, whereby the levy could be collected from all members who did not 'contract out'. Most union members did not bother to 'contract' one way or the other, so the money was collected after 1913 from all those who did not declare hostility to the Labour Party and seek exemption. After 1927, it was necessary actually to express support for Labour, and to seek to pay, with the result that less money was collected. (Attlee's Labour government in 1946 restored the 1913 position concerning this political levy.) The Conservatives took further revenge for the General Strike in another measure which cut unemployment benefit. They also seemed to suggest that some of the unemployed were idlers by insisting that, to qualify for benefit, they must 'genuinely' seek work, even though work was often nowhere in sight. The government had done much to restore stability after conflict, but such measures seemed petty rather than constructive.

(c) Conservative Reforms

Neville Chamberlain worked busily at the Ministry of Health and was responsible for two important reforms. The first was the Widows', Orphans' and Old Age Pensions Act of 1925. Lloyd George's coalition government had increased the old age pension to ten shillings (50p) a week in 1919 when prices were rising steeply. By 1921 the rise in prices had been checked and a period of deflation began, during which prices drifted downwards in the years before 1933. Wages tended to follow prices, but people receiving pensions and insurance benefits found the buying power of their incomes actually improving slightly. The government paid old age pensions entirely out of taxation and, with the increasing proportion of elderly people in British society found this a growing burden. The Act of 1925 provided for old age pensions as part of the system of national insurance, largely to be paid for by the insurance contributions of those in work, like sickness and unemployment benefits. These new pensions would become available at the age of sixty-five rather than seventy, and the insurance system was extended at the same time to cover widows and orphans.

Chamberlain claimed that the Act of 1925 completed a 'circle of security' for the British people. In fact, there were still hundreds of thousands who failed to qualify for insurance benefits and pensions, or who 'ran out' of rights to benefit because of long-term sickness or unemployment. Non-contributory old age pensions continued to exist for those too old to qualify under the new contributory system, and the poor law authorities continued to provide further assistance to elderly people in great need, and to others who were not entitled to benefits and pensions. The poor law authorities had been set up in 1834: they collected local rates for relief work, and this relief was administered by elected Guardians. It was usually difficult to collect enough rates to meet needs in the areas of greatest poverty, and many of the poor law authorities aimed to spend as little as possible. The poor in any case regarded relief by the Guardians as degrading, a last sort of charity for those who had failed. Above all, the poor feared that they might have to end their lives in the workhouse, where the poor law authorities housed those for whom there was no further hope.

In 1929 Chamberlain introduced his second important reform, the Local Government Act. Public Assistance Committees (PACs) of the county and county borough councils now replaced the old poor law authorities, 140 PACs compared with over 600 of the old authorities. The PACs therefore operated in larger areas and found it easier to collect adequate rates. The Act also changed the basis on which these local rates were collected, reducing or exempting industrial and agricultural payments and placing more of the burden on homes. Poorer areas were also able to get additional help from the Chancellor of the

FLAPPER: "WHICH ONE SHALL I THROW IT AT, FIDO?"

Fig. 3.6 Speculation about votes for the 'Flappers' prompted this thought by Strube in the Daily Express, *April 1927. The hopeful party leaders from left to right were Lloyd George, MacDonald and Baldwin*

Exchequer. The changes were administrative rather than humanitarian, however, and those in need of poor relief felt only small benefit. The PACs were hardly more popular than the former Guardians.

Joynson-Hicks, the Home Secretary, had some responsibility for another important reform when he was carried away by excitement at a public meeting, and promised equal voting rights for women. The Franchise Act of 1928 introduced universal adult suffrage, allowing women, like men, to vote at the age of twenty-one, and adding about five million 'Flappers' to the electorate, in spite of opposition from Churchill and others in the government (see Unit 2.1).

Otherwise, Baldwin's government proceeded quietly, and changed little. The British Broadcasting Company became the British Broadcasting Corporation in 1926, to be supervised (but not controlled) by governors appointed by the government, and with income from the sale of wireless licences. John Reith, the BBC's first Director-General, insisted on freedom from government control, so as not to endanger the Corporation's independence in presenting news and entertainment. Another public corporation, the Central Electricity Board, was set up in 1926 with the job of distributing electricity but not of generating or supplying it to the users, functions left mainly to private enterprise. In time the CEB was able to develop the National Grid, to bring electricity to most parts of Britain. The setting up of such public corporations by the Conservatives was actually a step towards nationalization. The

Merchandise Marks Act of 1926 required British manufacturers to mark imported products which carried their own name with their country of origin as well; and the Films Act of 1927 put a quota on foreign films in an effort to protect the infant British motion-picture industry. But by 1929 Baldwin's government was running out of reforming ideas – and another general election was due.

3.5   The General Election of 1929

The Conservatives had been losing by-elections in the run-up to 1929, but they nevertheless campaigned on the basis of Baldwin's record and reputation, and with the slogan 'Safety First'. Baldwin's face looked down from the hoardings, and the message to the voters was to trust him. Waldron Smithers, a Conservative MP with a passion for playing the organ, composed a lyric in praise of 'Stanley Boy' to the ready-made tune of 'Sonny Boy'. Liberals in Manchester wrote a less respectful lyric, and set it to the tune of 'Billy Boy'. Their man was Lloyd George, who campaigned vigorously. The Conservatives warned against the risk of change. Labour attacked the recent government's failure to do much about changing either the economy or society. And all parties hoped to attract the 'Flappers', voting for the first time. In electing the new House of Commons and, in effect the new government, the voters could choose between three men – Lloyd George, Baldwin and MacDonald – all of whom had already held office as Prime Minister, although the choice for most was between Conservative 'Safety First' and Labour 'Change'.

Lloyd George and the Liberals, nevertheless, struggled hardest to spell out a programme for curing the country's ills. Lloyd George produced money from his Political Fund to finance the Liberal campaign, and more than 500 candidates were put forward, together with a full programme for action:

The Liberal Policy is Work for the Workless, now. We can conquer Unemployment.

The policy looked ahead to ideas which became more acceptable in later years, and it outlined schemes for massive public works to employ the workless and add to the country's assets, by building houses and roads, modernizing the railways and increasing power-supplies. It included plans for more public corporations, for agricultural improvement and for town planning. It was a policy for action, and for spending, and it perhaps reminded the voters uneasily of the 'dynamic force' and alleged 'squandermania' they had rejected in 1922. But the Liberals not only suffered from the popular uneasiness about Lloyd George. From 1924 onwards they always found it difficult to win the negative voters who either voted Labour to keep out the Conservatives, or Conservative to keep out Labour.

Table 3.1 shows that the Liberals made only a small recovery from the election of 1924. The Conservatives lost seats, but most of them went to Labour, which gained more seats than the Conservatives despite a slightly smaller total vote. The Liberals won almost a quarter of the votes but less than a

Fig. 3.7 A Conservative Party poster at the general election of 1929. The voters proved disappointingly lacking in enthusiasm about the record of recent Conservative governments

tenth of the seats – and they complained bitterly about the first-past-the-post system. Labour had become the largest party in the Commons but again lacked an overall majority and, when MacDonald was sworn in as the new Prime Minister, his minority government depended on the Liberals to outvote the Conservative opposition, just as in 1924. Unemployment still stood at over a million, and there was soon to be the clearest evidence that the modest improvements in trade in the second half of the 1920s had already come to an end.

58   Success in British History since 1914

Further Reading
Seaman, L.C.B.: *Post-Victorian Britain, 1902–1951*. Methuen (London, 1966), chapters 15–20.
Cootes, R.J.: *The General Strike, 1926*. Longman (Harlow, 1964).
Hyde, M.M.: *Baldwin, the Unexpected P.M.* Hart-Davis (London, 1973).
Lyman, R.W.: *The First Labour Government, 1924*. Chapman and Hall (London, 1957).
Moore, R.: *The Emergence of the Labour Party, 1880–1924*. Hodder and Stoughton (London, 1978).
Mowat, C.L.: *The General Strike*. Oxford University Press (Oxford, 1966).

Documentary
Bettey, J.H.: *English Historical Documents, 1906–1939*. Routledge (London, 1967).
Mountfield, A.: *The General Strike*. Wayland (Hove, 1980).
Mowat, C.L.: *The General Strike, 1926*. Arnold Archive (London, 1969).

Exercises
1. Making use of Table 3.1, outline the changing electoral fortunes from 1922 to 1929 of (a) the Conservatives, (b) the Labour Party and (c) the Liberals. Summarize the main differences between the policies of the parties in this period.
2. Why were British voters required to go to the polls three times in the years 1922 to 1924? Why does the author call the elections of both 1923 and 1924 'premature' (page 44)?
3. Which of the views about the General Strike quoted in small print on pages 48 and 49 would you yourself most have wished to support in a speech in parliament? Outline the main points of your argument in giving such support.
4. What recent events led volunteer strike-breakers in 1926 to believe they were 'patriotically saving the country from 'the "Reds" ' (page 49)? How far was their belief justified?
5. What was the attitude to the General Strike of the cartoonist who drew Fig. 3.4, and how fittingly did he represent the part played by Baldwin at that time?
6. What were the main achievements and the main limitations of the domestic policy of Baldwin's government (1924–9)?
7. 'Safety First' was the Conservative slogan in the election of 1929. In the light of the record of Baldwin's government (1924–9), suggest *three* other slogans the Conservatives might have adopted at this election, arguing in support of each of them.
8. Summarize the likely opinions and the reasons for them of a British coalminer, looking back on the 1920s at the end of the decade, about (a) the coalowners, (b) trade unions and (c) government policies. (Refer to Units 2.3(c) and 3.4(b).)

Unit Four

The Years of Hope: Foreign and Imperial Policy, 1919–29

4.1 The Peace Settlement

(a) **Aims and Intentions**

Lloyd George went to Paris to play his part as peacemaker hardly a month after the general election of 1918, in which he had played the part of a demagogue (see Unit 2.2). Perhaps only someone as versatile as Lloyd George could have changed, in that time, from buying votes with sometimes petty speeches about revenge to striving constructively to bring about everlasting peace. The peace conference opened in January 1919, and its proceedings were influenced mainly by the leaders of the victorious Allies. President Wilson of the USA brought to Paris a mixed bag of ideals but a readiness, at the same time, to see the Central Powers punished. Clemenceau, the French Prime Minister, presided at the conference with great enthusiasm for punishment, and with a fixed determination to make Germany weaker. His point of view can be summarized in a brief exchange with Wilson:

> 'Pray, M. Clemenceau, have you ever been to Germany?'
> 'No, sir! But twice in my lifetime Germans have been to France.'

Clemenceau intended that they should never come again. Lloyd George summed up his own intentions when he said:

> We want peace. . . . We want a peace which will be just but not vindictive. We want a stern peace. . . . The crime demands it. But its severity must be designed not to gratify vengeance, but to vindicate justice.

There was therefore general agreement that Germany and its allies should suffer some punishment – though there was room for argument about the scale of it – but it was also intended that the peace settlement could achieve far more than that.

Lloyd George and Wilson had both listed their war aims in January 1918. They agreed on several specific points, such as the return of Alsace-Lorraine to France and the restoration of Belgian independence. They also agreed on certain general principles: that frontiers should be redrawn on the basis of nationality to free the peoples of Europe from foreign government; that armaments should be reduced; and that an international organization should be set up to preserve future peace. Most of the details of the peace settlement, however, had still to be worked out in Paris.

It was neither the best time nor the best place for peacemaking. Wartime anger had not yet abated, and it was especially strong in France. An influenza epidemic had followed the war, sweeping through Europe and beyond, killing more people than even the war had done. Russia had already experienced revolution, and other countries trembled on the brink of it. Almost every economy had been distorted by the costs of war, and disrupted societies faced daunting problems of reconstruction. People everywhere hoped for miracles from the peacemakers – an instant and lasting settlement to solve all problems. All that the peacemakers could actually do was to establish an international framework within which recovery could take place, so that the habits of peace could grow again. This was the task they set themselves in Paris and, not surprisingly, they found that there were many conflicting ideas about what precisely should be done.

One major difficulty was that, while working fast, the peacemakers had to decide both broad principles and, at the same time, innumerable specific and often minor details. Though assisted by their teams of experts, Lloyd George, Wilson and Clemenceau shouldered an enormous burden. Other Allied leaders were not allowed a major role; the Japanese became convinced that racial prejudice against non-whites in Paris meant that they were not all that welcome at the conference. The defeated powers were hardly consulted, except when they were required to sign the treaties which had been drawn up. Russia was unrepresented, since its Bolshevik government was considered either temporary or indecent. It is sometimes argued that the peacemakers were not only trying to prevent Germany from disturbing the future peace of Europe, but were also trying to build barriers against communism. Certainly, while the peace conference went on, all the Allies except Italy had troops in Russia giving encouragement, if not much active help, to the Russian counter-revolutionaries who were trying to overthrow Lenin and the Bolsheviks (see Unit 2.3(c)).

The peace settlement was constructed around several central pillars. One of these was the Treaty of Versailles with Germany, which aimed to curb Germany's ability further to threaten the security of France and Europe. Another was the division of the defeated Austro-Hungarian and Turkish Empires into smaller states, as far as possible on the basis of nationality. A third pillar was the League of Nations, to safeguard future peace. Britain's main interest in the settlement lay in so reconstructing Europe that future conflicts might be avoided, and Britain's involvement there might be small. By way of gain, Britain cast its eyes on the overseas territories which had belonged to Germany and the Turkish Empire. Woodrow Wilson had an American's suspicion of colonial empires, but a useful formula was found for these territories. They became known as mandated territories, and were transferred to Britain, France and other powers on a temporary basis, and under the supervision of the Mandates Commission of the League of Nations. Article 22 of the Covenant of the League stated that, to the peoples of these territories:

> there should be applied the principle that the well-being and development of such peoples form a sacred trust of civilization and that securities for the performance of this trust should be embodied in this Covenant.

Britain, therefore, took control of Palestine, Iraq and Transjordan by the Treaty of Sèvres with Turkey; and of Tanganyika and parts of Togoland and the Cameroons by the Treaty of Versailles with Germany.

(b) The Treaties

Five treaties made up the Paris Settlement: the Treaties of Versailles (with Germany), St Germain (with Austria), Trianon (with Hungary), Neuilly (with Bulgaria) and Sèvres (with Turkey). The first was signed in June 1919, the last in August 1920. The first twenty-six articles of each treaty set down the terms of the Covenant of the League of Nations. The treaties also had similar clauses requiring the defeated powers to cut down their armed forces and to pay reparations for wartime devastation; France and Belgium especially thought such payments were due from the Central Powers. Beyond that, the treaties were concerned mainly with territorial changes. Article 231 of the Treaty of Versailles, however, set out what became known as the 'War Guilt Clause' which appeared to saddle 'Germany and her allies' with 'responsibility' 'for causing all the loss and damage' of the recent war.

Apart from its overseas territories, Germany lost Alsace-Lorraine (to France), Eupen and Malmedy (to Belgium), Northern Schleswig (to Denmark), West Prussia and Upper Silesia (to Poland), and Memel, Danzig and the Saar (to League of Nations control). The Saar was a region rich in coal deposits, and for fifteen years its production was given over to the French, as compensation for the damage done to their coalfields in the war. The Saarlanders could then vote by plebiscite to decide their own future. Indeed, partly due to Lloyd George's influence, plebiscites were used in 1919 to determine the precise limits of Germany's losses, though no such procedure was allowed concerning Alsace-Lorraine. Nor was there a plebiscite in West Prussia, where the peacemakers insisted that a 'Corridor' was necessary to give access to the Baltic Sea to the new state of Poland, recreated from what had been possessions of Russia and Austria-Hungary in 1914. Germany lost almost half its iron production, about 15 per cent of its coal and agricultural production and some 10 per cent of its total industrial production. Germany and the German-speaking Republic of Austria were forbidden to unite, again with the intention of preventing future German pre-eminence. Allied troops were temporarily stationed on the Rhine and, further to protect France, the area west of the Rhine and thirty miles east of it was permanently to be demilitarized (free from military installations and personnel). In any case, Germany's army was limited to 100 000 men, and its other armed forces were crippled.

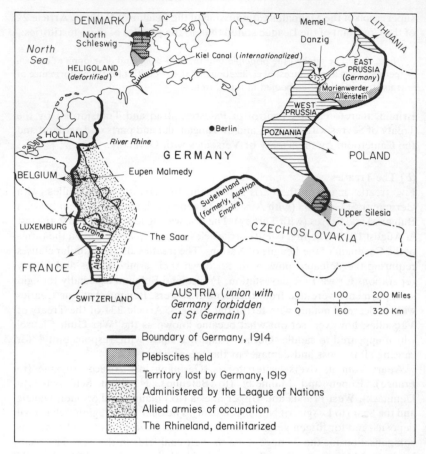

Fig. 4.1 The peace settlement: the treatment of Germany

There were squeals of anguish from Germany at this allegedly harsh treatment. Some Germans, Hitler among them, were determined to extract the maximum humiliation from the Treaty of Versailles, and to regard it as grossly unjust. They also complained, with some justification, that it was a *Diktat*, imposed upon them rather than negotiated. Yet, in the peace settlement as a whole, Germany remained one of the strongest powers in Europe. The peacemakers, unwittingly perhaps, increased the potential danger from Germany by creating small states in central and eastern Europe in other treaties of the Paris Settlement, trying hard to do justice to the ambitions of all nationalities. During the 1920s Germany had a democratic republican government which was law-abiding, but in the 1930s, when Hitler came to power, it became obvious that none of its neighbours was strong enough to resist Nazi aggression, and even France was beaten into surrender in 1940. The strength of Germany then made nonsense of the strident complaints that the country had been crippled in 1919. Nevertheless, the air was filled with recriminations after the signing of the Treaty of Versailles, with many Germans complaining that Germany had been treated vindictively. The French, including Clemenceau, suspected that Germany had been treated too leniently, a view shared by many of the Conservatives in the House of Commons on whom Lloyd George relied for support. In April 1919 he had to defend himself in the House, appealing for moderation while the delicate work of peacemaking was still going on, and asking MPs:

> not to soil this triumph of right in the angry passions of the moment, but to consecrate the sacrifices of millions to the permanent redemption of the human race from the scourge and agony of war.

The fiercest arguments about the Treaty of Versailles concerned the War Guilt Clause and reparations. The peacemakers passed the problem of the extent of reparation to the Allied Reparation Commission, and the Commission only completed its calculations in April 1921. Germany was then required to pay the sum of £6 600 million, plus interest, until the debt was settled. For Germany to pay this it would, of course, be necessary for the Germans to deliver goods of an equivalent value, or to sell such goods in order to obtain an acceptable currency. The Germans claimed that this was impossible, especially since they had been 'robbed' of territories and productive capacity. The French retorted that the recent war had been fought mainly on French and Belgian soil, not German, and that was where the massive devastation had occurred: the debt was fully deserved.

The economist, J.M. Keynes criticized reparations, forecasting that they would bedevil international trade and finance for years to come. The British coal industry, for example, felt some effects when Germany pushed its coal cheaply onto world markets in urgent search of foreign currency. Yet the Allies themselves had war debts, particularly to the USA, and the prospect of getting money from Germany to help pay them was naturally tempting. Reparations, though, merely added a further complication to the underlying economic problem of the 1920s – that all countries were engaged in cut-throat competition for markets where there was little demand. Most European countries were debtors after 1918, and what they all needed was to sell their goods to the USA, the richest creditor country, in order to earn dollars. That the USA imposed tariffs against foreign goods and made sales by Europeans very difficult, was a more fundamental problem than reparations. Reparations were finally abandoned in 1932, but it was significant that their payment only ran smoothly after 1924, when the Germans paid with money borrowed from the USA.

(c) The League of Nations
Lloyd George's list of *War Aims* had ended with the assertion that:

We must seek by the creation of some international organization to limit the burden of armaments and diminish the probability of war.

The idea for such an organization was not new, and there was widespread international support for it. Woodrow Wilson was able to create something of a myth that he invented the League of Nations, but much of the spadework was done in the British Foreign Office. Eric Drummond, a British civil servant, became the League's first Secretary-General, remaining in office until 1933 and doing much to secure the Secretariat's independence from the vested interests of individual nations. The aims and rules of the League were set out in the Covenant, which allowed all the member-countries an equal vote in the Assembly. A smaller body, the Council, was to meet and act in time of crisis, and this included both permanent and temporary members. The permanent members were the victorious Allies of 1918: Britain, France, Italy and Japan. The USA, having taken part in founding the League, refused to join it (see Unit 4.2(a)). Germany and the other defeated powers were not at first allowed to join the League, and the main burden of the organization always fell chiefly on the shoulders of Britain and France.

From the outset, the League had little power to deal with international crises. There was even some confusion about its general aims. The first preference of the British Foreign Office had been for a narrow League, to deal simply with threats to peace. Others wanted far more, a broader League which could also undertake humanitarian and economic work for the benefit of mankind. Lloyd George was willing to accept this wider objective, and the Covenant eventually compromised between the two points of view. The League set up Commissions, for Disarmament, Mandates, Minorities and Military Affairs, and numerous committees to deal with such matters as health, labour, communications, drugs, child welfare and women's rights.

But the crucial question was always what might be done if world peace were threatened by an aggressive power. The Covenant tackled this question in its Articles 10–17. Members of the League undertook to support one another against aggression, and disputes were to be submitted to the Council. Members undertook not to go to war for three months after any decision by the Council. The Covenant provided for the use of sanctions against any states that broke these rules, the main sanction being an economic boycott of the offending country. If that was not enough, the League had the right to request military forces from its members. The theories behind Articles 10–17 were sound enough, but there was too little spelling-out of exactly how the system would work. Optimistically, the peacemakers assumed that future wars would be threatened only by small and inexperienced states. In 1919 it seemed impossible that any major power would again want to go to war: condemnation by the League should therefore be enough to deter troublemakers. What was never really faced was the dilemma that, one day, the League might have to deal with a situation in which it could stop a war only by fighting a war. Hardly surprisingly, the peacemakers shrank from such a prospect.

Fig. 4.2 The remains of the Unknown Soldier carried past the newly unveiled Cenotaph in Whitehall, London, November 1920. Further war seemed unthinkable to those who paid homage to the dead of the war of 1914–18

4.2   British Foreign Policy in the 1920s

(a) Britain's Role

There were three main aims in British foreign policy after the First World War. One was to preserve the peace of Europe. The second was to support the League of Nations, both in Europe and further afield. The third, and some-times the most dominant aim, was to continue to defend the British Empire and to fulfil Britain's responsibilities towards the citizens of the colonies and the Dominions. Lloyd George hoped to pursue all these aims in the peace settlement. He particularly hoped that the settlement would establish the foundations for lasting peace in Europe, and that the League of Nations would guarantee this peace.

Lloyd George's government committed Britain to membership of the League. In the USA, however, the Democrats were defeated in elections, and the Republicans rejected US membership. This alarmed the French, who had counted on American support if they were ever again threatened by Germany. The 1920s, therefore, began with France in a state of some anxiety, and with Britain half-envious of the way in which the USA had been able to distance itself from Europe's problems. Geographical separation from the continent and worldwide imperial interests gave the British something of the American impatience with the squabbles of Europeans. Britain had no wish to become involved in the sort of European problems which had brought war in 1914. Yet 1914 had shown how difficult it was not to be involved. In the absence of the USA, the French now constantly demanded British support for French security, and the British found this rather tiresome. Once the peace treaties had been signed, it became a matter of debate just how far Britain should go in seeking to ensure the peace of Europe by giving the sort of guarantees the French demanded. At least superficially, it was a guarantee to Belgium which had led Britain into war in 1914.

There were similar arguments about how far Britain should go in supporting the League of Nations. There were many who seemed not to realize that the League could only be as strong as its members were willing to make it. The Covenant appeared to guarantee protection against aggression, but it was imprecise about how this should be done – and that perhaps was how Britain and other founder-members of the League wished to leave it. Throughout the inter-war period, from 1919 to 1939, British thinking was always complicated by questions of empire. Many in Britain thought that the country's real interests lay not in Europe but in its overseas possessions and the Dominions with which the British had close ties (see Unit 4.3). More than continental Europeans, therefore, the British viewed international problems from the standpoint of having interests which had to be defended in every continent. In order to be free to defend their interests there seemed still to be a case for arguing that Britain should avoid specific commitments to the French or, indeed, to anyone else.

(b) **The Coalition and the Conservatives**
Lord Curzon was Britain's Foreign Secretary from 1919 to January 1924. Though overshadowed in the coalition government by Lloyd George, Curzon was ever ready to play the part of an international statesman. He gave his name to the Curzon Line, the proposed boundary between Poland and Russia in 1920, but the Poles rejected it, seizing extensive lands further east during the Russo-Polish War which ended in 1921. (The Curzon Line was nevertheless the basis of the frontier after 1945.) Meanwhile, the coalition government tackled the problems left over from the war of 1914–18 and the peace conference. Lloyd George would have liked to quieten French fears, but his co-

operation with Briand came to nothing when Briand lost office to Poincaré. British troops were withdrawn from Russia during 1920, having done nothing of consequence to weaken Bolshevik rule. An Anglo-Russian trade pact in 1921 brought some improvement in relations. Eager for more general improvement in international relations, and aware of his own declining prestige, Lloyd George strongly supported the international conference which met at Genoa in April 1922.

The Genoa Conference proved disappointing, however. It was attended by Russians and Germans, among others, but hopes for agreements were frustrated by the French: Poincaré remained hostile to both Russia and Germany, Lloyd George was criticized at home by Churchill, and abroad by the French, for his new-found goodwill towards the Bolsheviks. The French again demanded British guarantees of their security, which the British were unwilling to give; and the French resolutely opposed any reduction in reparations, which the Germans demanded. Such underlying conflicts ensured the failure of the conference, and Lloyd George made none of the progress towards improving international trade he had hoped for. The most significant result of the Genoa Conference was that the Russians and Germans moved to nearby Rapallo, to sign a treaty of friendship which, as much as anything, was a snub to the rest of Europe.

On the surface more seemed to be achieved in Washington in 1921–2. The Washington Agreements took the form of three treaties. One was a five-power pact for reducing capital ships (battleships and cruisers) in the navies of the USA, Britain, Japan, France and Italy. None was to be built for ten years, and some older ships were to be scrapped. The powers would then arrive at a ratio of 5:5:3 for the USA, Britain and Japan, while France and Italy would each have just over half the Japanese tonnage. The USA, Britain, Japan and France also signed a four-power treaty, respecting their mutual interests in the Pacific and, finally, there was a nine-power treaty to respect the independence of China. But it was a feature of all the Agreements that no provision was made for upholding them. The USA wanted no commitments of that sort, and the British attitude was similar. The four-power treaty, in fact, actually enabled Britain to escape from the obligations towards Japan which had been undertaken in an alliance of 1902; and this was resented by the Japanese. The scrapping of British capital ships also fitted in nicely with the cuts in spending which Geddes had demanded (see Unit 2.3(a)).

Conferences were not the only method by which the powers tried to settle their problems after 1918. Nationalists in Turkey rebelled against the Treaty of Sèvres, and set about expelling Italians and Greeks from the country. Under the leadership of Mustapha Kemal, Turkish forces moved towards the Dardanelles, which had been placed under international supervision, and the Chanak Crisis developed (see Unit 2.4). Almost alone, Lloyd George was prepared to resist. Poincaré withdrew the French troops, and the Italians too departed. Fighting was avoided, however, by timely negotiation with Kemal and, after the fall of Britain's coalition government, Curzon helped to negotiate a new treaty with Turkey – the Treaty of Lausanne (1923) – which made some limited changes in the terms of the Treaty of Sèvres. The Dardanelles, while remaining demilitarized, would be supervised by the Turks themselves, an obligation which Kemal honourably fulfilled.

Lloyd George thus showed greater wisdom in foreign policy than many of his contemporaries in the years after the peace settlement. In recognizing the need to seek reconciliation with Russia and with Germany, he was too far-sighted for the French. And in recognizing the need to uphold international agreements against law-breakers, he was too far-sighted for many of his Conservative supporters in the Commons. Kemal, it turned out, had only limited objectives and offered no real threat to international peace, but the peace-loving powers were soon to face more aggressive dictators in Mussolini and Hitler. By 1922 such men were already noting that there seemed to be little enthusiasm in Europe for upholding treaties and right. Yet Lloyd George had also seemed impetuous, and there was some ill-feeling in the Dominions that he had done too little to consult Canadians and others in deciding on his policy.

In December 1922 Curzon complained that Bonar Law, Lloyd George's successor, went to the opposite extreme:

> willing to give up anything and everything rather than have a row.

Mussolini had become Italy's Prime Minister in 1922 and, in 1923, he bombarded and occupied Corfu, trying to force the Greeks to pay an alleged debt. The French too took the law into their own hands in 1923, marching into the Ruhr to help themselves from the mines and factories because Germany was failing to pay reparations. Britain protested against both lawless acts, but to little effect. Baldwin, who succeeded Bonar Law, had little interest in foreign affairs. An international conference gave Mussolini almost all that he wanted, and the French remained in the Ruhr. For the Opposition, MacDonald complained:

> (British) policy has been amateurish, feeble, uncertain. We have, therefore, almost ceased to count except as a hope (a no mean asset, however, if used).

The best that Baldwin and Curzon could do was to persuade the Americans to take part in an inquiry into reparations and the German economy. In January 1924, however, the general election gave MacDonald the chance himself to take charge of Britain's foreign policy (see Units 3.1 and 3.2).

(c) The First Labour Government

Ramsay MacDonald intended to play an active part in promoting better international understanding in three areas: to mediate in the Franco-German feud, to strengthen the powers of the League of Nations, and to reduce the isolation of the USSR. In fact, he was in office too briefly to achieve much at all.

The French showed no signs of leaving the Ruhr even though German workers refused to work for them. The French occupation had helped to weaken Germany's currency and to fuel rampant inflation in Germany. The underlying problem, of course, was one concerning reparations and it was this that MacDonald tackled. However it was the USA's willingness to lend money to Germany that was the key factor in relaxing tension and restoring the German currency. Political change in France also helped, when the moderate Herriot replaced Poincaré. A new scale of reparations was worked out in the Dawes Plan, named after the American General Dawes, and this was accepted at an international conference in London in August 1924. A loan to help the Germans was raised soon afterwards, with Americans providing most of the money. The French agreed to leave the Ruhr but took until 1925 to do so.

MacDonald was no more willing than his predecessors to guarantee French security, but he was keen to examine ways of strengthening the League's powers to deal with disputes. He himself led the British delegation to the League Assembly at Geneva. He felt obliged to reject a plan to bind all members of the League to give military help to the victims of aggression, since this would gain little support in Britain as being too inflexible. Instead, he worked with Herriot to produce the Geneva Protocol, to bind all members to accept compulsory arbitration in disputes. He also persuaded the French to stop further opposition to Germany's admission to the League. The Geneva Protocol was already running into opposition when the Labour government fell, however, and Baldwin's government quickly buried it.

MacDonald also ran into difficulties in his dealings with the USSR. Diplomatic recognition of Russia's Communist government aroused criticism and exposed MacDonald to the suspicions of the anti-communists. There was even more criticism in Britain when the Prime Minister proposed to extend Lloyd George's trade pact of 1921, and to lend money to the Russians. Details of the loan agreement were not complete by the time the Labour government lost the election of 1924 (see Unit 3.3). The next government was quick to cancel it, suspending the trade pact too and, in 1927, virtually withdrawing diplomatic recognition from the USSR.

(d) Austen Chamberlain and the Locarno Honeymoon
Austen Chamberlain was Britain's Foreign Secretary from 1924 to 1929. He readily severed MacDonald's links with the USSR and steered clear of more precise commitments to the League of Nations. But he was willing to continue efforts to improve international relations in western Europe as long as Britain's commitments remained limited. Chamberlain's years at the Foreign Office coincided with those of Gustav Stresemann as Germany's Foreign Minister and with the influence of Briand in French foreign policy. The three men worked well together.

Their first achievement was the Locarno Treaties of December 1925, regarded at the time as of great importance in guaranteeing European peace. In one of the Treaties, France, Germany and Belgium confirmed their acceptance of the frontiers in western Europe which had been laid down in the Treaty of

Versailles. To the delight of the French, Chamberlain agreed that Britain would guarantee to uphold these frontiers, and Mussolini undertook a similar commitment on behalf of Italy. It was also part of this agreement that the Rhineland would remain demilitarized. But Britain stood aside from the other agreements which were made at Locarno, merely encouraging the continentals to settle their own problems. Germany signed Arbitration Treaties with France, Belgium, Czechoslovakia and Poland, 'assuring the peaceful settlement of differences which might arise'. France made separate treaties with Czechoslovakia and Poland, exchanging mutual promises of support against aggression. The way was now clear for Germany to enter the League of Nations, and it took up membership in 1926, gaining a permanent seat on the Council with Britain's support.

The Locarno Treaties were greeted enthusiastically. At last France and Germany seemed to have been reconciled. Reparation payments were being made regularly, and there was a general climate of goodwill. Few at the time attached much importance to the fact that Germany had not pledged its total acceptance of frontiers in eastern Europe, in the same way as in the west. Even fewer worried that the Locarno Treaties, while often mentioning the League of Nations, had in effect by-passed it; and in overlapping the peace settlement of 1919–20, the Locarno Treaties had perhaps undermined that settlement, confirming only parts of it. Britain's guarantee of frontiers in western Europe also helped to blind observers to the fact that no such guarantees had been given for eastern Europe, an area in which Chamberlain was determined not to become involved. The guarantee to France and Belgium was perhaps after all no more than the recognition that Britain could hardly remain uninvolved anyway, if disturbances occurred so close to the British Isles. Britain had also enlisted Mussolini's support in this guarantee, perhaps luring him into a new peaceful policy after his violent attack on Corfu and seizure of Fiume from Jugoslavia in 1924.

The honeymoon period which followed the Locarno Treaties was given new expression in 1928 in the Pact of Paris (the Kellogg–Briand Pact). Briand suggested to Kellogg, the American Secretary of State, that they should give a moral lead. Kellogg suggested wider participation and sixty-five nations in all signed the Pact, Britain and the USSR among them:

> The High Contracting Parties solemnly declare, in the names of their respective peoples, that they condemn recourse to war for the solution of international controversies and renounce it as an instrument of national policy in their relations with one another.

Like the Washington Agreements, the Pact said nothing about how it was to be upheld. The British government was not alone in noting that it contained no new commitments which were likely to be embarrassing. Ringing declarations had now been substituted for clear thought about how international problems might be solved. Japan signed the Pact of Paris but went to war in Manchuria in

Fig. 4.3 Satisfaction after the signing of the Locarno agreements in London in December 1925: a group in the garden of 11 Downing Street. Baldwin, extreme right, and Mrs Baldwin, extreme left. The three Foreign Ministers who contributed most to the new spirit of international goodwill were Briand of France (centre, front row, with top hat and moustache), Stresemann of Germany (to the right in the row behind Briand) and Austen Chamberlain of Britain (to the left, row behind Stresemann). Winston Churchill and Mrs Churchill are at the back

1931 in hot pursuit of 'national policy'. The pieces of paper, and some minor successes by the League of Nations in settling disputes between small states, added to the general optimism in Britain as elsewhere. But the apparent calm of the late 1920s was mainly because no major power created a crisis.

The problem of disarmament was typical of the underlying issues which had not been settled. Hoping to build on the goodwill of Locarno, a Disarmament Committee set to work in 1926 to prepare a plan to put to an international conference. It laboured in vain for five years. The Germans pointed out that they had been disarmed after 1918, and it was time for others to follow suit. The others haggled and avoided decisions. In 1930 the USSR suggested total disarmament by all; and the idea was rejected. The Committee then drafted a plan, only to see it rejected by the USSR and Germany. In despair, the whole problem was referred to a new international Disarmament Conference which met in 1932 under the chairmanship of Arthur Henderson. The French now objected to the armaments which Germany might be allowed and, when Hitler became Chancellor of Germany in 1933, the Germans walked out. The Conference was abandoned the following year. Meanwhile in 1927, at Geneva, the USA tried to extend the naval disarmament previously agreed at Washington. The French and Italians refused to attend, and the British disagreed with the detailed figures; and that plan failed too. Something was rescued, however, during the second Labour government in 1930, when a Naval Conference was held in London. The USA, Britain and Japan agreed a ratio for their navies, including submarines, of 10:10:7. From Britain's point of view, this fulfilled the twin aims of curbing expenditure and preserving significant naval power.

4.3   The British Empire after the First World War

(a) The White Dominions

The declaration of war in 1914 was the last occasion on which Britain took a major foreign policy decision which bound Australia, Canada, New Zealand and South Africa – the Dominions. They already controlled their own internal affairs, and were considered rather like overseas settlements of Britons, although Canada had a substantial French population too. Their political systems were modelled, in varying degrees, on the British system, and political power lay with whites. When South Africa had been granted Dominion status in 1910, little notice was taken of the fact that most South Africans were black. Whites at that time assumed that it was natural for whites to rule and for blacks to obey. It also seemed natural to the British that the Dominions, like the dependencies within the British Empire, should fight alongside the mother country in war, and, like the entire Empire, the Dominions gave invaluable help to Britain against the Central Powers. Jan Smuts of South Africa even sat in Lloyd George's Imperial War Cabinet.

By 1918, however, the Dominions were eager to control their own foreign affairs. They sent their own representatives to the peace conference, and became individual founder-members of the League of Nations. Some took control of mandated territories. Australia eagerly took over mandates in the Pacific and South Africa took over what had been German South-West Africa. In 1922 South Africa and the other Dominions warned Lloyd George not to take their support for granted in the Chanak Crisis. But it was not entirely clear just how independent the Dominions were. As was often the case in the history of the British Empire, practice ran ahead of theory. It was clear which countries were Dominions, but it was less clear what their status was. Canadians and South Africans thought some definition was necessary, though Australians and New Zealanders pressed less hard for this. Jan Smuts claimed that the Dominions and Britain were members of 'our family', of 'our Commonwealth of Nations', a phrase used by Lord Rosebery as early as 1884, but again hardly a precise one. The question of definition was shelved at the Imperial Conference of 1923 (see Glossary), but it came up again in 1926.

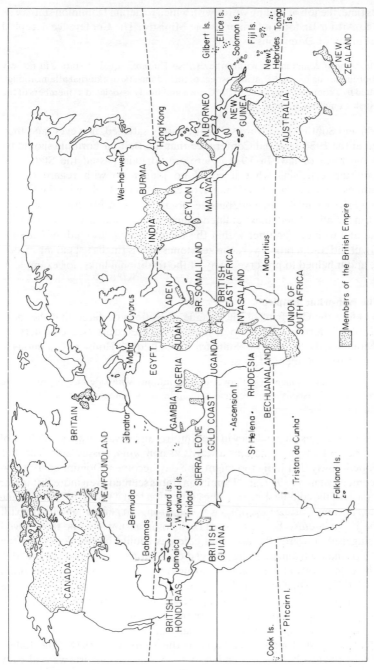

Fig. 4.4 The British Empire in 1914

Members of the British Empire

This time, the job of finding words with which to define Dominion status was given to Arthur Balfour, a former Prime Minister. The Conference accepted his definition of Dominions as:

> Autonomous communities within the British Empire, equal in status, in no way subordinate one to another in any aspect of their domestic or external affairs, though united by a common allegiance to the Crown and freely associated as members of the British Commonwealth of Nations.

Canada and South Africa were still not entirely satisfied, however, and they argued at the 1930 Imperial Conference that the Balfour Formula should be given the force of law. In 1931, therefore, Britain passed the Statute of Westminster, clarifying what it could no longer do with regard to the Dominions – what in fact it had long ago ceased doing. Links with the Crown and the Privy Council remained, but the Dominions were effectively independent. On the other hand, they retained a unique, but voluntary, link both with Britain and with one another within the British Commonwealth of Nations. Goodwill and co-operation were the keystones of this English-speaking association, and it helped to preserve many of the traditional links, for example in trade.

(b) The Non-white Empire

Even before the Covenant of the League of Nations declared that the mandated colonial territories were to be held as 'a sacred trust' (see Unit 4.1(a)), E.S. Montagu, the Secretary of State for India, told the House of Commons in 1917 that Britain intended to pursue:

> the gradual development of self-governing institutions, with a view to the progressive realization of responsible government in India as an integral part of the British Empire.

India was the largest dependency in the Empire, and it was always something of a test-case for Britain's intentions towards its non-white possessions. The idea developed slowly that India too might one day become a Dominion. But that day seemed distant in 1917, and Dominion status seemed even more distant for other parts of the colonial Empire. The conviction that it was Britain's right and duty to rule non-European peoples was still strong. In general, the British still put their own interests before those of their colonial subjects, and they moved only sluggishly towards the idea that colonies should be developed for the benefit of their inhabitants. They moved even more slowly towards the idea that the colonies should have self-government and, after that, their freedom. But in 1925 Ormsby-Gore, at the Colonial Office, proclaimed the principle that British policy in West and East Africa should take account of the welfare of Africans, and the Colonial Development Act of 1929 provided meagre funds for colonial improvements, especially in the West Indies.

Attention centred mainly on India in the years after 1918. The Indian National Congress had been founded in 1885, and nationalists were already demanding freedom. In April 1919, when tension was widespread, crowds gathered in the city of Amritsar in the Punjab. Few, if any, were armed, but General Dyer ordered his troops to open fire: 379 Indians were killed and over a thousand wounded, including women and children. The coalition government in Britain quickly recalled Dyer. Indians called the event the Massacre of Amritsar, but the British public raised £30 000 to show its support for the General. Lloyd George took a more constructive view and, before the end of the year, the Government of India Act was passed, to confer on the Indians what George V called 'a definite share in the government'. It was a very small share, in the government of India as a whole. Indians could elect a majority of the members of the country's parliament, but the power to take decisions lay entirely with the British Viceroy of India, a post once held by Curzon. India also had provincial governments, however, and the Act of 1919 set up a system in which British governors kept control of 'reserved subjects' (such as finance and law and order), while elected Indians managed 'transferred subjects' (such as sanitation and other social services). The theory behind this 'dyarchy' (dual administration) was that the Indians would gain experience, and practise the business of government on a limited scale. The scale was much too limited for politically minded Indians, however, and the scene was set for a tug-of-war between Indians and British which went on until India finally gained its freedom in 1947.

One of the leaders of the Indian campaign was Mohandas Gandhi, who preached non-violence but also non-co-operation with the British. The weapon of the boycott was used persistently. A tour of India by the Prince of Wales in 1921 was boycotted. British exports were boycotted. British laws were defied, and Gandhi was in and out of jail while the British struggled to find an answer to the problems he posed. In 1927 Baldwin's government sent the Simon Commission to examine the system of Indian government, but the Commission did not include Indians and it too was boycotted. Simon had still not reported by the time MacDonald returned to power in Britain in 1929 and, by that time, Gandhi was ready to launch a new campaign. 'I hold British rule to be a curse,' he declared (see Unit 8.1(a)).

Meanwhile, the mandated territories had made the British Empire even larger. These territories brought their own problems for British governments, and none more so than Palestine where the coalition government took up its mandate in 1920 (see Unit 12.3(b)). At that time, however, the problem of Ireland seemed much more urgent.

4.4 The Irish Settlement

In 1914 civil war in Ireland had seemed more probable than war in Europe. The Home Rule Bill of 1912, setting up an Irish parliament and government in Dublin, was due to take effect in 1914. Catholic Irishmen had long demanded Home Rule, and the Bill of 1912 was the third such measure to try to concede it. The first, in 1886, had not been accepted by the House of Commons after a split in the Liberal Party. The second, in 1893, had been vetoed by the House of Lords. In 1911, however, the Lords had lost their right of veto, and they could delay the third Home Rule Bill only until 1914. But Ulstermen were ready to resist it, regarding Home Rule as Rome rule, and they were bitterly hostile to the prospect of a government dominated by Catholics. Armed bands, both Protestant and Catholic, stood ready for conflict in Ireland, and Asquith's government in London seemed merely to be waiting apprehensively. When war with Germany began, Asquith seized the opportunity to withdraw the Home Rule Bill, and to postpone still further any settlement of the Irish question.

Irish nationalists wanted to be free from English rule, which they looked on as the rule of conquerors and heretics. For many years Irish nationalism and Catholicism had marched hand-in-hand in often violent protest against alien government by Englishmen. In the north-east of Ireland, however, there were descendants of Scottish and Protestant settlers who much preferred British rule to that of Catholic Irishmen. During the war of 1914–18 these northerners gave loyal support to Britain; the southerners, on the other hand, were divided. Many Irish Nationalists, led by John Redmond, backed the war effort, expecting Home Rule when the war ended. More extreme Irishmen took a different view. The Sinn Fein organization, founded in 1902 by Arthur Griffith, had always believed that Home Rule was a poor substitute for real independence. The movement now gained recruits from those who had no sympathy for Britain's war effort, and support for Redmond slipped away steadily. Sinn Fein also passed into the hands of yet more fiery leaders.

The movement gained considerable prestige with the Easter Rebellion in Dublin in 1916. The Irish rebels set up their headquarters in the Dublin post office and flew the green, white and orange flag of the Irish Republic. For a week there was the crackle of gunfire and the thunder of British artillery. But the contest was always one-sided: there was no hope of victory. When Patrick Pearse, the rebel commandant, eventually surrendered, however, some sixty dead had been added to the list of Irish martyrs, to be remembered in poetry, prose and innumerable songs. W.B. Yeats wrote that 'a terrible beauty was born', referring to an even more ferocious determination among Irishmen one day to be free. The British went on to make more martyrs, executing Pearse and fifteen ringleaders and arresting 4 000 others. One of the leaders, Eamon de Valera, was spared execution because his American birth raised doubts about his nationality, and Britain had no wish to offend the USA while the World War continued. In 1917 de Valera became the political leader of Sinn Fein, for which support now grew steadily. Another survivor of the Rebellion was Michael Collins, who became the leader of the Irish Republican Army (IRA) in 1919. Meanwhile, Sinn Fein won seventy-three Irish seats in the general election of 1918 (see Unit 2.2) and promptly declared Ireland independent, an act of defiance which Lloyd George's government could not ignore.

The IRA had about 2 000 'soldiers' who struck viciously at British property and at the authorities. The Royal Irish Constabulary (RIC) badly needed

*Fig. 4.5   An Irish stamp of 1941 commemorating the Easter Rising of 1916:
a nationalist soldier and the Dublin post office*

reinforcements: the new recruits were hastily kitted out in makeshift uniforms,
which won them the nickname of the Black and Tans. Like the IRA, the Black
and Tans fought viciously. Machine guns spluttered in ambushes. There were
bomb outrages and arson was not uncommon. Every atrocity was matched with
reprisals, and prisoners were ill treated and sometimes murdered. Much of the
city of Cork went up in flames when the Black and Tans ran amok. Opinion,
both in Britain and the USA with its strong Irish communities, was outraged.

*Fig. 4.6   A British tank used to smash open a door in the search for Irish
guerillas, 1916. A settlement of Irish affairs would need to be one of the priorities
of the British government when the First World War ended*

Jan Smuts was one of those who tried in vain to mediate, dismayed at this violence between members of the family of nations.

Lloyd George was fully aware of the need for a political solution, and a new Home Rule Bill was drafted, becoming law in December 1920 as the Government of Ireland Act. Ireland was divided, to meet the wishes of the Protestant north. The six northern counties were to have their own parliament in Belfast, with their own prime minister and cabinet for certain branches of government but with MPs at Westminster to play their part in the general government of the United Kingdom. George V opened the Northern Ireland parliament at Stormont, Belfast, in June 1921, and made sincere appeals for 'forbearance and conciliation' between religious sects and among Irishmen in general. Northern Ireland included a substantial Catholic minority, but Stormont would almost certainly be dominated by Protestants, which most Ulstermen found satisfying. Southern Ireland, however, could no longer be pacified with Home Rule, and the division of Ireland added a new grievance. Sinn Fein won 124 out of 128 seats in elections in southern Ireland in May 1921, and there could be no doubt that Home Rule was too little, too late.

Lloyd George negotiated with the Sinn Fein leaders, while Irishmen sang the praises of the Sinn Fein President:

> De Valera met the English as a soldier and beat them as a soldier. He has been meeting them now as a statesman and he will beat them as a statesman.

But it was Griffith who carried the talks to their conclusion in an Anglo-Irish Treaty at the end of 1921. The terms of the Treaty were then incorporated in the Irish Free State Agreement Act which became law in March 1922. The basis of this Act was that:

> Ireland shall have the same constitutional status in the Community of Nations known as the British Empire as the Dominion of Canada (and the other Dominions) . . . and shall be styled and known as the Irish Free State.

The Treaty was accepted much less readily in Ireland than in England. This was much more than Home Rule, but Ireland was not yet a republic. It had still to accept the British monarchy and the uncertainties which went with Dominion status (see Unit 4.3(a)). The Irish Free State was a very reluctant member of the Commonwealth family. Northern Ireland was left free to choose whether to join the Free State or remain apart, though the northerners were sure to reject union with the Free State, thus leaving Ireland divided. Irishmen also resented the fact that the British navy kept the right to use certain Irish ports. De Valera refused to accept the Treaty and others took a similar view, Countess Markievicz among them, but the Dail (the Irish parliament) accepted it by sixty-four votes to fifty-seven, and de Valera resigned in favour of Arthur Griffith. This was the signal for a new civil war in Ireland as the country divided for and against the Treaty. Collins, who supported it, was killed in an IRA ambush, and the conflict dragged on for over a year before the IRA ran short of

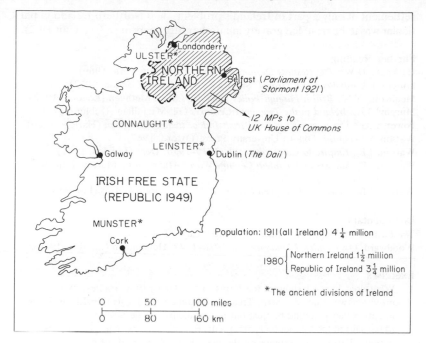

Fig. 4.7 The division of Ireland

ammunition and leaders, the latter being herded into prison and, in some cases, executed. Meanwhile Griffith had died unexpectedly, and the task of pacification fell to William Cosgrave, who led the Free State from 1922 to 1932. Cosgrave slowly healed the divisions, and the Irish Free State settled down, but it remained resentful of the continuing connection with Britain and of the division of Ireland. De Valera returned to parliamentary life in 1926, and became the Free State's Prime Minister in 1932, when new quarrels with Britain broke out about debts and trade (see Unit 8.1(b)).

The Irish settlement was perhaps one of Lloyd George's most remarkable achievements. Not only had he to grapple with the conflicting views of Irishmen themselves, he had to win support for the settlement in a House of Commons dominated by Conservatives. Conservatives and Unionists (see Unit 1.2(c)) insisted on the separation of Northern Ireland, but Lloyd George had to manoeuvre with some skill to persuade them at the same time to agree to substantial concessions to the southern Irish. In the past, the Conservatives had stubbornly resisted even Home Rule, and Dominion status went much further than that. The Prime Minister's concessions to Sinn Fein and the IRA, sensible as they were, were yet another cause of the ill feeling against Lloyd George which finally came to the surface at the Carleton Club in October 1922 (see Unit 2.4). In the long run, of course, the Irish settlement of 1920–2 was a settlement of only a part of Ireland's problems, and Northern Ireland in particular was to be troubled gravely in another fifty years or so (see Unit 19.2).

Further Reading
Harkness, D.W.: *The Restless Dominion*. Macmillan (New York, 1969).
Longford, Lord: *Peace By Ordeal*. Sidgwick and Jackson (London, 1972).
Medlicott, W.N.: *British Foreign Policy since Versailles*. Methuen (London, 1968).
Murphy, J.A.: *Ireland in the Twentieth Century*. Gill-Macmillan (Dublin, 1975).
Power, E.G.: *The Easter Rising and Irish Independence*. Longman (Harlow, 1980).
Watson, F.: *Gandhi*. Oxford University Press (Oxford, 1967).
Watson, J.B.: *Empire to Commonwealth, 1919–1970*. Dent (London, 1971).
Watson, J.B.: *Success in Twentieth Century World Affairs*. John Murray (London, 3rd edn. 1984).
Watson, J.B.: *Success in European History 1815–1941*. John Murray (London, 1981).

Documentary
The Easter Rebellion, 1916. Jackdaw Wallet. Cape (London).
Woodward, O.: *Divided Island: Ireland 1910–1949*. Heinemann (London, 1980).

Exercises
1. What does Fig. 4.1 show of the terms of the Treaty of Versailles? What further provisions were included in the Treaty? How far did the Treaty fulfil Lloyd George's intention that it should be 'just but not vindictive' (page 59)?
2. Make a list of the treaties and agreements Britain signed with foreign powers in the period 1919–30, and summarize the main terms of *each* of them.
3. Making use of this Unit and the Index to this book, show what you understand by *each* of the following: reparations; mandated territories; Imperial Conferences; Dominion Status; the British Commonwealth of Nations.
4. Outline Lloyd George's main achievements after 1918 in (*a*) foreign policy, (*b*) dealings with India and (*c*) dealings with Ireland.
5. What did MacDonald (Labour) and Austen Chamberlain (Conservative) contribute to British foreign policy in the years 1924–9? Explain how their policies differed with regard to (*a*) the Geneva Protocol and (*b*) the USSR.
6. What was agreed in the Locarno Treaties, and why were they 'greeted enthusiastically' (page 70)? How far was this enthusiasm justified? (You can extend your answer to the last part of this Question after reading Unit 8.)
7. What agreements about disarmament were reached at Washington and London? Why had more not been achieved by the time the Disarmament Conference was abandoned in 1934?
8. What was agreed in (*a*) the Government of Ireland Act of 1920 and (*b*) the Anglo-Irish Treaty of 1921? Why was the Treaty 'accepted much less readily in Ireland than in England' (page 78)?

Depression and Crisis, 1929–32

5.1 The Second Labour Government, 1929–31

MacDonald displayed his usual caution after the general election of 1929. His government was again a minority one, unable to pursue policies the Liberals would not accept and aware that the voters had given only qualified approval to the Labour programme. In his choice of ministers, MacDonald gave 'Safety First' as high a priority as Baldwin had. Snowden was again Chancellor of the Exchequer, a guarantee that there would be no rash spending. Henderson became Foreign Secretary, and appointments were found for Sidney Webb, Lord Sankey and Addison, who had parted company with Lloyd George over his housing programme in 1921. Housing, however, was now a matter for Arthur Greenwood at the Ministry of Health. MacDonald made an innovation at the Ministry of Labour, appointing Margaret Bondfield as Britain's first woman cabinet minister. The left (more radical) wing of the Labour Party was hardly represented at all, although the minor post of Commissioner of Works was given to George Lansbury.

The government's programme of legislation was equally unexciting and evasive and, before long, Churchill denounced MacDonald as a 'Boneless Wonder'. Unemployment had been an important issue. There had been a second hunger march to London at the beginning of 1929, repeating the demand of a march made in 1922 that government should find work for those without it. An observer described its start:

> Tens of thousands of Glasgow workers mobilized on Blytheswoode Square, Glasgow, to give a rousing send-off to 200 men, representing the Scottish coalfields, shipyards, textile towns, fishing industries and others affected by the blight of unemployment in Scotland. The marchers were something more than volunteers; they were representatives, because they had all been endorsed at great mass meetings held . . . throughout Scotland.

Such men hoped for effective action from a Labour government, especially one with a Scottish Prime Minister. MacDonald referred the problem of unemployment to a team of ministers, but little came of their discussions. A modest programme of public works, mainly on roads, merely scratched the surface of the problem; and a little more public money was made available for the relief of the unemployed. But, in general, Snowden insisted that there must be no

Table 5.1 British exports and unemployment, 1924–38

Date	Goods exported (value in £million)	Registered unemployed (millions)
1924	801	1.3
1925	773	1.2
1926	653	1.4
1927	709	1.1
1928	724	1.2
1929	729	1.2
1930	571	1.9
1931	391	2.7
1932	365	2.7
1933	368	2.5
1934	396	2.2
1935	426	2.0
1936	441	1.8
1937	521	1.5
1938	471	1.8

Source: adapted from Gregg, P.: *A Social and Economic History of Britain*. Harrap (London, 1950).

reckless spending. Table 5.1 shows that unemployment began to rise during 1930. But when Oswald Mosley, one of the team MacDonald had appointed to examine the problem, proposed sweeping reforms such as the ending of free trade, earlier retirement and public control of the banks, they were instantly rejected.

The legislation passed while the Labour government was in office had little to do with unemployment, though Greenwood's Housing Act of 1930 provided government money to help in clearing away slums. Addison introduced the Agricultural Marketing Act, which allowed producers to set up marketing boards to assist their sales. The Coal Mines Act of 1930 fixed the miners' working day at seven-and-a-half hours – more than the workers demanded but less than the eight hours the owners preferred. Herbert Morrison, who had had experience on the London County Council and whom MacDonald had made Minister of Transport, introduced the Road Traffic Act of 1930, abolishing the existing speed limit of twenty miles per hour. He also began work to set up a new public corporation, the London Passenger Transport Board (LPTB), to control the capital's passenger services; it came into operation after the government had fallen. So too did the Statute of Westminster which the Labour government also prepared (see Unit 4.3(*a*)). But the government could make no progress towards repealing the Trade Disputes Act of 1927. The Lords blocked an attempt to raise the school-leaving age to fifteen; and Labour proposals for changes in the system of voting were lost since they did not go far enough to satisfy the Liberals.

The Labour government's achievements in foreign policy were similarly limited, though Henderson was quick to restore diplomatic relations with the USSR. The London Naval Agreement was all there was to show for efforts to bring about disarmament (see Unit 4.2(*d*)). The port of Wei-hai-wei was restored to China, a gesture of goodwill, but Henderson was out of office before there was time fully to consider Japan's aggression against the Chinese state of Manchuria (see Unit 8.2(*a*)). Henderson devoted his remaining years to the service of the League of Nations and disarmament. MacDonald's government also struggled with the problem of India, and Gandhi came to a Round-table Conference in London in 1931; but here too the business had to be left unfinished (see Unit 8.1(*a*)). In 1931, however, everything was overshadowed by the deepening economic crisis.

5.2 The Great Depression

(*a*) The Trade Depression

Table 5.1 shows the worsening of Britain's export sales in 1929–31 and the level of unemployment. The trade depression was not a uniquely British problem. A World Economic Conference in Brussels in 1927 had recommended little but the reduction of tariffs, the removal of controls and careful budgeting by national governments, ignoring whatever positive steps governments might take to increase trade and thus reduce unemployment. The policy of interfering with private business as little as possible, typified by the Republicans in the USA, prevailed almost everywhere except in Russia. But while production increased in the later 1920s, there was only limited growth in the consumers' power to buy, and by 1929 there was over-production in relation to purchasing power. A serious slump on the American market in that year quickly spread to other markets. Prices fell, but still many goods remained unsold. The obvious next step seemed to be to reduce or even to halt production, so unemployment figures soared. The central feature of the Depression was thus a major slump in trade, production and employment; and the loss of income suffered by the unemployed itself led to a further drop in purchasing power, and a yet deeper depression. In 1932 the numbers out of work neared fourteen million in the USA, six million in Germany, and three million in Britain.

(*b*) The Financial Crisis

Part of the problem of the Great Depression was that the world was too dependent on the USA for its money supply. In 1929 the Americans were again involved in a re-examination of German reparations. The Young Plan was drawn up, cutting the original total to be paid and arranging new details for the settlement, but it was overtaken by events. There was already some concern in the USA about the amount of American money which had been loaned overseas, and the concern turned to panic with the Wall Street Crash, the collapse of the New York Stock Exchange, in October 1929. During the 1920s Americans had invested heavily on the stock exchange, buying shares in companies and often selling them again at a profit. Many did their buying with borrowed money, expecting to repay their debts from their gains. In 1929, however, doubts about trade in general raised doubts about share prices, which ceased to rise. There was panic in October when many investors tried to sell their shares to recover their money, found share prices falling, and clamoured all the more to get rid of their holdings. On 24 October, thirteen million shares changed hands – and prices continued to plunge for two years. Many were ruined. Not only were they unable to afford to buy goods, they could not repay their debts and mortgages. Savings were withdrawn to meet personal crises, and banks too were undermined in the general scramble for money. Institutions and even nations demanded payment of what was owed, and the USA especially looked to recover American money from Europe. Most important of all, confidence everywhere was undermined. Between nations, the demand was for gold, not paper money, and European gold reserves began rapidly to dwindle.

The strain was too much for Credit Anstalt, the main Austrian Bank which had to close in May 1931. Financiers in panic put pressure on other banks, and there was mounting concern in Germany about the strength of the Reichsbank. The crisis swiftly spread to London, where the gold reserves of the Bank of England fell alarmingly in July 1931. The Hoover Moratorium – a standstill on the payment of debts between nations, which took its name from the American President – did something to put a brake on the financial crisis, but it was not enough in itself to halt it, or to save Britain from a political crisis. The Bank of England needed help, and £50 million were raised in the USA and France. But the British government itself now came under scrutiny. Foreign investors wanted to take their money from the Bank of England in gold or dollars, not in sterling since there was now a crisis of confidence both in Britain's government and its currency. Governments were shaken almost everywhere. In Germany, the Depression played a considerable part in bringing Hitler and the Nazis to power in 1933 and, even in the USA, it helped to persuade American voters to reject Hoover and the Republicans and to turn to Roosevelt and the Democrats.

5.3   The Political Crisis and the General Election of 1931

Just as in 1921, there were many experts and non-experts in 1931 who believed that salvation must lie in cutting government spending, though it would do nothing to increase trade and reduce unemployment. It was thought 'necessary' to restore 'confidence'. The government must balance its budget and spend no more than it received in revenue. Confidence in the government, it was assumed, would then bring renewed confidence in sterling and in the Bank of

England. The May Committee had already been set up in March 1931 to examine government spending and, like Geddes ten years earlier, May recommended cuts. Those employed by the government should have their wages and salaries cut, and the unemployed should have their benefits cut. A cut of 20 per cent was proposed for teachers and the unemployed, and a variety of percentages, usually smaller, for civil servants, policemen, members of the armed forces and the government itself. It was thought that this would cause no great hardship, since prices had fallen during the 1920s while unemployment benefit and some wages had risen, though it was scarcely the reward for 'heroes' Lloyd George had once anticipated. Snowden, with his great belief in balanced budgets, thought the proposals sensible.

Merely by drawing attention to overspending the May Report caused further pressure on the Bank of England. In August the Bank desperately needed to borrow another £80 million to meet the demands upon it. The Americans would lend no more, however, until there were cuts. By now parliament was enjoying its summer recess, but MacDonald and Snowden had still to persuade the cabinet of the virtues of the May Report. The only alternative, they argued, would be to try to manage without a further loan, and to attempt to halt the run on the Bank of England by abandoning the gold standard and devaluing the pound. This would help British exports by making them cheaper, but it would be a gamble whether it would stop investors from trying to get rid of sterling, knowing they would receive fewer dollars for it. The main question was one of priorities. 'Official' advice, and that of most of the Conservatives, was to make the cuts and secure the loan to preserve the pound. Keynes condemned that policy, regarding the cuts as irrelevant to the central problems of trade depression and unemployment. Lloyd George might well have expressed a similar view, had he not been in hospital at the time. But the main opposition to cuts came from the Labour Party and the TUC. Bevin argued that it was grossly unjust to impose cuts, not on the whole nation, but on a section of it – public employees and the unemployed. Most people within the labour movement even thought it immoral to impose the double burden of unemployment and reduced benefits on those unfortunate enough to be out of work. Their priority was to help the unemployed, rather than to satisfy investors and the timid with token cuts 'to save the pound'. But MacDonald and Snowden believed that the cuts must come first. They were willing to reduce payments to the unemployed by only 10 per cent rather than 20 per cent, but it became clear that even this did not have the support of the majority of the Labour cabinet.

On 23 August MacDonald decided he must resign and went to inform the King. The general expectation was that George V would invite Baldwin to try to form a Conservative–Liberal coalition government. Instead, MacDonald returned to the Labour cabinet to announce that he had agreed to remain as Prime Minister with a National government 'of personalities'. This meant a government of Conservatives, Liberals and a handful of Labour supporters of cuts. The latter included Snowden, Sankey and Thomas, but to the previous cabinet and the Labour Party as a whole this appeared as an act of the basest

J'ACCUSE

'Prisoners, you have been found guilty of putting duty to the state and personal honour above party discipline. For so despicable a crime there is only one sentence – eternal banishment from our ranks!'

Fig. 5.1 Ramsay MacDonald and J.H. Thomas were pilloried by the Labour movement for their political somersault of 1931. The Conservative Daily Express *lost little time in presenting the former Labour politicians as patriots and statesmen, victimized by the TUC and their former colleagues (September 1931)*

treachery. Herbert Morrison described how he and the Labour Cabinet greeted the Prime Minister's announcement:

> Perhaps because I was the youngest member . . . I was the first to get my breath and find my voice. 'Prime Minister,' I said, 'I think you are wrong.' He seemed to be shocked and turned round to me and snapped, '*You* think I'm wrong!' 'I do,' I replied, ignoring the innuendo about my unimportance. 'Moreover, you will find it easier to get into this combination than to get out of it.' He said no more, yet his whole attitude made plain that he thought my forebodings ridiculous.

In fact, it is unlikely that MacDonald had any illusions about the noose into which he was putting his head, and about the storm which might be expected from the Labour Party. He thought it his personal duty to see the nation through the crisis but, at the same time, he was generous enough to advise some younger Labour politicians not to jeopardize their careers by following his example. Like Lloyd George in 1918, MacDonald was now a prisoner of the Conservatives and a man without a party. A contemporary observed that he now led 'the government of the unburied dead', a by no means uplifting alliance of MacDonald, Baldwin and Herbert Samuel (see Fig. 5.2).

Fig. 5.2 Ramsay MacDonald's new National government: the Cabinet, August 1931. MacDonald himself in the middle of the front row, Baldwin and Snowden to his right, Samuel and Lord Sankey to his left. From left to right in the back row: Cunliffe-Lister, Thomas, Lord Reading, Neville Chamberlain and Hoare

The Times led the chorus of approval from most of the press, however, and praised the new National government:

> All concerned are to be warmly congratulated on this result, so fully in accord with the patriotic spirit which has inspired a week's most anxious negotiations.

The *New Statesman* took a different view, rejecting arguments about patriotism and suggesting that MacDonald would be at war not just with the labour movement:

> but with all those, in all classes, who believe that the policy of reducing the purchasing power of the consumer to meet a situation of over-production is silly economics.

The cuts were duly made. Snowden also raised income tax, put higher duties on such items as beer, tobacco and petrol, and balanced his budget. The Bank of England got its loan of £80 million, but foreign investors were not apparently satisfied after all. They found a new reason for alarm when naval forces at Invergordon refused to obey orders to put to sea, in protest against cuts in their pay. The run on the pound continued. Snowden now cut his cuts, assuring all concerned that none would be higher than 10 per cent. At the same time, the National government did the very thing it had been formed not to do: it abandoned the gold standard. This allowed the pound to fall to a new level, equal to about 3.30 dollars. Since other countries also made changes in their currencies, however, the rate swung back by 1933 to about 5 dollars to the pound. Meanwhile, going off the gold standard produced none of the calamities the experts had forecast, and the run on the pound was at last checked. The Invergordon mutiny, always a gentlemanly affair, also ended quietly.

There was some uncertainty about what to do next. Most Conservatives wanted a general election, to catch the Labour Party in its confusion. In any case, Labour MPs were harassing the government by opposing whatever MacDonald put forward, and Lloyd George, out of hospital, was also hostile. A general election therefore took place in October 1931, and MacDonald asked the voters to give him a 'doctor's mandate', to cure the country's ills. The Conservatives supported MacDonald in their joint appeal 'to save the pound', suggesting darkly that Labour spending would destroy the value of savings. MacDonald toured the country with an old German banknote dating from the inflation of 1923, a dreadful warning, he claimed, of what might happen in Britain if the voters chose unwisely. Lloyd George called the whole thing 'a Tory ramp', and Labour called it 'a bankers' ramp'. Snowden decided not to stand for re-election, but nevertheless attacked the Labour Party, vigorously warning the country against voting for Bolshevism and 'irretrievable ruin'.

More than 500 Labour candidates were matched against the supporters of the National government, but they found themselves struggling against the tide. The Labour recommendations of economic planning, nationalization and the pursuit of greater equality won little favour among voters who were assured on all sides that such policies would lead to disaster, and who recalled Labour's record when in government without enthusiasm. Labour candidates suffered widespread defeats, including Henderson at Burnley. The Liberals too had their troubles. The issue of free trade or protection had come up again. Although MacDonald and Baldwin sat on the fence over this, most Conservatives now favoured protection, while Labour clung to free trade. The Liberals were divided. Samuel stood for free trade, Simon wanted protection, yet both contrived to support National government. Lloyd George was against National government, and against whatever MacDonald and Baldwin might be in favour of. Not surprisingly, the voters found some difficulty in seeing clearly what might be represented by a Liberal vote.

The outcome of the general election of 1931 was a massive vote of confidence in the National government: 554 MPs were elected to support it. Of these, 473 were Conservatives, while the rest were a mixture of Samuelite and Simonite Liberals, and National Labour followers of MacDonald. The voters administered a sharp rebuff both to Labour and to Lloyd George, since they returned only fifty-two Labour members and only four Liberal supporters of the Welshman. MacDonald remained in office as the Prime Minister and

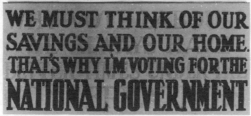

Fig. 5.3 An exercise in electoral blackmail: a poster in the general election of October 1931 suggesting the dreadful consequences of voting for any candidate who did not support National government

seemed to have won a great personal triumph. But he was now engaged in a strange dual-act with Baldwin, and his triumph would end when the Conservatives decided to get rid of him. Meanwhile, the country was still deep in the Depression. The National government had its mandate, but it was not yet clear whether it had a policy.

5.4   The Policy of the National Government

(a) Cheap Money and Balanced Budgets

Neville Chamberlain was the new Chancellor of the Exchequer and, rather fitfully, something of a policy emerged. The gold standard had already been abandoned, so that the value of the pound floated downwards, at least temporarily, helping exports. The Exchange Equalization Fund was set up in 1932, giving the government a device for steadying the pound against the activities of currency speculators, while leaving it free to find its natural level for trading purposes.

These changes had another effect. The government no longer needed to sustain the pound at the high level fixed in 1925 by the use of the Bank Rate (see Glossary). The Bank Rate now reflected the demand for loans, and since demand was very low during the Depression, Bank Rate could fall. Chamberlain seized the opportunity to reduce the interest on War Loan stock (see Glossary) from 5 to 3½ per cent. War Loan stock amounted to more than a quarter of the National Debt. The government was in no position to repay their loans to the holders of the stock, but the annual interest payments were costly. The cut would therefore reduce government spending and it appealed strongly to Chamberlain, as it would have appealed to Snowden. The general effect of the change, however, was to keep interest low on other government stock, and on all borrowing. Bank Rate fell to 2 per cent during 1932. Mainly by accident, Chamberlain had thus arrived at the policy of cheap money. Bank Rate stayed at around 2 per cent until 1951, so that money remained cheap for those who borrowed it. When interest rates climbed after 1951, however, the holders of War Loan stock felt they had been cheated, since they still could not recover the money they had loaned, and they received only 3½ per cent interest when interest rates generally were far higher.

Meanwhile, having arrived at the policy of cheap money, the National Government did almost nothing to make use of it. Public amenities, such as roads and schools, could have been built comparatively cheaply, and the government could thus have given a lead in reviving the economy and reducing unemployment, as did governments in the USA and many parts of Europe. The National government merely waited. Recovery, when it came, relied on private enterprise and local authorities rather than on the central government. The policy of MacDonald, Baldwin and Chamberlain lacked initiative and had little coherence. Restrictions were imposed on investing and lending abroad, to keep capital available for investment in renewed economic activity at home, but the government itself had no plans for using public money to stimulate that activity. It hoped that enterprise would automatically be encouraged by such negative policies as not increasing taxes for the benefit of the unemployed. Chamberlain carefully balanced his budget, and went on looking for ways of cutting official spending.

The means test provided one such way. It had been introduced along with Snowden's cuts in 1931, and MacDonald's government now encouraged the local authorities to apply it vigorously through the PACs (see Unit 3.4(c)). The unemployed who applied for dole found that close inquiries were made about their 'means of support'. The wages and savings of all members of the family were taken into account so that, wherever possible, the dole could be reduced or even denied altogether. The effects of this policy were recorded in 1934 by one of those who suffered from it:

Like most unemployed persons, especially those affected by the Means Test, the pledging of personal possessions became inevitable. The first articles of value, i.e. watches, rings . . . entered the pawnbrokers never to return. . . . Apparel and bed linen went next. My eldest son's best suit regularly enters the pledge office on Tuesday morning and is recovered on Sunday evening without his knowledge.

The means test heaped humiliation on top of poverty. An unemployed man was likely to find himself supported by his wife or others in his family, perhaps even dependent on the small sums earned by his children for delivering newspapers. The National government thus robbed men of their self-respect

Fig. 5.4 The classic face of unemployment in the 1930s: an unemployed miner in Wigan, 1939

and, far from abolishing the miserly system, the government took a tighter grip on it. The Unemployment Act of 1934 set up the central Unemployment Assistance Board to take over from the local PACs the work of dealing with, and means-testing, the long-term unemployed. Four years later, a report by the Pilgrim Trust described, as part of the consequences, the 'depression and apathy' in the homes of many of the 'long-unemployed men'.

(b) **Protection and Imperial Preference**
Towards the end of 1931 the National government decided to impose tariffs on certain foreign goods. Early in 1932 this was developed into the one deliberate policy which the government adopted to help Britain's depressed economy. Chamberlain introduced the Import Duties Act to bring in both protection and Imperial Preference, the policy for which his father, Joseph Chamberlain, had campaigned at the beginning of the century. A duty of 10 per cent was levied on all imports, except certain foodstuffs and the goods from the Empire and the Dominions, which were thus given preference over foreign goods. The Act also set up an Advisory Committee, which recommended higher tariffs on certain specific goods, and these were imposed. In general, however, the tariff was a low and cautious one: a levy of more than 20 per cent was imposed on only about 8 per cent of imports. The Import Duties Act did not produce any dramatic results. With the general slow recovery of trade after 1933 imports climbed back to a volume similar to that of the late 1920s. And it can even be argued that the Act had more ill effects on British exports than on imports – some retaliatory action was taken against Britain and, during the 1930s, British exports did not regain the levels of the late 1920s either by volume or value. There was, however, some shift in the direction of British trade. Table 5.2 shows a rising percentage of trade with the Empire and Commonwealth at the expense of trade with foreign countries.

This shift resulted from the Imperial Preference included in the Import Duties Act, and from the Ottawa Conference which met in 1932. Baldwin,

Table 5.2 Britain's trade with the Empire and Commonwealth

	Percentage of Britain's imports and exports as a whole	
Date	Imports from Empire/ Commonwealth	Exports to Empire/ Commonwealth
1913	25.0	32.9
1931	24.5	32.6
1933	34.3	36.0
1937	37.3	39.7

Source: Pollard, S.: *The Development of the British Economy, 1914–67*. Arnold (London, 1969).

Fig. 5.5 Two of Britain's ministers in search of a policy: MacDonald (Prime Minister) and Thomas (Secretary for the Dominions). Both resigned office in 1935, Thomas retiring after leaking budget secrets in 1936

Chamberlain and Thomas represented Britain at Ottawa. The Conference hoped for some grand plan to stimulate trade between the members of the British Commonwealth of Nations, who already had the advantage that they had agreed to the Sterling Area in 1931, and thus had a common trading currency (see Glossary). Baldwin told the Conference:

> We all have great expectations of the outcome of this great gathering of the representatives of the peoples of the Empire. . . . I most confidently believe that we shall not be disappointed, and I think we shall end . . . with definite arrangements for our mutual advantage.

But no grand plan resulted. Instead there was much bickering. Chamberlain complained that his patience was strained 'to the limit', and observers wrote of mediocre men. Britain and each of the Dominions wanted agreements to its own advantage. The British wanted to safeguard their own agriculture against the produce from Australia and New Zealand, for example, while having the freedom to sell their industrial goods throughout the Dominions. The Canadians resented Britain's reluctance to buy Canadian manufactures. The Conference therefore produced only a dozen limited deals, each of them between only two or three members. Nevertheless, by 1938, some 49 per cent of the exports of members of the Commonwealth of Nations went to other members of the association, and this was of some benefit at a time when markets remained difficult to find.

Protection found little favour with the free traders within the National government: MacDonald had to accept the resignations of Samuel, the Home Secretary, and Snowden, the Lord Privy Seal, who had been raised to the peerage in 1931. The loss of the Samuelites made little difference to the government's majority in the Commons, but it underlined the fact that, except for MacDonald, Sankey and Thomas, and the Simonite Liberals, the National government was virtually a Conservative government. By the end of 1932 it had no more ideas to contribute to a policy for overcoming the Depression, and it waited hopefully for the crisis to pass.

Further Reading

Seaman, L.C.B.: *Post-Victorian Britain, 1902–1951*. Methuen (London, 1966), chapters 21–3.

Skidelsky, R.: *Politicians and the Slump – the Labour Government of 1929–1931*. Macmillan (London, 1967).

Stevenson, J. and Cook, C.: *The Slump*. Quartet (London, 1977).

Documentary

Adelman, P.: *The Decline of the Liberal Party 1910–31*. Longman (Harlow, 1982).

Constantine, S.: *Unemployment in Britain Between the Wars*. Longman (Harlow, 1981).

Edwards, A.D.: *The Fall of the Labour Government, 1931*. Arnold Archive (London, 1975).

Yass, M.: *The Great Depression*. Wayland (Hove, 1973).

Exercises

1. Outline the main arguments you would have wished to put forward in London had you been one of the '200 men' whose 'send-off' from Glasgow is described in small print on page 81.

2. Explain the connection between the two columns (*Goods exported* and *Registered unemployed*) in Table 5.1, and account for the trend in *unemployed* in the years printed bold.

3. What problems faced the Labour government of 1929–31? Why, and how, did the Labour cabinet become divided? Why did Morrison tell the Prime Minister, 'I think you are wrong' (page 86)?

4. Explain the views expressed on page 87 by writers in (*a*) *The Times* and (*b*) the *New*

Statesman. State, with reasons, which of these two views you would prefer to support.

5. Why was 'the outcome of the general election of 1931' such 'a massive vote of confidence in the National government' (page 88)? Why did critics of the election call it a 'ramp' (page 88)?

6. How did the National government seek to deal with the Depression during 1931–2? To what extent had the government developed a convincing policy by the end of 1932?

7. Making use of the Glossary and, where necessary, a dictionary, make sure of your understanding of the following words and phrases used in this Unit: free trade; reduction of tariffs; mortgages; balanced budgets; devaluing the pound; run on the pound; nationalization; cheap money; Imperial Preference.

Unit Six

Politics and the Economy in the 1930s

6.1 The National Government Continued

(a) Ministerial Musical Chairs

After the general election of 1931 (see Units 5.3 and 5.4) the National government continued in name for the rest of the 1930s. In practice, it became essentially the government of the Conservatives. MacDonald and Baldwin changed places in June 1935, Baldwin becoming Prime Minister and MacDonald the Lord President of the Council. MacDonald's failing health provided the opportunity for this exchange of offices, but it also paved the way for the Conservatives to fight the coming general election with their leader

THE NEW ANNOUNCER

"—AND NOW, MY FRIENDS, I HAND YOU OVER TO YOUR NEW ANNOUNCER, MR. STANLEY BALDWIN —GUID-NICHT, EVERRYBODY—GUID-NICHT!"

Fig. 6.1 A cartoonist's comment on the change of Prime Minister in Britain in June 1935: MacDonald, the Scot, gave way to Baldwin but, like the BBC, National government seemed to have taken root as one of the nation's institutions

already in 10 Downing Street. MacDonald's usefulness to the Conservatives had dwindled since 1931 and, by 1935, they no longer needed him. Neville Chamberlain remained the Chancellor of the Exchequer, as Baldwin's tribute to his careful control of the budget. The Depression was beginning to lift. A year earlier, Chamberlain had made a small reduction in income tax and, in 1935–6, he completely restored the cuts which had been made in 1931. Baldwin moved Simon to the Home Office, making way for Hoare as Foreign Secretary, to grapple with what seemed to be increasing difficulties abroad (see Unit 8.2). Thomas meanwhile kept the post of Secretary for the Dominions which he had gained in 1931, and MacDonald's son, Malcolm, became Colonial Secretary, retaining some appearance of 'National' government when Sankey lost the office of Lord Chancellor to Viscount Hailsham.

The next general election was held in November 1935. Baldwin timed it well. He was able to claim that trade was beginning to revive, that unemployment was beginning to fall (see Table 5.1), and that this was somehow due to the policies of the National government. A few months earlier Britain had celebrated George V's Silver Jubilee in an outburst of patriotic fervour and flag-waving, and there was a feeling of genuine prosperity in those areas least

Fig. 6.2   The Silver Jubilee of the reign of George V: a British stamp of 1935

affected by unemployment. This was a tide on which the Conservatives could ride. Even more important, however, was the confusion within the Labour Party (see Unit 6.2(a)). Fierce conflict raged at the Labour Party Conference at Brighton in October 1935 over the Party's policy towards Mussolini's aggression against Abyssinia. There were violent attacks on the pacifists within the labour movement and, since he took his stand on Christian pacificism, on George Lansbury, leader of the Parliamentary Labour Party since 1931. Lansbury's conscience would not allow him to support retaliation against Italy, and he quoted the Scriptures:

'Vengeance is mine. I will repay,' saith the Lord.

Bevin, on the other hand, demanded support for sanctions (see Unit 8.2(c)), and he too quoted Biblical authority:

The man who has taken the sword is Mussolini, and because Mussolini has taken the
sword we stand by the Scriptural doctrine and say that he shall perish by economic
sanctions.

The Conference voted overwhelmingly with Bevin, who had charged Lansbury
with 'taking (his) conscience round from body to body asking to be told what
(he) ought to do with it'. Lansbury resigned and Clement Attlee took his place,
though he had not been confirmed as leader by his fellow-MPs when Baldwin
called the general election.

Baldwin's strategy was to ask for a broad vote of confidence in the National
government, with a message similar to that of 'Safety First' in 1929. International questions hovered on the fringe of the election campaign, and Baldwin
made a limited commitment to rearmament, while asserting: 'I give you my
word that there will be no great armaments'. No party spoke with a single voice
on foreign policy issues, but there were Labour accusations that the Conservatives would put Guns before Butter, and Herbert Morrison warned the
electorate against voting for war. Mysterious posters appeared in some constituencies, showing babies in Conservative gas masks. Most voters were
concerned mainly with domestic issues, however, and the comparatively prosperous areas of the country showed their satisfaction with the National government: 387 Conservatives were returned, with support from a further thirty-two
Simonites and eight National Labour MPs. Baldwin thus had a clear mandate
to continue with the National government.

Both MacDonald and his son lost their seats. Labour gained its revenge
against Ramsay MacDonald when Emmanuel Shinwell defeated him at
Seaham with a majority of over 20 000. Shinwell had been imprisoned for his
part in the Glasgow unrest of 1919, and another veteran of such protest, Willie
Gallacher, was also returned in 1935, as the only Communist in the new House
of Commons. The areas of high unemployment and poverty showed little
sympathy with the National government, and Labour did much better than in
1931, securing 158 seats. But the Liberals suffered again: Samuel lost his seat
at Darwen, and only twenty Liberals were returned, four of them members of
Lloyd George's family.

The death of George V occurred soon after the election, in January 1936. He
had reigned with much good sense since 1910, but his death led to the
Abdication Crisis. George was succeeded by his son, Edward VIII, whose
spasmodic sympathy with the poor had done little to endear him to influential
circles. Edward wanted to marry Mrs Simpson, by birth a commoner and an
American, and twice divorced. The Church of England was alarmed: such a
marriage would be unfitting for one who, as King, was also the supreme
head of the Church. The Prime Minister too was alarmed, lest Edward's
marriage proved a new divisive issue within the nation. Moreover, Baldwin
considered that the Dominions should share his alarm since Edward was also
their King. With his usual political skill, but with more speed than usual,
Baldwin confronted Edward with a choice between Mrs Simpson and the

crown and, when the King chose Mrs Simpson, arranged for his abdication. Edward and his bride retired to France, to be known in future as the Duke and Duchess of Windsor, and the crown passed to Edward's younger brother, George VI. The Abdication Crisis passed smoothly, though there was little to suggest that the country at large had shared the great anxiety of its political and religious leaders. Baldwin believed that he had performed an expert service; businessmen who had invested in souvenirs for Edward's coronation, which now did not take place, mourned the losses which many could ill afford; and the public in general showed some sympathy with Edward, but felt perhaps that one king was similar to another.

Fig. 6.3 Support for Edward VIII, December 1936. But it was Baldwin who had his way and Edward abdicated in favour of George VI

Baldwin himself retired in 1937, to be succeeded as Prime Minister by Neville Chamberlain. Ramsay MacDonald retired too. He had kept his place in the government after 1935, having returned to parliament in a by-election, but he was a spent force and died soon after retirement. Malcolm MacDonald had also won a by-election and, in minor office, kept a MacDonald in the National government until the outbreak of war in 1939. J.H. Thomas, on the other hand, resigned in 1936 after being implicated in a leak of budget secrets. When Chamberlain appointed his Cabinet in 1937, Simon, as Chancellor of the Exchequer, was the only non-Conservative to hold a major post.

Table 6.1 Leading ministers in the National governments in the 1930s

Prime Minister	Lord President	Chancellor of the Exchequer	Home Secretary	Foreign Secretary
MacDonald (Aug.–Nov. 1931)	*Baldwin**	Snowden	Samuel	Simon
MacDonald (Nov. 1931– 1935)	*Baldwin*	*N.Chamberlain*	Samuel	Simon
Baldwin (June 1935– 1937)	MacDonald	*N.Chamberlain*	Simon	*Hoare* *Eden* (Dec. 1935)
N.Chamberlain (May 1937– 1940)	*Halifax* *Hailsham* (Feb. 1938) Runciman (Oct. 1938)	Simon	*Hoare*	*Eden* *Halifax* (Feb. 1938)

* italics: Conservatives

(b) Domestic Policy

In 1936 Keynes' *General Theory of Employment, Interest and Money* was published, closely arguing the case for spending rather than saving in a time of economic depression. His followers urged the government to stimulate economic recovery by spending on public works, and by putting money into consumers' pockets – a policy which Lloyd George and others had advocated in 1929, and which Roosevelt was carrying out in the USA. The National government took no notice. MacDonald, Baldwin and Chamberlain did almost nothing to alter the National government's policy, which had taken shape in 1932, for dealing with the country's economic and social problems (see Unit 5.4). Successive governments continued to let economic recovery take care of itself. A few minor economic adjustments and social reforms were the spartan record of legislation in the years 1933–9.

Some limited help was given to British agriculture by placing quotas on imported foodstuffs, and British farmers were encouraged by government subsidies and marketing boards to help market milk, bacon, potatoes and beet-sugar. By 1939 the government was spending about £100 million a year to keep up the prices of foodstuffs to assist farmers, while keeping prices low for consumers. The farmers were a privileged group; little was done to give similar help to other industries.

Tariffs provided some protection for home industries against foreign

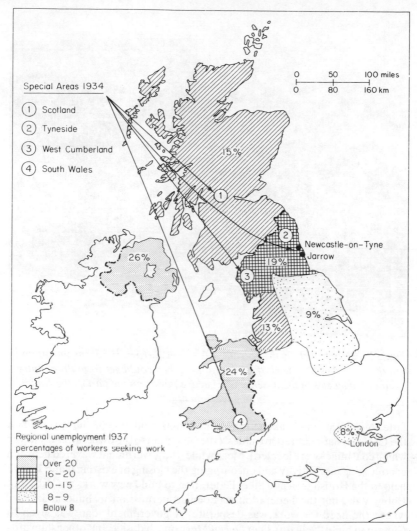

Fig. 6.4 *Regional unemployment and Special Areas*

competition but, rather than stimulating output, the National government fostered its reduction. Employers were encouraged to close uneconomic mills and shipyards as part of the reorganization of British industry to increase its competitiveness – a policy which became all too familiar some forty years later. But not much was done to modernize and expand other plant. The coal industry made few of the improvements recommended at the time of the General Strike, and the Coal Mines Reorganization Commission achieved

*Fig. 6.5 Relief work by the Salvation Army in Jarrow, 1933: the unemployed
and their families had need of all the support they could get from the country's
voluntary agencies in the absence of effective policy on the part of the National
government*

little. A small step was taken towards nationalization in 1938, however, when
the Coal Act nationalized 'royalties' (the sums paid to the owners of the land on
which coal mines were located). Meanwhile, the government wavered between
encouraging new activity and encouraging the closing of existing plant. It gave
help to the British Iron and Steel Federation to build new works at Corby and
Ebbw Vale, but the Federation was denied permission to build at Jarrow,
where the need for work was desperate. A government loan was given to
Cunard to build the luxury liner *Queen Mary* on Clydeside, but other shipyards
were closed. The basic fact was that there was little call for new ships, and the
government shrank from any serious effort to stimulate demand. Faltering
steps towards rearmament after the 1935 election provided some employment,
but rearmament was a political issue and had little to do with economic policy.

The Labour MP, Ellen Wilkinson, charged the National government with
the destruction of Jarrow in *The Town That Was Murdered*. It was towns like
Jarrow which suffered most from the government's inactivity. In Britain as a
whole in 1936 about a third of the workers in shipbuilding were unemployed,
along with one in four miners and about one in eight textile workers. The level

of unemployment again varied regionally: it was between 16 and 28 per cent in the North-West and North-East of England, Northern Ireland, Scotland and Wales, but only around 6 per cent in South-East England and most parts of London. The Special Areas Act had been introduced in 1934: it identified four distressed areas, to which the government tried to attract new industries (see Fig. 6.4). But it spent only £2 million to help employers move into these areas, or to help workers move out of them in search of jobs elsewhere. A similar Act slightly extended the scheme in 1937, but the results were negligible. The new industries that were attracted provided work for women rather than for their unemployed menfolk.

The Unemployment Assistance Board began work in 1936 (see Unit 5.4(a)). Means-tested assistance seemed more central to the government's thinking than any government-led economic revival. Table 5.1 shows that unemployment began to rise again in 1938, and in 1939 the TUC urged Chamberlain to set up a National Planning Board to try to take control of the economy. The Prime Minister replied that he had been considering it, but explained that he had done nothing because of the 'very heavy pressure of other business'. Foreign problems were certainly pressing by this time, but the government's legislative record could not be said to provide an adequate excuse. The Holidays-With-Pay Act of 1938 was probably the most important of its measures, entitling workers to a week's paid holiday each year.

6.2 The Opposition

(a) The Labour Party
The Labour Party's record in opposition during the 1930s was hardly more striking than that of the Conservatives and their allies in government. It took some time for the Party to recover from MacDonald's 'betrayal' in 1931 and, indeed, the events of that year left the Party with a lasting suspicion of its leadership. The moderate leadership of the 1920s seemed to have brought only disaster, and a resolution in 1932 approved a more definite commitment to socialist policies. On the other hand, the Party continued to reject all links with the British Communist Party, and lost the affiliation of the Independent Labour Party in 1932 when ILP members argued that the Labour Party was not sufficiently radical. In fact, the Labour Party continued to be a rather clumsy alliance of trade unionists, members of the working classes and socialist intellectuals; and the new generation of left-wing intellectuals, including men like Stafford Cripps, aroused little real enthusiasm for Marxism and for a red-blooded crusade against capitalism. The Labour Party as a whole moved only slowly towards that belief in economic planning which the TUC proposed to Chamberlain in 1939. For much of the 1930s it only offered a slightly more convincing programme for dealing with the Depression than that of the National government.

The Party devoted much energy to discussing its vision of the future and was not without idealism, but to the public it seemed to lack a clear and practical programme for the present and to be wasting its energies in furious wrangling. After 1931 the small band of Labour MPs was led, not very effectively, by Lansbury, while outside parliament the Party argued about the details of schemes for nationalization, and about theories of class warfare.

By the mid 1930s the Party was also debating what policy to adopt towards international lawlessness, a subject which came to a head at the 1935 Party Conference and resulted in Lansbury's resignation (see Unit 6.1(*a*)). Though the pacifists were defeated in 1935, the Labour Party was still slow to accept the need for positive action to deter aggression. It rested its faith in the League of Nations and in collective security, while resisting the National government's policy of rearmament. In 1937 Attlee tried to justify Labour's opposition to proposals to strengthen the RAF:

> Our policy is not one of seeking security through rearmament but through disarmament. Our aim is the reduction of armaments, and then the complete abolition of all national armaments under the League.

Even as late as spring 1939 the Labour Party, along with the Liberals, voted against peacetime conscription. Until the outbreak of war later that year it was always open to the charge that, though it voted to resist fascism in 1935, it failed to see the need to equip that resistance with teeth.

The TUC took a more positive stand. Trade unionists within the Labour movement accepted that force might be necessary to deal with Hitler and other aggressors. Walter Citrine, for many years President of the International Federation of Trade Unions, declared as early as 1935:

> There is only one way of dealing with a bully and that is by the use of force. . . . It may mean war, but that is the thing we have to face.

Bevin supported such views, and they were adopted by the TUC. But though Bevin and Citrine ensured that close links were maintained between the Labour Party and the trade unions, it took time to rid the Party of its lingering pacifist influences.

Debate continued meanwhile about the extent to which the Party should pursue Marxist goals. Cripps agitated for a Popular Front alliance with political groups to the left of the Labour Party, including the British Communists. He was eventually expelled from the Labour Party early in 1939, to be followed by certain other hard-liners, Aneurin Bevan among them. Both returned to the fold in later years.

By 1939 both the Labour Party and the trade union movement had begun to recover from the slump in their fortunes at the beginning of the decade. Labour won control of the London County Council in 1934, under the leadership of Herbert Morrison. He later wrote:

> In effect, they put us in power to try us out. . . . It was essential that we should provide London with clean, efficient, progressive, and public-spirited local government.

Labour launched programmes to improve the capital's housing and to widen educational opportunity, and planned a green belt around the city. Control of London, and elsewhere, increased the Party's prestige while, in the House of Commons, the quiet leadership of Attlee developed Labour into a more effective Opposition than it had been under the kindly Lansbury. It was typical of Lansbury that, after his retirement, he travelled to Germany to make an old man's personal plea to Hitler for peace and goodwill.

Trade union membership, meanwhile, began to climb again, to over six million by the end of the 1930s. There was a brief upsurge of strike activity around 1937, as the trade unions recovered their spirit, but industrial relations were peaceful in the 1930s, compared with the upheavals of the 1920s, and few working days were lost by strike action. The trade unions, nevertheless, gained recognition in a growing number of workplaces and, though they could do little about unemployment, they won minor victories which improved conditions for their members. In 1937, for example, the government agreed as part of a Factories Act to a forty-hour week for workers aged fourteen to sixteen, and for women a reduction from the usual forty-eight-hour week.

(b) The Liberal Party

The many upheavals after 1916 had left the Liberal Party disorganized, short of money and weak. Some seventy-two Liberals were elected to the Commons in 1931, but they were divided between the followers of Simon, Samuel and Lloyd George (see Unit 5.3). The Simonites became almost indistinguishable from the Conservatives, while the Samuelites won only a handful of seats in the 1935 election, having by that time moved into opposition to the National government (see Unit 6.1(a)). When Samuel lost his seat in 1935 the leadership of the Liberals passed to Archibald Sinclair. Lloyd George, however, like Winston Churchill, was almost a party in himself. Churchill sat as a Conservative, but he was regularly out of step with the leadership during the 1930s (see Unit 9.1). Lloyd George sat as a Liberal, but he spoke as an ex-Prime Minister and as an elder statesman rather than a Liberal loyalist. He continued to urge his plans for economic revival on the government and, like Churchill, became an outspoken critic of the government's foreign policy in the late 1930s. In May 1939 he complained that 'we have procrastinated seriously and dangerously', and he argued:

> There are two ways of ensuring peace. . . . It is necessary to have the dictators know that we have behind us the kind of forces that will make our ultimate triumph secure, so that they will not challenge the issue. . . . The second way is to secure the co-operation of as many independent nations as we can assemble in order to resist aggression.

In short, Lloyd George demanded more energetic rearmament and a more positive attempt to enlist the assistance of the USSR in standing up to Nazi Germany. As so often in the past, Lloyd George spoke to deaf ears, and the

USSR was left to make its own arrangements with Hitler (see Unit 8.4(*b*)). On this occasion, Attlee gave Lloyd George some support, but there was no close relationship between Labour and the Liberals in their general opposition to the National government. The Labour Party took the view that it provided the real opposition, and that the Liberals were mainly irrelevant.

(*c*) **Extremists**
The Communist Party opposed the National government on almost every issue. It championed the unemployed and resisted fascism, arguing that both were the products of capitalism. It even marched in support of Edward VIII. Its one MP, Gallacher, was the only Commons spokesman against Chamberlain's visit to Munich (see Unit 8.3(*a*)). But, excluded from any joint action with the Labour Party, the Communist Party remained on the fringe of British politics, one of a variety of Marxist groups highly critical of Britain's economy and society.

The extreme right of British politics in the 1930s was represented by the British Union of Fascists. The BUF was founded in 1932 by Oswald Mosley, whose career in the Labour Party had by then ended in expulsion. Two years earlier, he had vainly urged various plans on MacDonald (see Unit 5.1). Frustrated, he had then proposed founding a New Party, and eventually

Fig. 6.6 Mosley returns the Fascist salute of some of his followers during a demonstration of the BUF in London, October 1937. The Fascists won very little support from the British people as a whole

created the BUF, which showed admiration for Mussolini, wearing black shirts and saluting vigorously. The BUF claimed a membership of 20 000, but won no seats in parliament. It developed into a noisy rabble, imitating its Nazi counterpart in Germany by brawling with Communists and attacking minorities, such as the Jews of east London. In *The Greater Britain* Mosley set out his plans for a stronger government, which the British clearly did not want. The Public Order Act of 1936 curbed some of the BUF's activities and, when the Second World War began, Mosley was interned along with over 700 of his fascist supporters. Men of similarly intolerant opinions were to emerge in postwar Britain in movements like the National Front.

6.3 Economic Revival and Non-revival

(a) The Brighter Side
In 1935 some 300 000 dwellings were built in Britain by private enterprise and some 60 000 by public authorities. The latter almost doubled their building programme by 1939, but private enterprise continued to lead the revival in house-building, in keeping with the National government's view of the limited role government should play. Sharp economies during 1932 had resulted in the suspension of subsidies to local authorities, but the National government introduced new Housing Acts in 1933 and 1935, concentrating limited government help on building council housing to replace that destroyed by slum clearance. This was a continuation of the policy laid down in Greenwood's Housing Act of 1930. But local authority building did not provide much work or greatly contribute to reviving the economy. Much greater benefit came from private sector building; and the policy of cheap money proved particularly helpful, for builders could borrow at low rates of interest and buyers could obtain cheap mortgages (see Unit 5.4(*a*)). The nation was far better housed in 1939 than in 1918, although many still could not afford to buy homes, and council housing clearly lagged behind.

The expansion in housing was part of an economic revival which was sluggish and uneven. Nevertheless, the 1930s became comparatively prosperous for many: those with salaries and job-security benefited from the growing range of consumer goods and from falling prices. (The pound of 1900 was worth only about 50p in buying power in 1925. By 1935 it had climbed back to about 60p.) After 1933 the newer industries recovered, in response to reviving demand in the home market, and even increased their former output and expanded their work forces. The South of England and much of the Midlands began to experience a miniature boom, and life for many was comfortable. In the late 1930s there were more people at work in Britain than ever before, despite the vast army of unemployed.

The numbers employed in the chemical industry, for example, rose from about 150 000 before 1914 to almost 300 000 by the end of the 1930s, and those employed in electrical engineering grew from under 100 000 to over

300 000 in the same period. Industries such as vehicle-building and artificial fibres, especially rayon, expanded too, as did the service industries, such as banking. Moreover, much of the new industry was efficient. Smaller companies had been merged in 1926 to set up Imperial Chemical Industries (ICI), giving Britain one of the world's leading chemical organizations. Efficient production steadily reduced the price of motor-cars to the customer, and the number of vehicles doubled during the 1930s until there were about two million on the road in 1939. Electricity output also doubled during the 1930s, and in 1939 was six times what it had been in 1919. The aircraft industry was yet another growth area. On the eve of the Second World War it employed some 300 000 workers. At that time the government showed a flicker of interest in the country's developing airlines, setting up the British Overseas Airways Corporation, another public corporation.

(b) **The Darker Side**
The troubles of the older industries prolonged the Depression, however, in those parts of the country dependent on them (see Figs 2.3 and 6.4). Coal, textiles and shipbuilding suffered from the lack of export markets and were forced to trim their work forces severely. Coal output in 1938 was 227 million tons, compared with 258 and 287 million tons in 1929 and 1913 respectively. The reduction was due almost entirely to the fall in exports of coal, since power-stations in Britain were actually increasing their demand for it. The numbers employed in coal mining fell from over 1 100 000 in 1913 to below 800 000 in 1939, though output per man rose slightly. The level of technology in Britain's pits was still low compared with its more energetic competitors, despite the fact that in 1939 more than half of Britain's coal was being cut and conveyed underground by machinery.

The cotton industry presented a similar picture. In 1937 spinners were achieving much the same output as in the mid 1920s, but there was a dramatic slump in cotton cloth exports, and output was only about 70 per cent of what it had been in 1924. Again the labour force was reduced, from over 600 000 in 1913 to less than 400 000 at the end of the 1930s. Like the coalowners, textile firms modernized too little to increase the output per worker much, and they kept wages low, in an effort to be competitive. There was a limited revival of demand for cloth in the home market, but it was insufficient to prevent not only unemployment but a good deal of short-time working in textiles.

Iron and steel recovered better than shipbuilding. In 1937 the iron and steel industry even began to exceed its 1913 output, mainly because of demand from new industries such as vehicle-building. It was a precarious growth, however. In comparison with the industries of the USA and Germany, much of Britain's iron and steel industry remained old-fashioned. It relied mainly on the home market, protected by the tariffs which the National government had introduced. But such protection was of little help to the shipbuilders. They suffered from an almost universal lack of demand since international trade remained generally depressed. Shipbuilding only began to recover when rearmament

Fig. 6.7 Protest marches by the unemployed often attracted sympathy from the communities through which they passed, but they drew little response from government. Marchers from Jarrow passing through Bedfordshire on their way to put their case in London, October 1936

brought new orders at the end of the 1930s.

By 1939 Britain had made a patchy recovery from the Depression. New technology had given birth to new industries and new employment opportunities, and Britain's record here stood comparison with much that was happening elsewhere in the world. New technology, however, also tended to make old industries outdated. Modernization and up-to-date machinery were needed, but these required heavy capital investment which was lacking in much of British industry. There was also a need for flexible and imaginative management, and that too was lacking in many areas of British industry. Those who had opposed the introduction of protection could argue, indeed, that tariffs had sometimes made management complacent, content to serve the sheltered home market rather than compete against more efficient foreign producers.

Britain's share of world exports had fallen to below 10 per cent by 1937 (compare Unit 3.4(a)). Imports, on the other hand, remained comparatively high in spite of tariffs, considerably greater in volume than before 1914 and still over 17 per cent of the world's total. Table 6.2 shows that earnings from invisible exports prevented Britain from sinking deeply into debt on the balance of payments, but there were indications here too that it was losing

Table 6.2 Britain's balance of payments, 1929–38

Date	Trade balance exports/imports*	Earnings from invisible exports*	Current Account balance*
1929	−259	+362	103
1930	−282	+310	28
1931	−323	+218	−105
1932	−217	+166	−51
1933	−196	+196	0
1934	−221	+214	−7
1935	−185	+217	32
1936	−260	+243	−17
1937	−339	+283	−56
1938	−284	+230	−54

* £million
Source: adapted from Alford, B.W.E.: *Depression and Recovery? British Economic Growth, 1918–39*. Macmillan (London, 1972).

ground as a trading nation and storing up future difficulties. Government, employers and those who enjoyed prosperity in the 1930s not only showed too little concern for the distressed in the Special Areas, but also paid too little heed to the basic problems of the British economy. After the Second World War the country had to face the consequences of this earlier neglect.

Further Reading
Seaman, L.C.B.: *Post-Victorian Britain, 1902–1951*. Methuen (London, 1966), chapters 24–5.
Alford, B.W.E.: *Depression and Recovery? British Economic Growth, 1918–1939*. Macmillan (London, 1972).
Feiling, K.: *The Life of Neville Chamberlain*. Macmillan (London, 1946).
Pollard, S.: *The Development of the British Economy, 1914–1967*. Arnold (London, 1969).
Symons, J.: *The Thirties*. Faber (London, 1960).

Documentary
Brandon, L.G.: *John Maynard Keynes*. Arnold Archive (London, 1972).
Pilgrim Trust: *Men Without Work*. Cambridge University Press (Cambridge, 1938).
Yass, M.: *The Great Depression*. Wayland (Hove, 1973).

Exercises
1. 'Essentially the government of the Conservatives' (page 96): explain this view of the National government from 1931 to 1940 referring to both ministers (use Table 6.1) and policies.
2. Compare Fig. 6.4 with Fig. 2.3. How far does your answer to Question 3, Unit 2, already explain the relative figures for unemployed in 1937, and what further

explanations can you offer why the four areas named in Fig. 6.4 needed to be regarded as 'Special Areas' by 1937?

3. Design and write a double-page newspaper review looking back at the end of 1935 on the events of that year. Your headlines should include references to the Silver Jubilee, MacDonald's resignation, the Labour Party Conference, the general election and the British economy.

4. Making use of the Index to this book, write a survey of Stanley Baldwin's career to the time of his retirement in 1937. What do you consider were his *three* most important achievements?

5. What were 'the basic problems of the British economy' (page 110) during the 1930s? What were the policies of the National government for dealing with these problems? Did any of the parties referred to in Unit 6.2 offer convincing alternative policies?

6. Write *two* letters for publication in a newspaper at the time of MacDonald's retirement in 1937, *the first* from the point of view of a supporter grateful for his services to the country, *the second* from an embittered member of the Labour Party mindful of the events of 1931. Add an editorial comment aiming to strike a balance between the two viewpoints.

7. What different views of 'an economic revival which was sluggish and uneven' (page 107) might have been taken at the end of 1938 by (*a*) a worker in one of the new industries in South-East England and (*b*) a worker in one of the basic industries in North-East England? *In each case*, specify the industry you have in mind.

8. How far do Tables 5.1 and 6.2 support the argument that there was some economic recovery in Britain in the years after 1932? What doubts do the Tables raise about the extent of the recovery?

Unit Seven

Life in Inter-war Britain

7.1 The Social Structure

(a) Population Changes

At the time of the 1921 census the population of the United Kingdom was just over forty-two million. It increased by some five million during the next twenty years, mainly as a result of a fall in the death rate. Infant mortality declined sharply throughout the first half of the twentieth century, and advances in medicine, with improved housing and hygiene, curbed the toll taken by diseases such as tuberculosis and scarlet fever. One consequence of the reduced death rate was that society came to have a larger percentage of elderly people than previously, although the average expectation of life in 1930 was still only sixty-three for women and fifty-nine for men. The birth rate also fell, after a brief boom immediately after 1918. The changing status of women, the use of birth control and an increasing awareness of the connection between large families and poverty reduced the average number of children in a family to two in the 1930s. A Baby Austin, it was said, was often more attractive than a human baby. Emigration, mainly to the Dominions, tended to lower the population during the 1920s, but the movement was reversed in the 1930s when many European refugees came to Britain. The overall growth of population occurred mainly in London, South-East England and the Midlands, and the total population changed little in the more economically depressed areas of Britain.

(b) Standards of Living

Unemployment was a constant threat, especially in the basic industries, and even when prices fell after 1929, working-class families on low wages often experienced hardship. Though their standard of living was higher than in the nineteenth century, the labouring classes often endured a life of drudgery which ended in premature death. In 1936 Seebohm Rowntree conducted a social survey in York, to make comparisons with his earlier survey in 1899 (see Unit 1.2(b)). His new findings were not comforting. Though there had been a slight improvement, 31 per cent of the working population were still 'under the poverty line', and conditions for the elderly seemed to have grown even worse, despite state pensions. The long-term unemployed and their families

Fig. 7.1 For the poor in the inter-war years a visit to the pawnbroker was no uncommon event: a miner's wife on such a visit, 1921. What could be borrowed on clothes or household goods often enabled a family to eat

frequently lived in the deepest misery and want, and the means-tested dole was woefully inadequate.

The average wage in Britain was a little under £4 a week in 1936, and more than 70 per cent of the population lived on less than £5 a week. Rowntree calculated that £2.65 would be just enough to keep a family of five 'in health', provided that there was 'constant watchfulness and a high degree of skill on the part of the housewife'. He recommended that there should be a national minimum wage, but such an idea was too radical for the National government – or for any British government since that time. Wages varied considerably. The better paid work was in prosperous industries, such as electrical engineering and vehicle-building. Miners, on the other hand, even when they had steady work, were paid less than the average wage and, unless their families were small, were in danger of earning too little to keep 'in health'. Agricultural labourers were even worse off in financial terms, though their employment was more regular: most earned less than £2 a week. Incomes were also low in the textile industries, where the many women workers were even worse paid than the men. Unemployment benefit and the dole varied according to the size of the family and as a result of the means test; but a married man with two children was fortunate to collect £1.50 a week, even when the cuts of 1931 had been restored.

About 20 per cent of incomes were between £5 and £10 a week in the late 1930s, and they were mostly earned by white-collar workers, such as bank clerks and teachers. Among the working classes, only supervisors and those with vital skills were likely to get into this group. Another 8 per cent or so earned more than £10 a week, about one in a hundred more than £40 a week. Gross inequalities therefore existed. But there were many among the higher-income groups who complained bitterly about the rate of taxation. The standard rate of income tax, paid on incomes above a certain level, had been raised to 30p in the pound in 1919, but was reduced to 20p in 1926. The economic crisis took it up to 25p in 1932, but Chamberlain settled for 22½p in 1935, returning to 25p in 1938 to help pay for rearmament. The level of taxation on the well-to-do was by no means high, in comparison with the years after 1940, though it was heavier than it had been before 1914. In his budget of 1909 Lloyd George had begun to use taxation as a means of redistributing wealth, to finance old age pensions, for example. Death duties on large estates, first introduced in 1889, worked in a similar direction. By 1939, however, such policies had hardly narrowed the gap between rich and poor. Many landed families remained, like the monarchy, extremely wealthy. The Duke of Westminster held vast and profitable estates. The Duke of Rutland received £1 500 000 for the sale of just half of his Belvoir estate. Other families had accumulated wealth from industry. Stanley Baldwin inherited business interests in Baldwins Ltd, whose empire included iron and steel, mines and railways. In 1919 he gave £150 000 to the nation, a fifth of his fortune.

For all those with steady incomes above £4 a week, the 1930s offered increasing comforts. There had been a marked decline in the numbers of domestic servants since the First World War (see Unit 1.4), but even in the 1930s they were not at all uncommon. Everyone who could afford it aspired to employ helpers, though fewer could be found to 'live in'. But low prices brought more labour-saving homes and household utensils within reach. A compact and easy-to-manage semi-detached house could be bought for little more than £300 in the late 1930s. Vacuum cleaners and electric irons were used in more and more homes, and some of the better-off had washing machines and refrigerators. Some of the new 'semis' also had garages, since a motor-car could be bought for little more than £100 by 1939. Woolworth's stores advertised that they sold 'Nothing over Sixpence' (2½p), and mass-produced suits could be bought at the Fifty Shilling Tailor for £2.50 and less. It was a comment on the times that Woolworth sold spectacles for 'Sixpence': the poor could rummage and serve themselves. The more fortunate could buy wirelesses and gramophones and enjoy a greater choice of foodstuffs since the new high street stores stocked a growing range of branded goods. For those preferring to eat out, a good meal could be had for less than 10p.

Unfortunately, there were two nations: meals out, new suits and even electric irons were beyond the reach of millions. George Orwell spoke for many of the poor, describing in *The Road to Wigan Pier* (1937) not just their misery but their dignity:

> They have made things tolerable by lowering their standards. . . . You can't get much meat for threepence, but you can get a lot of fish and chips. . . . Milk costs threepence a pint and even 'mild' beer costs fourpence, but . . . you can wring forty cups of tea out of a quarter-pound packet.

Cups of tea, chips and carrots played a prominent part in the lives of the unemployed and poorly paid. A Welsh miner, B.L. Coombes, wrote of his own experiences in *These Poor Hands* (1939):

> Early last Saturday morning three young men stopped outside this house. . . . (One) asked quietly if we could give them a spot of warm tea. . . . He said they could manage for food. I had eaten all the bread for breakfast after coming from work, so my wife cut them three large slices of apple cake to go with the tea. . . . They meant to walk to London, in the hopes of getting work. . . . (They had) a Lyle's sugar packet, and their 'food' was inside – one large crust of bread that was terribly hard and had been dusted with pepper as a substitute for butter.

Many social surveys besides Rowntree's recorded the living conditions of the poor. The Pilgrim Trust reported on Liverpool in *Men Without Work* (1938):

> One thing which will remain in the memory of anyone going round among the Liverpool unemployed will be the appalling housing conditions and the low domestic standards. . . . There is the 'general labourer' of 33 living with a wife and four children (a daughter of 6 at school, another daughter crippled, a daughter of 2, and a son just born) in two rooms, small, dark, damp, with plaster decayed, nowhere to wash . . . (and a) gap between their net income of 34s (£1.70) and the 38s (£1.90) or so required by our 'poverty line' standard.

This was the other face of Britain, in what Orwell described as 'a land of snobbery and privilege, ruled largely by the old and silly'.

The findings of the social surveys and the complaints of the trade unions produced as little widespread interest in Britain as did the activities of the totalitarian and aggressive powers in Europe and the Far East. Complacency reigned. Neither the nation's leaders nor the media provided much leadership, and society as a whole was content to mind its own business. J.B. Priestley visited Jarrow, recording in his *English Journey* (1933):

> One out of every two shops appeared to be permanently closed. Wherever we went there were men hanging about . . . hundreds and thousands of them. The whole town

looked as if it had entered a perpetual penniless bleak Sabbath. The men wore the drawn masks of prisoners of war.

Philip Gibbs later recalled in *The Pageant of the Years* (1946):

> I went up to the distressed areas in Yorkshire, Northumberland, and Durham. It was all very tragic up there, especially in the mining villages with their rows of little houses reaching out to the slag heaps. In some of them there was complete unemployment.

Units 5 and 6 have shown how little was done to help the unemployed, and equally little was done to remedy the more precise injustices of which men like B.L. Coombes wrote:

> There are 78 000 boys working in the British mines. 58 boys under sixteen were killed at colliery work during the first half of 1938, and the records of 1937 show that 5 750 were disabled for more than three days. They may lose a limb or have their features scarred, so that they are handicapped before they have really started to know life.

This was the real cost of a society which went on believing in 'leaving things as they are' and in the politics of not spending the taxpayer's money.

(*c*) **The Status of Women and Fashion**
Nevertheless, slow changes were taking place in British society. Lord Birkenhead told the House of Lords in 1928:

> I was against the extension of the franchise to women (in 1918). I am against the extension of the franchise to women. I shall always be against the extension of the franchise to women.

But he grudgingly accepted that the descent of what he called 'the slipping slope' was inevitable. It was sometimes claimed that the First World War helped to break down barriers between the classes, though inequalities in wealth worked powerfully to preserve them. The War did, however, break down some of the barriers between the sexes. The right to vote, which women gained in 1918 and 1928, was just one aspect of their changing status (see Units 2.1 and 3.4(*c*)).

In 1934 F.W. Hirst observed in *The Consequences of the War to Great Britain*:

> The line which formerly demarcated so clearly the province of women from that of men has now become so blurred as to be often scarcely visible. During the war . . . women undertook men's jobs and showed unexpected capability. Since then they have managed, not without a good deal of ill-feeling, to retain their footing in business and most of the professions, not to mention the now all-important world of sport.

*Fig. 7.2   Fashions at Ascot, 1928, and a different nation from that of the miner's
wife in Fig. 7.1 and the slum dwellers in Fig. 7.3(a) and (b)*

She was writing mainly of middle-class women. Most professions were now
open to women, except for the Stock Exchange and the Church, but even in
'business' and 'the professions' they were often paid less than men and seldom
secured the highest appointments. Working-class women continued to be
employed in factories, especially in textiles, and with their nimble fingers they
found increasing opportunities in many of the new industries. Opportunities
for office work expanded with the growth of service industries, and a skilled
secretary often earned more than a miner, and certainly more than a farm
worker. Even so, except among the working classes, married women were not
expected to go out to work in the years before 1939. Indeed, some wives, those
of teachers and civil servants were forbidden to do so. The role of the middle-
class wife was still that of looking after the home.

A degree of financial independence enabled some women to behave in an
ever more scandalous fashion. The 'Flappers' of the 1920s adopted styles of
dress, and sometimes of behaviour, that caused grave alarm. Skirts became
shorter and, for a brief time in the mid 1920s, knees were to be seen. Girls
danced the Charleston frenetically, cut and bobbed their hair, smoked cigar-
ettes, went out without chaperones, and were alleged, without foundation, to

Fig. 7.3   Two glimpses of poverty and slum housing in the 1920s:
(a) The cramped quarters of a family living in Bethnal Green, London, photo-
graphed in 1923

be as immoral as they were apparently immodest. Rapidly changing fashions both in outer clothes and underwear, exploiting rayon and other new fabrics, not only heralded female emancipation but also provided a stimulus to industry, as did the increased use of cosmetics. By the 1930s, however, women were abandoning their short skirts and tubular dresses – fashion again empha- sized feminine curves – and women were once more growing their hair long.

While all these excitements were happening, male fashions changed very little. Office workers turned from starched to soft collars, and to wrist watches rather than pocket watches. Manual workers were slow to abandon the cloth cap for the trilby, though some had done so by 1939. For a time the bowler hat reigned as the status-symbol of the foreman – and of the nation's foremen too, since it was worn by Lloyd George and, particularly, by Stanley Baldwin. For more formal occasions, of course, there was the top hat, the wearing of which by MacDonald alarmed his followers as much as the emancipation of females alarmed Birkenhead.

(b) Housing in the industrial north of England at about the same time

7.2 The Changing Environment

(a) Towns and Housing

Britain was already highly industrialized and urbanized before 1914 (see Unit 1.2(b)). During the inter-war years the agricultural labour force continued to shrink while, at least in the prosperous areas, towns expanded into the surrounding countryside. The suburbs became fashionable for those who could afford to move to them. Deliberate planning was rare, however, and there was much ribbon-development, with houses and premises springing up along the main roads. Welwyn Garden City, planned in 1920 by Ebenezer Howard for a community of some 50 000 living pleasantly alongside industry and work, was exceptional, as was Morrison's idea of the green belt around London. Also exceptional were the communities which developed in the 1930s around the new steel works at Corby, and at Aycliffe and Cwmbran in the Special Areas, as the result of introducing trading estates with their light industry. The general tendency was for older properties in the heart of urban communities to deteriorate, while new properties were built on the outskirts. Many slums were cleared, especially during the 1930s (see Unit 6.3), but more than half a million slum homes remained in 1939, and almost as many again were deteriorating fast. Orwell wrote of the mining areas:

hundreds of miles of streets inhabited by miners, every one of whom . . . in work, gets black from head to foot every day, without ever . . . a house in which one could have a bath.

In the old industrial towns, the majority of workers continued to live in rented, back-to-back terraced houses, with outside WCs and without hot-water systems.

Cheap money and the services of building societies led to a considerable increase in owner-occupation. The building societies were cautious about lending to wage-earners, however, and most mortgages went to the salaried. It was white-collar workers, therefore, who were likely to move to the suburbs, with their semi-detached houses with 'mod cons' (modern conveniences, in estate agents' jargon – all the necessary interior plumbing, electricity and probably gas, usually a garden and perhaps a garage). Further embellishments were popular, especially bay windows, leaded lights and 'decorative twiddles', many of them mock-Tudor. The new owner-occupiers were likely to move from older town properties, so the less prosperous who remained behind were able to rent the houses they had vacated, thus relieving the overcrowding in many areas.

Council housing provided many other people with the opportunity of moving to new homes. Of the four-and-a-half million houses built in Britain

Fig. 7.4   Owner occupation and a family car in the 1930s in a street (or more likely 'avenue') still lit by gas. Life during the Depression was far from uncomfortable for those with a steady income

between the wars, almost a third were built by local authorities. Not all their building was for the poor, and council estates varied from almost luxurious semi-detached housing to functional, and often jerry-built, 'boxes with bathrooms', bathrooms being required by law. Life on some council estates, such as Rose Hill at Burnley, differed very little from life in privately owned suburban properties, most of the tenants being employed in non-manual work. Such tenants zealously mowed their lawns, planted their gardens and 'beautified' (a common inter-war term for 'decorated') their houses. Their estates were spacious and well maintained by the councils. Other estates, however, were built to rehouse slum dwellers, and even 'better-class' ones were often conceived as working-class ghettos. These estates were likely to be concrete jungles, recreating rows of terraced houses and, in some ways, continuing nineteenth-century ideas about basic housing for the workers. That 'basic' now meant providing an inside bathroom affronted some ratepayers, and gave rise to the myth that workers would keep coal in their baths.

Britain also began trying to solve its housing problems in some areas by building blocks of flats, both private and public. The towers were to grow ever higher in the years after 1945, though it was already being argued before 1939 that high flats were unsuitable for families with young children. For the authorities, however, they had the alleged advantages of cheapness and of taking up limited ground-space, and high blocks of flats were built in many parts of London – in Camberwell and Lambeth, for example – as well as in other cities. Other blocks of flats, like those at Quarry Hill in Leeds and Collyhurst in Manchester, aimed to combine compact housing with community amenities and were less forbidding. In general, by 1939, Britain was better equipped with housing than ever before, most of it rented at 50p, or less, a week. But compared with the properties from which their tenants had moved, the new council estates were often remote from workplaces, cinemas and even shops. Moreover, one common effect of such movement was to break up working-class communities which, enduring past hardships together, had developed a warm spirit of comradeship.

(b) **Transport**
A spectacular change in inter-war Britain was the increase of motor traffic, necessary in many towns because of suburban growth and the siting of new housing estates. By 1937 firms such as Austin, Morris and Ford had an annual output of more than half a million motor-vehicles, excluding motor-cycles, and annual spending on Britain's roads had risen to about £70 million. Horse-drawn vehicles became less universal after the First World War, until they were only used to deliver milk, coal, beer and railway parcels, and to collect rags and bones. City centres were often clogged with buses, trams, trolley-buses, lorries, vans and, increasingly, private transport. From the early 1920s to the late 1930s public transport vehicles increased from about 75 000 to about 100 000, goods vehicles rose threefold to about half a million, and private cars sixfold to nearly two million. Motor-cycles also numbered about half a million by

Fig. 7.5 The Elephant and Castle, London, 1933: trams and buses provided cheap transport for the masses at a time when private cars were still a luxury. Already, however, the congestion in London's streets was increasing and policemen were required to play an increasing part in traffic control

1939, though there were already over 300 000 at the beginning of the 1920s. Fares were cheap, like prices generally in the 1930s, and the masses relied heavily on public transport. Birmingham's buses and trams carried some 400 million passengers a year in the late 1930s, while fleets of coaches (more luxurious versions of the earlier charabancs) competed with the railways for long-distance passengers, many of whom were taking seaside holidays. But although fares were low, the lure of personal motorized transport was strong among those who could afford it.

Like the railways in the nineteenth century, motor-vehicles in the twentieth brought changes not only to the economy but also to social habits. Many more places became accessible, both to live in and as centres for recreation. Easier local travel helped to increase cinema audiences and attendance at football matches and other sports fixtures. The transport authorities generally were quick to run 'Specials' to all sorts of events catering for mass audiences. 'Outings' of all kinds became possible – to the seaside, to gardens, to zoos, and to pleasure parks such as Manchester's Belle Vue. Shoppers could now go further afield in search of things to buy, and department stores could make more deliveries over a wider area.

The railways suffered from this motorized competition, both for passengers and parcels. Local lines were already so unprofitable in the 1930s that some were closed. The railways began to concentrate increasingly on what were later called 'inter-city' services, seeking their profits from the speed and comfort of long-distance expresses (such as the Manchester–London 'Comet'), and from the bulk travel of 'excursion' trains to resorts such as Blackpool. They retained some business because of the poor state of many roads. Cobbled streets in the towns jolted passengers in vehicles, and tramlines were a hazard for cyclists and drivers of light cars. Road-building and maintenance were often patchy between towns and road travel was far more dangerous than rail. Lloyd George's Road Act of 1920 earmarked receipts from Road Fund licences for road improvements, but the Fund was raided by Churchill in 1926 when money was needed for other things, and it was wound up in 1936. Roads were always an obvious target when governments wished to cut spending. Of the new roads which were built, most were in the south of England. Road accidents increased steadily to the middle of the 1930s when Hore-Belisha, Minister of Transport from 1934 to 1937, introduced new Road Traffic Acts. The Act of 1930 had made third-party insurance compulsory, but had abolished the earlier speed limit of twenty miles per hour. The new Acts imposed a limit of thirty miles per hour in built-up areas, though it was not well enforced. New drivers were also required to pass a test of competence and devices such as traffic lights were adopted for the control of traffic and to reduce the chaos and carnage at road junctions. Percy Shaw, a Halifax man, invented cat's eyes, to reflect the lights on vehicles, and to mark the middle and edges of roads after dark. Pedestrians too gained some respite with marked road-crossings, indicated by 'Belisha beacons'. Such innovations helped to reduce the death toll, which had reached an annual total of 7 000 by 1934. Britain's roads, though among the most crowded, became safer than most, though numerous accidents had become a feature of twentieth-century living.

(c) The Media

With education now compulsory until fourteen, the age of mass literacy had arrived. The 'Press Lords' – Beaverbrook, Northcliffe (until his death in 1922) and then Rothermere – competed furiously to sell their cheap newspapers to a mass readership. By 1939 Beaverbrook's *Daily Express* had a circulation nearing three million, while Lord Riddell's *News of the World* sold four million copies on Sundays to the seekers of sensations, especially sexual ones. The cheap press preferred scoops and scandals to the serious and orderly presentation of substantial news, and it laced what news there was with extensive, and often irrational, editorial comment. The Northcliffe-Rothermere *Daily Mail* waged its own vendetta against a sensible peace settlement in 1919, against trade unions and strikes, against socialism, communism and the League of Nations and, though it reached a million sales in the 1920s, it only rose to one-and-a-half million by 1939. The *Daily Herald*, as the mouthpiece for the labour movement, helped to redress the balance. In financial difficulties in the

1920s, it was financed jointly after 1929 by the TUC and Odhams Press, and sold two million copies ten years later. The *News Chronicle*, controlled by the Cadbury family, fared rather less well with a daily sale of one-and-a-quarter million copies. It aimed to preserve moral values and liberalism, and was anti-fascist and anti-Conservative. Two tabloid newspapers – full of pictures on smaller pages, and originally conceived as suitable for female readers who might be confused by a lot of print – were the *Daily Mirror* and *Daily Sketch*. The former made headway in the 1930s with increasingly massive headlines, and with a strip-cartoon about the misfortunes of Jane, a young lady forever dressing and undressing.

The 'heavies' existed for more serious readers. *The Times* usually spoke for the establishment, and tried hard to remain discreet, with unobtrusive headlines and few pictures. The *Daily Telegraph* spoke unashamedly for the Conservatives, favoured substantial news coverage, and appealed very successfully to businessmen, with the largest circulation of the weightier papers (over 600 000 in the late 1930s). The *Manchester Guardian*, like the *Scotsman*, had a regional image but a much wider circulation, and the *Guardian*'s cause was Liberalism. On Sundays, serious readers could buy the *Observer* or the *Sunday Times*, to escape from the more lurid Sunday equivalents of the popular dailies. *Reynolds News*, which spoke for the Co-operative movement, was alone in its condemnation of Chamberlain's Munich Agreement, and had only a small circulation. The *Daily Worker*, founded in 1930, was the only British newspaper to be financed almost entirely by a political party. Its 100 000 copies sold mainly to the supporters of the British Communist Party. *The Week*, edited by Claud Cockburn, presented a Marxist interpretation of the week's news. There were also growing numbers of periodicals both for information and entertainment.

Newspapers and periodicals had to compete with broadcasting after the First World War. The British Broadcasting Company was given a monopoly in 1922, and became a public corporation four years later (see Unit 3.4(c)), financed by wireless licences costing 50p a year. Seven million licences a year were being issued by 1935, rising to nine million by 1939 when only the poorest homes remained without a wireless set of some sort. The first television broadcasts were made in 1936, but television was still an expensive luxury and only a small minority received them before services were interrupted by the Second World War.

The BBC's first wireless broadcasts were mainly news, concerts and, starting at an early stage, children's programmes. Listeners found them new and exciting, and demanded more. Plays, light music and comedy added to the variety and during the 1930s 'listening to the wireless' became an almost universal pastime, revolutionizing leisure. Religious services and sports commentaries were also popular and the wireless became indispensable not only to the sick and housebound but to the public in general. From the outset, the BBC offered its listeners a mixture of information and entertainment, but the popular press often complained that it was too 'highbrow', not aware enough of mass taste.

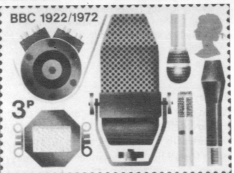

Fig. 7.6 Stanley Baldwin was one of the first politicians to recognize the importance of broadcasting and to make use of it. (a) He is photographed here broadcasting at the time of his retirement in May 1937 (b) The British stamp of 1972 commemorated the origins of the BBC with a display of developments in microphones

John Reith, the BBC's first Director-General, endured a good deal of criticism for his alleged efforts to influence public taste and to avoid at all costs the controversial and undignified. Ellen Wilkinson attacked him in 1931:

> In six short years, Sir John Reith has made himself more even than the guardian of public morals. He has become the Judge of What We Ought to Want.

Another critic called him 'the Napoleon of Broadcasting', deploring both the Director-General's strict moral code and the 'impeccable' accents of the BBC announcers, whose pronunciation of standard English and syntax had little in common with those of the mass of their listeners.

Yet the BBC became a national institution, respected and even loved. It also provided a new link between the people and their rulers. As early as 1924 George V's voice was heard on the wireless when he opened the Wembley Exhibition. Six years later, the King spoke directly not only to his subjects in Britain but 'to all my people everywhere', when the BBC broadcast his Christmas message to many parts of the Empire. Again as early as 1924, it was realized that broadcasting could be used for election purposes and the principle was quickly established that the BBC must not favour one political party more than another. Nevertheless, Baldwin was quicker to master the techniques of broadcasting than MacDonald, and his quiet talk on the wireless to the electors might well have helped him to win the election of 1924. Radio became vital for matters of national interest in the 1930s. Edward VIII spoke to the nation in an abdication broadcast and, in September 1939, people everywhere gathered anxiously round their wireless sets to hear Neville Chamberlain announce the state of war between Britain and Nazi Germany. Meanwhile in 1938, a BBC spokesman reported another event:

> Sir John Reith is shortly leaving the BBC to become the . . . Chairman of Imperial Airways. . . . A sad day for the Corporation, to lose the man who really was the BBC, and who has been mainly responsible for its creation.

(d) The Nation at Play

The wireless provided entertainment in the home, but the inter-war years also saw a tremendous increase in entertainments outside it. Cinemas, dance halls and spectator sports attracted increasing custom. In 1920 London already had over 250 cinemas. By the 1930s the very names of cinemas promised enchantment, plushness and luxury: *Palace, Plaza, Princess, Regal, Rialto* and *Trocadero*. They offered a taste of the high life and escape – from the drabness of long hours of work and homes which were often still cold, cramped and spartan. In the country as a whole there were more than 4 500 cinemas by the end of the Second World War. Films in the 1920s were silent, and the film critic who wrote under the heading of *Film Flickers* chose a fitting title for his column. But films brought romantic visions of a different (and often illusory) world. The choice in Blackpool in 1920 included romance from the South Seas in *A Woman There Was*, while *Auction of Souls* promised scenes from Turkish harems and eastern slave markets. The highlight of the season, however, was a visit in person from Nazimova, 'the Screen Wonder Woman', one of the many idols the film industry created for the masses to worship. Mary Pickford and Greta Garbo were other stars who attracted dedicated followings in the 1920s,

Fig. 7.7 Rudolph Valentino attracted unprecedented female adulation in the 1920s. The Sheik was made in 1921. The Son of the Sheik followed, and when Valentino died in 1926 there was universal grief among his admirers

while women swooned over Rudolph Valentino and John Gilbert. Their skills in slapstick and gymnastics ensured a mass following for Buster Keaton, the Keystone Cops and a host of other comedians. Chaplin and, a little later, Laurel and Hardy had an appeal which was almost universal.

Talking-pictures arrived in the late 1920s with Al Jolson in *The Jazz Singer*, and this brought a new revolution in entertainment. Town-centre cinemas were built to seat audiences of 3 000 and more, and countless smaller cinemas catered for immediately local patrons. It was not uncommon for families in working-class districts to visit cinemas four or five times a week. Some films began to be made in colour, enticing even more people into the cinemas. Seats in the local picture-houses could be had for a few pence and, even in the grandest and most opulent cinemas luxury cost little more than 10p. The larger cinemas had the added attraction of organ recitals on the Mighty Wurlitzers, and some combined new films with old music-hall, offering both pictures and stage acts. Live theatre was sometimes overshadowed but seldom entirely eclipsed by the new picture palaces. There was no doubt, however, that it was to the cinema that the masses flocked, especially to the ritual queueing for the two 'houses' (performances) on Saturday evenings.

Dance, as well as film, had palaces. The 'Palais de Danse' was often plush, and romantically and optimistically named: the *Empire Ballroom, Mecca, Tivoli* and *Locarno*. With an exciting succession of new rhythms and dances, the 'Pally' drew the young, and demonstrated the new-found freedom of young women to go where they wished, unchaperoned. The steady output of dance music provided the BBC with innumerable programmes and the gramophone-record industry with a stream of profit-making 'hits'.

Sport too attracted larger audiences than before 1914. A million and more watched Saturday football matches – 5p was enough to gain admission. The crowds grew at cricket matches, not only at test and county level, but also at the many local league games, especially popular in the textile areas of Lancashire and West Yorkshire. Many towns acquired greyhound-racing tracks, mainly for working-class patrons for whom horse-racing might be too remote or too expensive. Betting had a wide appeal, on football pools, at 'the dogs' and on horse-racing too, many of the transactions being carried on, in theory illegally, by means of betting slips surreptitiously conveyed to local bookmakers. Some towns acquired 'dirt-track' (speedway) racing. And for the many who wanted to play games themselves, local parks developed more facilities for tennis, bowls, putting and 'crazy golf', and preserved patches of grass on which one could improvise almost anything.

The seaside was more of a magnet for the average holiday-maker than ever before. Authorities in Blackpool claimed that the town had more than half a million visitors at the August Bank Holiday 1937, brought in hundreds of packed trains and thousands of motor-coaches as well as by cars and motor-cycles. Blackpool's range of attractions seemed to grow annually. Immediately after the First World War there was a craze for roller-skating, spreading from London. The less energetic could at that time sail from Blackpool to half a dozen places along the coast, south to Llandudno and north to Barrow, or across the sea to the Isle of Man. The Victorian Tower had its circus. There were cinemas, theatres, waxworks, ballrooms, piers, pleasure parks with their tennis courts and gardens, and amusement parks with their 'rides' and slot-machines. To the expanding Illuminations were added by 1939 an icedrome, indoor swimming, wrestling contests and greyhound-racing, pleasure flights in aeroplanes and even, for a time, baseball. But the first Butlin's holiday camp was opened in 1939 at Skegness, with an inclusive price per person per week of just over £2.50. Whatever the state of the British economy in the inter-war years, the entertainments industry had become an important part of it.

7.3 Education and Religion

There was less obvious expansion in education during the inter-war years, and probably even less growth in Britain's religious observance. The financial policies of successive governments meant that little was done to expand education after the Fisher Act of 1918 (see Unit 2.3(*b*)). Most children now received an elementary education to the age of fourteen. Almost half of them, in 1939, were still in all-age schools, though some local authorities had built council schools for the eleven-to-fourteen age group. Fewer than 10 per cent of children received secondary education in high and grammar schools, where it was usual to attempt the General School Examination at the age of sixteen. Many entered secondary schools simply because their parents could afford and were willing to pay fees for them, but gifted children of poor families could take a ten-plus examination and win scholarships. These provided for the payment of fees, but the parents still had to meet many other expenses (for uniforms and quite often books, for example) and they also had to manage without the wages which might have been earned at fourteen. Only a small minority of working-class children therefore achieved the School Certificate, and fewer still went on to university at eighteen. Here again, however, state scholarships from 1920 allowed some students from poor homes to continue their education, while some more enlightened local authorities developed their own systems of grants to give similar help. Such grants were neither numerous nor lavish – there were only two hundred state scholarships a year, for example – and cuts in spending were always likely to reduce or to suspend help to students. The dice were heavily loaded against the children of poor families, however gifted they might be.

New universities or university colleges were opened between the wars, at Swansea, Leicester, Reading and Hull, for example. But there were fewer than 30 000 students in English universities in the mid 1920s and only one child in 250 could hope for a university education in the mid 1930s. The opportunities for girls and for working-class children were very limited indeed. Yet schools in general were becoming less like barns and prisons. Some authorities were more forward than others in erecting new buildings; and the better schools were recognizing the advantages of light and space. The schools also showed concern for the general health of their children. School meals and medical inspections dated from legislation in the years before 1914, but the Milk Act of 1934 made a third of a pint of milk available daily for a halfpenny, or free to the very poor. Such milk was vitally important to the under-nourished children of the unemployed. The nation assumed, however, that it could not afford to do more for its children. The Hadow Report of 1926 recommended compulsory education to the age of fifteen, and the improvement of education from the age of eleven. But the Report was shelved. Chamberlain's government considered raising the school-leaving age in 1939, but war with Nazi Germany now prevented the change.

The Churches, meanwhile, seemed to share the complacency which afflicted so many inter-war governments. Only the Roman Catholic Church had much success in attracting new members. In 1928 a proposal to revise the Anglican Prayer Book was defeated in parliament. Four years later the Methodist movement was reunited when various groups such as the Primitive Methodists rejoined the Wesleyans. But Sundays went on becoming holidays rather than holy days for most British people, and religious services were much less well attended than before 1914, at least in some parts of the country. Individual churchmen, and groups like the Salvation Army, showed concern for suffering, but the Churches offered little leadership. The reader of popular newspapers was much more interested in the career of the luckless Rector of Stiffkey. After being unfrocked for his colourful attempts to rescue young ladies from moral danger, he became a showground performer. He endured a prolonged fast in a barrel at Blackpool, but his life was ended abruptly at Skegness, when he chose to address the holidaymakers from an animal cage, and was mauled by lions. As the headlines about the inquest expressed it:

EX-RECTOR ASKED FOR TWO LIONS
SAID ONE WAS 'TOO SLOW'

Further Reading
Blythe, R.: *The Age of Illusion*. Hamish Hamilton (London, 1963).
Cootes, R.J.: *The Making of the Welfare State*. Longman (Harlow, 1966).
Marwick, A.: *Britain in the Century of Total War – War, Peace and Social Change, 1900–1967*. Penguin (Harmondsworth, 1970).
Seaman, L.C.B.: *Life in Britain Between the Wars*. Batsford (London, 1970).

Documentary
Briggs, A.: *They Saw it Happen, 1897–1940*. Blackwell (Oxford, 1960).
James, M.: *The Emancipation of Women in Great Britain*. Arnold Archive (London, 1973).

Exercises
1. Write a paragraph about *each* of the illustrations in this Unit and Unit 6, explaining what each illustration shows of British society between the wars.
2. 'There were two nations' (page 115): what evidence in this Unit supports this statement about Britain between the wars?
3. Making use of the Index to this book and earlier Units, show how far you think the status of women in Britain had risen by 1939, compared with the early years of the century.
4. What housing problems remained in Britain at the end of the 1930s? Making use of the Index to this book (*Acts*), summarize the Housing Acts which had been passed since 1918. Why were these Acts not more far-reaching?
5. Selecting a variety of headings (such as 'railways', 'public road transport', 'private cars'), compare transport in the late 1930s with that at the present time. How far does this comparison support the opinion that change has brought universal improvement?
6. Making use of Unit 7.2(*c*), suggest how differently the following news items might have been treated by the named newspapers:
   (*a*) The General Strike, 1926 – the *Daily Mail* and *Daily Herald*;
   (*b*) The formation of MacDonald's National government, 1931 – the *Daily Telegraph* and *Daily Worker*;
   (*c*) The general election result, 1935 – the *News Chronicle* and *Daily Mirror*;
   (*d*) The Munich Agreement, 1938 – *Reynolds News* and the *News of the World*;

(*e*) Persisting unemployment, 1938 – *The Times* and the *Manchester Guardian*.

7. Suggest in the form of daily entries in a diary how you might have spent a week free from work in the late 1930s with sufficient money to afford the various recreations and entertainments then popular.

8. 'The dice were heavily loaded against the children of poor families, however gifted' (page 129). Explain and illustrate this statement with reference to Britain's educational system in the 1930s and to the general opportunities open to such children at that time.

Unit Eight

The Years of Dismay: Foreign and Imperial Policy, 1930–9

8.1 The Empire and the Dominions

(a) India

Gandhi chose salt taxes as the target for his new campaign against British rule in India at the end of the 1920s (see Unit 4.3(*b*)). With his followers, he made a well-publicized march to the sea at Dandi, on India's west coast, praying and spinning thread along the way. (The spinning wheel was an important symbol in Gandhi's campaigns. It represented self-help, simple but dignified labour and home production in preference to British imports.) When they began, inexpertly and illegally, to make salt from the sea the police made arrests, and vigorous police baton charges were duly recorded on film. The British imprisoned more than 50 000 Indian nationalists in 1930, including Gandhi, but having arrested him they had no alternative but to release him again. Civil disobedience was a powerful weapon, and peace would only be restored by negotiation. Meanwhile, the Simon Report was completed in May 1930, and MacDonald summoned a Round-table Conference in London to discuss the way ahead. The Indian National Congress boycotted the first Conference, but Gandhi agreed to attend the second, and arrived in London in the autumn of 1931.

Gandhi chose to stay in east London and made visits to the slums. He spoke to students at Oxford, and travelled to Lancashire, to explain to the mill-workers why India was boycotting their exports, in both cases winning sympathy for his cause. A rather curious figure in chilly England in his loincloth, wrap and sandals, critics dubbed him the 'Mickey Mouse of India'. Official alarm was expressed when he visited George V, 'with no proper clothes on, and bare knees', as the King put it. ('The King had enough on for both of us,' Gandhi commented.) Churchill was particularly indignant, referring to the Indian leader as:

> a seditious Middle Temple lawyer, now posing as a fakir of a type well known in the East.

The Round-table Conference achieved little, and Gandhi went home 'empty-handed'. The third Conference in 1932 again met without the leaders of Congress. The struggle within India continued, while the National government

Fig. 8.1(a) and (b)   Mohandas Gandhi photographed at the Friends' Meeting House, Euston Road, on his visit to London in September 1931, and his birth commemorated on a British stamp of 1969. Gandhi's dress hardly seemed suitable for England's climate but it attracted attention and helped him to publicize India's cause

considered what further changes should be made in India's administration.

The result was the Government of India Act of 1935. MacDonald's government had accepted that the goal should be India's 'attainment of Dominion status', but believed that this would be premature in 1935, so the Act made further compromises. Provincial self-government was granted but the principle of dyarchy was applied to the central government: the Viceroy kept control of defence and foreign policy, and reserved certain further powers, while Indian ministers were allowed to run other departments. The new system worked well in the eleven provinces, control of the majority of which was won by the Indian National Congress and its allies in elections in 1937. Congress was now led by Jawaharlal Nehru as its President, but he and Gandhi considered the arrangements for India's central government were inadequate. They demanded immediate Dominion status, and continued to obstruct the British authorities. They were angered still further when the Viceroy, Lord Linlithgow, committed India to war against Germany in 1939, without consulting Indian opinion. The Act of 1935 thus fell short of Indian hopes, but it went too far for Churchill. British government, he asserted, was 'incomparably the best Government that India has ever had or ever will see', and he declared:

> We shall try to inculcate this idea . . . that we are there for ever as honoured partners with our Indian fellow subjects.

Churchill had little feeling for twentieth-century nationalism among non-Europeans. Moreover, a new problem was developing in India. The Indian National Congress was largely Hindu, and its successes in the elections of 1937 disturbed the country's Moslems. The cry went up that 'Islam is in danger', and the Moslem League became alarmed lest, in a free India, the Moslems might be dominated by the Hindus (see Unit 12.3(a)).

(b) The Dominions and the British Commonwealth of Nations

In 1931 the Statute of Westminster had provided a satisfactory definition of Dominion status (see Unit 4.3(a)), but trading arrangements within the British Commonwealth remained less satisfactory. In 1924 Britain had mounted the Empire Exhibition at Wembley and, two years later, set up the Empire Marketing Board. A million pounds a year were spent promoting Commonwealth goods, and 'Empire Made' became a familiar trading label. The campaign was abandoned in 1932, however, partly to save money, but also because the Dominions refused to contribute to the Marketing Board's expenses. In that year, too, the Ottawa conference failed to find a comprehensive solution to the problem of the trade recession (see Unit 5.4(b)).

Other ties to consolidate what George V called a 'Commonwealth of Peace' were developed more successfully. The first Empire Games were held in 1930. By 1939 regular test matches were taking place between Britain, Australia, India, New Zealand, South Africa and the West Indies, a development of the cricket matches between England and Australia which had begun in the 1870s. There were innumerable links throughout the Commonwealth between professional groups such as journalists, doctors, teachers and parliamentarians. Broadcasting created a new bond, as did air travel. It was no accident that Britain's main airline company took the name Imperial Airways, and that the pride of its fleet was the Empire Flying Boat. By 1938 it was possible to fly from

Fig. 8.2   A British stamp of 1974 commemorating the importance of the Empire Flying Boat in postal history

Britain to South Africa in six days for £125, or to Sydney, Australia, in ten days for £160. When Commonwealth ties were tested in 1939, they were strong enough for all the Dominions, except the Irish Free State, voluntarily to rally to Britain's support in war.

Ireland remained the reluctant Dominion (see Unit 4.4). After becoming the Irish Prime Minister in 1932, de Valera dropped the oath of allegiance to the British crown, and suspended payments to Britain of debts arising from old land deals. The National government hit back by imposing tariffs on Irish exports. In 1937 the Free State adopted the name of Eire, amending its constitution to make it more like the Republic which Irish politicians wanted; and Irish ties with Britain and the Commonwealth grew weaker. Chamberlain, nevertheless, decided to practise appeasement, and a not ungenerous settlement of Anglo-Irish disputes was reached in 1938. The trade war was called off. Britain gave up the Irish ports which had been reserved for naval use in the Treaty of 1921, and Eire's debts were cancelled in exchange for a token payment. Chamberlain still failed to secure much Irish goodwill. Eire remained neutral during the Second World War and, in 1949, became the Republic of Ireland, resigning from the Commonwealth at the same time. Northern Ireland, on the other hand, remained tenaciously British.

The inter-war years saw only the first stirrings of nationalist protest in the rest of the British Empire with popular nationalist movements less advanced than in India. Independence was granted to Iraq, one of the mandated territories, in 1932, and the Anglo-Egyptian Treaty of 1936 conceded independence to Egypt. Neither Iraq nor Egypt applied to join the Commonwealth of Nations partly because neither had had long experience of British rule. But in more representative parts of the British Empire, in the West Indies, Africa and Asia, the inter-war years were little more than a prelude to the outbursts of nationalist agitation for freedom which were to follow the Second World War (see Units 12.1 and 12.3). In Britain, meanwhile, the 1935 Jubilee provided an occasion for patriotic display and rejoicing in an Empire that was still vast.

8.2 The Decline of the League of Nations

(a) The Manchurian Crisis

The Japanese seizure of the Chinese province of Manchuria, towards the end of 1931, revealed the uselessness of the various pieces of paper which Britain and other powers had signed during the 1920s (see Unit 4.2). China appealed to the League of Nations, which sent a commission of inquiry to the Far East in February 1932. It was led by Lord Lytton, and made a leisurely journey by sea. The Lytton Report was not made until October 1932, and the League Assembly did not formally approve it until February 1933. The Report stated the obvious: Japan was guilty of aggression. By the time the League had condemned Japan, however, and demanded withdrawal, the Japanese had renamed Manchuria Manchukuo and installed a puppet regime under Pu Yi. In March 1933 the Japanese went on to invade the province of Jehol, and gave notice of their intention to withdraw not from their conquests but from the League.

The attack on Manchuria had, of course, coincided with the Depression. The major powers could also plead some confusion, since the Japanese had certain legitimate interests in the Manchurian railway system and alleged that the Chinese had attacked their property. But Manchuria was some five times the size of Britain and no amount of Japanese propaganda could disguise the fact that the Japanese military were bent on conquest. Stimson, the US Secretary of State, recommended a doctrine of non-recognition, to deny Japan's right to its conquests, and to impose a moral boycott. With severe economic problems at home, the USA was not disposed to do more. The European powers were similarly anxious not to become involved. Simon, at the British Foreign Office, was more eager to show that he was consistent than that he was effective:

> From beginning to end, without the slightest change of attitude, we have said that conciliation is the first task. It is the provision of Article 15 of the Covenant that you should endeavour to conciliate. Let us do it by every manner of means.

Like the League as a whole, Simon discovered that conciliation was useless against a major power bent on expansion. Japan left the League, kept its conquests and penetrated even further into northern China by the mid 1930s. It also renounced the Washington and London Naval Agreements. Simon's only success was that he was able to prod the League into prodding Japan to abandon its further ambitions on Shanghai, at least for the time being. The era of great power aggression had begun, however. Resorting only to words, the League had been found wanting.

When Japan started a full-scale war against China in 1937, absurdly referring to it as the 'China Incident', the League again remained inactive. It was not difficult for Britain and other League members to find excuses. Economic problems, public opinion, the remoteness of China from Europe, the alleged lack of weapons, the inactivity of other powers – all were offered in explanation. British politicians expressed anxiety, mainly about the safety of the British Empire, but seemed to conclude that the best course of action, or inaction, was not to offend the Japanese. Meanwhile they could pretend that Manchuria was still part of China, and the National government could focus its inactivity on ignoring 'more urgent' problems nearer home.

(b) Enter the Nazis

Hitler became Chancellor of Germany in January 1933, and its *Führer* in August 1934. Almost his first international move was to withdraw from the Disarmament Conference in October 1933, hammering the last nail into its coffin (see Unit 4.2(*d*)). Germany also withdrew from the League, and Hitler and his Nazi followers made no secret of their intention to undermine the Treaty of Versailles. There were many in Britain and elsewhere who were now ready to agree that that Treaty had been unjust; nevertheless, Hitler moved cautiously. His first policy was rearmament, but conscription and a massive programme of armaments were not announced until 1935, the year in which, in the plebiscite provided for at Versailles, the Saarlanders voted for reunion with the German Reich.

The change of government in Germany, though alarming, was none of

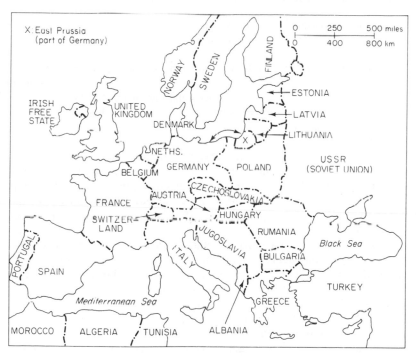

Fig. 8.3 Europe in 1931

Britain's business. But Hitler's international ambitions had been well publicized, and the problem for the National government was to decide how best to deter him. Mussolini wanted some sort of pact between Italy, Britain, France and Germany, but that came to nothing. MacDonald and Simon tried to capitalize on Mussolini's interest, however, and the result was the Stresa Conference of April 1935, at which Britain, Italy and France condemned the revival of German militarism and any repudiation of the Treaty of Versailles, except by agreement, and tried to deter Hitler with a verbal warning. At almost the same time, MacDonald and Simon were hoping to conciliate Hitler with an agreement about which they chose not to consult the French, since the latter would almost certainly have objected. The result of this conciliation was the Anglo-German Naval Agreement which Hoare, Simon's successor at the British Foreign Office, carried through in mid June 1935. Britain agreed that Germany should have a navy with a tonnage up to 35 per cent of the naval forces of the British Commonwealth of Nations, including a submarine fleet up to 45 per cent of the Commonwealth's submarines, or – if the Germans thought it 'necessary' and gave 'notice to this effect' – 100 per cent. Hitler was delighted. The French were furious.

Hoare optimistically asserted in a Note to Ribbentrop, the German Ambassador in London, that this very flexible treaty would:

> facilitate the conclusion of a general agreement on the subject of naval limitation between all the naval Powers of the world.

No such 'general agreement' followed, and if the National government thought Japan might now be brought to the conference table to revive the London Naval Agreement of 1930 and improve relations in the Pacific, it was disappointed. The Anglo-German Naval Treaty's major achievement was to sabotage the Stresa Front, although there were already grave doubts about the reliability of Mussolini's Italy; it had taken some effort at Stresa to ignore the brewing conflict between Italy and Abyssinia. In that sense the Naval Treaty was something of an insurance policy. If it was not possible to deter Hitler, it would perhaps be possible to teach him the rules of international good manners by persuading him to negotiate for what he wanted. Neither France nor the USSR had faith in such a policy. In 1935 they signed a treaty for mutual support in case of war.

It is unlikely that the leaders of the National government were much influenced by public opinion in Britain at this time. Essentially their policy was to pursue Britain's traditional aim of reducing international tension by conciliation. Eleven million Britons nevertheless expressed something of their opinions in the 'Peace Ballot', organized by the League of Nations Union in 1934–5. Almost all who voted expressed approval of the League of Nations and of a general reduction in armaments. A large majority voted in favour of non-military sanctions against aggressors, almost seven million also voted in favour of military sanctions, 'if necessary'. The politicians too would now have to declare their attitudes towards aggression – but it was Mussolini, not Hitler, who first put them to the test.

(c) Mussolini Changes Sides

Mussolini played a more important part in European affairs in the mid 1930s than either Simon or Hoare. His first response to Hitler's rise to power was displeasure: he himself was the senior fascist in Europe, and he despised German culture. When it seemed that Hitler was manoeuvring for the control of Austria in 1934, Italian troops were moved to the Brenner Pass to warn off the Germans. The crisis passed, and Mussolini looked briefly more like an international policeman than the lawbreaker he had been in earlier times. But a skirmish between Italians and Abyssinians around the oasis of Walwal, on the border of Italian Somaliland, occurred in December 1934. Mussolini now demanded both Walwal and compensation for Italian casualties. The old Mussolini was reasserting himself, the leader who was not against bullying the weak, as he had done at Corfu in 1923 (see Unit 4.2(a)). Throughout the summer of 1935 Italian troops streamed through the Suez Canal on their way to East Africa. The League of Nations recommended Haile Selassie, the Emperor of Abyssinia, to negotiate with Mussolini. Not much came of that and, in September 1935, Hoare reassured the Assembly of the League that Britain stood ready to play its part in maintaining collective security:

> In conformity with its precise and explicit obligations, the League stands, and my country stands with it, for the collective maintenance of the Covenant in its entirety, and particularly to all acts of unprovoked aggression.

Mussolini was not deterred. The Italians invaded Abyssinia early in October.

The League acted comparatively swiftly. Britain supported the economic sanctions which were imposed on Italy, Baldwin and Hoare perhaps influenced now by the results of the Peace Ballot. But there were other influences at work. The Suez Canal, in which Britain had a substantial financial stake, remained open to Italian transport, and the sanctions were not extended to oil, coal and steel, the commodities Italy most needed. Hoare also looked for ways of satisfying Mussolini. With Laval of France, he devised the Hoare–Laval Plan, offering the Italians about two-thirds of Abyssinia and Haile Selassie the compensation of access to the sea. Both Italians and Abyssinians rejected the Plan. Moreover, it caused such an outcry that both Hoare and Laval had to resign. Eden became the new British Foreign Secretary; but still nothing was done to extend sanctions to oil. What sanctions there were clearly proved useless, and they were solemnly abandoned when the Abyssinian capital fell to the Italians in May 1936. A month later, Baldwin told the Commons:

> I hope that the League of Nations will still be able to make collective security a reality, but there are real difficulties about it.

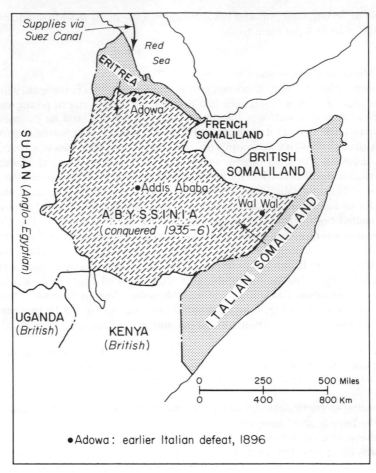

Supplies via
Suez Canal

Red
Sea

ERITREA

Adowa

FRENCH
SOMALILAND

BRITISH
SOMALILAND

SUDAN (Anglo-Egyptian)

Addis Ababa

A·B·Y·S·S·I·N·I·A
(conquered 1935-6)

Wal Wal

ITALIAN SOMALILAND

UGANDA
(British)

KENYA
(British)

| 0 | 250 | 500 Miles |
| 0 | 400 | 800 Km |

●Adowa: earlier Italian defeat, 1896

Fig. 8.4 The conquest of Abyssinia

He spoke in favour of rearmament, so that the League might have more teeth at some future time. But it was already too late. The League offered no realistic deterrent to aggression. Britain and other members had failed it, and Italy followed Japan and Germany in withdrawing from it.

Throughout the Abyssinian affair Baldwin, Hoare and Eden had been aware of the danger that Mussolini might be driven into the arms of Hitler. Nazi Germany, like Austria and Hungary, had refused to apply any sanctions at all against Italy and, during 1936, the Fascists and Nazis drew closer together. British attempts to conciliate Mussolini, or to deter him with half-hearted sanctions, had failed. Mussolini's fancy was taken by a line between Rome and Berlin which he called the *Axis*, around which he dreamed the rest of Europe would revolve. By the end of 1936 Italy and Germany were together helping Franco in the Spanish Civil War; Mussolini had finally settled for joining the lawbreakers.

Meanwhile, the Abyssinian War provided a cloak for a further move by Hitler. In March 1936 German troops marched into the demilitarized Rhineland, flagrantly breaking both the Versailles and Locarno Treaties. The French did not dare to intervene without support from Britain. The British gave no support, preferring to argue that the demilitarization had been unfair to Germany anyway. Eden told the Commons:

> Our objective throughout this difficult period has been to seek a peaceful and agreed solution. . . . Our objectives . . . are threefold – first, to avert the danger of war, second to create conditions in which negotiations can take place and third, to bring about the success of those negotiations so that they may strengthen collective security.

But there was nothing to negotiate about. Britain was not prepared to do more than protest; Hitler simply left his troops in the Rhineland. The Germans now built the Siegfried Line, along the border with France, facing the Maginot Line which the French had completed in 1934. Eden explained to the Commons:

> I assure the House that it is the appeasement of Europe as a whole that we have constantly before us.

Only the word had changed. 'Appeasement' was merely the continuation of 'conciliation', and it was this policy which Neville Chamberlain was to pursue so zealously when he became Prime Minister in 1937.

8.3 Appeasement

(a) Austria and Czechoslovakia

Chamberlain started out from the dogged conviction that appeasement could be successful. What was needed, in his view, was to settle the legitimate grievances of the aggrieved and thus arrive at tranquillity. He was aware, and was reminded by his military advisers during 1937, of the weaknesses in Britain's armed forces. Rearmament had not yet made much headway, for all Baldwin's mentions of it. Nazi Germany, on the other hand, expertly nourished the impression that Germany's armed might was far greater than was actually the case in the late 1930s. It was assumed, in the event of war, that German bombers would almost instantly wipe out Britain's cities. Chamberlain did not act from cowardice, however. He hardly doubted that Britain would eventually win any war in which it engaged, but he had a decent man's horror of war as well as the horror he thought proper in a former Chancellor of the Exchequer of spending money on weapons. Above all, he believed in his own powers of diplomacy to pacify Europe.

One of the first results of his ambitions was a clash with Eden. Chamberlain rebuffed President Roosevelt when the latter suggested an international conference with a US presence to discuss international problems. He courted Mussolini, and seemed so intent on running his own foreign policy that Eden resigned. The new Foreign Secretary, Lord Halifax, was more a Chamberlain's man, and the Prime Minister charted their course:

> I cannot believe that with a little goodwill it is not possible to remove genuine grievances and to clear away suspicion which may be entirely unfounded.

In March 1938, less than a month after Eden's resignation, Nazi Germany annexed Austria, in defiance of the Treaties of Versailles and St Germain. A plebiscite appeared to show that 99 per cent of the Austrian people were in favour of this *Anschluss*. It was easy to ignore Austria's Jews, Social Democrats, liberals and communists whom the Nazis murdered or took away to concentration camps. This time Mussolini gave his blessing to the Nazi seizure of Austria, while Chamberlain, having first protested, explained that nothing could have been done to prevent it except by the use of 'force'. The British government, he said, would review its defence programme in the light of the new developments.

Possession of Austria enabled Hitler to press on Czechoslovakia from three sides. The break-up of the Austro-Hungarian Empire after the First World War had left some three million German-speaking subjects within Czechoslovakia, in the Sudetenland. There was a well-orchestrated clamour among these Sudetenlanders during the summer of 1938, against alleged misrule and in favour either of independence or union with the German Reich. Much of the noise was made by Henlein, the local Nazi leader. Hitler made a series of violent speeches suggesting that conflict between Germany and Czechoslovakia was likely, and this frightened the French who had treaty obligations to assist the Czechs against aggression.

Britain had no such obligations, but Chamberlain assumed that he could resolve the problem. Lord Runciman was sent to Prague in August 1938, apparently to persuade President Beneš, the Czech leader, to make concessions. Beneš offered the Sudetenlanders what was virtually Home Rule. This made no difference to the Nazis, and Chamberlain decided to make a personal visit to Hitler. He had already largely discounted any resort to war, however, having written in his diary in March:

> You have only to look at the map to see that nothing that France or we could do could possibly save Czechoslovakia from being overrun by the Germans, if they wanted to do it. . . . Russia is 100 miles away. Therefore we could not help Czechoslovakia – she would simply be a pretext for going to war with Germany.

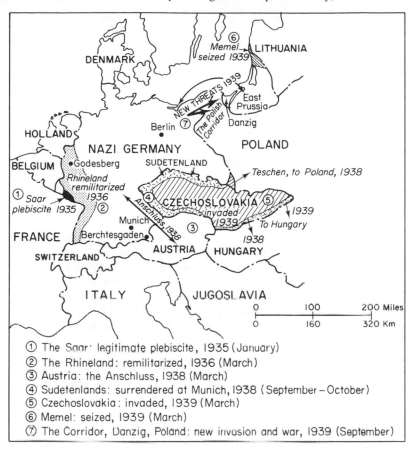

Fig. 8.5 The expansion of Nazi Germany, 1935–9

The French were very willing to let Chamberlain snatch a settlement from the crisis, to rescue them from their treaty obligations. The USSR had similar obligations, but only needed to honour its own treaty with Czechoslovakia once the French had honoured theirs. Chamberlain preferred to ignore the USSR. Even if Poland or Rumania would allow Russian troops access to Czechoslovakia, the western powers had no wish to see the Red Army in central Europe. Chamberlain met Hitler at Berchtesgaden on 15 September, and again at Godesberg a week later. Between the meetings, Chamberlain and Daladier, the French Prime Minister, produced a plan for the Czechs to transfer to the German Reich those Sudeten areas with populations more than 50 per cent German. Beneš was informed, and his reluctant agreement was extracted. To Chamberlain's dismay, Hitler added further areas to his shopping-list, when they met at Godesberg, setting 1 October as the deadline for a settlement.

Chamberlain gloomily contemplated the awful prospect of war after all. He spoke to the nation on the radio:

> How horrible, fantastic, incredible it is that we should be digging trenches and trying on gas masks here because of a quarrel in a far-away country between people of whom we know nothing. . . . War is a fearful thing, and we must be very clear, before we embark on it, that it is really the great issues that are at stake.

But rescue was at hand, and Czechoslovakia's fate was conveniently removed from 'the great issues'. Mussolini was persuaded to help arrange a third meeting, and Hitler agreed to receive Mussolini, Chamberlain and Daladier at Munich on 29 September. The USSR was not invited, and Czech representatives had to wait in a nearby hotel while their country's fate was decided. This involved little more than agreeing to Hitler's terms – almost everything he had demanded at Godesberg, except for some minor details that would be considered later by an international commission. The Czechs were told that they could now expect no further 'help' from the west, and the Sudetenland was added to the Reich. Chamberlain stayed a few hours longer in Munich to secure Hitler's signature to another piece of paper. It declared that the Anglo-German Naval Treaty and Munich Agreement were 'symbolic' of the desire of 'our two peoples' not to fight one another again; and it went on:

> We are resolved that the method of consultation shall be the method adopted to deal with any other question that may concern our two countries.

Chamberlain waved this paper triumphantly at the airport, on his return to Britain. The rejoicing was almost universal. 'I believe it is peace for our time,' the Prime Minister declared; and the crowds in Downing Street sang, 'O God, Our Help in Ages Past'. The House of Commons showed similar enthusiasm, though Gallacher muttered 'What about Russia?' and Churchill spoke his own critical summary of the events:

> £1 was demanded at the pistol's point. When it was given, £2 were demanded at the pistol's point. Finally the Dictator consented to take £1.17.6 and the rest in promises of goodwill for the future.

Churchill also forecast, rightly, that all Czechoslovakia would be 'engulfed in the Nazi regime'. The loss of the Sudetenland deprived the country of important industry and defendable frontiers. In March 1939 Hitler demanded special rights for any Germans still under Czech rule, and German troops marched into Prague. Nazi rule was imposed on Bohemia and Moravia, and a puppet state was set up in Slovakia. Chamberlain's protests were brushed aside and, a week later, the Germans also seized Memel from Lithuania. Doubts about the

No. 9,177   SATURDAY, OCTOBER 1, 1938   ONE PENNY

PREMIER SAYS 'PEACE FOR OUR TIME'-P. 3

Give Thanks In Church To-morrow

TO-MORROW is Peace Sunday.

Hardly more than a few hours ago it seemed as if it would have been the first Sunday of the most senseless and savage war in history.

The "Daily Sketch" suggests that the Nation should attend church to-morrow and give thanks.

THE fathers and mothers who might have lost their sons, the young people who would have paid the cost of war with their lives, the children who have been spared the horror of modern warfare —let them all attend Divine Service and kneel in humility and thankfulness.

To-morrow should not be allowed to pass without a sincere and reverent recognition of its significance.

MR. CHAMBERLAIN shows the paper that represents his great triumph for European peace to the thousands who gave him such a thunderous welcome at Heston yesterday. It is the historic Anglo-German Pact signed by himself and the Fuehrer, Herr Hitler.

'Determined To Ensure Peace'

WHEN Mr. Chamberlain arrived at Heston last night he said:

"This morning I had another talk with the German Chancellor, Herr Hitler. Here is a paper which bears his name as well as mine. I would like to read it to you:

"'We, the German Fuehrer and Chancellor and the British Prime Minister, have had a further meeting to-day and are agreed in recognising that the question of Anglo-German relations is of the first importance for the two countries and for Europe.

"'We regard the agreement signed last night and the Anglo-German Naval Agreement as symbolic of the desire of our two peoples never to war with one another again.

"'We are resolved that the method of consultation shall be the method adopted to deal with any other questions that may concern our two countries and we are determined to continue our efforts to remove possible sources of difference and thus to contribute to the assurance of peace in Europe.'"

Fig. 8.6   The front page of the Daily Sketch, *1 October 1938 – a 'Peace Souvenir Issue' which joined in the general adulation of Neville Chamberlain and his assumed services to international goodwill. On an inside page the* Sketch *reported the praise for the Prime Minister of the President of the League of Nations Council: 'His name today is blessed in all the homes of the world'.*

willingness of the British people to resist the Nazis were now beginning to disappear, though the press, with honourable exceptions such as the *News Chronicle* and the *Manchester Guardian*, still made little effort to inform readers about the full extent of Nazi barbarism within the lands they ruled. It can also be argued, though not very convincingly, that the Munich Agreement bought time for Britain to rearm. The RAF was expanded, especially with fighter aircraft. Peacetime conscription began in spring 1939, and plans were made to equip an Expeditionary Force. But the suspicion must remain that Chamberlain had been completely outmanoeuvred during 1938 in his attempts to appease Hitler.

(*b*) The Axis

Mussolini's attachment to Hitler strengthened in the years 1936–9. Both actively supported Franco in Spain, recognizing him as a kindred spirit, for his aim was to become a dictator with the title *El Caudillo*. Franco's Nationalist forces were in rebellion against Spain's Republican government, and the country became a battleground of ideologies. The Republicans were supported by volunteer International Brigades of communists, socialists and liberals, united – up to a point – in an anti-fascist front. They also received cautious support from Stalin, the leader of the USSR. Some two thousand British volunteers took part in the vain attempt to uphold the Republic, George Orwell among them, and he recorded his experiences in *Homage to Catalonia*. In Britain, many more were jolted out of their complacency by the savagery with which the struggle for Spain was fought. An organization called Friends of Nationalist Spain showed admiration for Franco, but it was heavily out-numbered by sympathizers with the Republic.

The British government preferred to support neither side, adopting a policy of neutrality and non-intervention. It secured support for this policy, on paper, from France, Germany, Italy and the USSR; their Non-Intervention Agreement of August 1936 ignored the League of Nations. Having signed it, Germany, Italy and the USSR ignored the Agreement although, while the conflict lasted, these 'non-interventionist' countries who were in fact intervening reassured the British several times of their good intentions. In 1937 a conference met at Nyon to consider:

> (attacks) in the Mediterranean by submarines against merchant ships not belonging to either of the conflicting Spanish parties.

Britain, France, the USSR and several Mediterranean governments agreed on policing action to provide some protection for shipping, but the conference took care not to identify the offending submarines, even though it was common knowledge they were Italian. In their further anxiety not to offend Mussolini, the British then agreed that Italy too should be allowed to patrol a sector of the dangerous waters. Chamberlain went yet further: he promised to recognize Mussolini's conquests in Abyssinia once Italian 'volunteers' withdrew from

Spain. The Italians and Germans did not, in fact, withdraw from Spain until Franco's victory in 1939. As soon as that victory was in sight, however, the British and French governments rushed to close the whole sorry episode by recognizing Franco as the official ruler of Spain in February 1939.

By that time, the British had conspicuously failed to detach Mussolini from Hitler. There were ominous signs, too, that the European Axis powers were drawing closer to Japan, whose continuing expansionism in the Pacific also caused alarm in Britain. Germany and Japan signed an Anti-Comintern Pact in November 1936, and Mussolini joined it a year later. The Pact was a ritualistic declaration of hostility to communism and the USSR, with a pledge to resist 'interference by the Communistic International in the internal affairs of nations' (see Glossary: Comintern). There were many in Britain and the west who found such anti-communism by no means undesirable; nevertheless, it was a setback to British policy when those Britain had tried to appease seemed bent on uniting in trouble-making. Mussolini embarked on the rather laborious conquest of Albania in April 1939, his appetite whetted by jealousy of Hitler's successes. A month later he made the Pact of Steel for 'continuous contact' with the Führer, and for 'full political and diplomatic support' in this, 'the XVIIth year of the Fascist Era'. The German-Italian-Japanese alliance was finally consolidated by the Tripartite Axis Pact in September 1940.

8.4 Guarantees, the Russian Problem and War

(a) Appeasement Abandoned
Within weeks of the German entry into Prague in March 1939, Chamberlain was spurred into action. Britain gave guarantees of support in the event of attack to Poland, Rumania, Greece and Turkey. Where Chamberlain had earlier been ultra-cautious, he was now extravagantly reckless. Hitler was already rehearsing new grievances and demands. In particular, he wanted Danzig and, at the very least, access to East Prussia across the Polish Corridor (see Fig. 4.1). Here too Hitler found Germans who – so he chose to declare – were badly treated. Germany had signed a Non-Aggression Pact with Poland in 1934, but no one now trusted this to restrain the Nazis. Lloyd George, however, reminded Chamberlain of the geography he appeared to have forgotten (see Unit 6.2(b)). Poland could only be defended successfully against German aggression by the USSR. Chamberlain had thought that geography made it impracticable to defend Czechoslovakia in 1938; in 1939 he seemed to be assuming that the British and French could somehow act in Poland.

(b) The Russian Problem
The USSR had joined the League of Nations in 1934, and soon afterwards signed various mutual-security treaties, including one with France in 1935. Such actions seemed to show that the Russians were alarmed by the rise of the Nazis. But the National government in Britain had not sought closer ties with Moscow, and Chamberlain left the Russians out of the Munich Agreement.

Stalin seemed as much of a tyrant as Hitler although, apart from the rather muted activities of the Comintern, the USSR showed no aggressive inclinations. Nevertheless, a fierce reign of terror wracked the USSR, and purges of the Red Army raised doubts in 1939 about its fighting qualities. On the other hand, there was bitter hatred between fascists and communists, and there was no reason to doubt that the USSR feared and detested Nazi Germany. It seemed logical for the new militant Chamberlain to enlist Russian support in his efforts to deter Hitler by the threat of force.

A PIECE MISSING, TOVARISH

Fig. 8.7   The comment by the cartoonist David Low on collective security and peace-keeping, April 1939. If Chamberlain and Beck, Poland's Foreign Minister, now hoped to deter Nazi Germany from further aggression, collective action with the Soviet Union seemed essential, however unfavourably the Western Powers might regard it

Stalin later claimed that he believed the real intention of western statesmen had been to foster a war between Germany and the USSR, in which communism might be destroyed. It is unlikely that any such plan was seriously considered by western governments and certainly, in 1939, it was Britain and France who took the lead in guaranteeing support for the possible future victims of the Nazis. Hitler had long asserted his own intention of crusading against communism, but Chamberlain was still too distrustful of the USSR fully to seek Stalin's co-operation against Germany. Moreover, the Poles remembered the past Russian domination of their country, and they hoped to remain independent both of Germany and the USSR. The result was that discussions between the west and the Russians proceeded only slowly and uncertainly: virtually nothing had been achieved by the end of July 1939, for which each side blamed the other. Meanwhile, the Jewish and fiercely anti-Nazi Litvinov was replaced as Soviet Foreign Minister by Molotov. Like Stalin, Molotov simply wanted to extract the best possible deal for the USSR from the European crisis; he therefore began talking with the Germans.

Germany could offer Russia what the west could not: a share of Poland, freedom of action for the Russians in Baltic states such as Latvia and, at least

SOMEONE IS TAKING SOMEONE FOR A WALK

Fig. 8.8 A further comment by Low, this time on the Nazi–Soviet Pact of August 1939 and the strange deal between Stalin and Hitler

for the time being, non-involvement in war. The Nazi–Soviet Pact was signed on 23 August 1939, pledging mutual non-aggression, and with a Secret Additional Protocol allowing the USSR to take back most of what had been lost in the Treaties of Brest-Litovsk and Riga. With fortitude Chamberlain instantly confirmed Britain's guarantee to Poland but, with the USSR now in his net, Hitler was confident that Britain and France could not save the Poles. Privately the Führer reassured his followers that he had not abandoned the long-term aim of destroying communism: Stalin too had been duped. The Soviet leader perhaps imagined the capitalist powers were now about to destroy one another, while the USSR quietly extended its frontiers.

(c) 'A Sad Day for All of Us'

The German invasion of Poland began on 1 September. Last-minute

Page 10   THE DAILY MIRROR   Monday, September 4, 1939

WANTED!

FOR MURDER . . . FOR KIDNAPPING . . . FOR THEFT AND FOR ARSON

ADOLF HITLER
ALIAS
Adolf Schicklegruber,
Adolf Hittler or Hidler

Last heard of in Berlin, September 3, 1939.   Aged fifty, height 5ft. 8½in., dark hair, frequently brushes one lock over left forehead.   Blue eyes.   Sallow complexion, stout build, weighs about 11st. 3lb.   Suffering from acute monomania, with periodic fits of melancholia.   Frequently bursts into tears when crossed.   Harsh, guttural voice, and has a habit of raising right hand to shoulder level. DANGEROUS !

Profile from a recent photograph. Black moustache. Jowl inclines to fatness. Wide nostrils. Deep-set, menacing eyes.

FOR MURDER Wanted for the murder of over a thousand of his fellow countrymen on the night of the Blood Bath, June 30, 1934. Wanted for the murder of countless political opponents in concentration camps.
He is indicted for the murder of Jews, Germans, Austrians, Czechs, Spaniards and Poles. He is now urgently wanted for homicide against citizens of the British Empire.
Hitler is a gunman who shoots to kill. He acts first and talks afterwards. No appeals to sentiment can move him. This gangster, surrounded by armed hoodlums, is a natural killer. The reward for his apprehension, dead or alive, is the peace of mankind.

FOR KIDNAPPING Wanted for the kidnapping of Dr. Kurt Schuschnigg, late Chancellor of Austria. Wanted for the kidnapping of Pastor Niemoller, a heroic martyr who was not afraid to put God before Hitler. Wanted for the attempted kidnapping of Dr. Benes, late President of Czechoslovakia. The kidnapping tendencies of this established criminal are marked and violent. The symptoms before an attempt are threats, blackmail and ultimatums. He offers his victims the alternatives of complete surrender or timeless incarceration in the horrors of concentration camps.

FOR THEFT Wanted for the larceny of eighty millions of Czech gold in March, 1939. Wanted for the armed robbery of material resources of the Czech State. Wanted for the stealing of Memelland. Wanted for robbing mankind of peace, of humanity, and for the attempted assault on civilisation itself. This dangerous lunatic masks his raids by spurious appeals to honour, to patriotism and to duty. At the moment when his protestations of peace and friendship are at their most vehement, he is most likely to commit his smash and grab.
His tactics are known and easily recognised. But Europe has already been wrecked and plundered by the depredations of this armed thug who smashes in without scruple.

FOR ARSON Wanted as the incendiary who started the Reichstag fire on the night of February 27, 1933. This crime was the key point, and the starting signal for a series of outrages and brutalities that are unsurpassed in the records of criminal degenerates. As a direct and immediate result of this calculated act of arson, an innocent dupe, Van der Lubbe, was murdered in cold blood. But as an indirect outcome of this carefully-planned offence, Europe itself is ablaze. The fires that this man has kindled cannot be extinguished until he himself is apprehended—dead or alive !

THIS RECKLESS CRIMINAL IS WANTED—DEAD OR ALIVE!

Fig. 8.9 The Daily Mirror's *view of Hitler, the morning following the declaration of war, 4 September 1939*

diplomatic exchanges proved fruitless, though Mussolini told Hitler that Italy was not yet ready for a major war. For a moment it seemed that not only Mussolini was wobbling: with the Germans already on Polish soil, Chamberlain sent them a 'last warning'. By 2 September Mussolini was proposing an international conference (another Munich, perhaps), but Chamberlain declared in the Commons that, unless the Germans withdrew, Britain would 'be bound to take action'. The Prime Minister's critics complained that taking 'action' was taking a long time, but a deadline was finally appointed for the Germans to promise withdrawal from Poland – 11 am on 3 September. Hitler made no reply. Shortly after 11 o'clock Chamberlain broadcast to the British people, to inform them that a state of war now existed between Britain and Germany:

> You can imagine what a bitter blow it is to me that all my long struggle to win peace has failed. . . . Everything that I have worked for, everything that I have hoped for, everything that I have believed in during my public life, has crashed into ruins.

An hour later, he gave a similar message to the House of Commons, informing MPs of France's co-operation with Britain, and adding:

> This is a sad day for all of us, and to none is it sadder than to me.

Italy kept out of the war for the time being. Germany quickly overran western Poland, and the USSR moved into the eastern part of the country. But the war began slowly for Britain and France – so slowly, in fact, that the British had energy to spare for an outburst of rage when the USSR attacked Finland in November 1939. There was talk of sending help to the Finns, and the League of Nations suddenly roused itself to expel the USSR, for aggression.

It took the Russians until March 1940 to force Finland to submit but, by that time, the war in western Europe was about to burst into life. Britain then had little time to brood on ideological differences with the USSR. Instead, it brooded on the shortcomings of Neville Chamberlain. His days as Prime Minister were numbered. Whatever his shortcomings as a statesman, however, the war was the product of the Nazi system and of Nazi aggression. That British and French statesmen had found no way of curbing Hitler's ambitions was due much less to their inadequacy than to Hitler's ruthlessness and deceitfulness. It was sensible and honourable to try to avoid war, for which millions would have to pay in suffering and with their lives. The real tragedy of the 'sad day' was that there were politicians in Europe and Japan for whom war was an instrument of policy. But what soon became clear was that Chamberlain was an unconvincing leader of a nation involved in war.

Further Reading

Seaman, L.C.B.: *Post-Victorian Britain, 1902–1951*. Methuen (London, 1966), chapters 26–33.
Bloncourt, P.: *The Embattled Peace, 1919–1939*. Faber (London, 1968).
Medlicott, W.N.: *British Foreign Policy since Versailles*. Methuen (London, 1968).
Rock, W.R.: *British Appeasement in the 1930s*. Arnold (London, 1977).
Stone, R.: *The Drift to War*. Heinemann (London, 1975).
Taylor, A.J.P.: *The Origins of the Second World War*. Penguin (Harmondsworth, 1964).
Watson, J.B.: *Success in European History 1815–1941*. John Murray (London, 1981).

Watson, J.B.: *Success in Twentieth Century World Affairs*. John Murray (London, 3rd edn. 1984).

Documentary

Bettey, J.H.: *English Historical Documents, 1906–1939*. Routledge (London, 1967).
Evans, L. and Pledger, P.J.: *Contemporary Sources and Opinions in Modern British History*, Volume Two. Warne (London, 1967).
Parkinson, R.: *Origins of World War Two*. Wayland (Hove, 1970).

Exercises

1. 'An Empire that was still vast' (page 135): referring both to this Unit and to Unit 4, describe the extent of the British Empire in 1935. In what ways was the Empire in 1935 different from that shown in Fig. 4.4?
2. How do Units 4.4 and 8.1(*b*) help to explain why 'Ireland remained the reluctant Dominion' (page 134) and why it later resigned from the Commonwealth?
3. Table 6.1 lists Britain's Foreign Secretaries in the 1930s. Divide a large sheet of paper into three columns. Write in the first column the names of the Foreign Secretaries; in the second column, alongside each name, the main international problems with which he had to deal; and in the third column, Britain's policy in response to each problem. Using this information, write a survey of the work of Britain's Foreign Secretaries in the years 1931–9, considering at the end whether any Foreign Secretary pursued a policy markedly different from that of the others.
4. Hoare stated in September 1935 'that Britain stood ready to play its part in maintaining collective security' (page 139). What do you understand by *collective security*? (Compare your answer with the Glossary definition.) Show what *part* Britain did play at this time, and explain why it had little success.
5. As a result of the Anglo-German Naval Agreement, 'Hitler was delighted' and 'the French were furious' (page 138). Explain why this was so. How far could the same comments have been made about the Munich Agreement (Unit 8.3(*a*))?
6. Making use of the Index to this book as well as this Unit, show what you understand by *appeasement*. Write *two* letters to a newspaper, dated soon after the Munich Conference, *the first* arguing in support of the appeasement practised at Munich, *the second* arguing in support of Churchill's criticism quoted on page 144.
7. Explain what Fig. 8.5 shows of Hitler's foreign policy and how Britain responded to that policy at *each* of the seven stages listed at the foot of the map.
8. What does this Unit show of British policy towards the USSR in the 1930s? What was the importance for Britain of the Nazi-Soviet Pact of August 1939? Explain what Figs 8.7 and 8.8 suggest about the USSR's involvement in international relations in 1939.

The Second World War

9.1 'Phoney War' and Cabinets

With the outbreak of war, Chamberlain set up his War Cabinet during September 1939. It was smaller than his peacetime Cabinet, but it had the same senior members: Simon, Halifax and Hoare. Winston Churchill was a newcomer, recalled as First Lord of the Admiralty, the office he had held from 1911 to 1915. He had been out of office since 1929, and was often out of step with the Conservative leadership during the 1930s – on issues such as India, Edward VIII's abdication and appeasement. His pugnacity made him a natural

Fig. 9.1 The National government geared for war: Chamberlain's War Cabinet, September 1939. Chamberlain in the centre of the front row, Simon and Halifax (end of row) to his right, Hoare and Lord Chatfield to his left; back row, left to right – Kingsley Wood, Churchill, Hore-Belisha and Lord Hankey. The Cabinet approached the war with a quiet dignity

TWO-GUN WINSTON
—by *Illingworth*.

choice for wartime office but, not surprisingly, he fretted at his colleagues'
apparent lack of urgency in conducting the opening stages of the war. A British
Expeditionary Force had been quickly sent to France where, along with the
French, it simply waited for a German attack. The Germans were busy in
Poland, however, and so little happened on the Western Front that the description the 'Phoney War' became current. Having steeled themselves to endure
massive air raids and a furious Nazi assault against the west, the British were
puzzled. On 4 April 1940 Chamberlain complacently told a Conservative
audience that Hitler had 'missed the bus'.

Hitler had half expected that, once Poland had been occupied, the British
and French would negotiate a settlement. But the Allies shrank from yet
further compromise so, within days of Chamberlain's optimistic comment, the
Germans swept into Denmark and Norway. There was nothing the British
could do to dislodge them, and Allied raids at Trondheim and elsewhere
achieved little. Many Conservatives were now questioning Chamberlain's fit-
ness to remain as Prime Minister, and matters came to a head early in May.

Fig. 9.2 Britain under new management: Churchill became both Prime Minister and Minister of Defence in May 1940. (a) (opposite) A cartoonist's view (b) A photograph of Churchill in 1940 on a British commemorative stamp of 1974

Leopold Amery quoted the words Cromwell had once used to the Rump Parliament:

> You have sat here too long for any good you have been doing. Depart, I say, and let us have done with you. In the name of God, go.

Lloyd George added his weight to the opposition, reminding the Prime Minister that he had 'always been worsted' in his dealings with Hitler:

> I say solemnly that the Prime Minister should give an example of sacrifice, because there is nothing which can contribute more to victory in this war than that he should sacrifice the seals of office.

In the face of this opposition from Labour, the Liberals and some members of his own party, Chamberlain duly resigned. He died only six months later.

Churchill became the new Prime Minister of a Coalition government on 10 May. Eden returned as Foreign Secretary, and the various jobs of organizing supplies were given to Lord Beaverbrook. The tiny War Cabinet also included Attlee and, within a few months, Bevin as Minister of Labour. Other Labour leaders were given appointments as the war went on, Cripps and Morrison among them. The first priority was to inject new energy into the war effort: the urgency of this was underlined when the Germans attacked the Netherlands, Belgium and Luxemburg on the very day that Churchill took office. The new Prime Minister made no false promises to the British people. He said, 'I have nothing to offer but blood, toil, tears and sweat'. The 'Phoney War' was over and the years of severe trial were beginning.

9.2 The Nazi Domination of Europe

The Netherlands surrendered within five days of the Nazi onslaught and, with fast-moving *Panzer* troops, the Germans raced across Belgium. The French Maginot Line, which did not defend the Franco-Belgian border, proved irrelevant; and happy-go-lucky British singing about 'hanging out the washing on the Siegfried Line' was, at best, hopelessly optimistic. German troops drove across northern France, reaching the Channel coast south of Calais. Disaster seemed imminent, for the British and Allied forces were now cut off. Belgium capitulated on 28 May, and all the British could do was to try to evacuate as many men as possible before the German trap shut fast. Only the beaches of Dunkirk in northern France were available. The 'Miracle' began on 29 May: 200 000 British and 140 000 Allied troops were taken from the Dunkirk beaches by 4 June, partly because Hitler blundered and slowed the Nazi advance, and partly through a supreme effort of improvisation. Hundreds of small craft ferried men to larger vessels lying in deep water, while a rearguard kept the enemy at bay and the RAF did its best to protect the Allied troops from the air. Calm seas helped the operation, and German bombs were rendered less effective because of the sand which softened their blast. Even so, almost all the army's equipment had to be left behind. It was miracle enough that so many men were rescued, and the Dunkirk Evacuation became Britain's first major achievement in the war. The retreating forces could only leave Europe at the mercy of the Nazis, however. Mussolini now plucked up courage to declare war on the already

Fig. 9.3 The beaches at Dunkirk, June 1940: some 340 000 men were evacuated by over 800 vessels, many of them tiny craft built for Britain's inland waterways rather than the sea

beaten France on 10 June. Four days later the Germans entered Paris, and France surrendered on 22 June.

There was no question in Churchill's mind of a similar surrender, and the Dominions gave full support to his determination to fight on. He declared:

> The Battle of France is over. I expect that the Battle of Britain is about to begin. Upon this battle depends the survival of Christian civilization. Upon it depends our own British life, and the long continuity of our institutions and our Empire.

There was not long to wait. In July 1940 the *Luftwaffe* (German air force) began bombarding Britain's airfields and shipping, in preparation for the launching of Operation Sealion. The pre-war development of the RAF proved to have been just adequate. Under the command of Air Chief Marshal Dowding, with Beaverbrook in charge of aircraft production, with the valuable help

Fig. 9.4 North-western Europe, 1940–4

Fig. 9.5 (a) A British stamp of 1965 commemorating the Battle of Britain and (b) Hurricanes, planes which played a vital part in that Battle. St Paul's Cathedral and the skies over London where part of the Battle of Britain was fought. These Hurricanes were photographed in 1941 on active service in the Far East

of radar and, above all, with the heroism of the 'few' fighter pilots who flew the *Hurricanes* and *Spitfires*, the RAF defied the might of Goering's *Luftwaffe*. Heavy losses were inflicted on the German aircraft during August and the first half of September. Again, Hitler blundered. Stung by the impertinent RAF bomber raids on Berlin, he diverted his own bombers to raid London. The RAF was thus saved from the very real danger of running out of fighter aircraft through German raids on Britain's airfields. The Germans could not invade the British Isles without control of the skies or the seas and, in mid-September, Operation Sealion was postponed indefinitely. The invasion troops, which had stood ready, were dispersed. Churchill had already immortalized Britain's fighter pilots for 'their prowess' and 'their devotion':

Never in the field of human conflict was so much owed by so many to so few.

The RAF included men from the Dominions and from European Allies too. Over 400 lost their lives, more than a third of their numbers. But they had won the Battle of Britain.

On the continent, however, the Germans were supreme. The whole of the Balkans were under Nazi control by early 1941. Some states, such as Bulgaria, collaborated with the Germans. Others were conquered, and although 60 000 British troops were sent to help Greece, they were again forced to leave the European mainland and, eventually in May 1941, Crete as well. These successes inspired Hitler to launch the crusade against Communist Russia which the Nazis had long been promised. Operation Barbarossa began in June 1941, and Britain now had a European ally with the same determination as Churchill's, never to admit defeat. The Germans advanced deep into Russia, but they advanced over 'scorched earth'. This was a war of annihilation, in which no quarter was given. The Russians devastated their own land rather than yield anything to the invaders, and the casualties were enormous. But when the Germans reached the gates of Leningrad, Moscow and Stalingrad, they could make no further headway against the Red Army, and the tide turned during 1943. Operation Barbarossa had proved to be an enormous blunder, and Germany's Russian Front a bottomless pit which relentlessly swallowed the Nazi resources.

Britain, meanwhile, had benefited not only from the human and material resources of the Empire and Commonwealth, but also from the goodwill of the USA. At the start of the war President Roosevelt supplied Britain and France on the 'Cash and Carry' system. In 1940 Britain received fifty old US destroyers, in exchange for bases in Newfoundland and on West Indian islands. By the end of that year Roosevelt was planning 'Lend-Lease', by which war supplies would be leased to Britain, to be returned or replaced at a later date. The American President made no secret of his own anti-Nazism, and asserted that the USA would be 'the great arsenal of democracy'. He met Churchill in August 1941 to draw up the Atlantic Charter, in which they looked forward to the postwar world, when Nazi tyranny had been destroyed, when all peoples would be free to choose their own governments, and when international co-operation would safeguard peace and promote prosperity. Soon afterwards Lend-Lease was extended to the USSR. It seemed only a matter of time before the USA would enter the war. The Grand Alliance was beginning to take shape.

9.3 Japanese Expansion and the War in Asia

Japan had been at war with China since 1937 (see Unit 8.2(*a*)). As Hitler was to discover in Russia, the conquest of a vast country which refused to surrender meant a lengthy and costly struggle. By 1941 Japan had occupied the Chinese coast and penetrated several hundred miles inland, but the Chinese fought on under the leadership of Chiang Kai-shek. Increasingly dominated by the military during the 1930s, Japan's ambition was to solve its economic problems by expansion – to set up a 'Co-Prosperity Sphere' in Asia, where the Japanese would have access to abundant raw materials and captive markets. The Co-Prosperity Sphere was the phrase the Japanese used for what Hitler, in Europe, called *Lebensraum*. Both were based on the arrogant assumption that a 'superior' race was entitled to take what it coveted by force. Churchill too could practise appeasement, however: in July 1940 the British forbade the sending of supplies to the Chinese through Burma, perhaps even at this stage in the hope of persuading Japan to respect Britain's colonial properties in Asia.

The Nazi successes in Europe not only distracted attention from the Far East; they whetted Japan's appetite and brought it the windfall of French Indochina. After the fall of France in 1940 a collaborationist regime was set up under Pétain. He authorized Japan's penetration into Indochina during 1941, so Japan came closer to Britain's possessions in India and Malaya. By this time, however, the USA had begun to show keen concern about Japanese activities. Steps were taken to restrict supplies to the Japanese and, in the summer of 1941, Britain co-operated with Roosevelt in denying oil to Japan and in freezing Japanese assets in the west. The Co-Prosperity Sphere took on a new urgency. In particular, the Japanese wanted the Dutch East Indies, where oil could be obtained. General Tojo decided to gamble. Since the USA seemed unlikely to stand aside while Japan launched new invasions, the Japanese struck at the US base at Pearl Harbor in Hawaii hoping, at least temporarily, to cripple the American war machine in the Pacific. The attack took place on 7 December 1941. At the same time, the Japanese attacked targets in the US Philippines, and in British Hong Kong, Malaya and Singapore. On the following day the USA and Britain declared war on Japan. Germany and Italy honoured their commitments in the Tripartite Axis Pact, declaring war on the USA. The Second World War had now been fully launched. Churchill wrote later that this was the decisive moment in the struggle:

> I knew that the United States was in the war, up to the neck and in to the death. So we had won after all! . . . England would live; Britain would live; the Commonwealth of Nations and the Empire would live.

But a long struggle still lay ahead. And, on Christmas Day 1941, the Japanese drove the British from Hong Kong.

9.4 The Grand Alliance

(a) War on Land, at Sea and in the Air

Churchill hastened to Washington to see Roosevelt again in December 1941. They agreed that priority must be given to victory in Europe, but Churchill

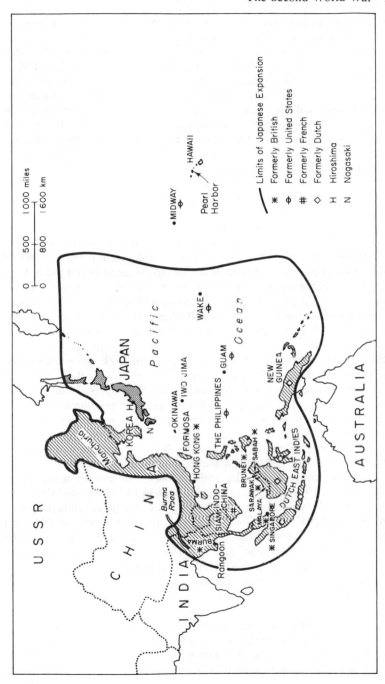

Fig. 9.6 Japan's 'Co-Prosperity Sphere'

argued that it was too soon to try to invade the European continent. Instead, the Americans agreed to Operation Torch, whereby forces were landed in Algeria to attack the German and Italian forces in north Africa from the west. The fighting in north Africa had developed from an Italian attack on Egypt. Mussolini's Empire collapsed elsewhere in Africa, but the Italians had German help when British and Commonwealth forces chased them from Egypt and threatened their colony in Libya. General Montgomery nevertheless held Rommel's Afrika Korps at El Alamein, and then drove the Axis troops back across Libya and into Tunisia. Operation Torch completed the Axis defeat, and the battle for north Africa was over by May 1943. Meanwhile, the Japanese too had been halted. Britain had lost Malaya, Singapore and much of Burma by the summer of 1942, but the Japanese could not reach India. During 1943, a start was made on pushing them back. General Slim and British troops adapted to jungle warfare as Montgomery had adapted to desert warfare, and the slow liberation of Burma was begun. At the same time, the Americans began forcing the Japanese from the islands they had occupied in South-East Asia.

Communications were vital in this global war and, just as in the First World War, the Germans suffered from their inability to gain control of the seas. From September 1939 the war at sea was a desperate one, the main battle being for command of the Atlantic. The Germans relied on U-boats and surface raiders, but their pocket-battleships were steadily hunted down and destroyed. The *Graf Spee* was an early casualty, trapped and scuttled by her own crew at Montevideo in December 1939. On the other hand, Britain had already lost HMS *Royal Oak*. Germany's largest warship, the *Bismarck*, was not destroyed until May 1941, after a chase of nearly 2 000 miles, and the *Tirpitz* and *Scharnhorst* survived until 1943. Meanwhile, the British navy suffered heavy casualties too, not all of them at German hands: Japanese aircraft sank the *Prince of Wales* and *Repulse* in December 1941, demonstrating both the vulnerability of warships to attack from the air, and the problems of defending the widely scattered Empire which pre-war British statesmen had feared.

What was really at stake now, however, was the safe passage of merchant ships loaded with essential supplies, and German U-boats took a heavy toll. At the beginning of 1941 Britain was losing more than 150 000 tons of shipping a month. The total rose to almost 200 000 in April 1941, and continued at a high level. In March 1943 Britain lost some half a million tons and, in 1943 as a whole, more than three times that amount. Its Allies lost even more. But in the last three months of 1943 more than fifty U-boats were destroyed and, after that, the Germans were much less effective. Much of the success in countering the U-boat menace came from the co-ordination of Allied naval and air services, making use of sophisticated methods of detection and more powerful depth-charges. Even so, and in spite of the almost universal use of the convoy system, 30 000 British merchant seamen lost their lives in keeping supplies moving. Meanwhile, the Americans began to win control of the Pacific.

Aircraft were important in determining the outcome of the Second World War, though bombers were never the decisive weapon of mass destruction that had been expected. British cities endured a massive bombardment for six months after September 1940, with high-explosive and incendiary bombs causing extensive damage and heavy casualties. London was the Germans' regular target, but their bombers struck much further afield – at Glasgow, Liverpool, Bristol and other ports, and at industrial centres such as Coventry and Manchester. They did not destroy the morale of the civilian population, however. People took refuge in air raid shelters and, in London, in the underground transport system. More than 500 people were killed in the prolonged raid which destroyed the centre of Coventry. Many were made homeless. But the disruption of industry and of communications was much less than had been feared and, not until late in the war, with the Allied raids on Germany, did bombers seriously curtail industrial production.

By that time, the Allied air forces had been augmented and thousand-bomber raids were commonplace: many German cities were pulverized. In February 1945 the city of Dresden was devastated in a spectacular fire-storm which killed tens of thousands. This was terror-bombing at its most savage. Dresden was of little military importance, but similar raids on Berlin, Hamburg and the industrial towns of the Ruhr worsened the chaos which was now developing within Germany. Hitler searched desperately for a new weapon with which to create similar havoc in Britain, since the *Luftwaffe*, like the U-boats, had lost its own battle, leaving the skies largely under the control of the Allies. V1s, noisy but pilotless aircraft, loaded with explosives and quickly nicknamed 'doodlebugs' by the British public, had begun to rain on Britain in June 1944. When their engines stopped, they dived to the ground. They killed thousands of civilians but they were hardly a decisive new weapon: they were too erratic, and counter-measures were quickly devised to deal with them. More menacing were the V2s which heralded the new age of rocket warfare. These came too late to save Germany since, at this stage, they had not yet been perfected and could not yet be directed with confidence to specific targets. Before that could happen, Allied forces, advancing into Europe, overran their launching sites.

(b) Victory in Europe

Although Roosevelt suspected that Churchill was an imperialist who took too much pride in the British Empire, the two men continued to co-operate closely in organizing the Allied war effort. In 1943 they met at Casablanca and again at Quebec, where Mackenzie King, the Canadian leader, was also present. In the previous year Churchill had visited Moscow, to talk with Stalin. Commonwealth leaders and de Gaulle, who led the Free French, sometimes thought that Churchill was dictatorial and not willing enough to consult them, but the war demanded united leadership and the Big Three – Roosevelt, Churchill and Stalin – aimed to achieve that. Stalin had reservations about his capitalist Allies, however, and Churchill especially was suspicious of Stalin. The Big Three did not actually meet until November 1943. Stalin's main concern at their Teheran meeting was that his Allies should invade Europe in the west, and open a Second Front to take some of the strain of the Nazi military effort from the USSR. Churchill, however, insisted on proceeding cautiously.

The first invasion of Europe, therefore, occurred in Sicily in July 1943, following up the Allied success in north Africa. It produced the almost instant downfall of Mussolini, who was deposed. When the Allies crossed to the Italian mainland in September, Italy capitulated. That was not enough to save Italy from becoming a battlefield. The British Eighth Army and its Allies advanced only slowly against stubborn German resistance. They entered Rome in June 1944, but there was still a long way to go before Germany could be reached. Mussolini, meanwhile, had taken refuge behind the German lines.

The opening of the long-planned Second Front occurred two days after the taking of Rome. The first D-Day landings were made in Normandy on 6 June with 130 000 lavishly equipped men. A bridgehead was established and heroically defended and, within a month, the Allies had a million troops in France. Supreme command of the invasion had been entrusted to the American General Eisenhower, while the British among his forces were under Montgomery. Forces were also supplied by many other Allied powers. Almost nothing had been left to chance. Fuel was supplied by PLUTO (Pipe-line under the ocean), and prefabricated (Mulberry) harbours were towed across the Channel to help with the unloading of equipment. The Germans resisted fiercely but the whole of France had been liberated by October. When paratroops were landed prematurely at Arnhem in the Netherlands, however, in an effort to secure a crossing of the Rhine, the British suffered heavy losses.

Churchill busied himself with a further meeting with Roosevelt at Quebec, and with another visit to Moscow. The Germans were now struggling to hold back the Allies in the west and the Red Army in the east, as well as to hold northern Italy. The Allied ring tightened remorselessly and, though still capable of temporarily successful counter-attacks, such as that in the Ardennes in the winter of 1944–5, the German defeat had become almost certain. When the Allies at last crossed the Rhine in March 1945 the Russians were already in east Germany, and the Red Army reached Berlin on 20 April. On 30 April, while the battle for the city raged, Hitler committed suicide. Italian partisans killed Mussolini at almost the same time. The Nazi-Fascist New Order in Europe was at an end, and Germany surrendered unconditionally on 7 May. Victory in Europe had been won.

(c) **Victory in Asia**
Victory in Asia seemed more remote. The Americans came within bombing distance of Japan with the capture of Okinawa in April 1945. But island-hopping was proving costly: the liberation of each Pacific island added to the toll of lives. On the mainland the British had freed Burma, with the help of skilled jungle fighters such as Wingate's Chindits who operated behind the Japanese lines. They had reopened a supply route to the Chinese along the Burma Road, and they reached Rangoon by May 1945. The liberation of Malaya and China was likely to be slow and costly, however. The USSR,

meanwhile, was in no hurry to declare war on Japan, and to open the new front which would have helped the Allies; and, within weeks of the taking of Okinawa, President Roosevelt suddenly died.

The task of ending the war in Asia fell to America's new President, Harry S. Truman. Almost at once he faced an agonizing decision. The war could be continued, no doubt at great cost in lives – or he could use the new weapon which his scientists had made available during July. This atomic bomb, the world's first nuclear weapon, would unleash forces of unprecedented power, whose results could not all be calculated. But, if it persuaded Japan to submit, it would save the lives of innumerable Allied soldiers. Truman made his choice, and an atomic bomb was dropped on the Japanese town of Hiroshima on 6 August. The whole town was devastated. Nearly 100 000 of its population of a quarter of a million were killed instantly. Another 100 000 were injured, often hideously, many of them condemned to great suffering and lingering death as a result of the radiation the bomb had released. Stalin quickly realized the situation had changed, and the USSR now hastened to declare war on Japan. But the Japanese suffered a second atomic explosion at Nagasaki on 9 August before they surrendered. Victory in Asia had now been won too. US troops occupied Japan without further casualties; and the British took back all their colonies in the Far East which had been overrun by the Japanese.

Further Reading

Seaman, L.C.B.: *Post-Victorian Britain, 1902–1951*. Methuen (London, 1966), chapters 34–45.

Gilbert, M.: *Winston Churchill*. Oxford University Press (London, 1966).

Hobbs, A.: *The Battle of Britain*. Wayland (Hove, 1973).

Jardine, C. Bayne: *World War Two*. Longman (Harlow, 1968).

Liddell Hart, B.H.: *History of the Second World War*. Cassell (London, 1970).

Pelling, H.: *Winston Churchill*. Macmillan (London, 1974).

Watson, J.B.: *Success in Twentieth Century World Affairs*. John Murray (London, 3rd edn. 1984).

Documentary

Peacock, R.: *The Second World War*. Arnold Archive (London, 1970).

Exercises

1. Why did Neville Chamberlain resign in 1940? Making use of the Index to this book and of the biography in Alan Palmer's *Dictionary of Twentieth-Century History* (see Bibliography), write a review of Chamberlain's career such as might have been broadcast on the radio at the time of his death.
2. Write an account of the War in North-West Europe, 1940–4, making use of Fig. 9.4
3. Explain how Britain benefited in the Second World War from (a) the help of the Empire and Commonwealth, (b) alliance with the USSR and (c) alliance with the USA. What did Britain itself contribute to the outcome of the war?
4. (a) Why, and how, did Britain come to be involved in war with Japan?
   (b) What parts of the British Empire were overrun by the Japanese during the

Second World War (Fig. 9.6), and in what circumstances were they regained?

5. What were the strengths and achievements of Winston Churchill as a war leader? How well were his strengths portrayed by the cartoonist in Fig. 9.2(*a*)? Making use of the Index to this book, trace Churchill's career from 1914 to 1940 and explain why he held so few government appointments before he became Prime Minister.

6. Find out more about *each* of the following and estimate its importance in determining the outcome of the Second World War in Europe: the evacuation from Dunkirk; the Battle of Britain; the invasion of Italy; the war at sea.

Britain at War

10.1 Total War

(a) A Nation Organized

A bustle of official activity accompanied the outbreak of war in 1939. The government armed itself with the Emergency Powers (Defence) Act a few days before war was declared, and set up new ministries to take charge of such matters as Munitions, Food and Information. Conscription had already been introduced in April 1939, to provide six months' military training for men aged twenty. The National Service (Armed Forces) Act now made all males aged eighteen to forty-one liable for military duties, unless they were in some vital occupation such as coal mining. The machinery worked at less than top speed until Churchill became Prime Minister, but a million-and-a-half men had nevertheless been enlisted by spring 1940. A National Register was also drawn up, numbering all of Britain's forty-six million citizens and issuing them with identity cards. Most citizens had received gas masks by the beginning of 1939, and an early wartime precaution was the evacuation of children from cities which seemed likely to be devastated by bombs. Early in 1940, however, there were still complaints of 'creeping paralysis', and of the 'slightly leisurely air' with which Chamberlain's government conducted the nation's business. By May 1940 only those aged twenty-seven or less had been registered for military service, and unemployment had still not been eliminated.

It took time to harness the nation's manpower but, as the war went on, almost everyone became involved in some way, either in military or civilian duties. Those not yet conscripted, or excluded from military duties because of occupation, age or poor health, did part-time work in organizations such as the AFS (Auxiliary Fire Service, later the National Fire Service) or the ARP (Air Raid Precautions), and took part in fire-watching rotas (keeping a nightly watch in readiness for dealing with fires caused by enemy bombs). In the summer of 1940 a million or so joined the LDV (Local Defence Volunteers, later known as the Home Guard), mostly older men, ready with their enthusiasm, though poorly armed and equipped to fight off Nazi invaders. Those too young to fight could join the junior branches of the armed forces, to receive preliminary training as cadets. There were branches of the armed services for women, and other women joined the Land Army, to help produce more foodstuffs. Women filled the places in industry vacated by men called into the

Fig. 10.1 The Second World War, like the First, produced a need for women munitions workers. This young woman made parts for field guns

forces, just as in the First World War. In 1941 conscription was extended to young unmarried women to ensure that all did useful service. There were also innumerable opportunities for voluntary work, from knitting 'comforts' for the troops to assisting in hospitals and organizing collections of anything which might be useful to the war effort. Lady Reading had founded the WVS (Women's Voluntary Service) in 1938, an organization which worked energetically through the war and beyond. Even entertainers were organized, with ENSA (Entertainments National Service Association) promoting morale-boosting concert-parties, theatre and film shows. Though it was typical of wartime humour to assert that ENSA stood for 'Every Night Something Awful', the Association gave over two-and-a-half million performances. The BBC also worked for victory, relaying ministerial broadcasts, official announcements, regular news bulletins (suitably spiced where appropriate with propaganda) and daily cheer such as *Music While You Work*, which it was hoped would boost output in factories, particularly among young women. The BBC also provided important services, broadcasting to Nazi-occupied Europe and other war zones, helping to keep alive hope and a spirit of resistance. The British people meanwhile readily accepted that, in the struggle to preserve freedom, it was necessary to surrender much of it 'for the duration' – the duration, that is, of the war.

Bevin was a dictatorial but admirably energetic Minister of Labour. Priorities were laid down for the use of manpower in 1940–1, and the depressed industries of the 1930s, such as shipbuilding and mining, were now highly rated. Even conscientious objectors were mobilized, many of them directed into the mines as 'Bevin Boys'. Workers could neither change jobs nor be dismissed without official approval, and Bevin ensured that, for the first time, the TUC was closely and regularly consulted by government. Unemployment was virtually eliminated, and there were fewer strikes than at any other time during the twentieth century. TUC members, with a better understanding of the workers than most politicians and civil servants, made useful advice available on a wide range of issues, including the organization of rationing. From 1941 the TUC also emphasized that the USSR was as important an ally as the USA. 'Help for Russia' was organized, though it was hazardous and costly to get tanks and other supplies to the USSR. German U-boats preyed relentlessly on the Arctic convoys.

As much as possible was produced within the United Kingdom, to reduce the need for imports across dangerous seas. Manpower and machines were worked to capacity: the output of war supplies and foodstuffs soared, while that of luxuries and non-essentials dwindled. Even so, Britain depended heavily on supplies from all parts of the Empire and Commonwealth, and from the USA. Again, planning was needed to determine priorities and to ensure that all resources were fully used. A Production Executive was set up at the start of 1941. While Bevin organized manpower, Beaverbrook played the leading part in organizing other resources, though theirs was an uneasy alliance – between the representatives, respectively, of labour and capital. Beaverbrook retired in 1942, when the foundations had been laid, and his work was taken over by Oliver Lyttleton. During 1943 Britain built nearly 9 000 tanks, more than 26 000 aircraft and almost 300 000 tons of shipping. Agricultural output increased too, going a long way towards feeding the nation. People as a whole were exhorted to 'Dig for Victory' and to grow vegetables whenever and wherever they could. They were also ordered to hand over for scrap whatever metals they could spare – old kettles and pans for example – and many railings were removed from houses and parks to be melted down for the war effort. This was an age of determination and action in which even children played their part, gathering waste paper, glass jars and rags for recycling on a scale previously unknown. The first characteristic of total war was the total commitment to the war effort which it demanded.

(b) Endurance

Total war also demanded endurance and sacrifice. Most families were affected by conscription and by the direction of labour. Many found their lives disrupted by enemy bombing, and all found them restricted by limitations on freedom and by shortages. Evacuation caused one of the first upheavals. At the start of the war, children, the mothers of the very young, and teachers, were evacuated from the cities to safer areas of the countryside and, in some cases, the seaside.

The authorities moved about one-and-a-half million, and as many again went by private arrangements, often to stay with relatives. Some millions refused to move, however. Although 'planned', the first evacuation arranged little except the transport of the children, usually by special trains. There was sometimes near-chaos at the receiving end of the journey. Most of the children came from poor families, and it was not always easy to find homes for them. It was the poor who housed the poor, more often than not. But the upper and middle classes, remote from the industrial centres, now saw something of how the urban poor lived. Some were shocked, and evacuation played its part in helping to change social attitudes, bringing a new sympathy for the poor among those who in the 1930s had lived in blissful ignorance of the realities of life in the cities. In the short term, however, evacuation caused emotional upsets and disrupted both family life and education.

When the expected massive bombing did not occur many evacuees returned to London and other cities. Some were then evacuated again, when the *Luftwaffe* began its pounding of Britain later in 1940, but this time the authorities played little part in organizing their movements. On the other hand, authorities did move certain key personnel out of London, and dispersed a number of institutions and national treasures. The Bank of England made its headquarters in Hampshire, for example, and art treasures were stored in slate caverns in north Wales.

When the bombing came it took a considerable toll of lives and property, but it neither broke the spirit of the British people nor halted production (see Unit 9.4(*a*)). Builders were drafted into London and other bombed areas to patch up houses that were still habitable. Welfare services were expanded to help the injured and those 'bombed out' and, in a spirit of comradeship and mutual support, city people endured the ordeal with dogged determination. In June 1940 Churchill expressed something of that determination:

> We shall defend our island whatever the cost may be. . . . We shall never surrender.

A year later, when Britain had experienced the full strength of German bombing, he still inspired confidence:

> I feel sure we have no need to fear the tempest. Let it roar; let it rage; we shall come through.

Air raids, even when they came nightly, only added to the will of the British people to resist. They accepted the bombing, as they accepted all the other hardships and inconveniences of the war – the total darkness of the blackout at night, to ensure that enemy aircraft could find no landmarks; the removal of signposts and station name-plates, to baffle any invaders who might arrive; and hundreds of other changes from their peacetime lives. Bombs killed about 60 000 British civilians during the war. When bombing was at its height in the winter of 1940–1, some 5 000 people a month died. Millions of homes were

Fig. 10.2 The anxious faces of children caught up in the adult business of total war: evacuation at a London station in 1940. The children in the lower half of the photograph carry their gas masks in boxes slung round their necks

destroyed or severely damaged; even the House of Commons was gutted. But the later and heavier bombing was to fall on Germany. In June 1942, Churchill accurately forecast that:

> German cities, harbours and centres of war production, will (from now on) be subjected to an ordeal the like of which has never been experienced by any country, in continuity, severity, or magnitude.

Meanwhile, rationing had been introduced in Britain. Petrol was rationed first; hardly any fuel was obtainable for pleasure motoring. Food rationing began in January 1940. Lord Woolton was appointed Minister of Food, and the system of food rationing became comprehensive, with basic rations of substances such as meat, bacon, sugar and tea, and a points system for choosing between other foods such as biscuits and tinned milk. Amounts varied; the meat ration, for example, varied between one and two shillings' worth per head weekly. Housewives soon learned how to make the best of the rations, rushing to take advantage of whatever might become temporarily available 'off the ration'. Woolton took the advice of nutritional experts, and it is likely that many poorer families were in fact better fed during the war than in the 1930s.

Fig. 10.3 Civilian preparations for the onslaught: an imaginative way of taping a London shop window, September 1939, to prevent flying glass in case of bomb blast. The shopkeeper had an eye to business too with a hasty advertisement of 'gas mask cases'

Basic food was available for all, at prices they could afford; and government regulations even extended to prescribing what should go into bread and into sausages. Clothing was also rationed, and 'utility' standards were laid down for the manufacture of essential goods, including furniture, to combine quality with the minimum use of materials. Basic clothing was manufactured as 'austerity wear'.

Food rations could be supplemented, however. More school meals were served, and most works had canteens. Cheap, wholesome meals could also be bought in British Restaurants, run by local authorities. For the first time in its history, British society was making a serious attempt to ensure everyone was treated equally, and minimum standards of basic essentials were maintained even for the poorest.

The British people adapted to wartime life in many other ways. They were encouraged to take 'Holidays at Home', and local parks became fairgrounds, sports centres and the focal points of countless 'talent competitions'. People used less water in their baths, to save the fuel of heating it, and they searched out Colorado beetles and other pests that damaged crops. Not everyone was patriotic and devoted to the war effort, however. Rationing led to the development of a 'black market', where society's 'spivs' and 'drones' (terms which came into common use at the end of the war) were to be found. Many deals were undoubtedly done 'under the counter'. On the other hand, the nation had never before shown such a united sense of purpose and awareness of the common good. Endurance had more than merely negative aspects.

(c) The Price of Victory

Britain suffered far fewer military casualties in the Second World War than in the First. Some 250 000 were killed, with a further 110 000 dead from Empire and Commonwealth forces. In both cases rather more had been wounded, many disabled for life. The USA had a total of dead similar to Britain's, but the USSR suffered horrendously, with about twenty million dead, military and civilian. The German dead numbered more than four million. Financially, the British government spent some £28 000 million in winning the war. The whole economy had been disrupted. Massive debts had once more accumulated, in spite of increased taxation with income tax at 50p in the pound. The volume of exports fell during the war, to about 30 per cent of the 1938 level. Imports had fallen too, but only to about 70 per cent of the 1938 volume. Military victory was only the prelude to further years of struggle to rebuild the economy, though men and machines had again been strained to their limits. Much repair work was also needed, some of it to replace devastated housing and to rebuild the bombed areas of London and such places as Coventry and Plymouth.

Striking a balance between restoring personal liberties and continuing governmental organization was another postwar problem. People were now accustomed to government controls and had seen some of the advantages of organization and co-operation. Once the danger of invasion seemed to have passed, preparations were begun for the organization of postwar society. These too contributed to the war effort, since people who could look forward to a fairer society than that of the 1930s were likely to commit themselves to victory even more wholeheartedly. At the same time, there was less of the false optimism that had been so widespread in 1918. There was great rejoicing on 'VE Day' (Victory in Europe, 8 May 1945), and there were further celebrations three months later to mark Victory over Japan. Between VE Day and VJ Day a general election took place, and the British quickly prepared themselves to face the difficulties of peace.

10.2 Wartime Preparations for Peace

Several Committees had been appointed during the war, to look into peace-time reconstruction. They reported on such matters as education, health, housing and town planning. But it was the Beveridge Report of 1942 which captured the nation's attention. The 'Committee on Social Insurance and Allied Services' had been set up, under William Beveridge, in June 1941. The Report took as one of its sub-headings 'Abolition of Want as a Practicable Post-War Aim', and it provided a framework for social revolution. It was based on three principles: that this was a moment 'for revolutions, not for patching'; that the 'organization of social insurance should be treated as one part only of a comprehensive policy of social progress'; and that 'social security must be achieved by co-operation between the State and the individual'. Beveridge recommended a comprehensive system of national insurance, built on the pre-war provision, which would include all Britain's citizens and 'provide income security'. The plan was for universal co-operation, not for charity. Everyone in work would contribute, along with their employers and the government. Benefits would be received 'as of right and without means test'. The able were to pay into the Insurance Fund, and everyone would have entitlement to benefit when in need – at times of sickness, unemployment, widowhood and old age, for example.

Beveridge went much further, however. Insurance was seen as:

> an attack on Want. But Want is only one of five giants on the road to reconstruction, and in some ways the easiest to attack. The others are Disease, Ignorance, Squalor and Idleness.

Further changes were therefore needed. Beveridge recommended a national health service to provide treatment for all, not merely for those who could afford to pay for it. He recommended help for large families by the payment of family allowances. He built death grants into his scheme to remove anxiety over funeral expenses. He assumed that improvements would be made in education and housing but, above all, he assumed that there would be a planned attack on unemployment, the giant he called 'Idleness'. The Report recognized that unemployment was wasteful; and it was an important require-ment for all Beveridge's proposals that the nation should increase its output to produce the wealth that was necessary to make the reforms possible. Beveridge took it for granted that postwar governments would lead and organize the nation, and that there would be no return to the politics of inactivity that had characterized the 1930s.

R.A. Butler, the President of the Board of Education, believed that educa-tion should be 'the spearhead of social reform'. The (Butler) Education Act of 1944 was therefore passed even before the war ended, and it set the pattern of education in England for the next twenty-five years or so. A Ministry of Edu-cation was to be set up. The school-leaving age was to be raised to fifteen, and eventually to sixteen, and the first of these steps was taken in 1947. The Act also made secondary education free, like primary education, with the division between the two to be made at the age of eleven, and schooling geared to 'age, ability, and aptitude'. In dealing with the organization of schools, the Act tried to knit the voluntary schools, which were supervised by religious bodies, more securely into the state system. At the same time, more than 150 independent schools gained a new status as direct-grant schools: in addition to their fee-paying 'private' students, they admitted children from the state system and received a grant of money direct from the central government. Among the Act's other clauses was one requiring schools to include Religious Instruction in their curriculum.

The main result of the Butler Act was the reorganization of secondary schooling. Most local authorities now adopted eleven-plus systems of selection, to sort their children for grammar, technical or modern schools. The theory behind this was that such schools would cater for differing abilities and apti-tudes. But the provision of technical schools was patchy, and the numbers admitted to grammar schools depended as much on the number of places available locally as on a child's ability to cope with academic work. Moreover, secondary modern schools tended to be associated with a child's failure at the age of eleven to qualify for something 'better'. When the school-leaving age was raised to sixteen in 1972, many authorities were abandoning the three sorts of secondary school in favour of comprehensive schools, which included all levels of ability. Meanwhile, only slow progress was made in fulfilling the 1944 Act's other aims – to provide nursery schools for the under-fives and further education for the over-fifteens.

The Family Allowances Act of 1945 was also passed before the general election took place. It made provision for the payment of 25p a week 'in respect of each child . . . other than the elder or eldest', while still at school or until the end of an apprenticeship. But whether more of Beveridge's recommendations would be carried out now seemed likely to depend on the outcome of the general election.

10.3 The General Election of 1945

Victory in Europe at once led to discussion about the timing of the long overdue general election. Attlee, the Labour leader, would have preferred an autumn election. Sinclair and the Liberals were hesitant. In the end, it was mainly Churchill's decision that the election should take place in July and the coalition government was therefore brought to an end in May 1945. Pending the election, Churchill led a caretaker government, mainly of Conservatives. Butler replaced Bevin as Minister of Labour, for example.

The election of 1945 gave the British people a straightforward choice between the parties. Lloyd George did not contest the election. He was created a peer, but died before the year was out. In almost every constituency the electors were at last freed from confusion about different groups of Liberals and about 'National' candidates.* The Conservatives and the Labour Party each fielded more than six hundred candidates, and the Liberals more than three hundred. It seemed certain that the next prime minister would be either Churchill or Attlee, the Labour leader.

To some extent the voters were also voting on the Beveridge Report.

---

* 'Help Him to Finish the Job – Vote National!' Churchill's supporters still used the term 'National', but it clearly meant 'Conservative'.

Table 10.1 General elections, 1945–79

Date	CONSERVATIVES Total vote (millions)	% of votes cast	Seats won	LABOUR Total vote (millions)	% of votes cast	Seats won	LIBERALS Total vote (millions)	% of votes cast	Seats won	OTHERS Total vote (millions)	Seats won	Total MPs elected
1945	10.0	39.8	213	12.0	47.8	393	2.2	9.0	12	0.9	22*	640
1950	12.5	43.5	298	13.3	46.1	315	2.6	9.1	9	0.4	3	625
1951	13.7	48.0	321	13.9	48.8	295	0.7	2.5	6	0.2	3	625
1955	13.3	49.7	344	12.4	46.4	277	0.7	2.7	6	0.3	3	630
1959	13.7	49.4	365	12.2	43.8	258	1.6	5.9	6	0.1	1	630
1964	12.0	43.4	304	12.2	44.1	317	3.1	11.2	9	0.3	0	630
1966	11.4	41.9	253	13.1	48.0	363	2.3	8.5	12	0.5	2	630
1970	13.1	46.4	330	12.2	43.0	287	2.1	7.5	6	0.9	7+	630
1974 (Feb.)	11.9	37.9	297	11.6	37.1	301	6.1	19.3	14	1.8	23**	635
1974 (Oct.)	10.5	35.9	277	11.5	39.2	319	5.3	18.3	13	1.9	26++	635
1979	13.7	43.9	339	11.5	36.9	269	4.3	13.8	11	1.8	16=	635

bold: the Party which won the election and formed the next government.

Notes:

The figures for the Conservatives include their Ulster Unionist Allies from 1945 to 1970. From February 1974 Northern Ireland MPs are included under Others.

The total number of MPs in the last column varies because of changes brought about by Boundary Commissions which periodically seek to equalize the size of constituencies.

*   includes 2 Communists. No Communist MPs have been elected in general elections since 1945

\+   includes 1 SNP (Scottish Nationalist Party)

**   includes 7 SNP and 2 PC (Plaid Cymru)

\+\+   includes 11 SNP and 3 PC

=   includes 2 SNP and 2 PC

Source: this Table has been derived mainly from Butler, D. and Sloman, A.: *British Political Facts, 1900–1979*. Macmillan (London, 1980).

Churchill and many of the Conservatives gave the impression of being luke-warm about it, sometimes echoing the voices of the 1930s with warnings about costs and 'the heavy burden' of taxation. In the election campaign, however, they seemed to be reverting to the mood of 1918, demanding a vote of confidence and gratitude for Churchill, like a latter-day Lloyd George. The nation was undoubtedly grateful to Churchill for his wartime leadership; but it was now choosing a leader for peacetime reconstruction. Voters wanted more than slogans. (The Conservative candidate in Eccles typically proclaimed that 'A Vote for Cary is a Vote for Churchill'.) Churchill did not play his elec-tioneering cards well. His comment that Labour might have to fall back on 'some form of Gestapo' seemed not only insulting but silly when related to the mild and unassuming Attlee. And his interpretation of comments by Laski, the Chairman of the Labour Party, that seemed to suggest that a Labour govern-ment would have to take orders from the Party's National Executive, proved of little interest to the voters.

The voters also paid scant attention to the Empire and international prob-lems. They were, however, passionately interested in plans for their future lives – and both Labour and the Liberals had far more to say on this subject than the Conservatives. The Labour Manifesto struck the right note with its title, *Let Us Face The Future*, promising active and reforming government, while the Liberals presented *Twenty Points*. Labour was also able to make use of pre-war history, and it was not difficult to persuade many of the voters that Conserva-tive and 'National' politicians had failed them during the 1930s. By constantly emphasizing that a Labour government was likely to be an interfering and even totalitarian one, Churchill managed to suggest that the Conservatives would be less active, perhaps even complacent.

Most of the country voted on 5 July although, by an unusual arrangement, the votes were not counted until 26 July. Certain towns such as Bolton could not vote on 5 July, because of annual holidays, and the delay also allowed time to collect votes from those in the forces (see Glossary: ABCA). The Gallup Poll, however, forecast the result with remarkable accuracy a fortnight before the count, showing that public opinion polls were likely to become a regular feature of British elections. In 1945, for the first time, a Labour government was returned with an overall majority. Table 10.1 shows that it was not only the Conservatives who had reason to be shocked by the result. The Liberals suffered a major defeat, winning only twelve seats and losing sixty-four deposits. A new era had begun in British politics.

Further Reading

Seaman, L.C.B.: *Post-Victorian Britain, 1902–1951*. Methuen (London, 1966), chapter 46.

Chamberlin, E.R.: *Life in Wartime Britain*. Batsford (London, 1972).

Marwick, A.: *Britain in the Century of Total War – War, Peace and Social Change, 1900–1967*. Penguin (Harmondsworth, 1970).

Documentary
Beveridge and After. Longman History Pack (Harlow, 1974).
Yass, M.: *The Home Front: England 1939–45*. Wayland (Hove, 1971).

Exercises
1.   After reading Unit 1.3 again, list the ways in which the British civilian population was organized (*a*) during the First World War and (*b*) during the Second World War. What similarities and what differences do these lists reveal?
2.   Write an account of the year's events in the life of a typical Londoner during 1940.
3.   Summarize the main recommendations of the Beveridge Report. What was the significance of the Report's emphasis on benefits 'as of right and without means test' (page 174)? Why did this Report capture 'the nation's attention' (page 173)?
4.   What does this Unit show of the services to Britain during wartime of (*a*) Bevin and (*b*) Butler?
5.   Compare Units 1.4 and 10.1(*c*). In what common and what different ways did the two world wars affect (*a*) Britain's economy and (*b*) the expectations of British society?
6.   (*a*) Draw three columns headed Conservatives/Labour/Liberals. Write in each column the reasons why the party in question might have secured your vote in the general election of 1945.
     (*b*) How far does your answer to (*a*) adequately explain why the Labour Party won the election of 1945?
     (*c*) Referring to Table 10.1 and the Glossary (*Voting*), explain why the number of seats won by the Liberals in the House of Commons bore little relation to the number of votes given to the Party.

Unit Eleven

Reconstruction: Labour Government, 1945–51

11.1 Men and Measures

The ritual photograph for which Attlee's cabinet posed in the garden of 10 Downing Street in 1945 showed a number of ministers already well known to the public (Fig. 11.1). Attlee had been, in effect, Churchill's Deputy Prime Minister during the war. Immediately to the right of him sat Bevin who, after long service as the Minister of Labour, now became Foreign Secretary – a rather unexpected appointment. Morrison, Home Secretary under Churchill, sat on Attlee's left, and was now the Lord President. Cripps was another

Fig. 11.1 Attlee's cabinet, 1945, Attlee himself in the middle of the front row. To Attlee's right, Bevin, Greenwood, Cripps, Jowitt and Addison. To Attlee's left, Morrison, Dalton, Alexander, Chuter Ede and Ellen Wilkinson. In the back row, Aneurin Bevan on the extreme left, Shinwell second from right. This was the first Labour government with an overall majority in the House of Commons

minister with wartime experience. He had made his peace with the Labour Party and became President of the Board of Trade in 1945, and in 1947 replaced Dalton as Chancellor of the Exchequer. Perhaps the next most important minister in the government was Aneurin Bevan, who showed a fiery commitment to his job as Minister of Health. The first Minister of Education was Ellen Wilkinson, filling the post newly created by the Education Act of 1944.

Attlee's team was a talented one, and Attlee himself managed it expertly despite taunts that he was like a 'little mouse'. His task was not an easy one. There was a feud between Bevin and Morrison, and the government included ministers in Cripps and Bevan with a reputation for strong, allegedly left-wing views. Attlee had chosen rather elderly men for office on the whole, including Arthur Greenwood, who had served in the Labour government of 1929–31. Bevan, not yet fifty, was a comparative youngster in the cabinet. It was a hard-working team; both Bevan and Cripps greatly shortened their lives struggling with the government's daunting postwar problems.

Members of the government were well aware that this was the first time Labour was in power with a parliamentary majority. They wanted to make up for lost time. In spite of the country's many economic problems, their aim was to establish a welfare state, to avoid unemployment, to settle the problems of India and, perhaps, to settle some old scores as well; the government's lesser measures included the repeal of the Trade Disputes Act of 1927, and a further reduction in the powers of the House of Lords. Their highest priority, however, was to restore the British economy.

Attlee's government found itself struggling continuously with the country's many-sided economic problems – a struggle which no government since 1945 has been able to avoid, except very briefly. In 1945 Britain tottered on the edge of bankruptcy. Its debts to foreign creditors stood at over £3 300 million. Gold and dollar reserves had been almost exhausted during the war, and over £1 100 million worth of foreign assets had been sold. This reduced the earnings from invisible exports, which fell from almost £250 million in 1938 to only £120 million in 1946. It was therefore even more vital to find export markets for British goods, in order to pay for imports; but the war had played havoc with existing markets. Moreover, the war had helped to increase costs in Britain, thus threatening to make its goods uncompetitive in overseas markets. Rationing and price controls kept wartime inflation at a lower level between 1939 and 1945 than between 1914 and 1918. Nevertheless, the Retail Prices Index rose by some 70 per cent between 1935 and 1945, and this might mean that Britain would need to devalue the pound, if difficulties could not be overcome by other methods.

The country faced numerous other problems in 1945. About a third of its merchant shipping had been destroyed. It had worn-out plant and machinery. There was a history of neglect in some industries, with too little investment for the future: the railways and the coal industry, for example, cried out for modernization. It would require not just hard work but great skill to cope with these problems and, at the same time, carry out extensive social reform. But this was the job the voters had entrusted to the government. Churchill had played a major part in winning the war. It was Attlee's job to win the peace.

Attlee and his ministers readily accepted that government must now play a far more active part in organizing the nation, than had been normal in the 1930s. Morrison had emphasized this as early as 1943:

> Through its governmental and public authorities, the nation is consciously planning . . . the use and direction of its material resources with a degree of efficiency never hitherto achieved. . . . What are we going to do about this sensible planning at the end of the war? Scrap it? Go back to economic anarchy? . . . If that happens we shall be heading for muddle and disaster. . . . Labour must lead the glorious fight for constructive sense.

Britain could therefore benefit from the wartime experience of planning and organization – and the nation in general was willing to join with the government in constructive efforts to overcome problems and build a more equal society. The Labour government also began its work with the goodwill of the trade union movement and, for its part, was willing to consult the TUC on many issues. It would be impossible to overcome Britain's economic problems without high productivity and without keeping down costs: the co-operation of the workers was therefore vitally important. Attlee's government believed that full employment and consultation were essential in gaining this co-operation. Only by removing the fear of unemployment could new technology be introduced, for example, since the unions were otherwise likely to resist it as a threat to jobs.

But the country's problems were deep-rooted and persistent, and the five years after 1945 produced disappointments as well as successes. By 1950 both the government and the nation were tiring of the struggle. The government narrowly survived the general election of that year. A year later, however, though Labour won its largest vote in any general election before or since, the scales were tipped, and the Conservatives returned to office (see Table 10.1). Time was to show that the tragedy of postwar Britain was its inability to find more than temporary solutions to its economic problems, so that the country eventually moved into the 1980s in growing desperation. In the years of Attlee's government, however, the problems were tackled soberly, and the nation added peacetime hardships to its wartime experiences, in an effort to establish what it hoped would be the foundations for a prosperous future.

11.2 Economic Reconstruction

(a) Debts and Austerity

The ending of American Lend-Lease arrangements in August 1945 caused Dalton urgently to seek a new loan to tide Britain over its immediate problems. The USA advanced some £1 100 million, enough to cover the debts arising from Lend-Lease and to leave Britain with a reserve of dollars for trading purposes. Canada also loaned about £300 million. By the middle of 1947, however, most of this money had been spent, and reserves were again dangerously low, despite exports now being well above the 1938 level. Some areas of the home market had been starved of supplies – cars, for example – in order to boost sales abroad. But payments for imports of food and raw materials for industry still drained Britain's reserves, especially of dollars. Britain had a persistent 'dollar gap' – that is, the gap between the dollars that could be earned and those needed to pay for imports from the USA.

There were other crises, too. In 1946, there was a shortfall in world food supplies, and bread rationing was introduced in Britain in July – a hardship which had been avoided even in wartime. Then came the exceptionally severe winter of 1946–7. The coal industry was producing less than in 1939, and fuel stocks were already low. Snow and ice almost paralysed communications, making the problem worse. Urgent economies had to be made in the supply and consumption of electricity, and the nation shivered. The BBC reduced its programmes; street lighting was restricted; but, worst of all, two million workers were laid off early in 1947, when their workplaces were without fuel. Production and exports were interrupted. People endured these hardships with comparatively little grumbling, and it was evidence of the change of mood since the 1930s that the government was criticized for too little planning rather than too much. Shinwell was made the scapegoat and dismissed, rather unjustly, from the Ministry of Fuel and Power, where Hugh Gaitskell then gained his first major appointment. When the thaw came, the country suffered from floods – and there was a shortage of potatoes, and they too were rationed.

In November 1947, while Britain still struggled to balance its overseas trade, Dalton had to resign. His downfall was the result of a leak of parts of his budget speech in the press, an hour or so before he spoke in the Commons. The new Chancellor of the Exchequer was Cripps, who had already been playing a leading part in the management of the economy. The name of Cripps now became inseparable from his policy of Austerity. He demanded higher productivity, and insisted on sacrifices from all classes, to bring the balance of payments under control. Income tax remained at 45p in the pound and, in 1948, a levy was imposed on capital. Cripps also demanded longer hours of work, for example from the miners; and he was remarkably successful in convincing the workers and trade unions that they should accept wage restraint, lest exports became too expensive. Cripps held back inflationary pressures in a similar way, by curbing government spending. While disappointed that the hoped-for recovery was coming only slowly, people co-operated well with this policy of Austerity. There were very few strikes. In the later 1940s they remained at almost the same low level as during the war.

Britain received further help towards economic recovery from Marshall Aid, an American programme which assisted western Europe generally after 1947. Even so, the country continued to struggle. Table 11.1 shows that a surplus was achieved on the current account of the balance of payments (compare

Illingworth comes back from the Alps

'What ?   Everything   frozen   here,   too ?'

Fig. 11.2 Illingworth's comment on Britain in the severe winter of 1946–7, Cripps threatening 'Greater Austerity', Shinwell unable to produce sufficient fuel, Bevan's housing drive impeded and the government about to abdicate its responsibilities in Palestine

Table 6.2), but the dollar gap soon threatened to widen again and, in 1949, another large deficit seemed likely. Cripps therefore devalued the pound in September 1949, setting the new exchange rate at £1:2.80 dollars, instead of the previous £1:4.03 dollars. This made exports cheaper and imports dearer, thus discouraging the latter, and this produced a healthy surplus in 1950. Cripps resigned in that year because of failing health, and Gaitskell replaced him as Chancellor. Almost at once, however, in 1951, the surplus turned into a substantial deficit, mainly because the war in Korea created shortages of commodities and sharply increased the cost of Britain's imports yet again.

Britain exported almost three times as much in 1951 as in 1946 but a healthy trading position still proved elusive. The British people had certainly made an effort. They had steadfastly accepted higher taxation than in pre-war years, and endured controls, shortages and the continuation of rationing, which was lifted only gradually. Clothing, for example, was rationed until 1949. The continuation of conscription for young men was also tolerated, because of international tension. At the age of eighteen they had to undergo some two years of National Service. For its part, the government used controls and subsidies to keep down prices, and continued the policy of cheap money to hold down interest rates. It also fulfilled its promise of full employment. Unemployment was almost wholly short-term in the years 1945–51, and it was always below 400 000. In spite of their disappointments, almost fourteen million voters gave their support to the Labour Party in the election of October 1951.

Table 11.1 Britain's balance of payments, 1946–51

Date	Exports*	Visible trade balance*	Current Account	
			Deficits*	Surpluses*
1946	917	−165	−295	
1947	1 145	−415	−442	
1948	1 602	−192		+ 7
1949	1 841	−137		+ 38
1950	2 250	−133		+297
1951	2 748	−733	−419	

* £million
Source: Pollard, S.: *The Development of the British Economy*. Arnold (London, 1969).

(b) Nationalization and Growth

Clause Four of the Labour Party's constitution of 1918 had committed the Party to the public ownership – nationalization – of important sectors of the economy (see Unit 3.2). When the Labour Party won the general election of 1945 it had its first opportunity to implement Clause Four. In the case of various important industries, nationalization accorded with Labour's view of the 'national interest': it would provide a useful foundation for planned development where modernization was likely to need heavy investment, beyond the scope of private owners, and it might indeed be vital not only for future growth but even for the survival of certain basic industries. The specific problems it was hoped nationalization would help to solve varied from one industry to another. The coal industry, for example, needed investment for modernization, while the sorry history of the industry had long caused the Miners' Federation to demand nationalization in the hope of improving miners' conditions, regarded by some as the main purpose of nationalizing the pits.

The Bank of England was the first important institution to be nationalized, in 1946. One of the few national banks anywhere in the world still remaining in the hands of private shareholders, it was placed under public ownership and its shareholders were compensated. The same happened with all the industries that were nationalized. In effect, the nation gave the shareholders government stock in exchange for their shares.

Electricity and gas were nationalized by the Electricity Supply Act of 1947 and the Gas Act of 1948. Baldwin's government had gone some way towards the state control of electricity in 1926 (see Unit 3.4(c)), but the industry's organization was still somewhat haphazard at the end of the Second World War, and some areas were still without electricity. The 1947 Act set up the British Electricity Authority with fifteen regional boards, to provide a coherent system of generation and supply. Gas came under the Gas Council, with twelve regional boards.

The Labour government also aimed to lay the foundations for a national transport policy. Nationalization would make it possible to consider not only the economic aim of making a profit but the transport *needs* of the community as a whole as part of overall social policy. The country's main airlines were nationalized and, by 1949, there were two public corporations, BOAC (see Unit 6.3) and BEA (British European Airways). These were merged into British Airways in 1973. A more ambitious undertaking was the nationalization of domestic transport. The British Transport Commission was set up in 1948, with six boards to control not only the railways and their hotels but road services (except local bus services), dock services and inland waterways. It cost the nation over £1 200 million to buy out the previous owners, but the intention was to develop an overall plan to co-ordinate Britain's rail, road and water transport. The Conservatives, however, protested that the package included well-run, profitable services. In 1953 Churchill's government began to sell back the profitable road-haulage services to private owners.

The Conservatives made no serious complaints about the Coal Industry Nationalization Act of 1946, however. The Reid Report, a year earlier, had commented on the coal industry's poor technology and weak organization. The coal owners received £165 million in compensation, a generous sum since many of the mines had been neglected, and few were profitable. Coal nationalization was a personal achievement for Shinwell, before he ceased to be the Minister of Fuel and Power. (Such was Shinwell's satisfaction that comics alleged he exclaimed, 'It's mine, all mine', when visiting a National Coal Board colliery.) But when the NCB took control of the industry in 1947, it faced great problems. In addition to the need for investment to modernize, the industry had to be adapted to falling demand in the face of competition from electricity and oil. There was a temporary increase in demand during the 1950s, but consumption fell from 214 million tons in 1949 to some 200 million tons in 1960, and then to only 122 million tons in 1972. Only the electricity-supply industry increased its use of coal in these years. The railways, iron and steel, and the gas-supply industry almost stopped using coal. Factories and homes reduced their demand, and after 1939 coal exports all but ceased. The Coal Board thus had to cut manpower, from about 725 000 in 1948 to about 270 000 in 1972. At the same time it increased productivity by more than doubling the output per man per shift. In the 1970s, however, problems over the supply of oil gave coal renewed importance, and it was fortunate that the NCB had preserved a British coal industry which, by this time, was also efficient.

Fig. 11.3 The end of a long struggle by the mineworkers: the coal industry was nationalized with effect from the beginning of 1947

The Iron and Steel Act of 1949 completed the Labour government's programme of nationalization, but it was the start of a period of confusion for that industry. The government argued for public ownership because expensive modernization was needed, and because of the high rate of unemployment in iron and steel in the past. But the Labour Party was not united on the details of nationalizing the industry, and legislation had been left almost to the end of the government's life. The Conservatives resisted fiercely, and the House of Lords created difficulties, so that the Act did not become law until after the general election of 1950 when about a hundred companies were taken over by the British Iron and Steel Corporation. Then, almost as soon as the Iron and Steel Corporation was born, the Conservatives won the election of 1951.

Churchill's Iron and Steel Act of 1953 began the process of selling the companies back to private owners, though buyers could not now be found for all of them, for example, for the firm of Richard Thomas and Baldwins. Labour in turn threatened to renationalize the industry when it was next in power and, indeed, proceeded to do so in 1967. Even in 1953, however, the Conservatives retained some oversight of the industry by setting up the Iron and Steel Board, in the hope of combining reorganization 'under private enterprise' with 'public supervision'. There was a growing demand for iron and steel, but there was also fierce foreign competition. After 1967 the British Steel Corporation found itself on the familiar treadmill: huge amounts of capital were needed to introduce new technology in order to be competitive, and to increase productivity it was necessary to close inefficient plant, and employ fewer workers. Like the Coal Board, the Steel Corporation inherited enormous problems. At the end of the 1970s even the Corby Steelworks, though in the vanguard when it was built in the 1930s, had to be shut down as outdated with very damaging results for the town which had depended on it. The Steel Corporation was now deep in debt, and struggling to resist foreign steel imports.

Nationalization was only part of the policy of general economic management to which Attlee's government was committed. Many boards and councils were set up to consider how best to modernize their industries, to increase productivity, maintain good labour relations and keep full employment. By 1950 industrial production had increased by more than a third, compared with 1946, when it was still at much the same level as in the late 1930s. The growth was especially marked in vehicle-building, engineering and chemicals and, in general, there were now sound foundations for further development in the 1950s.

Fig. 11.4

The Labour government had taken active steps to stimulate and direct both public and private investment. The Investment (Controls and Guarantees) Act ensured that investment was directed into areas of national importance. The repair of the whole economy was important to safeguard prosperity in future years, as well as to win a healthy trading position in the late 1940s. Germany and Japan, the defeated powers, could not compete seriously with British exports in the years immediately after 1945, but that state of affairs would not last and, in the second half of the twentieth century, Britain was likely to face fiercer competition than ever before. By 1951 substantial growth had been achieved, together with improvements in productivity, and a start had been made on modernizing outdated industries. But by no means all the problems had been overcome, and continued effort would be needed. However, 1951 was exactly a hundred years after Britain had celebrated its Victorian prosperity in the Great Exhibition. It seemed a suitable moment to celebrate again, and the Festival of Britain took place. The Post Office, Britain's oldest state-owned industry, commemorated the event in stamps with a curious allegorical mish-mash, said to represent 'Commerce and Prosperity' (Fig. 11.4).

11.3 Social Policy and Reform

(a) The Welfare State
British society returned to a peacetime footing far more smoothly after the Second World War than after the First. The Beveridge Report had pointed the way to social progress (see Unit 10.2), and the government's aim was to complete the building of a welfare state (see Glossary) as quickly as possible. Greenwood, Bevan and James Griffiths, the Minister of National Insurance, were mainly responsible for this task.

National insurance lay at the centre of the new system, and the National Insurance Act of 1946 carried out many of the Beveridge Report recommendations. For just under 25p a week, deducted from the worker's wage packet, he or she was entitled to benefit in times of sickness and unemployment, and at retirement, and a family was covered for maternity benefit, widow's and orphans' allowances and the death grant. A separate act dealt with compensation for industrial injury. The whole scheme came into operation in July 1948, bringing into one coherent system, under the Ministry of National Insurance, the various state schemes which had existed before the war, and also extending them. *The Times* commented:

> The British public join together in a single national friendly society for mutual support during the common misfortunes of life. . . . The new social security system is, as the Prime Minister said . . . the most comprehensive of its kind ever introduced in any country. . . . (It) treat(s) the individual as a citizen, not as a 'pauper', an object of charity, or a member of a particular social class.

No one was allowed to remain outside the scheme, which led to some criticism among the minority who thought they had no personal need of insurance. There was also some concern that a large staff of officials would be required to administer the scheme. Above all, there were regrets that friendly societies now lost the place they had held in the earlier National Insurance scheme, in distributing sickness benefits. But the Conservatives supported the government, and Butler declared:

> I think we should take pride that the British race has been able (so soon after the war) to show the whole world that we are able to produce a social insurance scheme of this character.

The National Insurance scheme was designed to be self-supporting, financed by contributions from employees, employers and the government, so certain conditions had to be met in order to qualify for benefits, and there were limits on the duration of some benefits. A further measure was needed to help those with special financial needs, such as deserted wives and the disabled. The National Assistance Act of 1948 set up the National Assistance Board (NAB):

> to assist persons in Great Britain who are without resources to meet their requirements, or whose resources . . . must be supplemented in order to meet their requirements.

National Assistance was financed out of national taxes, and it provided a safety net for all those in need. In 1953, however, it was evidence of the shortcomings of the National Insurance scheme that the NAB had to give extra help to a quarter of those receiving retirement or widows' pensions. The NAB replaced the old poor law machinery and the Unemployment Assistance Board, and the new system was less harsh and more flexible. Workhouses became a thing of the past. National Insurance, full employment and, when necessary, National Assistance made the 'dole' obsolete too. The NAB looked into an applicant's means, but it did not apply the means test of the 1930s, which had also inquired into the wages and savings of relatives. Yet National Assistance was still seen as a sort of charity, for which the proudly self-reliant were reluctant to apply, and which some taxpayers alleged was a waste of money.

Aneurin Bevan, once a South Wales miner, passionately championed the National Health Service Act of 1946, perhaps the most vital part of the social revolution. Churchill's coalition government had made preliminary plans for a free and comprehensive health service and these were now implemented, with some amendments. The introduction of the National Health Service (NHS) placed Britain in the forefront of reforming and caring nations, and people as a whole were enthusiastic. Many, like Bevan, had seen real suffering and death because sick people could not afford treatment, and had experienced the anxiety which resulted from the dread of large hospital bills. There had, of course, been some provision in pre-war Britain for the medical treatment of the poor, and many doctors had deliberately undercharged them. But there was general agreement that much more was now needed.

Essentially the 1946 Act meant that every British citizen could now receive medical, dental and optical services free of charge. 'Free' meant that the NHS was paid for out of taxation, like defence services and the whole apparatus of government. Those in need could receive treatment in hospitals and health centres, and could call on the services of general practitioners (family doctors) and dentists, opticians and midwives. Some 3 000 hospitals were taken over from existing organizations and local authorities, and were now run by the state, while many other local authority services were fitted into the national system of care. At the same time, however, those who wished to pay for private treatment remained free to do so. The British Medical Association fiercely opposed various aspects of the scheme, and many doctors feared that they were in danger of becoming civil servants. But Bevan, working strenuously to ensure that the system would run smoothly, coaxed some 90 per cent of the medical profession into the NHS. When the scheme began in July 1948, the rush for treatment showed what need there was for the NHS. Within a year 187 million prescriptions for medicine had been written, and more than five million pairs of glasses supplied.

The NHS cost just over £200 million in its first year of operation but costs rose sharply in later years. In 1965 they were over £1 200 million and, in 1975, over £5 200. The cost of equipping and running hospitals rose most sharply of all. The NHS clearly fulfilled a need but, from the outset, it was handicapped by many old and inadequate buildings, and it soon became clear how difficult it would be to find all the money the Service required. Of all twentieth-century reforms, however, the creation of the NHS must rank among the boldest and most important, and millions of British citizens have had reason to be grateful for it. When Bevan died in 1960 the *British Medical Journal* wrote that he was 'the most brilliant Minister of Health this country ever had'. Nevertheless, Attlee moved him to the Ministry of Labour in 1951; and Bevan was further angered when Gaitskell, the new Chancellor, imposed charges on NHS users in part-payment for dentures and glasses. These charges only saved the government about £13 million, a trivial sum in the budget as a whole; but they destroyed the principle Bevan had held sacred, that the Health Service should be free.

As the Minister of Health, Bevan was also responsible for housing in the years 1945–51. Here too he had an impressive record. Wartime damage and the decay of older properties had left the country in need of almost a million new homes. About 160 000 temporary prefabricated homes ('prefabs') were put up in the immediate postwar years, to deal with urgent needs while permanent houses were being built. Bevan then concentrated resources on council housing, steadily pushing up the rate of building until about a quarter of a million new homes were completed during 1948. Financial problems led to a slight falling back after that, but Bevan always insisted that the new houses should be of good quality. The Housing Act of 1949 laid down the principle that council houses should be built for all classes, not only for the poor. The government also continued rent control, to protect tenants of local councils and private landlords.

Two further Acts showed the government's concern for the environment. The aim of the New Towns Act of 1946 was to create model communities where people could be rehoused, and where they would also have ready access to employment and leisure facilities. Each new town was to be organized by a development corporation. The first such corporation was set up at Stevenage, in 1946, and fourteen in all, two of them in Scotland and one in Wales, were set up during the lifetime of the Labour government. Others followed in later years. The Town and Country Planning Act of 1947 continued the attack on the Giant that Beveridge had called 'Squalor'. Local authorities were required to draw up development plans, and steps were taken to control the use of land and to preserve historic buildings. But less was achieved than might have been

Fig. 11.5 New Town Development Corporations by 1951

hoped. Many parts of Britain continued to be disfigured by the decaying remains of nineteenth-century industry, and also by the ugly clutter of many of the new buildings of the more affluent society of the twentieth century. Planning by local authorities often showed little awareness of what eyesores might result.

The Children Act of 1948 was for the protection of deprived children. It required local authorities to observe uniform standards of care, both in children's homes and of children who were 'boarded out'. The reorganization of education meanwhile proceeded under the Act of 1944, while the Family Allowances Act of 1945 provided assistance to parents with more than one child (see Unit 10.2). By 1951 more radical changes had been made within a mere seven years than ever before, and Britain had become a state which cared for its people's welfare to an extent which few other countries could equal.

(b) Further Reforms

The Trade Disputes Act of 1946 repealed the Act of 1927 (see Unit 3.4(b)), which gave satisfaction to the trade unions and also helped the finances of the Labour Party. The Representation of the People Act of 1948 revised the boundaries of parliamentary constituencies, in line with changes in population, completed the movement to single-member constituencies, and abolished the separate representation of the universities in the House of Commons. It also abolished the practice of plural voting on account of the possession of a university degree or of business premises (see Unit 2.1). The principle of 'one man, one vote' was now firmly applied, and it was extended to local government too, where the vote was no longer limited to ratepayers. No change was made in the first-past-the-post system, however, and general elections continued to produce some illogical results. In 1951 and February 1974, for example, elections were lost by parties which gained the most votes (see Table 10.1). In 1949 the Parliament Act was finally approved, having been held up by the Lords since 1947. This Act reduced the Lords' delaying power from two years to one. It was intended partly to speed up the passing of the government's Iron and Steel Act, but it also increased the authority of the Commons, the elected House. Radical members of the Labour Party were hardly satisfied. They wanted the abolition of the House of Lords, which they saw as an outdated relic of the past – an unelected assembly of noblemen, unique among the countries which claimed to be democratic and progressive. The government had no wish to become involved in such a controversy, however. It would be difficult to decide what would replace the Lords, and it might well lead to arguments about whether the monarchy should remain, when so many countries had become republics. On the other hand, it was argued that the Lords was a symbol of Britain's nostalgic attachment to class distinctions which Attlee's government was attempting to undermine in its other reforms.

Meanwhile, the Atomic Energy Act of 1946 authorized the Ministry of Supply to develop the peaceful uses of nuclear power. Secretly, a year later, the government decided that Britain should develop atomic weapons, another issue sure to arouse controversy within the Labour Party when it became public knowledge. The Monopolies Act of 1948 was on safer ground. It set up the Monopolies Commission to protect the public against the monopolistic practices of big business, a policy attractive to Labour supporters, who tended to ignore the fact that nationalization itself created monopolies.

By 1950 the strain of five testing years in office was beginning to tell on the government. An election would have to be held no later than July 1950, and the Conservatives talked increasingly during 1949 of 'setting the people free' from Labour controls, regulations and planning. Attlee decided to hold the general election in February 1950.

11.4 The General Elections of 1950 and 1951

The Labour Party narrowly survived the election of 1950 but, when Attlee had been in office for a further twenty months, it narrowly lost the election of October 1951 (see Table 10.1). In the 1950 campaign Labour virtually admitted that the task of reconstruction was still unfinished, calling its Manifesto *Let Us Win Through Together*. A more radical section of the Party clearly indicated its suspicion of the leadership in a pamphlet called *Keeping Left*. The Conservatives, for their part, focused their attack on nationalization and Labour's alleged restraints on liberties, rather than on the popular welfare state or Labour's foreign policy, with which they were in broad agreement (see Unit 12.2). *This Is the Road* (which would lead to 'freedom') was the theme of the Conservative Manifesto. Churchill and his supporters also attacked the Liberals, now led by Clement Davies, accusing them of splitting the anti-Labour vote. The Liberals attacked conscription, and urged the virtues of schemes for employers to share profits with their workers. *No Easy Way* was a prophetic title for the Liberal Manifesto. The vast majority of voters saw the election as a straight choice between Labour and Conservative. The turnout was high, almost 84 per cent, but there was little support for the Liberals. They lost 319 deposits, and the Party was only saved from financial ruin by its foresight in taking out insurance against such disastrous election results, at a premium of £5 000. There were now only nine Liberal MPs in the Commons.

The Labour government of 1950–1 was only a pale shadow of Attlee's earlier administration. It had little to offer at home, apart from completing the nationalizing of the iron and steel industry. Foreign problems tended to predominate, especially the war in Korea which began in June 1950 (see Unit 12.2(*c*)). One effect of this war was to upset Britain's balance of payments again (see Unit 11.2(*a*)) and, along with devaluation, it also added to rising prices within Britain. The value of money in Britain had fallen by about 20 per cent in the six years from 1945 to 1951, in spite of the government's efforts to hold prices down, and the trade unions were now demanding higher wages to compensate.

Attlee's second government also suffered from internal conflicts and ministerial changes. Attlee chose Gaitskell to succeed Cripps as Chancellor and Morrison to succeed Bevin as Foreign Secretary. He overlooked Aneurin Bevan and seemed clearly to prefer men on the right of the Labour Party. Bevan was the hero of a group of radical Bevanites and something of a thorn in the flesh of the Labour leadership, as well as being a passionate enemy of the Conservatives whom he once referred to as 'lower than vermin'. In 1951 he resigned from the government, along with Harold Wilson, who had taken over the Board of Trade in 1947. The issue at that moment was not wholly clear.

Bevan had been displeased when Attlee moved him to the Ministry of Labour, angered by Gaitskell's charges on NHS users and critical of the government's programme of rearmament. More broadly however, he was now out of sympathy with a Labour government which seemed to be losing its radical fire. The weariness of the government was all too evident. It was harassed by the Conservatives in the Commons, and forced to defend its tiny majority in many late-night sittings.

Attlee decided to submit to another general election in October 1951. There was still much loyalty to the government among the voters, but the Conservatives nevertheless won a majority of the seats in the Commons. It seemed that the Conservatives had done better than Labour in winning the collapsing Liberal vote (see Table 10.1). Attlee resigned and, at the age of seventy-seven, Churchill at last got his chance to lead a peacetime Conservative government.

Further Reading

Seaman, L.C.B.: *Post-Victorian Britain, 1902–1951*. Methuen (London, 1966), chapters 47–50 and 54.
Bartlett, C.J.: *A History of Postwar Britain, 1945–1974*. Longman (Harlow, 1977).
Chester, N.: *The Nationalization of British Industry, 1945–1951*. HMSO (London, 1977).
Childs, D.: *Britain since 1945, A Political History*. Benn (London, 1979).
Cootes, R.J.: *The Making of the Welfare State*. Longman (Harlow, 1966).
Eatwell, R.: *The 1945–1951 Labour Government*. Batsford (London, 1979).
Gregg, P.: *The Welfare State from 1945 to the Present Day*. Harrap (London, 1967).
Sked, A. and Cook, C.: *Post-War Britain, A Political History*. Penguin (Harmondsworth, 1979).
Stephens, M.: *Ernest Bevin, Unskilled Labourer and World Statesman*. Transport and General Workers' Union (London, 1981).
Williams, F.: *A Prime Minister Remembers*. Heinemann (London, 1961).

Documentary

Evans, L. and Pledger, P.J.: *Contemporary Sources and Opinions in Modern British History*, Volume One. Warne (London, 1967).

Exercises

1. 'Daunting postwar problems' (page 181): list the domestic problems Britain faced in the postwar years and, alongside *each*, state the policies with which the government aimed to deal with the problem. (After reading Unit 12, extend this list to include foreign and imperial problems and policies.)
2. List the industries nationalized in the years 1945–51. Asterisk those industries whose nationalization was particularly unpopular with the Conservatives. Suggest for *each* industry what benefits nationalization was expected to bring. Add two paragraphs to explain (*a*) why the Labour Party generally favoured nationalization and (*b*) why the Conservatives generally disapproved of it.
3. What does Table 11.1 show of Britain's international trade in the years 1946–51. Account for the *deficits* in 1946–7 and 1951, and for the *surpluses* in 1948–50.
4. Write a definition of the term *welfare state*. What measures during the 1940s

contributed to the establishing of such a state in Britain? Select the *three* of these measures you consider to have been the most important, arguing in support of your selection.

5. Show what part was played in government in the years 1945–51 by *each* of the following: Aneurin Bevan; Stafford Cripps; James Griffiths; Emmanuel Shinwell.

6. Summarize the reasons why a Labour voter in 1945 would in 1950 *either* have voted Labour again *or* have switched his/her vote to a different party.

7. 'The Labour government of 1950–1 was only a pale shadow of Attlee's earlier administration' (page 194). Examine the evidence which supports this opinion.

8. Making reference to Table 10.1, describe and account for the results of the general elections of 1950 and 1951.

Unit Twelve

Foreign and Imperial Policy under Labour, 1945–51

12.1 The Changing World

After the Second World War the world was increasingly dominated by the 'super powers', the USA and the USSR. No individual European country could now hope to compete with them in terms of military strength and political influence. The world became sharply divided between capitalists and communists, between the USA and the USSR, with the division quickly manifesting itself in a 'Cold War' of mutual suspicion, economic rivalry, propaganda blasts and counterblasts, and frantic jockeying for position, first in Europe and then further afield. Both the USA and the USSR had been Britain's wartime Allies (see Unit 9) but, after 1945, the Labour government quickly found that it had to choose between them.

A less immediately apparent result of the war was that it signalled the end of the colonial empires of the Europeans. Two barbaric twentieth-century wars had discredited Europeans in the eyes of non-Europeans. As Ndabaningi Sithole, a Rhodesian nationalist, wrote:

> African soldiers (fighting for their mother countries) saw white soldiers wounded, dying and dead. The bullet had the same effect on black and white alike. After spending four years hunting white enemy soldiers, the African never again regarded them as gods.

Europeans could no longer hope to assert their former claim to moral superiority. Both super powers condemned colonial empires as immoral and outdated, and nationalist ambitions for freedom were growing fast within almost all of Europe's colonies.

Britain therefore faced a period of painful readjustment. Creech Jones argued in 1945 that:

> The time has come when Britain must renounce an imperialistic relationship with the colonial peoples, and government must be inspired by new conceptions of purpose. . . . At bottom must be the idea of 'freedom'.

The Labour government was ready to grant freedom to India, though Churchill deplored 'the clattering down' of the British Empire. But India, in any case, was only the first dependency to clamour for independence. The clear-sighted already saw that the whole Empire would have to be decolonized, though traditionalists went on for many more years believing that this could somehow be avoided.

Britain had to find a new role for itself in the fast-changing postwar world. The first to tackle the problem was Bevin, Foreign Secretary from 1945 until his retirement with severe heart disease in 1951. Left-wingers in the Labour Party were uneasy about the way in which Bevin resolutely attached Britain to the American side in the Cold War. Conservatives, on the other hand, warmly supported this policy, which resulted in Britain becoming firmly committed to NATO (the North Atlantic Treaty Organization). There was a general welcome for Indian independence, but some misgivings arose about the way Bevin handled the problem of Palestine.

12.2 The Super Powers and Their Struggle

(a) The German Problem
Roosevelt, Stalin and Churchill (the Big Three) had met at Yalta, in the Crimea, in February 1945, to discuss the final stages of the war and the postwar world. They agreed that Germany would be de-nazified and stripped of its capacity to wage a future war; and that this should be achieved in the short term

Fig. 12.1 The Big Three during a lighter moment at Yalta, February 1945: Churchill, Roosevelt and Stalin

Fig. 12.2   The new Big Three at Potsdam, July 1945: Attlee, Truman and Stalin. The civilians behind the seated leaders, from left to right, Bevin, Byrnes and Molotov, the Foreign Ministers respectively of Britain, the USA and the Soviet Union. Bevin at least was prepared for tough negotiations with the Russians and, as a veteran trade unionist, he was used to hard bargaining

by dividing the country into zones of occupation. They also agreed to co-operate in setting up a new international organization, and a conference took place at San Francisco in April 1945, where the Charter of the United Nations Organization (UNO) was drafted. But there were many other details to be decided about postwar Europe, and the Big Three arranged to meet again at Potsdam, Berlin, in July 1945. By that time Germany had surrendered and, since Roosevelt was dead, President Truman represented the USA. The British general election in July 1945 meant that Attlee replaced Churchill at the Potsdam Conference towards the end of the month. With Attlee came Bevin who, with characteristic bluntness, promptly declared, 'I'm not going to have Britain barged about.'

Germany's future was still the main issue, however. Its division into four zones was confirmed. Berlin, deep inside the Russian Zone, was similarly divided into sectors. New arrangements were agreed for Germany's eastern frontier on the Line of the Oder and Neisse Rivers, thus transferring some German territory to Poland and part of East Prussia to the USSR. Germany was to pay reparations to those countries, like the USSR, which had suffered the heaviest devastation in the war. There was also an understanding that

200 Success in British History since 1914

Germany would be treated as a single economic unit, in spite of the zones. It was assumed that Germany would one day become a single free nation again, when it had shown itself to be trustworthy.

This was the heart of the problem. Stalin had no intention of allowing Germany ever again to threaten the USSR. He believed such a threat could be forestalled if Germany were prevented from returning to a capitalist system. The USA, however, had no intention of allowing Germany to become communist, and this was also Bevin's stance. After the Potsdam Conference it soon became obvious that the German problem had not been settled at all. The USA, the USSR, Britain and France established their zones, and their sectors of Berlin, but disputes soon followed. Stalin demanded reparations from the Western zones, since the Russian one was comparatively poor. This was agreed but, in return, the Russian Zone was to send foodstuffs to the West. When that did not happen, the West argued that it was having to support West Germany and thus, in effect, was helping to provide reparations for the USSR. France had more sympathy for the Russians than had the USA and Britain, but there were other anti-Russian complaints. In eastern Europe the USSR was promoting communist parties to power. It seemed that two Europes were rapidly developing. The western states had capitalist systems, most of them with democracies similar to those in the USA and Britain. The eastern states were becoming communist, on Stalinist lines. Truman expressed his exasperation in a letter to his Secretary of State, in January 1946, recommending 'an iron fist and strong language' in dealing with Stalin, and ending:

> We should insist on the return of our ships from Russia and force a settlement of the Lend-Lease debt of Russia. I'm tired of babying the Soviets.

Such attitudes only made the problem worse. The USSR was deeply suspicious of the capitalist powers, and its own actions could well have been merely defensive ones. Nevertheless, Churchill accurately* described the situation which was developing in Europe when he spoke at Fulton, in the USA, in March 1946:

> From Stettin in the Baltic, to Trieste in the Adriatic, an iron curtain has descended across the continent. Behind that line lie all the capitals of the ancient States of Central and Eastern Europe – Warsaw, Berlin, Prague, Vienna. . . . All these famous cities lie in the Soviet sphere . . . subject . . . to . . . increasing . . . control from Moscow.

The West began to believe that Stalin had almost unlimited ambitions to extend Russian power. At the end of 1946 the USA and Britain merged their zones of Germany as 'Bizonia' and, after some hesitation, the French attached their zone to it. A separate West Germany was in the making, while the Russians kept a tight hold on East Germany.

* Almost accurately: he meant Lübeck rather than Stettin.

Fig. 12.3 The division of Germany and the Iron Curtain

(b) The Atlantic Alliance

It was, therefore, impossible to sign a peace treaty with Germany like that at Versailles in 1919, though Bevin helped to bring about treaties with Germany's former allies, such as Italy, Hungary and Finland, in 1947. Britain's influence in world events was clearly shrinking, however. The Treaty of San Francisco, the settlement with Japan, was arranged almost singlehandedly by the USA; Britain, like other powers, was simply invited to sign it, in 1951. Even the role Britain chose for itself began to prove too much of a burden. For some time

Britain supported the non-communists in a civil war raging in Greece, but in February 1947 Bevin reported to the USA that the British government could no longer afford to sustain this effort. The USSR kept aloof from the Greek struggle, but the West tended to assume that any communist uprising must inevitably be part of a plot hatched in Moscow. Truman therefore took over from Britain the job of helping Greece and Turkey to resist communism. He demanded four hundred million dollars from the US Congress, 'to support free peoples who are resisting attempted subjugation by armed minorities or outside pressure'. This declaration of policy became known as the Truman Doctrine.

Marshall Aid followed hot on the heels of the Truman Doctrine. George Marshall, the US Secretary of State, offered American bounties to help friendly countries fight against the 'hunger, poverty, desperation, and chaos' which the US government assumed to be the breeding-grounds of communism. But Marshall insisted that Europeans must prepare a plan in order to make the best use of this Aid. Here was a role for Bevin. He welcomed the Marshall Plan and held preliminary talks about it with the French and Russians. The latter decided not to take part, but sixteen capitalist countries drew up the European Recovery Programme (ERP) by September 1947. The ERP was approved by the US government, and the Organization for European Economic Co-operation (OEEC) was set up in 1948 to implement it.

Western Europeans were also beginning to co-operate politically. Britain and France signed the Treaty of Dunkirk in 1947, promising mutual support against Germany more positively than they had ever done before the Second World War. This led to the Brussels Treaty Organization in 1948, in which Britain, France, Belgium, Luxemburg and the Netherlands pledged support for one another against any armed attack. This alliance was renamed the Western European Union (WEU) when Italy and Germany joined it in 1955. Britain thus undertook clearer obligations in Europe than before 1939, but it was becoming evident that the alliances were intended mainly as a defence against the USSR.

Relations between West and East in Germany deteriorated further. By June 1948 there were arguments about access to the Western sectors of Berlin, and when the West decided to introduce a new currency in their zones, the Russians refused to accept it in the Russian Zone. This provoked further arguments about treating Germany as a single economic unit. The dispute focused on Berlin, when Stalin suddenly severed all land links between Berlin and the West. One of his aims was probably to persuade the West to withdraw from the city, to end their embarrassing presence 'behind' the iron curtain. But the USA chose instead to mount the massive Berlin Airlift, pouring supplies into West Berlin in transport planes. The RAF helped in this mammoth task, carrying about a quarter of the supplies, which averaged more than 6 000 tons a day. Lives were lost in accidents but the Russians made no attempt to interfere and Stalin reopened the land links after about eleven months. Britain's part in the Airlift cost almost £9 million, but Bevin had shown that Britain was the USA's

Fig. 12.4 Supplies for West Berlin: British troops loading coal into a Dakota for airlifting from the British Zone to West Berlin at a critical time for the city's fuel stocks

staunchest ally in the Cold War. Other west European countries had preferred not to take part.

The crisis over Berlin, coupled with a communist takeover in Czechoslovakia, previously regarded as not wholly within Soviet influence, led to the setting up of NATO in April 1949. The Brussels Treaty Organization, the USA, Canada and several other states joined together for the joint defence of western Europe and the north Atlantic. Britain and its fellow-members of NATO asserted their determination:

> to safeguard the freedom, common heritage and civilization of their peoples, founded on the principles of democracy, individual liberty and the rule of law.

With the founding of the North Atlantic Treaty Organization, Bevin now had the satisfaction of knowing that the USA too was fully committed to the defence of western Europe and Britain. In May 1949 it was agreed to transform the American, British and French Zones in Germany into the new state of West Germany, known as the German Federal Republic. The Russians replied later in the year by setting up East Germany, the German Democratic Republic.

NATO claimed to be purely defensive and to offer no threat to the Russians. The Russians too claimed to be acting purely defensively when, six years later, they set up the communist counterpart of NATO, the Warsaw Pact. Both sides remained heavily armed. Until the end of the Korean War, in 1953, Britain maintained its armed services at around 400 000 men, relying on National Service to provide sufficient recruits since there were too few volunteers. Government spending on defence was a drain on Britain's resources. Attlee's government never achieved its target of reducing defence costs to 5 per cent of the annual Gross National Product. Only in 1947 did it cut spending to below £1 000 million and, by 1951, a new programme set the costs at some £4 700 million over the next three years. This caused much disquiet in the Labour Party: many thought the money could have been better spent. But Bevin had few doubts. He wholeheartedly committed both himself and Britain to the Atlantic Alliance against communism.

Britain held back from other movements towards unity in western Europe, however. Bevin joined the Council of Europe in 1949 but, although it eventually set up a Commission and Court of Human Rights, it was little more than a debating society. He stood aside from the planning of the European Coal and Steel Community (ECSC), and his successors also refused to join when the ECSC was set up in 1952. Membership would have involved some loss of national independence in making decisions about these industries, which was unacceptable to the British government. Bevin thus charted another course for Britain to follow. Britain did not seek membership of the ECSC, and the European Economic Community (EEC) which developed from it, until many years later (see Unit 20.3).

(c) China, Korea and Iran

Bevin took a different path from that of the USA on one issue. In 1949 Mao Tse-tung and the Chinese Communist Party completed the overthrow of Chiang Kai-shek, and set up the People's Republic of China. Mao now ruled some six hundred million Chinese, while Chiang retreated to the comparatively tiny island of Taiwan (Formosa). The USA insisted that Chiang was still the rightful ruler of China and assumed, against all the evidence, that Mao must be a puppet of Moscow. Bevin took a more sensible view, and recognized the Communist government of China. He would also have supported Red China's admission to the United Nations Organization, but the USA rallied votes to prevent this. Chiang Kai-shek continued to occupy China's seat in the UN Security Council, and Communist China was not admitted until 1971.

When Japan was defeated in 1945, Korea had been divided. For some time the USSR occupied the North and the USA the South; both then withdrew, leaving a communist North and a capitalist South. In 1950 North Korea attacked South Korea, to the great indignation of the Americans. The matter was referred to the United Nations Security Council, where the five major Allies in the Second World War (the USA, the USSR, Britain, France and China) held permanent seats and had the right of veto. At that moment, however, the USSR was absent from the Security Council, protesting at the exclusion of Red China. The Council could therefore condemn North Korea for aggression and, on 27 July 1950, it called upon UN members to assist South

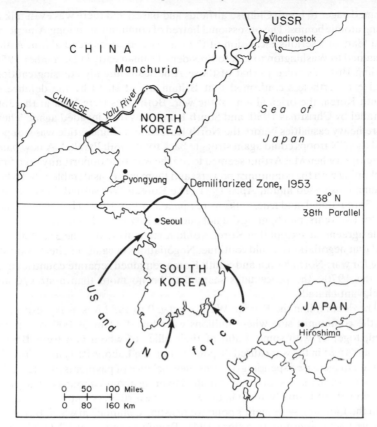

Fig. 12.5 The division of Korea

Korea. The USA had begun to do so already, pouring in men and supplies. More than a dozen other nations now sent troops, to serve under General MacArthur and to drive back the North Koreans. Bevin made sure that Britain was one of these nations. The USSR, however, kept out of the conflict. Within three months the North Koreans had been driven back to the 38th Parallel, and almost all of South Korea had been liberated.

At the insistence of the USA, and with British support, the United Nations Organization now agreed to change the aims of the war: North Korea would be invaded in order to reunite the whole country under an 'acceptable' system. By November UN forces were nearing the Yalu River which divided North Korea from Communist China. They were at once confronted by well over 200 000 'Chinese People's Volunteers', who had rushed from China to help the North Koreans. The Americans and their allies were flung into rapid retreat, and that triggered off heated debates as to what to do about Red China. MacArthur seemed eager to bomb Chinese airfields and bases, and there was even talk of using atomic bombs. The obsessional hatred of communism among Americans and fears of a serious escalation of the war caused widespread alarm. Attlee hastened to Washington to talk to President Truman early in December 1950, adding Britain's voice to that of those Americans already advising caution. Attlee nevertheless confirmed that Britain would stand by the defence of South Korea, the original aim of the war. Both sides were back at the 38th Parallel by Christmas 1950, and South Korea was then invaded again. There were heavy casualties before the North Korean and Chinese tide was stopped and the UN troops could again struggle back to the 38th Parallel. A new panic developed when MacArthur seemed to see the war as an opportunity for a final reckoning with the communist powers, and there was considerable relief when Truman dismissed him in April 1951. The Korean War settled down around the 38th Parallel, and truce talks were opened in July 1951. The talks dragged on for two years, and fighting did not end until July 1953. Even then there was little agreement, except that Korea would remain divided at the 38th Parallel, and that negotiations would continue. Negotiations became, in effect, a substitute for war: North Korea and South Korea remained separate countries and, by the 1970s, the peace talks seemed to be no more than a strange and irrelevant charade.

The death toll in the Korean War from 1950 to 1953 was heavy, especially on the communist side where millions were killed. Over 30 000 Americans died, together with some 4 500 of their allies of whom 686 were British. Britain's part in the war caused disputes within the Labour Party and, since the war led to increased spending on arms, new balance of payments problems and further rises in the cost of living, it helped to bring about Labour's defeat in the election of 1951. Involvement in the war was, nevertheless, entirely in keeping with the Labour government's policy of resisting communism which Bevin had pursued with determination since 1945. Britain's support of UNO disguised only thinly the fact that Britain was, in effect, supporting the USA. The Conservatives agreed with this policy and, in 1954, Churchill's government committed Britain to membership of the South-East Asia Treaty Organization (SEATO), a counterpart of NATO to defend South-East Asia against communism.

The example of Persia (now known as Iran) showed that assumptions about communist expansionism were not always correct, however. Britain and the USSR had guaranteed the country's independence in 1942, when Persia declared war on the Axis powers. After the end of the Second World War, Russian troops remained in Azerbaijan, where Persian communists were trying to set up a republic, free from the rule of the Shah. Britain took the matter to UNO. The Russians withdrew, leaving the communists of Azerbaijan to be crushed by the Persian government in 1949.

A different problem for Attlee's government arose in Persia in 1951, providing a foretaste of the readjustments Britain had to make in a world of developing nations. Dr Musaddiq was Persia's new Prime Minister in 1951 and, between fainting fits and tears, he pursued a vendetta against foreign interests in his country. The Anglo-Persian Oil Company was nationalized. British personnel had to be withdrawn and the refinery at Abadan was abandoned. Morrison could do little about it, but he was fiercely criticized for not protecting British interests in Persian oil. The matter could not be settled until 1954, when Churchill's government was able to take advantage of further changes in Persia's politics. An agreement was negotiated, giving Britain and other capitalist countries a new stake in the Persian oil industry, but Persian nationalists continued to resent it. The wider question raised by the issue was that of the conflict of interests between the foreign investments of the comparatively rich capitalist powers, such as Britain, and the developing nations, such as Persia, which wanted to reap the full benefit from their own resources, in this case oil. A similar problem was to arise in 1956, when the Egyptian government nationalized the Suez Canal Company (see Unit 14.1(b)). Moreover, a Moslem uprising in Iran in 1978 overthrew the Shah, and again led to the expulsion of foreign oil companies.

12.3 The Empire and Commonwealth

(a) Indian Independence
Indians continued to resent British government and the way that India had been involved in the Second World War in 1939 without consultation (see Unit 8.1(a)). The British again made arrests, to stifle their protests. Gandhi was imprisoned again, in 1942, when his simple message to the British was 'Quit India'. He was released two years later and, by that time, had spent more than 2 000 days in British jails at various periods in his life, and had seen his wife Kasturba die in prison. Almost as soon as the war began, however, the British tried to buy Indian loyalty with promises of Dominion status when it ended. Cripps led a mission to India in 1942, carrying that message. In general, Britain received valuable help from India, especially in the war against Japan, but Indian independence could not be delayed much longer. Attlee's government intended to grant it. Pethick Lawrence, the Secretary for India, and Cripps led a new mission to work out the details, but they found the divisions in India between Hindus and Moslems now presented a serious obstacle. Pethick Lawrence broadcast to the British people in May 1946:

> During our stay in India we have tried by every means to secure such an accommodation between the parties as would enable constitution-making to proceed. Recently we were able to bring them together at Simla in a conference with ourselves, but . . . it was not found possible to reach complete agreement.

The Moslem League, led by Jinnah, insisted on a separate Moslem state in Pakistan. The Indian National Congress and the Hindus demanded a single independent India. Though a Hindu and a leading member of Congress, Gandhi worked strenuously for tolerance and goodwill. But Jinnah remained inflexible, 'a man with a difficulty for every solution'. The Moslem cry was 'Pakistan or Perish', and 16 August 1946 was named Direct Action Day, to protest against the appointment of Nehru, the leader of Congress, as India's Prime Minister. When Nehru took office the Moslems put out black flags of mourning, and the north of the Indian subcontinent seemed to be on the brink of civil war. Even Gandhi could only check the violence and killing in his own immediate vicinity. Attlee called the Indian leaders to London, but still no agreement could be achieved. He therefore resorted to shock tactics, declaring in February 1947 that a solution must be found by June 1948, when the British would no longer be responsible for India. He also appointed Lord Mountbatten as Viceroy in place of Lord Wavell, relying on Mountbatten's popularity, for he had helped to defend India from the Japanese during the war.

Mountbatten took the view that there was no alternative to division, rightly anticipating that Congress would accept this in preference to civil war. He also insisted that action must be swift. A Bill was quickly prepared for the British parliament, and British rule in India ended on 15 August 1947. Congress accepted partition by 153 votes to 29, and Nehru became the Prime Minister of independent India, while Jinnah became the Governor-General of independent Pakistan. On the eve of the transfer of power, Nehru addressed the Indian parliament:

> Long years ago we made a tryst with destiny, and now the time comes when we shall redeem our pledge. . . . At the stroke of the midnight hour, while the world sleeps, India will awake to life and freedom. A moment comes, which comes but rarely in history, when we step from the old to the new, when an age ends.

The moment was indeed historic. Not only was it a moment of rebirth for the more than four hundred million people of the Indian subcontinent, it marked the beginning of the decolonization of Britain's vast non-white Empire, and was an achievement in which Attlee's government took much pride. *The Times* reviewed what it saw as the past strengths of British rule in India, and took pleasure from the fact that both India and Pakistan joined the Commonwealth of Nations:

> The Indian Empire disappears from the political map and the circle of the Dominions is enlarged in idea as well as in fact by the admission of two Asiatic States which, as the Viceroy said . . . yesterday, derive from their own ancient and lofty civilizations their title to the full sovereign privileges implicit in Dominion status.

India, in fact, broke new ground again in 1950 when, though it became a Republic, it won approval for remaining within the Commonwealth. Until that time it had been assumed that states within the Commonwealth always retained the British monarchy. Pakistan also became a Republic in 1956, likewise at that time staying within the Commonwealth, although it withdrew in 1972 in protest at the admission of Bangladesh. Meanwhile, independence and mem-

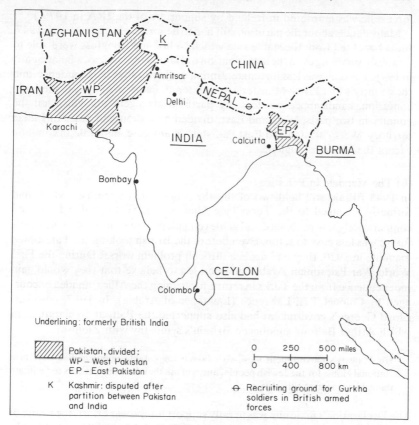

Fig. 12.6 The partition of the Indian subcontinent

bership of the Commonwealth were also granted to Ceylon, in 1948, and the British left Burma, which chose not to join the Commonwealth.

Although Labour politicians congratulated themselves on this radical decolonization of the Indian Empire, the haste with which the British left the subcontinent in 1947 contributed to the fact that the transfer of power was accompanied by much suffering. Some twelve million people became refugees, fleeing to the safety of Moslem communities in Pakistan or Hindu communities in India. Probably about a quarter of a million were killed in religious slaughter, since it took time for the new authorities to impose order. One can only speculate on whether the British might have handled the transfer of power more efficiently. The difficulties were great, and the British were under pressure to depart quickly; and, where deeply-rooted religious traditions are in conflict with one another, hysteria and intolerance run high and may well defy rational political solutions. (Mountbatten himself was the victim of irrational forces: he was murdered in Ireland by supporters of the IRA in 1979.)

Many details about the partition still had to be sorted out after August 1947. India benefited from the stable rule which Nehru and Congress were able to establish, surviving even the assassination of Gandhi by a religious fanatic early in 1948. Pakistan was less fortunate. Jinnah died soon after independence, and the country's first Prime Minister was murdered. Pakistan quickly drifted into confusion, handicapped not least by partition arrangements which left the country in two parts, West and East, divided by a thousand miles of Indian territory. West Pakistan and East Pakistan, in any case, had little in common except the Moslem religion.

(b) The Mandate in Palestine

In 1945 Britain still held two of the three mandated territories which had formerly belonged to the Turks (see Unit 4.1(*a*)). Transjordan presented comparatively few problems, and achieved independence in 1946. Palestine's future was less easy to settle. Even before the British took up the Palestinian mandate in 1920, they had made a difficult problem worse. During the First World War Palestinian Arabs had been led to believe that they would gain independence from the Turks in return for helping the Allies, an idea encouraged by Colonel T.E. Lawrence (Lawrence of Arabia). In 1917, however, Lloyd George's government had also supported the Balfour Declaration, in which Arthur Balfour announced Britain's sympathy with Zionism:

His Majesty's Government view with favour the establishment in Palestine of a National Home for the Jewish people, and will use their best endeavours to facilitate the achievement of this object.

The Declaration's main aim was to rally support for the war effort; the future of Palestine had not been clearly thought out. Balfour referred only vaguely to the rights of non-Jews, and he did not squarely face the fact that Zionists fully intended to set up a Jewish state in Palestine, since it was a land with which the Jews had strong religious and historical ties. Churchill, as Colonial Secretary in 1922, attempted a further definition of British policy. Balfour's 'National Home', he asserted, did not actually mean a 'National State', and the British had not intended that Palestine should become 'wholly Jewish'. But Britain was now facing the problem that both Jews and Arabs expected the mandate to lead to an independent Palestine, of which both peoples wanted exclusive control.

The British faced continuous arguments about the extent of Jewish immigration into Palestine, and continuous difficulties about the country's constitutional development. It also seemed that British governments could not make up their minds about what they were trying to achieve. In 1922 there were almost 600 000 Arabs but fewer than 100 000 Jews in Palestine. By 1928 the number of Jews had risen to 150 000. MacDonald decided to restrict further Jewish immigration, but then reversed this policy after the 1931 election. By 1937 there were 400 000 Palestinian Jews, and the policies of the Nazis in

Germany were steadily increasing the pressures on Jews to emigrate from Europe. The British imposed new restrictions on entry into Palestine, with a humbug-like effort to limit immigration to Jews who were wealthy. The Jews inside Palestine often bought land from absentee Arab landlords, and further inflamed racial hostility by evicting poor Arab tenants. From 1936 many Arabs were in revolt, resorting to guerilla warfare, while the Jews hit back with terrorist gangs. The British sent 20 000 troops to try to keep the peace, and set up the Peel Commission. But the Peel Report recommended partitioning Palestine, which was unacceptable to Jews and Arabs alike. Chamberlain then renounced partition and produced a new White Paper, promising first the reduction and then the stopping of Jewish immigration, and a new Palestinian

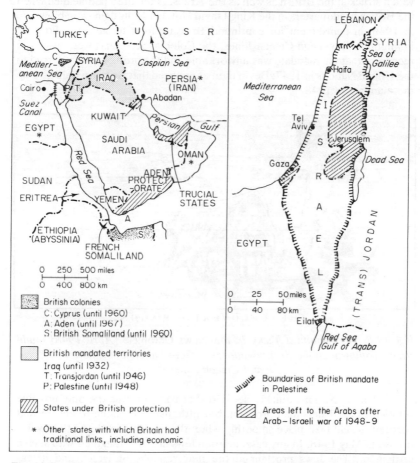

*Fig. 12.7   The Middle East: (a) British interests in the Middle East after 1945
(b) The mandate in Palestine*

constitution in ten years with rights guaranteed both for Jews and Arabs. This too was almost universally rejected, but the outbreak of war in Europe in 1939 enabled the British to shelve the Palestinian problem. The Arabs remained embittered and restless, not least because Jewish immigration continued. The Jews supported the war against Nazism, but they also prepared for their takeover of Palestine.

This was the problem the Labour government inherited in 1945. By that time, however, Nazi attempts to exterminate the Jews had created widespread emotional support for Zionism, and Britain came under pressure from the USA to admit even more Jewish refugees to Palestine. Within Palestine the Jews had organized more ferocious terrorist groups, including the Stern Gang which struck at the British as well as the Arabs. A hundred people died when the British headquarters in the King David Hotel in Jerusalem were blown up in 1946, in punishment for continued British efforts to stem the flood of immigrants. Bevin and Creech Jones, the Colonial Secretary, were forced to recognize that the mandate was unworkable and the problem was referred to the United Nations in 1947; Bevin then announced that Britain would give up the mandate in 1948.

THE   UNCOVERED   WAGON

Fig. 12.8 The cartoonist Vicky in the News Chronicle *(April 1948) made critical comment on the British withdrawal from Palestine, the policy of Bevin and Creech Jones*

The United Nations quickly decided that partition was the only possible solution to the Palestinian problem, but little had been done to ensure that partition would take place smoothly when the British completed their withdrawal in May 1948. In any case, neither Jews nor Arabs agreed with such a settlement. The Jews proclaimed the new republic of Israel, and it was promptly attacked by a coalition of Arab states, in the first of the Arab–Israeli wars. When Count Bernadotte arrived in Jerusalem to try to mediate on behalf of UNO, he was murdered by Jewish terrorists. The Arabs had to admit defeat in February 1949, by which time Israel had taken over the lion's share of Palestine. About a million Arabs had fled, most of them becoming homeless refugees. Ten years later, Israel had a population of almost two million Jews, outnumbering the remaining Arabs by about ten to one. Britain's abandonment of Palestine had been hasty and impatient but the problem was partly the legacy of pre-war neglect in many areas, which Attlee's government had inherited.

(c) Colonies and Dominions

There were problems elsewhere in the British Empire after 1945, but nationalist pressures for independence were as yet less advanced than in the Indian subcontinent and Palestine. In keeping with the Colonial Development Act of 1940, the Labour government made some effort to improve living standards in the colonies, especially in the West Indies, where the Moyne Report on the eve of the Second World War had painted a dismal picture of poverty, squalor, unemployment and juvenile delinquency. The whole Empire, as Lloyd George had put it, resembled a 'vast slum'. But it was difficult to find the money for the hospitals, schools, communications and social services that were needed. Here too was a history of neglect. Nehru complained that many of India's problems had grown up during British rule. As a nationalist he perhaps had reason to exaggerate, but among the problems he listed were:

> the lack of industry and neglect of agriculture; the extreme backwardness in the social services; and, above all, the tragic poverty of the people.

Attlee's government, struggling with the British economy, could only scratch the surface of this problem in the Empire as a whole.

Meanwhile, Jamaica had achieved a new constitution in 1944, moving a little nearer to independence, and the Labour government encouraged discussions about the future of the whole of the British West Indies, perhaps in a single federation. There was little immediate progress either here or in the rest of the Empire, though India's independence suggested that other new nations would shortly emerge. The British Empire after 1945 was still generally quiet, unlike the Dutch Empire in Indonesia and the French Empire in Indochina. One exception was Malaya where a communist uprising in 1948 forced the British to embark on more than ten years of jungle warfare against a guerilla army.

The British Commonwealth of Nations was now changing. The Republic of Ireland resigned in 1949 (see Unit 8.1(b)), but the admission of India, Pakistan and Ceylon meant that the Commonwealth was no longer a white man's club. Patrick Gordon Walker, Britain's Commonwealth Secretary in 1950, declared, 'We are today as much an Asian as a Western Commonwealth.' In that year Britain and other members of the Commonwealth took the lead in setting up the Colombo Plan, to assist the development of states in southern Asia with money, expertise and training facilities. The Plan was supported by the USA, and it was a successful forerunner of many such organizations to help the poorer nations. In due course it became an important feature of the Commonwealth that its more prosperous members assisted the weaker. As membership of the Commonwealth grew with the admission of more new nations from 1957 onwards, it developed a unique understanding of the problems of development, and of the relationships in the modern world between wealthy and poor countries, and between whites and non-whites. Beginning with the independence of India, and in spite of the sometimes sorry history of the British Empire, the Commonwealth carried into the late twentieth century quite remarkable mutual goodwill between Britain and its former colonies. Though he had been critical of British rule in India, Nehru declared in 1950:

> Member nations of this Commonwealth sometimes disagree . . . sometimes pull in different directions; nevertheless the basic fact remains that they meet as friends, try to understand each other and try, as far as possible, to find a common way of working.

This was exactly how Attlee's government wished the developing Commonwealth of Nations to be.

Further Reading

Seaman, L.C.B.: *Post-Victorian Britain, 1902–1951*. Methuen (London, 1966), chapters 51–3.
Barker, E.: *Britain and a Divided Europe, 1945–1970*. Weidenfeld and Nicolson (London, 1971).
Crane, E.A. and Roy, W.T.: *Birth of the Indian Nations*. Heinemann (London, 1972).
Medlicott, W.N.: *British Foreign Policy since Versailles*. Methuen (London, 1968).
Roberts, E.M.: *Gandhi, Nehru and Modern India*. Methuen (London, 1975).
Watson, J.B.: *Empire to Commonwealth, 1919–1970*. Dent (London, 1971).
Watson, J.B.: *Success in Twentieth Century World Affairs*. John Murray (London, 3rd edn. 1984).
Williams, F.: *Ernest Bevin*. Hutchinson (London, 1952).

Documentary

Morgan, R.: *The Unsettled Peace*. BBC Publications (London, 1974).

Exercises

1. Why did different representatives from Britain attend the Conferences to which Figs 12.1 and 12.2 refer? What did these Conferences meet to decide? What European problems did they fail to solve?
2. Explain the divisions of Germany, Austria and Korea shown on Figs 12.3 and 12.5. How did these divisions involve Britain in international problems?
3. Making reference to Fig. 12.3, show what you understand by the 'iron curtain' of which Churchill spoke (page 200), and by 'Bizonia' (page 200). How would you use this map to explain the need for the Berlin Airlift of 1948–9?
4. What commitments in Europe did Britain undertake in the postwar years? How did this policy compare with Britain's policy towards European commitments between 1918 and 1939?

5. Making use of the Index to this book and of the biography in Alan Palmer's *Dictionary of Twentieth-Century History*, summarize the career and achievements of Ernest Bevin. What guidelines for future British policy overseas did Bevin establish in the years 1945–51?

6. 'The beginning of the decolonization of Britain's vast non-white Empire' (page 208): show what you understand by *decolonization*. Why did such decolonization follow the Second World War and why did it begin in the Indian subcontinent?

7. Making use of the Index to this book, trace the history of India from 1917 to independence and show the parts played in it by Gandhi and Nehru.

8. 'Hasty and impatient' (page 213): how far do you agree with this description of the way in which Britain gave up control of Palestine? Explain the cartoonist's comment on this withdrawal (Fig. 12.8). How far could the phrase 'hasty and impatient' also be applied to the way in which Britain gave up control of the Indian subcontinent.

9. 'The British Commonwealth of Nations was now changing' (page 213): what was the British Commonwealth of Nations, and how had it changed by 1951?

10. Making use of the Index to this book, outline Clement Attlee's career and main achievements by 1951. What do you consider were his distinctive personal qualities? Compare what you have written with Alan Palmer's biography in the *Dictionary of Twentieth-Century History* or with a good encyclopaedia.

Unit Thirteen

Politics and the Economy: Conservative Government, 1951–64

13.1 Elections, Economics and Ministers

(a) The Economy and Political Arguments

Having won the general election of 1951, the Conservatives went on to win those of 1955 and 1959 too, and so remained in power for thirteen years. Conservative supporters spoke enthusiastically of an 'age of affluence' in these years, and Harold Macmillan once remarked that the British 'had never had it so good'. 'Life is Better under the Conservatives' was the message at the 1959 general election. In 1964, however, Labour critics charged the Conservatives with 'thirteen wasted years', during which fundamental economic problems had been neglected. Both sides supported their claims with mountains of statistics.

The Conservatives pointed to the boom in housebuilding, the increasing ownership of television sets, motor cars and other goods once considered luxuries, and increased spending in areas such as education, with the opening of new universities. They showed that Britain's GNP had grown by some 50 per cent during the period 1951–64, and that people were earning more, with incomes running ahead of rises in prices. Unemployment remained low, only marginally higher than the immediate postwar years, and seldom climbing above 500 000. Similarly, the number of days lost in strikes was not much higher than during Attlee's years of government, though there were occasional outbursts of industrial strife. Moreover, the Conservatives were able to show that the balance of payments was usually in surplus, in spite of some alarming deficits from time to time – in 1955, 1960–1, and again in 1964.

Trade deficits were seized on by the Conservatives' opponents, who argued that they were evidence of underlying problems. Only in one year – 1956 – had Britain achieved a surplus on its visible trade, and they maintained that Britain's trading position was worsening. Its share of the world's total export trade was about 11 per cent in the late 1940s, but it had fallen to about 8 per cent by 1964. Its share of the world's exports of industrial goods fell even more markedly, from over 20 per cent in 1951 to below 15 per cent in 1964. This decline was linked with Britain's comparatively low rate of growth (see Table 13.1, showing Britain's performance after 1951 compared with that of other developed countries). Britain's rising standard of living seemed not fully to be supported by a matching rise in output and this had an inflationary effect: the value of money in Britain fell by more than a third in the years 1951–64. Production costs had risen so British exports became less competitive.

Labour accused the Conservatives of exercising too little control over the economy. The Conservatives retorted that Labour wanted far too many regulations. This issue was to remain fundamental to British politics in the postwar years. In the 1950s and 1960s, however, all parties accepted that government must intervene more than it had before 1939. There were some who argued that the usefulness of such intervention was over-rated, and that governments might unintentionally make matters worse. Preserving jobs in outdated industries, for example, while avoiding unemployment in the short run, might simply mean inefficient use of manpower, making it more difficult for Britain to stand up to foreign competition. Conservative Chancellors nevertheless busied themselves with efforts to regulate the economy, and the majority of critics, especially on the Opposition benches of the House of Commons, complained not that they tried but that they did not try hard enough.

Table 13.1 Average annual growth rates, 1951–76

	Percentage of Gross Domestic Product*
Japan	8.5
West Germany	5.5
Italy	4.9
France	4.8
USA	3.1
Britain	**2.5**

* at 1970 prices
Source: Treasury *Economic Progress Report*, July 1978.

(*b*) **Prime Ministers and Chancellors**
The rising standard of living certainly helped to keep the Conservatives in power from 1951 until 1964. Table 13.2 shows some of the chief ministers during these thirteen years. Churchill retired from office in 1955 to spend his remaining ten years on the back benches, and it was Eden who led the Conservatives to success in the general election of 1955. He resigned as Prime Minister in January 1957, in poor health and in the wake of the Suez Crisis (see Unit 14.1(*b*)), and Harold Macmillan was Prime Minister for the next six years.

In the 1930s Macmillan had sat in the Commons as the MP for Stockton-on-Tees, where he had first-hand experience of the results of the Depression. As early as 1933 he tried to prod the National government into action with his *Reconstruction: A Plea for a National Policy*. He supported planning and was strongly in favour of social reform. In the late 1930s he was also strongly critical

of Chamberlain, and of the government's hesitant policies towards rearmament and the European dictators. A firm supporter of Churchill, Macmillan's
rise was rapid during the 1950s (see Unit 13.2). As Prime Minister, he was
often known to the nation as 'Supermac', inspiring not only devotion among
Conservatives but even some affection among their opponents.

Macmillan's retirement in 1963 caused problems for the Conservative Party.
Unlike other parties, the Conservatives had no machinery for electing their
leader until 1965. Conservative leaders 'emerged' as the result of 'consultation'. When Lord Home emerged in 1963, it was a final blow to the ambitions
of R.A. (Rab) Butler who had been consistently overlooked. Table 13.2 shows
some of the offices Butler held, and he had also been Lord Privy Seal and
Home Secretary in the late 1950s and Macmillan's Deputy Prime Minister in
1962. The policy pursued by Butler when Chancellor of the Exchequer was so
similar to that of Labour's Gaitskell that the term *Butskellism* was coined.
Butskellism implied moderation and, just as Gaitskell had his critics on the
Labour left, so Butler's moderation was not much to the liking of doctrinaire
right-wing Conservatives. The choice of Home as leader was a rebuff to Butler.
It was probably also a disservice to the Conservative Party.

"NOW, I'LL TAKE OFF MY CORONET TO GIVE THE PARTY THAT NEW, MODERN,
PROGRESSIVE IMAGE."

*Fig. 13.1 A less than flattering greeting to Lord Home, the new Conservative
leader, from Vicky in the* Evening Standard, *October 1963. The cartoonist's
sympathies perhaps lay with the luckless Butler whom the Conservatives again
rejected*

Home had to renounce his peerage and win election to the Commons as Alec Douglas-Home.* His selection as their leader revived the old view of the Conservatives as an aristocratic party. Moreover, the new Prime Minister's public reference to his use of matchsticks when trying to understand economic problems, though it perhaps evoked sympathy, hardly inspired confidence. Nor did Douglas-Home promote his cause by talk of making a 'donation' to help retirement pensioners; in the welfare state, they had learned to regard their pensions as a right. The loss of the general election of 1964 proved fatal to Douglas-Home's leadership. The Conservatives quickly set up machinery for electing a leader and Edward Heath, a former grammar school boy, was the successful candidate defeating his main rival, Reginald Maudling. Butler, meanwhile, had left the Commons.

Table 13.2 Conservative ministries, 1951–64

Date	Prime Minister	Chancellor of the Exchequer	Foreign Secretary
1951–5	Churchill	Butler	Eden
1955–7	Eden	Butler (1955) Macmillan (1955–7)	Macmillan (1955) Lloyd (1955–7)
1957–63	Macmillan	Thorneycroft (1957–8) Heathcote Amory (1958–61) Lloyd (1961–2) Maudling (1962–3)	Lloyd (1957–60) Douglas-Home (1960–3)
1963–4	Douglas-Home	Maudling	Butler

In the early 1950s, however, it was Butler who had begun the 'Stop-Go' policies for which Conservative Chancellors became renowned. To deal with balance of payments deficits, they checked the demand for imported goods by monetary and tax policies which imposed restraints on purchasing power (the policy of 'Stop'). Once Britain's trade position had improved these restraints were lifted so people had more money to spend (the policy of 'Go'). Butler inherited a balance of payments deficit in 1951 (see Unit 11.2(a) and Table 11.1), and he began with 'Stop'. In 1953 he was ready for 'Go', and it became a pattern that 'Go' policies had a habit of coinciding with general elections. Butler's budget of 1955 helped to sustain the Conservative vote in that year

* This trail was blazed in 1960 by Labour MP Anthony Wedgwood Benn, who preferred to remain in the House of Commons rather than inherit his father's title as Lord Stansgate. Until Benn fought for and won this right, peerages could not be renounced.

(see Table 10.1), but it also led to a new trade deficit of over £150 million. Similarly, Heathcote Amory's 'Go' helped the Conservatives to win the election of 1959, but led to a deficit of over £260 million in 1960. Maudling made a 'run for growth' with more 'Go' after 1962, and the deficit in 1964 was almost £400 million. Maudling had hoped that this policy might help to stimulate investment in British industry and thus increase GDP, but the balance of payments deficit proved an electoral handicap in the election of 1964 and the Conservatives were defeated.

The fact was that, as fast as money was put into people's pockets, they tended to spend it on imported goods – further evidence that Britain's own output was not competitive enough. By 1964 it was beginning to be argued that wages were too high and were driving up the costs of production; eventually this led to more industrial conflicts, not least because wages in Britain were often low compared with those in other developed countries. But Britain's affluence went into buying consumer goods rather than into investment for industrial modernization and expansion. There were growing doubts about the efficiency of Conservative management, and about the extent to which the British economy had made any real progress since Stafford Cripps and the years of Austerity. After 1964, indeed, far from having solved its economic problems, it seemed that Britain began to plunge into difficulties more deeply and more often.

13.2 Conservative Freedom

When King George VI died in February 1952, soon after the Conservative success in the general election of 1951, and Queen Elizabeth II inherited the throne, there was optimistic talk of a new Elizabethan age. The Conservatives believed the new age should be built on freedom, with the demolition of many of the controls and regulations brought in by Attlee's government. In fact Wilson, at the Board of Trade, had already made a 'bonfire of controls' in 1949, and it was logical that further relaxation would follow as Britain recovered from the effects of the Second World War. The Conservatives did not rush this. Gradually the remaining controls on scarce resources, such as building materials, were lifted by Churchill's government, and all food rationing was ended during 1954.

It took another six years to get rid of conscription, however, since that would lead to a serious reduction in the manpower of the armed forces. To make up for this the Conservatives decided that Britain should continue as a nuclear power, and add hydrogen bombs to atomic bombs. Randolph Churchill, Winston's son, welcomed the decision and declared in 1958:

> Britain can knock down twelve cities in the region of Stalingrad and Moscow from bases in Britain, and another dozen in the Crimea from bases in Cyprus. . . . We are a major power again.

Fig. 13.2 London to Aldermaston march, April 1958: Aldermaston, near Reading, was made the target of CND protests since it was the site of Britain's Atomic Weapons Research Establishment. British governments nevertheless clung to Britain's nuclear weaponry

The government argued that nuclear weapons made it possible to curb spending on defence, but others were less happy than Randolph Churchill. The Liberals and some members of the Labour Party thought it immoral to build such weapons, and the Campaign for Nuclear Disarmament (CND) mounted a spirited, but unsuccessful, protest movement.

There were protests, too, at the Rent Act of 1957, which followed severe cuts in government subsidies for council house building. The Rent Act removed controls on the rents that many private landlords could charge. The welfare state was left intact, however. Graduated pensions were introduced in 1959, to allow those with higher earnings to qualify for a higher retirement pension by paying larger contributions. Otherwise, no major changes were made. A slightly larger proportion of the GNP was devoted to social security and the Health Service after 1957, but only slow progress was made in modernizing hospitals and building health centres.

More dramatic successes were achieved in housebuilding. The Conservatives had asserted in 1951 that housing was 'the first of the social services', and had set a target of 300 000 new homes a year. Churchill appointed Harold

Macmillan the Minister of Local Government and Planning, and made him responsible for the building programme. He also hinted strongly that Macmillan's future career would depend on his success. The Town Development Act was passed in 1952 to assist the growth of small towns, such as Bletchley, willing to help in re-housing overcrowded city dwellers. But Macmillan's main task was to encourage local authorities and private enterprise to build as many new homes as possible. The target figure was reached in 1953, when some 240 000 council homes and over 70 000 private homes were built. The Conservatives achieved their target almost annually thereafter, though council building declined until after the general election of 1964. The shift towards private building was deliberate, since it was part of the Conservative belief in freedom to encourage more people to become owner-occupiers. Nevertheless, higher interest rates had to be paid on mortgages. In 1951 the Conservatives had immediately begun to use Bank Rate as an instrument of economic policy, bringing to an end the age of cheap money which had lasted since 1932 (see Unit 5.4). Bank Rate had remained at only 2 per cent, even during the years of Austerity, but it was now adjusted frequently, and it reached 7 per cent several times during the years 1957–64. Macmillan's success with housing had meanwhile brought him rapid advancement. In 1954–5 he was successively Minister of Defence, Foreign Secretary and Chancellor of the Exchequer. He became Prime Minister in 1957, surrendering the office only when forced to retire because of failing health. He presided over British affairs with a carefully cultivated, urbane and even leisurely style that was almost Edwardian, giving the impression of one born to rule. He seemed to Labour supporters to symbolize the almost casual arrogance of Britain's well-entrenched patrician classes, and critics who alleged that a strong connection existed between social divisions and private education in Britain noted that Macmillan was an old Etonian.

An attack on the nationalized industries was expected as part of government policy, since the Conservatives strongly preferred private enterprise. As promised, they denationalized the iron and steel industry as far as was possible (see Unit 11.2(b)). The Transport Act of 1953 also denationalized road transport, though British Road Services had to be set up in 1956 to reorganize the transport undertakings which could not be sold. The Act of 1953 and another Transport Act of 1962 also undermined and then disbanded the Transport Commission, so that the advantages of overall planning were lost and the remaining state services became fragmented under such bodies as the British Railways Board and the British Waterways Board.

The Railways Board faced grave problems. The rail network could not pay its way in the face of competition from road transport, and the Board was unable to obtain sufficient capital for the vast programme of modernization that was needed. Moreover, railway finances were burdened by debts – the interest on government stock which had been used to buy out the former owners at the time of nationalization. In 1955 a start was made on phasing out steam locomotives and replacing them with more efficient diesel and electric

Fig. 13.3 Vicky's view of the resilience of Harold Macmillan, coming up stain-free for the general election of 1959 in spite of the economic 'Squeeze' in recent years, the Suez Crisis and problems in Britain's colonies. It was Vicky who helped to develop the image of 'Supermac' (Evening Standard, *10 September 1959)*

units. This took both time and money. Track electrification was even more costly, and proceeded very slowly. The first long-distance electric service, the Inter-City line between London and Manchester, was not operational until 1966. Meanwhile, in 1961, the Conservatives insisted that the railways must be made profitable, rejecting the argument that they should be treated as a social service. Dr Beeching became the Chairman of the Railways Board in that year, to carry out the necessary surgery. The Beeching Report (1963) proposed closing some 5 000 miles of unprofitable track (about a quarter of the network), and more than 2 000 stations, with matching cuts in manpower. Most of the cuts took place before Beeching gave up his chairmanship in 1966, by which time 40 per cent of the railway's labour force had been shed. Although British Rail was now more efficient, it continued to operate at a loss, like railways everywhere that had to compete with modern road transport. There were jobs which only railways could do, such as moving certain types of heavy freight, carrying London's armies of commuters and providing fast long-distance transport. But the costs of maintaining even a reduced railway network remained huge, and modernization involved British Rail in an unending struggle to find the capital to keep pace with improving technology.

The Conservatives left the other nationalized industries untouched after 1951, but their preference for competition and choice could be seen in the Television Act of 1954. This set up the Independent Television Authority (ITA) to provide a rival service to BBC Television. Like the BBC, the ITA was a public corporation, but it issued contracts to transmit television broadcasts to private programme companies, such as Granada and Thames. These companies received their income from the sale of advertising time not, like the BBC, from licences. The companies prospered, and advertising slogans and jingles steadily penetrated into millions of homes where television sets became increasingly commonplace. Not everyone welcomed this invasion of what had been the BBC's monopoly. Critics argued that commercial television would lower standards by pursuing the mass audiences needed to attract advertising revenue. *TV Times* seemed to confirm their fears, claiming in its first issue that:

> Viewers will no longer have to accept what is deemed best for them. The new independent television programme planners aim at giving viewers what viewers want – at the time viewers want it.

There was an immediate deluge of ready-made American cowboy and gangster programmes. American-style quiz programmes became popular too, rewarding competitors handsomely for meeting such challenging questions as 'Who was king in Henry VIII's reign?' Between the programmes, the advertisers added new dimensions to the English language, claiming it was possible to achieve something 'whiter than white' and to 'improve' on 'perfect' whiteness. Independent television matured, however, after its first frantic grab for viewers. Its supporters argued that competition revitalized BBC television, forcing it to breathe more life into its presentation of news, for example, lest it was left behind in the popularity stakes by more spirited ITV 'newscasters'.

The Conservatives, meanwhile, carried through the Restrictive Practices Act, to promote competition in industry and trade. Macmillan, as Chancellor, introduced Premium Bonds: those who saved through the Post Office could now compete for prize money, allotted by the random selection of winning Bonds, instead of accumulating interest. Again there were critics, complaining that the state was encouraging gambling and a something-for-nothing attitude. The Conservatives argued that they were widening choice and that the traditional forms of National Savings were still available for those who preferred them. The Betting and Gaming Act of 1960 caused another storm. By authorizing the opening of betting-shops and casinos, it brought into the open (and, opponents argued, encouraged) the previously illegal activities of neighbourhood bookmakers. The Street Offences Act of 1959, on the other hand, imposed more severe punishments on prostitutes who solicited for custom in public places. Bookmakers could emerge from the shadows, but prostitutes were better concealed, it seemed. The government could argue that it was merely responding to the moods and wishes of the country; and few of these reforms showed any great poineering spirit.

There were deeper currents stirring, however. In 1956 the Commons voted to abolish the death penalty, a cause long championed by Sidney Silverman, a Labour MP. The Lords rejected abolition but Eden's government carried a compromise Homicide Act, limiting capital punishment to certain types of murder. The next Labour government went further, the Murder Act of 1965 suspending the death penalty for a trial period, but in practice abolishing it. In this instance politicians were running ahead of public opinion, since opinion polls continued to show extensive support for hanging. The view prevailed in parliament that, as the Howard League for Penal Reform had argued in 1950:

> The death penalty is harmful to the whole community because periodically it stirs up unhealthy emotions, concentrates public interest on brutality, violence and vengeance. . . . In killing the murderer it sanctions killing and weakens respect for life.

The debate went on, however, since the postwar world and postwar Britain seemed plagued by increasing violence.

The Conservative government yielded to public pressure on one issue, restricting freedom in a way that was unprecedented. The Commonwealth Immigrants Act was passed in 1962, at a time of furious debate about the growing number of non-whites who were settling in Britain (see Units 17.1 and 17.2(a)).

13.3 Conservative Economic Management

The two faces of the British economy under the Conservatives were broadly considered in Unit 13.1. One face was that of a prosperous society, and Table 13.3(a) shows the rise in real earnings after 1953. It also shows something of the other face, a tendency to lose ground compared with other countries. Britain's rate of rise in real earnings was less than that of the Japanese and west Europeans, and Table 13.3(b) also shows how Britain lagged behind in investing for the future. Government, businessmen and workers – indeed, the nation as a whole – shared responsibility for this. The British people enjoyed their rising standard of living and asked for more, assuming that the future would somehow take care of itself. They were encouraged in this attitude by Conservative governments, by slogans about the good life, and by politicians in general who traded optimistic promises about the future in exchange for votes. Conservative chancellors in the 1950s usually took a short-term view of economic problems, considering it their job to deal with immediate difficulties by applying a dab to the accelerator or a touch on the brakes, but otherwise letting market forces operate freely.

Butler's first task as Chancellor in 1951 was to deal with the deficit on the balance of payments. He used credit controls, Bank Rate and higher taxes to reduce demand. The trading position improved, helped by favourable movements

Table 13.3 Earnings and investment

(a) *The growth in real earnings, 1953–75*

Country	1953*	1966	1975
West Germany	100	209	311
Japan	100	166	315
France	100	161	269
Italy	100	158	439
Britain	**100**	**151**	**207**
USA	100	130	139

* The base year for all countries in this Index. This does not, of course, mean that the countries were equally wealthy in 1953. This Table shows the *rate of growth*. The USA's earnings grew least, but the USA nevertheless was richer than other nations.

Source: Hey, J.D.: *Britain in Context*. Blackwell (Oxford, 1979).

(b) *Investment 1950–4 and 1970–5* (percentage of GDP)

Country	1950–4	1970–5
Japan	21.5	33.5
West Germany	20	24
Italy	19	21
France	18	24
USA	17.5	17.5
Britain	**14**	**19**

Source: Treasury *Economic Progress Report*, July 1978.

in the terms of trade as the world overcame the problems caused by the Korean War. Butler could now relax the pressure. It was a Conservative aim to reduce income tax so that, though Butler had begun by raising the normal rate from 45p in the pound to 47½p, it was eventually lowered to 39p in 1960. Butler also gave modest government help to industrialists who were willing to invest in new machinery. Butler's 'Go' soon arrived at another 'Stop', however. He himself, and then Macmillan, used various measures to damp down demand after the election of 1955. In 1957, Thorneycroft applied a further touch on the brakes when he increased the charges for welfare services and raised Bank Rate to 7 per cent. But the periods of 'Stop' now increasingly conflicted with the workers' demands for higher wages, and attempts to resist wage increases led to a rash of strikes. London's buses were paralysed and the country's rail service was disrupted before the level of wage increases was brought down. By that time Thorneycroft had resigned, and Heathcote Amory became Chancellor. It was 'Go' again, until new strains appeared after the election of 1959.

Selwyn Lloyd took over the Exchequer in 1961: Bank Rate went up to 7 per cent again, and the Chancellor placed much of the blame for Britain's troubles on wage increases. He demanded a 'Pay Pause'. The government tried to stop wage increases among those whom it employed directly, but it won little sympathy when it chose to fight its first major battle against the nurses. Nevertheless, it was beginning to be realized that there were deep-rooted problems to be solved, and the government at last turned its eyes to the longer view.

The National Economic Development Council was set up in 1961, to seek ways of improving Britain's comparatively low growth rate.* After the 'Pay Pause' the government called for further 'wage restraint', suggesting that, since growth was around 2½ per cent, wages should rise only at that rate. The government had some control over the public services, but little over private enterprise. The National Incomes Commission (NIC, known as 'Nicky') was therefore set up in 1962 to seek ways of controlling incomes, and of carrying out a wages policy, but it was destined to be short-lived. Wage restraint brought new conflicts, with postmen and railwaymen among others, and Macmillan decided to make changes in his cabinet. Selwyn Lloyd was removed from the Exchequer, to be remembered as the Chancellor who taxed ice cream and sweets while relieving the tax burden of the well-to-do, one of several ways in which he lost the goodwill of trade unionists.

By this time Macmillan's government was exploring the possibility of joining the European Economic Community, though only the Liberals had shown interest in membership when the EEC was set up in 1958. Pro-Europeans argued that membership would benefit the British economy, and the negotiations were entrusted to Edward Heath, as Lord Privy Seal. Heath declared, though it was by no means certain that the country as a whole agreed, that Britain was now eager:

> to become a full, wholehearted and active member of the European Community in the widest sense.

But in January 1963 President de Gaulle of France vetoed Britain's application, and Britain had to remain outside the EEC for the present (see Unit 20.3). Macmillan's new Chancellor, Reginald Maudling, had meanwhile decided to make a dash for growth: the early result was another balance of payments crisis, and Maudling's term at the Exchequer was cut short by the general election of 1964.

In the early 1960s there was thus greater awareness that Britain had stubborn economic problems, but there was virtually no agreement on how to solve them. Instead, the British showed as much inclination to look for scapegoats as

---

* The NEDC soon became known popularly (and in a typically British way) as 'Neddy'. Its disappointing achievements led to the suggestion that 'Noddy' might have been more appropriate.

"YOU KNOW, I'M BEGINNING TO FEEL THIS NATIONAL
SPORT'S GETTING REALLY CRUEL . . ."

*Fig. 13.4   The problems of Macmillan's government compared with the Grand
National steeplechase: Vicky comments on Britain's economic problems, March
1963 (*Evening Standard)

for solutions, and much energy was wasted in the 1960s and 1970s on debating
where to place the blame. Stop-Go policies had led to widespread frustration,
in spite of Britain's generally greater prosperity. The political parties blamed
one another, and it became popular to blame all politicians. Some found fault
with 'systems', such as the capitalist system, the class system or the electoral
system. Exaggerated ideas circulated about a class war in Britain. Employers
and managers were blamed, as well as politicians. Above all, however,
encouraged by the media, the belief became widespread that the main fault lay
with trade unions.

13.4 Trade Unions

Trade unions exist first and foremost to serve the interests of their members –
to protect them from injustice and to achieve collective strength with which to
secure improved conditions of work. Membership of trade unions in Britain
grew steadily from about 1932. By 1945 the unions had some eight million
members, by 1960 about ten million and by 1980 about twelve million. During
the postwar years the unions became a force to be reckoned with. Many other

workers, however, especially in white-collar employment, did not belong to trade unions. Individual unions were pressure-groups concerned with the sectional interests of their members. Collectively, most unions were members of the Trades Union Congress (TUC, founded 1868), a pressure-group on behalf of the trade union movement as a whole and workers in general. The employers had their 'unions' too, in the various trade federations and, the counterpart of the TUC, the Confederation of British Industries (CBI, founded in 1916). The TUC and CBI thus represented the two sides of industry, workers and employers. By 1945 the tradition had long been established that the TUC and trade unions had close links with the Labour Party, and the CBI less formal but nevertheless strong links with the Conservative Party.

British trade unionists played an important part in setting up a new trade union movement in West Germany after the Second World War, building a modern movement with fewer than a score of large unions, influential enough to defend their members and at the same time to make a useful contribution to West Germany's growth and prosperity (see Tables 13.1 and 13.4). In Germany, however, the Nazis had destroyed the earlier trade unions and in 1945 it was possible to start with a clean sheet. In Britain the sheet was not clean, and the problem after 1945 was to adapt a long-established union movement to modern needs. Tradition itself had a firm place in British industrial relations, and many industrial problems were so rooted in the past that it was a far from easy task to overcome them. Even the structure of the British trade union movement began to seem ramshackle after the Second World War. In 1930 there had been over 1 100 trade unions in Britain, many of them tiny. Though amalgamations reduced the number to below 700 by 1960, many small unions still clung successfully to their separate identities. The result was that in certain industries, such as vehicle-building, there were several unions within a single plant, representing different trades and different grades of workers. Arguments about 'demarcation' (who should do which work) and 'differentials' (how one rate of pay should be related with another) were the result. To the outsider such arguments could seem trivial, but they were rooted in Britain's industrial history and the issues were often complicated. Both sides of industry agreed that a further reduction in the number of unions was desirable, but many groups of workers preferred to keep the smaller associations which they thought best protected their particular interests. Most engine-drivers, for example, preferred membership of the Associated Society of Locomotive Engineers and Firemen (ASLEF) to membership of the National Union of Railwaymen (NUR). Most grammar school teachers similarly preferred their own associations to the National Union of Teachers (NUT). The criticism that the trade union movement was too slow to reform its own structure took little account of the fact that, in a society claiming to be democratic, change requires agreement.

The majority of those who blamed the trade unions for Britain's economic ills were less concerned with technicalities about structures than with what they saw as union militancy. In the late 1940s trade unions had responded well to the Labour government's appeals to hold down wages in the national interest; but the climate began to change in the 1950s. Many workers had known little but promises of 'jam tomorrow', repeated by politicians, it seemed, during the pre-war years of hardship, the Second World War itself and the postwar years of austerity. Britain still had a vast army of low-paid workers, and manual workers seldom shared in the privileges, security and comfortable working facilities which salaried employees took for granted. Within the framework of free enterprise and the pursuit of affluence which governments encouraged after 1951, the lower classes set their sights higher than in the past. They looked to their unions to negotiate better wages and conditions.

Prices were rising and larger incomes were needed simply to keep pace with them. On the other hand, wages were a factor in the costs of production, and it was argued that wage increases themselves pushed up prices. The extent to which this was true varied considerably from one industry to another. It applied more to industries that depended heavily on manpower rather than on advanced machinery (that is, where industries were labour-intensive rather than capital-intensive). Wage restraint was nevertheless not popular with trade unions: it was not popular with their members. Nor, though they paid lip-service to it, was it popular with politicians who were well aware that rising incomes tended to produce satisfied voters. Free enterprise – 'free collective bargaining', in the jargon of union negotiators – often meant, however, that the strongest and most militant unions won the largest wage awards, regardless of the effects on the costs of production. This was why the NIC was eventually set up in 1962. It seemed that government needed an incomes policy, though there was little agreement on how it might work. Meanwhile, the over-simplification gained ground that the trade unions were undermining the economy by excessive wage claims.

From the unions' point of view, the problem looked rather different. Unions existed to try to ensure that their members received a fair share of the country's wealth. Millions of workers had not achieved this in the past, and many were also still being called upon to make sacrifices for the national good. Those who criticized the unions most noisily often forgot that many were co-operating in painful reductions in manpower in industries such as coalmining and the railways. Technological changes were already bringing new threats to jobs and, yet again, raising fears of unemployment. This was a problem which seemed likely to get worse, stiffening the resolve of the labour movement to do what it could to cushion the workers against hardship and injustice. It was sometimes argued that wage increases themselves put men out of work, by making industries uncompetitive, but this was another over-simplification: textile workers were neither militant nor did they gain any excessive pay increases, yet in the late 1970s they suffered as much unemployment as other groups of workers.

By the early 1960s there was already talk of a 'British disease', one symptom of which was the country's low rate of growth. Strikes were another symptom.

Table 13.4 shows that, at least until the late 1960s, Britain actually suffered less from strikes than did many of its overseas competitors. A comparison of Tables 13.1 and 13.4 shows that there is also little correlation between strikes and the rate of growth. Strikes were nevertheless an emotional issue, which critics of the trade unions seized upon as a further explanation of what was wrong with Britain. There is little evidence that strikes at this time had much effect on the

Table 13.4 International comparison of working days lost annually because of industrial disputes, 1950s to 1970s

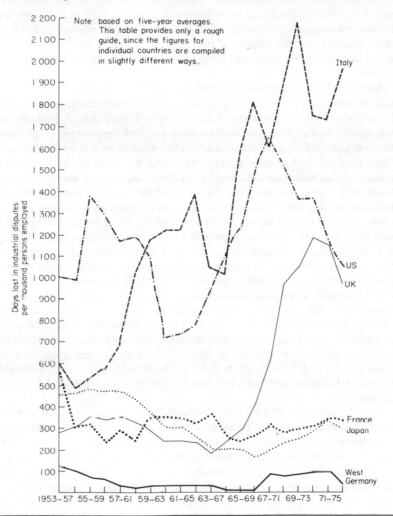

Source: adapted from Hey, J.D.: *Britain in Context.* Blackwell (Oxford, 1979).

British economy. Production in British engineering industries almost doubled in the years 1951–64, in spite of strikes. The textile industry, though relatively strike-free, scarcely increased production at all. Strikes were hardly at the root of Britain's economic problems, though they sometimes interrupted deliveries and lost the country some export orders.

What was most remarkable about British strikes was not their extent or the damage they did but their nature. The vast majority were 'unofficial' in that they were not called by trade union leaders. They resulted from walkouts by angry workers and were sometimes referred to as 'wildcat' strikes. Most were very brief. Europeans found them intriguing since they seemed distinctively British, resulting not from the strength and militancy of trade unions but from their seeming inability to control their own members. Union leaders spent much of their time getting men back to work rather than leading them into strikes.

So much local disruption and spontaneous downing of tools suggested a malaise in at least parts of British industry and in labour relations. Those who looked for simple explanations of Britain's problems readily found another scapegoat: their attention focused on shop stewards, seemingly in the belief that workers could not act for themselves but must be misled by their leaders. Shop stewards had become prominent during the First World War. Their earliest duties had been little more than collecting union subscriptions. But both employers and workers had felt the need for local negotiators who were less remote than union officials at headquarters. Shop stewards thus became spokesmen for the workers in their individual places of work. Anti-unionists now often alleged – sometimes accurately – that shop stewards were communists, and that this somehow explained Britain's industrial troubles. Again, however, this judgment assumed too readily that the stewards wielded almost magical powers over the workers they represented. Militant shop stewards could and did occasionally foment disruption, but this provided no general explanation of Britain's ills. Like the blanket condemnations of 'unions' and 'workers', or those of 'managers' and 'politicians', such simple explanations made no useful contribution to solving Britain's tangled economic problems. The world of the shop steward did, however, provide Peter Sellers with the opportunity to make an entertaining film, *I'm All Right, Jack*, in 1960. This too gave rise to sweeping claims, and some argued that it summed up the philosophy of Britain as a whole at this time.

British trade unions differed from those in Europe not only in number but in another important respect. From its foundation, the Labour Party was much inter-linked with trade unionism. It depended on the unions for much of its finance. At party conferences, the unions cast their block votes on behalf of their affiliated members and influenced Labour policy. In 1980 the Transport and General Workers' Union commanded a million and a quarter votes, the largest block. The Amalgamated Union of Engineering Workers had just under a million, dwarfing the 180 000 of the NUR. But all these major unions dwarfed the votes of the constituency parties. This, of course, affected the nature of the Labour Party (see Unit 1.2(c)). It also meant that trade union issues in Britain were bound up with matters of party politics. It became a normal feature of British government in the years after 1945 that trade unions, in their own right, were entitled to be consulted by government in the management of the British economy, just as the CBI was consulted. However, when it began to be argued during the 1960s that legislation was needed to improve British industrial relations and perhaps even to 'reform' the trade unions, the Labour Party found itself in difficulties, perhaps being too close to the union movement. The Conservatives, on the other hand, were still perhaps too remote and too much the party of the employers, so that Conservative measures were readily seen by the unions as those of the enemy. Almost everything to do with trade unions gave rise to heated arguments in the 1960s and 1970s.

Table 13.5 Working days lost annually in Britain through industrial disputes, 1949–64 (millions)

1949	1.8	1957	8.4
1950	1.4	1958	3.5
1951	1.7	1959	5.3
1952	1.8	1960	3.0
1953	2.2	1961	3.0
1954	2.4	1962	5.8
1955	2.7	1963	1.7
1956	2.0	1964	2.0

13.5 The Opposition in Confusion

Conservative successes in the general elections of 1955 and 1959 were made easier by the confusion within the Labour Party. The falling Labour vote showed the voters' loss of faith in the Party (see Table 10.1). As early as May 1949, the *New Statesman* shrewdly anticipated the problem:

> The plain fact is that the Labour Party is reaching the end of the road which it first set itself to traverse in 1918 . . . . What next?

The Labour Party had completed the building of the welfare state, nationalized some key industries and achieved full employment in peacetime. It now needed to rethink its political aims. Intellectuals within the Party, such as Anthony Crosland, searched for a new coherent philosophy, appropriate to the second half of the twentieth century. In the meantime, however, there was wrangling between right and left. Disputes began while Attlee's government was still in office (see Units 11.3 and 11.4), and continued after the general election of 1951. Political parties of the left are generally more stormy than those of the right, since it is easier to agree on preserving things than on how to make changes, or on what changes to make. The Labour Party always claimed to be a party of change, but it was weakened throughout the 1950s by seeming to have few clear ideas about the direction in which it wanted to go.

The right wing of the Party, represented for example by Gaitskell and Morrison, and including many trade unionists, had no wish for much further nationalization, and were not passionately hostile to the foreign policy of Churchill's government or to Butler's economic policies (see Unit 13.1(b)). The left wing, on the other hand, still saw nationalization as a weapon against capitalism and wanted more rapid movement towards socialism and equality. The left were also against spending on arms, and some disapproved of the close alliance with the USA. Above all, the left objected to British nuclear weapons, responding angrily when Britain's first atomic bombs were tested in 1952. The left rallied around Aneurin Bevan, and the Party divided between Gaitskellites and Bevanites. Attlee's policy seemed to be to paper over the divisions and to try to keep the peace.

Attlee chose to retire during 1955 and the Parliamentary Labour Party (PLP) elected a new leader. Gaitskell won 157 votes, Bevan 70 and Morrison 40. The limited support for Bevan was not surprising, since the PLP stood generally to the right of the Party as a whole. It did, however, cause tension between the PLP and other sections of the Party such as the National Executive Committee, as well as some trade unionists such as Frank Cousins, leader of the TGWU. But Bevan apparently ceased to be a Bevanite in 1957. Gaitskell made him the Opposition spokesman on foreign affairs, and Bevan gave his support to the British hydrogen bomb lest Britain should go 'naked into the conference chamber'. Internal wrangling continued, and Labour could win no lasting advantage even from the Suez Crisis in 1956, which led to Eden's resignation (see Unit 14.1(b)). Opposition to the Rent Act of 1957 produced a flicker of spirit and some Labour unity but the Party again lost votes in the general election of 1959. Some blame was attached to Gaitskell who made rash promises of tax cuts which Butler ridiculed with the comment, 'A bribe a day keeps the Tories away'. Nor did Gaitskell perform well on television, which was now beginning to play an important part in British general elections: he was earnest and honest, but lacked the charm of 'Supermac'. Bevan once referred to Gaitskell as 'a desiccated calculating-machine'.

The Labour Party had now lost three successive general elections and inquests followed. It seemed that Labour was making little appeal to young voters and to growing social groups such as owner-occupiers. Gaitskell thought that Clause Four of the Party's constitution was to blame (see Unit 3.2). He argued that further nationalization had little relevance to the campaign for greater equality in Britain, and that Clause Four should be dropped. Harold Wilson retorted that that was like taking 'Genesis out of the Bible'. The Party was deeply divided on the issue, and Clause Four remained. Almost at once Gaitskell faced a new difficulty. In 1960 Cousins and the Labour supporters of the CND wanted a promise to abolish Britain's nuclear weapons. The Labour leadership resisted this vigorously, and Gaitskell proclaimed that he would 'fight, fight, and fight again' to uphold 'sanity and honesty' in the Party. The left criticized him for, in effect, upholding the policies in which he himself believed but which many in the Party opposed. The arguments dragged on, damaging Labour's image as a party in which the voters could place their faith. But the Party found a rallying flag in opposing Heath's efforts to secure Britain's admission to the EEC. Gaitskell's sudden death in January 1963 occurred at the very moment when the Party at last seemed to be closing ranks in his support. He was still comparatively young – only fifty-six – and his death robbed the country of a probable future prime minister whose economic expertise might have been invaluable.

A new generation of Labour MPs contested the leadership. Bevan had died in 1960. Morrison had retired after his defeat in 1955. The PLP now elected Harold Wilson in preference to George Brown and James Callaghan. Like Gaitskell, Wilson was an economist but he had more skill in political manoeuvring than his predecessor; he also inherited an improving position for the Party. Opposition to the EEC brought unity to the Labour Party, while the Conservatives were falling into confusion. There was growing evidence that disillusioned Conservative voters were flocking to the Liberals. In 1962 the Liberals won a by-election at Orpington, a seat the Conservatives had thought absolutely safe. Macmillan dismissed a third of his cabinet, including Selwyn Lloyd, in an effort to restore Conservative fortunes. But ill health forced the Prime Minister himself to retire, and the choice of Douglas-Home caused further disruption (see Unit 13.1).

By the end of 1962 scandals involving national security were being uncovered. Further revelations followed during 1963, involving not only prostitutes and Soviet agents but also John Profumo, the Minister for War. Profumo resigned after confessing that he had made an untrue statement to the Commons, though there was no reason to believe that he had given away any national secrets. The media had a field day with spicy stories and pompous editorials about public morality. Conservative discomfort was increased by a vigorous Opposition attack on 'Rachmanism'. Rachman was a slum landlord whose sordid activities came to light during investigations into the other scandals. With Alsatian dogs and a gang of thugs, Rachman was alleged to have intimidated difficult tenants and to be involved in racketeering in the Paddington area of London. Wilson argued that Rachman and his like flourished because of the freedom given to them by the Rent Act of 1957. Such a cause helped to put more spirit into the Labour Party. In fact, like Labour in 1951, the Conservatives were running out of steam and their opponents eagerly looked forward to the next general election, due to be held in 1964 (see Unit 15.1).

The Liberals had increased their vote in the 1959 election but not their number of seats in the Commons (see Table 10.1). A pattern was beginning to emerge which became a feature of postwar British politics. Dissatisfaction with the Conservatives often increased the Liberal vote, especially in by-elections, as if the Liberals provided a refuge for 'Conservatives with consciences'. In the

Fig. 13.5 Douglas-Home acknowledges applause at the Conservative Party Conference in Blackpool, soon after 'emerging' as the Conservative leader, October 1963. Among those congratulating the seated Prime Minister are Edward Heath (second from the left) and Iain Macleod (extreme right)

early 1960s it seemed as if the Liberals were set to become a major party again, actually leading all parties in an opinion poll in March 1962. Jo Grimond, who had been elected to the Liberal leadership in 1956, provided new vigour, ever ready 'to march towards the sound of gunfire'. The Liberals looked forward to the general election, conscious of widespread sympathy. It remained to be seen, however, whether they could break out of the strait-jacket in which they had been confined at past general elections, when voters seemed to believe that it was necessary either to vote Conservative to keep out Labour, or Labour to keep out the Conservatives.

Further Reading

Sked, A. and Cook, C.: *Post-War Britain, A Political History*. Penguin (Harmondsworth, 1979), chapters 4–7.

Bogdanor, V. and Skidelsky, R.: *The Age of Affluence, 1951–1964*. Macmillan (London, 1970).

Haseler, S.: *The Gaitskellites*. Macmillan (London, 1969).

Hey, J.D.: *Britain in Context*. Blackwell (Oxford, 1979).

Lindsay, T.F. and Harrington, M.: *The Conservative Party 1918–1979*. Macmillan (London, 1979).

Pollard, S.: *The Development of the British Economy, 1914–1967*. Arnold (London, 1969).

Proudfoot, M.: *British Politics and Government, 1951–1970*. Faber (London, 1974).
Williamson, H.: *The Trade Unions*. Heinemann (London, 1970).

Exercises

1. Making use of the Index to this book, outline the career of Winston Churchill from 1914 to 1955. How far do you agree that he was more successful in wartime than in peacetime?

2. Explain the term *Butskellism* (page 218). What parts did Butler and Gaitskell play in the politics of the 1950s, and why did *each* encounter opposition from other members of his own party?

3. What do you understand by policies of 'Stop' and 'Go'? Why did governments in the 1950s sometimes adopt one of these policies and sometimes adopt the other? How fittingly did the cartoonist in Fig. 13.4 comment on Britain's difficulties?

4. 'Bringing to an end the age of cheap money' (page 222): show what you understand by these words, and explain why Bank Rate 'was now adjusted frequently' (page 222).

5. Draw four columns headed by the names of the Prime Ministers shown in Table 13.2. List in each column the reforms introduced during the time the Prime Minister was in office. Select the *three* reforms you consider to have been the most important in the years 1951–64, arguing in support of your choice.

6. What do the Tables in this Unit show of Britain's 'stubborn economic problems' (page 227) in the years 1951–64? Why was it difficult to solve the problems you have identified?

7. What complaints were made about each of the following in the years before 1964: 'unions'; 'workers'; 'managers'; 'politicians' (page 232)? Write a defence for *each of two* of these groups against the charge that they were mainly to blame for Britain's economic problems.

8. Explain (a) what you understand by *Bevanites*, (b) why the Labour Party was turbulent after the retirement of Attlee and (c) why the Party nevertheless 'eagerly looked forward' (page 235) to the general election of 1964.

Unit Fourteen

Foreign and Imperial Policy under the Conservatives, 1951–64

14.1 Foreign Policy in the Eden Years, 1951–7

(a) The Atlantic Alliance

Anthony Eden was Foreign Secretary from 1951 to 1955, when he succeeded Churchill as Prime Minister. He was no newcomer to foreign affairs, having been Foreign Secretary from 1935 to 1938, when he resigned from Chamberlain's government (see Unit 8.3(a)), and Churchill's Foreign Secretary during the war, from 1940 to 1945. Like Churchill, he believed in the alliance with the USA, the alliance of English-speaking peoples; and neither he nor Churchill wanted greatly to change the policies which Bevin had followed during Labour's years of government (see Unit 12.2). Britain therefore continued to support the USA in the Korean War, remained within NATO and joined SEATO when it was founded in 1954.

Alliance with the USA did not always mean tame subservience, however. Eden discouraged American intervention in Indochina in 1954. By that time it had become clear that France could no longer hold its colonial possessions against nationalist resistance there. Resistance was led by the Viet Minh, an organization of North Vietnamese Communists and nationalists, and a new anti-communist campaign like that in Korea seemed possible. Eden played a prominent part in the Geneva Agreements of 1954, when the French agreed to withdraw from Indochina and arrangements were made for the area's future. It was not Eden's fault that these agreements later broke down and that the USA, after all, became involved in a bitter and costly struggle in Vietnam, from which the British always remained apart.

Germany continued to be the main problem in Europe in the early 1950s. After West Germany and East Germany had been set up as two separate nations in 1949, debates began as to how West Germany could best contribute to its own defence, sharing the burden of the NATO powers. Rather than permit a new German military machine to develop, it seemed desirable that West Germany should become part of a European Defence Community (EDC), in which west Europeans could pool their forces. Eden again followed in Bevin's footsteps. Britain had not joined the ECSC, which would have involved some loss of independence concerning coal and steel; and it would not now join the EDC, which would involve the surrender of some control over Britain's armed forces. Plans for the EDC therefore collapsed, since France would not join without Britain. A solution to the problem of West German rearmament was found in 1955, however, when the German Federal Republic joined the Western European Union (WEU), an expanded version of the Brussels Treaty Organization. West Germany was allowed to contribute forces to western defence within this alliance. British troops remained in Germany but no longer as occupation forces: they were there by invitation, as part of the West's defence system.

The Austrian State Treaty was signed in 1955, agreeing to the total evacuation of occupation forces and giving Austria its independence. British troops left southern Austria and the British Sector of Vienna (see Fig. 12.3), and it now became possible to make some reductions in the size of Britain's armed forces.

Meanwhile, Eisenhower had been elected President of the USA in 1952 and Stalin had died in 1953. Both Americans and Russians began to show interest in British proposals for 'summit meetings' between the leaders of the major powers. The first took place in 1955 at Geneva, where Eden and other western leaders met Bulganin of the USSR. Eden hopefully suggested that the two Germanies should be reunited, but the idea was unrealistic and little came of the meeting. Bulganin visited London in April 1956, accompanied by Nikita Khrushchev, soon to emerge as the new Soviet leader. A patchy thaw in East–West relations seemed to have begun. Eden had shown skill as a negotiator and had contributed to this slight easing of East–West tension. But it was clear that Britain's voice was no longer decisive in world affairs and, in appearing to accept this, Bevin, Churchill and Eden had won international respect. However, 1956 was to show that there was still some confusion in Britain about the country's role in the modern world. Eden's reputation, and Britain's, crumbled almost overnight in the Suez Crisis.

(b) The Suez Crisis

The events of the 1930s had left a lasting impression on Eden. He remembered vividly how the appeasement of Hitler had led to the Second World War. At the same time, like Churchill, he was uneasy about Britain's retreat from its age of imperial glory. Both had yet to come to terms with the aggressive nationalism of developing countries which sometimes threatened Britain's interests. Events in Persia had already humiliated Britain (see Unit 12.2(c)) and in 1955 Eden was further frustrated when he helped to create the Baghdad Pact, as a regional defence system against communism in the Middle East. Britain's partners were Turkey, Iraq, Persia and Pakistan and, since it seemed to be a logical bridge between NATO and SEATO, the USA was also expected to join the Pact. To Eden's dismay the Americans welcomed it, but remained outside. Then Jordan seemed to snub the British. King Hussein dismissed Brigadier Glubb from command of the Arab Legion in March 1956. Glubb Pasha had long been a symbol of British influence in Jordan, which had survived the ending of the mandate. His dismissal pleased Jordanian nationalists, who complained that Glubb seemed to regard himself as the Emperor of Jordan. A general assault on British interests in the area followed. Britain had much stronger ties with the Middle East than had the USA (see Fig. 12.7(a)), and increasingly Eden came to believe that sinister forces were afoot there, which it was Britain's duty to resist.

Eden's anxiety focused on Egypt. The British had agreed to Egyptian independence in 1936, after more than half a century of great influence there. But British troops had remained in the Canal Zone, guarding the Suez Canal in which the British had a major financial interest, and which was a vital route for British trade. A new Anglo-Egyptian Treaty in October 1954 agreed that these troops would be withdrawn within twenty months. Gamal Abdel Nasser was the Egyptian Prime Minister and, in 1956, he became the country's President. Nasser was a forceful Arab nationalist. The French suspected that he had a good deal to do with the increasing Algerian clamour for independence from France, and Eden suspected him of undermining British interests in Jordan and elsewhere in the Middle East. With his liking for drama and rhetoric, Nasser reminded Eden of Hitler and Mussolini. Moreover, he was also a military leader, usually surrounded by soldiers, and he showed a tendency to make deals with the USSR. In fact, Nasser was a not untypical leader of the nationalist movements which were becoming common in those parts of the world once dominated by Europeans. Like many such leaders, he realized that acts of defiance against former masters would make for popularity. When the British began to leave the Canal Zone Egyptians hailed Nasser as a liberator, no doubt boosting his confidence.

But Nasser was also anxious to improve the lot of the millions of poor Egyptians. Building the Aswan High Dam, to provide hydroelectric power and a regular water supply to parched farmlands, was vital to his plans. The USA outbid the USSR in offering to help finance this massive undertaking, but Nasser then made himself unpopular in the USA by recognizing China's Communist government, and unpopular in Britain by criticizing the Baghdad Pact. Western aid was withdrawn when he also bought arms from Czechoslovakia and the Eastern bloc. Although the USSR was willing to step in with help, Nasser saw a way in which Egyptians could help themselves. In July 1956 he nationalized the Suez Canal Company, telling the Egyptian people:

> The Suez Canal was dug by the efforts of the sons of Egypt – 120 000 Egyptians died in the process. The Suez Canal Company is a usurping company. . . . We shall build the High Dam and we shall gain our usurped rights. . . . The Canal Company annually takes £35 million. Why shouldn't we take it for ourselves?

The shareholders in the Canal Company were to be compensated at the then prices on the French stock exchange, but both the British and the French governments protested furiously. With their presidential elections almost due, the Americans preferred a quieter response.

Eden, Selwyn Lloyd (his Foreign Secretary) and the French confidently expected the Canal to cease operating efficiently under Egyptian management.

Intervention to keep this vital waterway open could then be justified. But the Canal continued to function normally, even when western personnel were withdrawn in September 1956. International negotiations and appeals to the United Nations proved fruitless. Britain and France seemed powerless; but few nations shared their belief that some great wrong had been done. To Eden, it nevertheless seemed vital to teach Nasser a lesson, perhaps even to depose him. What was needed was a better pretext for intervention than the mere compulsory purchase of the Suez Canal Company shares – and this was provided when Israel attacked Egypt towards the end of October 1956. Since 1949 there had been no more than an uneasy truce between Israel and its Arab neighbours (see Unit 12.3(*b*)) and renewed fighting was not unexpected. There seems to be little doubt, however, that the Israeli attack was the result of collusion between the Israelis, the French and the British. Once the Israelis advanced across Sinai, Anglo-French forces could be unleashed 'to protect the Suez Canal'. The appeal of such an arrangement for the Israelis was that the Europeans, while they were about it, could destroy the Egyptian air force.

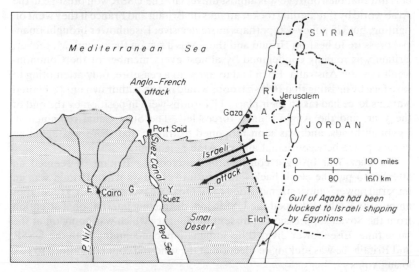

Fig. 14.1 The Suez war, 1956

The Israelis advanced. On 30 October Britain and France issued an ultimatum, solemnly declaring:

> This event threatens to disrupt the freedom of navigation through the Suez Canal on which the economic life of so many nations depends.

Britain and France therefore demanded that 'the Government of Egypt' should:

withdraw all Egyptian military forces to a distance of ten miles from the Canal . . .
(and) accept the temporary occupation by Anglo-French forces of key positions at
Port Said, Ismalia and Suez.

The Egyptians were informed that a similar document had been sent to Israel.
This extraordinary ultimatum nevertheless seemed to bring a new principle
into the conduct of international affairs, that the powers would intervene to
punish the *victim* of aggression. The Egyptians rejected it, but Eden did not
intend to be stopped now. Britain and France vetoed a UN Security Council
resolution condemning Israel for aggression, and they defied an overwhelming
vote (64 to 5) in the General Assembly which urged them to observe a
ceasefire. On 5 November British paratroops landed at Port Said, and com-
mando troops stormed ashore the next day to begin the task of driving the
Egyptians from the Canal. The Egyptians promptly sank nearly fifty ships to
ensure the Canal would be blocked.

The Anglo-French military operation came to an abrupt end on 7 November. International outrage was almost universal. The USSR won prestige in the
Arab world by threatening rocket attacks on Britain and France if they went on
fighting, but US policy was perhaps more decisive. Eisenhower brought financial pressure to bear on Britain and there was a run on the pound. Moreover,
Britain was roundly condemned by almost every member of the Commonwealth except Australia. Eden had to agree to a ceasefire, only attempting to
save face by insisting that British troops would not be withdrawn until a United
Nations force had taken their place. UN troops were in position by the end of
the year, and the Anglo-French forces left. The Suez Canal remained in
Egyptian hands, and was soon reopened to traffic; and there was again an
uneasy peace between Israel and its Arab neighbours.

The Suez War brought considerable discredit to Britain. It seemed an
attempt to put the clock back – to return to the days when Britain was an
imperial power – and it strengthened rather than weakened Nasser's reputation
among the Arabs. It helped the USSR too, distracting international attention
from the Soviet suppression of dissent in Hungary which was going on at the
same time. Eisenhower divided his indignation, condemning both the USSR
and Britain; he was seeking re-election at the time and could not afford to risk
losing votes.

Eden resigned in January 1957 on medical advice, but he remained unrepen-
tant:

> We make no apology and shall make no apology for the action that we and our
> French allies took together.

In spite of fierce criticism within Britain as well as outside it, Eden still had a
good deal of support from his Party and among the British public. There was
even some satisfaction about the way the military operations had been conducted. One military spokesman observed:

Fig. 14.2 An Australian cartoon of 1956, suggesting something of the international reception given to Eden's Suez Policy and his attempt to provide Churchillian leadership

> Tempers ran so high over the ethics of the Franco-British intervention at Port Said that its technical brilliance has been obscured.

Harold Macmillan, the new Prime Minister, had no record of opposition to the Suez War. Indeed, there had been very little opposition among members of Eden's government, and only two junior ministers had resigned.

The Suez War had claimed twenty-six British lives and cost millions of pounds and much goodwill which Britain could ill afford to lose. Egypt and Israel suffered much more heavily in terms of casualties and damage, but the conflict changed hardly anything in the Middle East. For a time, Egypt drew closer to the USSR, but even that was only temporary. It proved an illusion that Nasser was either another Hitler or a Soviet puppet.

14.2 Foreign Policy in the Macmillan Years, 1957–63

The USA was more inclined to support Britain in the Middle East after the Suez Crisis and the presidential election. The Eisenhower Doctrine was announced in January 1957, offering US support to any Middle Eastern country threatened by 'overt armed aggression from any nation controlled by international communism'. British and American forces were sent to Jordan in 1958 when political changes in Iraq weakened the Baghdad Pact. Iraq withdrew from the Pact and the alliance was reorganized in 1959 as the Central Treaty Organization (CENTO). The USA still declined to become a full member of CENTO, but nevertheless guaranteed the security of Turkey, Persia and Pakistan.

The thaw in East–West relations continued, though rather erratically. Specific agreements were few. Macmillan still argued the British view that Germany should be reunified, but there was little prospect of that. Berlin too was now sharply divided between East and West. The USSR and East Germany hoped to manoeuvre Western forces out of the city, but the British gave firm support to the Americans who insisted on staying there. West Berlin remained a capitalist outpost in eastern Europe, and a refuge for those who sought to escape from communism. In 1961 the East Germans therefore built the Berlin Wall, to make passage from one side of the city to the other almost impossible except through checkpoints. Britain protested, but even the USA could take no effective action to interfere. East and West had accepted that there were now two Europes, and that neither side would seriously meddle in the affairs of the other; but international leaders continued to meet and talk. Macmillan visited Moscow in March 1959, and even broadcast to the Soviet people. Another summit meeting was arranged for May 1960, this time in Paris, but it collapsed in bitter disputes over an American U-2 spy-plane which had just been shot down over the USSR. British influence counted for little on such occasions. Macmillan was little more than a bystander as a new feud developed between Eisenhower and Khrushchev, though he had worked hard to bring about the Paris summit and had had ambitious plans for it.

British proposals for a reduction of armaments were similarly lost in the welter of superpower proposals and counter-proposals. Britain nevertheless clung to its own hydrogen-bomb programme. It also tried in a limited way to compete in the space race, which quickened in 1961 when Yuri Gagarin successfully orbited the earth in a Soviet space capsule.

The Cuban Missiles Crisis once more showed Britain's near-irrelevance to the rivalry of the superpowers, however. Macmillan was only an onlooker while President Kennedy, Eisenhower's successor, engaged in a dramatic test of strength with Khrushchev. For a moment in October 1962 it seemed that the world was on the brink of nuclear war, but the Crisis passed when Khrushchev gave way and removed the Soviet missiles which had been placed in Cuba and pointed towards US cities. The Missiles Crisis even had beneficial results. In 1963 the USA, the USSR and Britain signed the Test Ban Treaty:

> Each of the Parties to this Treaty undertakes to prohibit, to prevent and not to carry out any nuclear test, explosion, or any other nuclear explosion, at any place under its jurisdiction . . . in the atmosphere; . . . outer space; or under water.

The powers were at last attempting to check nuclear pollution, and the West

Fig. 14.3 Harold Macmillan (extreme right) and Selwyn Lloyd (second from the left) in Moscow, 1959; Nikita Khrushchev, second from the right. A jovial reception hardly disguised the fact that Britain now carried limited weight in the affairs of the super powers

reached a degree of understanding with Khrushchev, who shared a general fear of nuclear war. The Chinese and de Gaulle, the French President, however, refused to sign the Treaty. De Gaulle, critical of American influence, had begun to take his own course in foreign policy, and France was virtually to withdraw from NATO in 1966. It also became clear after 1960 that a deep rift had developed between the USSR and Communist China.

Macmillan held fast to the Anglo-American alliance while trying to settle problems within the British Empire, and he developed a close personal relationship with President Kennedy. Even so, he could do little to restrain the US government from becoming ever more deeply involved in the affairs of Vietnam. The Geneva Agreements on Indochina in 1954 had produced no lasting solutions (see Unit 14.1(*a*)). The USA drifted into a bitter struggle against Vietnamese communists, perhaps with an even more distorted view of Vietnam's affairs than the British had had in Egypt in 1956. When Kennedy was assassinated in 1963 President Johnson stepped up the struggle, sending in ever more troops. Britain refused to take part in the war, settling into the role of mediator and adviser, though with comparatively little influence.

In any case, an era was coming to an end and there would soon be new leaders on the world stage. At almost the same moment that the Conservatives lost the general election of 1964, Khrushchev fell from power in the USSR. By

"Careful, Mr. Acheson! <u>We</u> turned up for that funeral, but our own came first."

Fig. 14.4 Cummings replies in the Sunday Express *to the suggestion in December 1962 by Dean Acheson, a former US Secretary of State, that Britain was 'just about played out'*

the end of that year the age of Khrushchev, of Eisenhower and Kennedy, of Macmillan and Douglas-Home, had ended. Whether the East–West thaw would continue now depended on other statesmen.

14.3 The British Empire: Federations and Decolonization

Although Britain's voice in the affairs of the super powers was hardly decisive in the years 1951–64, the British had the special responsibility in this period for deciding the future of the British Empire. Attlee's government appeared to have set the Empire on the road to decolonization and independence (see Unit 12.3), but it was not a road along which Churchill was eager to travel. Progress was slow in the early 1950s. Individual colonies moved towards self-government – the Gold Coast, for example, where Kwame Nkrumah became Prime Minister in 1951 – but there were no further grants of independence until 1957. Attempts were also made to tackle other questions. In 1952 General Templer was sent to Malaya, to govern and to step up the war against communist guerillas. He performed both tasks with distinction, laying the foundations for independence in 1957 and for the eventual ending of the jungle war in 1960.

Thought was also given to the future of some of the colonies which might be too small or too poor ever to become independent nations. The Conservatives began to experiment with federations, grouping colonies together into what they hoped would be successful federal unions. The Federation of the Rhodesias and Nyasaland (the Central African Federation) was set up in 1953, the West Indies Federation in 1958, and what came to be known as the South

Arabian Federation in 1959. None proved successful. It was suspected that such federations arose not merely from Britain's anxiety about the welfare of these territories but from some other considerations. Northern Rhodesia and Nyasaland, not without reason, saw the Central African Federation as a device for extending to themselves the control which a privileged white minority already exercised in Southern Rhodesia. Jamaica and Trinidad were suspicious of the West Indies Federation, fearing that Britain wanted to saddle them with the upkeep of the tiny and impoverished Caribbean islands which were included in the Federation. Both Federations collapsed in the early 1960s, and Liberals in the House of Commons claimed to have discovered a new political truth: that whomsoever the Conservatives joined together were sure to fall apart.

The Suez Crisis seemed to weaken the British government's will to hold on to the Empire. In 1957 Ghana (earlier known as the Gold Coast) and Malaya moved smoothly to independence, but doubts still persisted about Conservative readiness to accept the equality of races and to liberate all non-whites from white rule. In 1959 Selwyn Lloyd tried to reassure the UN General Assembly:

> We reject the idea of any inherent superiority of one race over another. Our policy is therefore non-racial. It offers a future in which Africans, Europeans, Asians, the peoples of the Pacific, and others with whom we are concerned, will all play their full part as citizens in the countries where they live and in which feelings of race will be submerged in loyalty to the new nations.

At about the same time, Macmillan appointed Iain Macleod as Britain's Colonial Secretary.

Macleod had already earned a reputation for liberalism at the Ministries of Health and Labour, and had come near to resigning in protest during the Suez Crisis. His appointment was symbolic of a new commitment to ending British imperial rule. He showed skill in making constitutions for new nations, though his liberal policies towards Africa soon attracted criticism from the right wing of the Conservative Party. Independence was granted to Nigeria in 1960, and then to Sierra Leone and Tanganyika in 1961; and the policy of withdrawal from the Empire was continued throughout the 1960s and 1970s by Macleod's successors, both Conservative and Labour. There were comparatively few problems when colonies had few white settlers: constitutional arrangements were made, and power was transferred to governments acceptable to the colonial peoples. The timing of independence produced some difficulties, however, since it sometimes seemed that the British were unnecessarily slow in arranging the orderly transfer of power on which they insisted. Local nationalists were eager for their colonial rulers to be gone, and when they did not go quickly enough, clashes were likely, as had happened in India before 1947. But, on the whole, the decolonization of the British Empire was accomplished more smoothly, and with less bitterness than that of any other European colonial empire.

Violent confrontations nevertheless occurred in Kenya and Cyprus. Nationalist supporters of the Mau Mau took a Killing Oath as part of their campaign to terrorize the British into leaving Kenya. A bitter struggle lasted throughout the 1950s until the Mau Mau were crushed in 1960. Fewer than a hundred whites were killed, but some 2 000 Africans died in the service of the British government, and almost 10 000 Mau Mau supporters. Britain's withdrawal from Kenya was complicated by tribal rivalries and by the presence there of substantial minorities of whites and Asians. Some of the whites wanted safeguards for their privileges, which were not consistent with a belief in racial equality. For some years the British hesitated to transfer power to a black majority government, and thus to appear to be abandoning their 'kith and kin'. However, it was to a predominantly black African government under Jomo Kenyatta that the British eventually transferred power, when the decision was finally taken to make Kenya independent in 1963.

The confrontation in Cyprus had different origins, and displayed some similarities to the problems Britain had faced in Palestine. Cyprus was divided between Greek and Turkish communities, neither of whom wanted to be dominated by the other; yet the Greeks in particular clamoured for independence. A further complication was a movement among some Greek Cypriots for *Enosis*, union with Greece, with a militant wing of the movement, known as EOKA, resorting to terrorism to press their demands. Once again the British were involved in conflict, although it became evident during the 1950s that the best hopes for peace in Cyprus lay with Archbishop Makarios, a Greek Cypriot leader who commanded widespread respect. Talks with Greece and Turkey as well as with the Cypriots brought some peace to Cyprus during 1959, and Makarios was elected the island's President. Britain then conceded Cyprus its independence in 1960. The island's long-term problems had not been solved, however, and since Macmillan's government had insisted on retaining military bases on the island, Britain inevitably became involved again in later years.

Delays in granting independence also occurred elsewhere. The West Indies Federation had been intended to lead to the independence of a union of British Caribbean islands, but disputes among its members caused it to be dissolved in 1962. Jamaica and Trinidad-Tobago then gained their independence as individual nations. Barbados and some of the smaller islands followed in their footsteps until, by the 1980s, Britain was left with only a handful of the tiniest islands.

The independence of British Guiana, on the mainland of South America, was delayed for a different reason. Guiana had not joined the West Indies Federation, but moved gradually towards self-government during the 1950s. In elections the people of Guiana showed a tendency to support Cheddi Jagan and his followers. Jagan had once been a dentist. Politically, he was a Marxist. When he became the Prime Minister in 1961 neither the British Conservatives nor their American allies felt it would be proper to transfer power to a government which leaned towards communism. The British therefore withheld independence, claiming the excuse of unrest within Guiana. It was not until 1966 that the people of Guiana elected a government sufficiently 'respectable' and with a strong enough majority to satisfy the British. Only then did the British Labour government concede independence. Under the new leadership of Forbes Burnham, Guiana adopted the name of Guyana.

The Central African Federation had meanwhile collapsed in 1963. Two of its members, Northern Rhodesia and Nyasaland, became independent under black governments a year later. Yet neither was as advanced and prosperous as Southern Rhodesia, the third member of the Federation, from which independence was withheld. Southern Rhodesia was about to become the most difficult problem of all in the decolonization of the British Empire. It is a problem which needs to be looked at in the context of southern Africa as a whole, and also in the light of the growing awareness of the importance of race relations in the world of the later twentieth century.

14.4 The Wind of Change in Southern Africa

(a) South Africa and the Changing Commonwealth

The new nations which gained their independence in the 1950s and 1960s almost all sought and obtained admission to the Commonwealth (see Table 14.1). The British Commonwealth thus became increasingly multi-racial and, since it was a partnership of equals, 'British' was quietly dropped from its title. 1960 was an important year in the Commonwealth's history: the admission of Nigeria meant that for the first time non-white members outnumbered the white members who had founded it originally. By 1968, of twenty-eight member nations twelve were African. There was no room in such a changing association, nor in the world as a whole, for lingering beliefs in white superiority. Moreover nations such as Britain, which depended on overseas markets and goodwill, simply could not afford to offend the developing non-white nations by clinging to outworn attitudes. The Suez Crisis had taught Britain one lesson about the ways in which the world was changing. The British were tested again over the issue of non-white immigration into the United Kingdom (see Unit 17). It was a relatively simple matter for Selwyn Lloyd to reject racial superiority in a speech to the United Nations, but Britain was likely to be judged on its actions rather than on words. This was nowhere more true than in southern Africa.

The Union of South Africa had become a Dominion shortly before the First World War and was a founder-member of the British Commonwealth of Nations (see Unit 4.3(a)). Since all political power in South Africa lay with the whites it was regarded as a White Dominion at that time. In fact, only about 20 per cent of the South African population was white, though the country was organized to the great advantage of this minority. The non-whites, especially the twelve million or so of Bantu descent who made up almost 70 per cent of the population, were repressed and regimented to serve the interests of their

Table 14.1 The developing Commonwealth

Country	Estimated population 1980 (millions)	Year of admission	Year of resignation
The White Man's Club			
Britain	56	*	
Canada	24	*	
Australia	15	*	
New Zealand	3	*	
South Africa	28	*	1961
Irish Free State	3	1921	1949
The European-Asian Commonwealth			
India	630	1947	
Pakistan	77	1947	1972
Ceylon (Sri Lanka)	14	1948	
The Multi-racial Commonwealth			
Ghana	11	1957	
Malaya (Malaysia, 1963)	13	1957	
Nigeria	80	1960	
Cyprus	0.8	1961	
Sierra Leone	3	1961	
Tanganyika (Tanzania, 1964)	17	1961	
Jamaica	2	1962	
Trinidad-Tobago	1	1962	
Uganda	13	1962	
Kenya	15	1963	
Malawi	6	1964	
Malta	0.4	1964	
Zambia	6	1964	
The Gambia	0.6	1965	
Singapore	3	1965	
Guyana	1	1966	
Botswana	0.8	1966	
Lesotho	1	1966	
Barbados	0.3	1966	
Mauritius	1	1968	
Swaziland	0.6	1968	
Nauru	†	1968	
Tonga	0.1	1970	
Fiji	0.6	1970	

Country	Estimated population 1980 (millions)	Year of admission	Year of resignation
Western Samoa	0.2	1970	
Bangladesh (formerly East Pakistan)	83	1972	
The Bahamas	0.3	1973	
Grenada	0.1	1974	
Papua New Guinea	3	1975	
The Seychelles	0.1	1976	
Solomon Islands	0.2	1978	
Tuvalu	†	1978	
Dominica	0.1	1978	
St Lucia	0.1	1979	
Kiribati	†	1979	
St Vincent	0.1	1979	
Zimbabwe	7.4	1980	
Vanuatu	0.1	1980	
Belize	0.2	1981	
Antigua	0.1	1981	

* founder-members before 1914
† below 70 000
The Commonwealth Secretariat was set up in 1965, with its headquarters in London.

white 'superiors'. The system was that of *baaskap*, of white supremacy, and black South Africans had neither political nor economic power. A more elaborate system was developed after the Nationalist Party won the South African elections in 1948. Based on the doctrines of *apartheid*, it provided for the separate development of the races, even to the extent of eventually setting up *bantustans*, areas in which the blacks could organize and control their own affairs. The rulers of South Africa argued that the system provided for the development of the Bantu – but only 13 per cent of South African land was allocated to them. For blacks everywhere, South African apartheid was a symbol of the degradation of their race, and it was detested throughout the world. South Africa further offended world opinion by retaining its hold on South-West Africa (Namibia), a mandated territory after the First World War but now another area where apartheid was practised.

Inevitably the question was asked during the 1950s whether apartheid had any place in the developing Commonwealth. The new members of the Commonwealth, supported by the Canadians, demanded changes in South African policies. Interest began to focus on Britain's attitude. After all, it was Britain that had transferred power to the white minority in South Africa in 1910. Macmillan visited South Africa early in 1960, and spoke in Cape Town:

> The most striking of all the impressions I have formed since I left London a month ago is of the strength of . . . African national consciousness. . . . The wind of change is blowing through the continent. Whether we like it or not, this growth of national consciousness is a political fact. Our national policies must take account of it.

Macmillan made it clear that Britain could not support apartheid, but the South African government showed no great concern. Later in 1960, however, the Commonwealth Conference asserted that 'the Commonwealth . . . is a multi-racial association'. When South Africa gave notice that it was intending to drop the British monarchy and become a republic, the Commonwealth seized the opportunity to insist that, when that happened, South Africa would have to apply to members of the Commonwealth for the renewal of its membership. The Republic was approved by South Africa's white voters, and Dr Verwoerd, the Prime Minister, made his first overseas journey for more than thirty years to argue South Africa's case for membership of the Commonwealth Conference of 1961 in London.

Most members of the Commonwealth wanted a compromise. Like Nehru and Nkrumah, they demanded some promise that apartheid would at least be softened. Canada and New Zealand took a similar stance. Only Australia and Britain tried to sit on the fence, condemning apartheid but apparently preferring to do nothing about it. Verwoerd refused to make any concessions at all. A decision became more urgent, however, when Julius Nyerere, the Tanganyikan leader, sent a message to the Conference. Tanganyika was about to become independent, and Nyerere declared that his country would not join the Commonwealth if South Africa remained a member. It was essential now to decide whether its members genuinely supported a multi-racial Commonwealth. For Nyerere, it was a vital matter of principle. Not to join the Commonwealth, he told his people, was:

> a sacrifice we must be prepared to make in our fight to preserve the dignity of man in Africa and wipe out racialism.

It seemed that the Commonwealth must now choose between South Africa and Tanganyika, since Verwoerd still defended apartheid. It also seemed likely that many more states would adopt Nyerere's attitude, when they became independent.

Macmillan still hesitated, and it was Verwoerd himself who finally resolved the dilemma. With some relief, the Commonwealth leaders reported:

The Prime Minister of South Africa informed the other Prime Ministers this evening that in the light of the views expressed on behalf of other member Governments . . . regarding the racial policy of the (South African) Government, he had decided to withdraw his application for South Africa's continuing membership of the Commonwealth.

South Africa thus left the Commonwealth. Tanganyika and many other new nations duly joined it. Macmillan nevertheless still tried to give comfort to Verwoerd by an agreement that Britain and South Africa would continue to co-operate 'in all possible ways'. Britain had extensive commercial and financial interests in South Africa which the British government believed it had a duty to protect. Many Conservatives also believed that friendship towards South African whites might eventually lead to some relaxation of the laws of apartheid. Most of their Labour and Liberal opponents were more forthright in condemning the South African system, and Britain's policy towards South Africa continued to be a matter for political controversy in Britain.

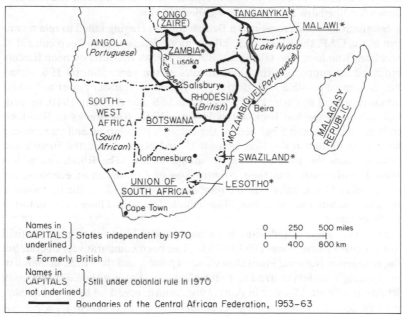

Fig. 14.5   The Wind of Change in Southern Africa by 1970

(b) The Rhodesian Problem

It was against this background that the problem of Southern Rhodesia came to the boil. In the 1960s Southern Rhodesia had a population of some four-and-a-half million, of whom just over 200 000 were white. The colony had had self-government since 1923 but that meant rule by the white minority, similar in some ways to the white rule of South Africa. Not until 1961 were black Rhodesians guaranteed any seats in parliament, and comparatively few of them qualified for the right to vote. While the Central African Federation (CAF) lasted, that too was dominated by whites. First Godfrey Huggins, a Southern Rhodesian, and then Roy Welensky, a Northern Rhodesian, tried to entrench white power in the Federal government, and black nationalist leaders were imprisoned. This solved nothing in Northern Rhodesia and Nyasaland, however, for the white settlers were too few to be able to resist the 'wind of change' for long. Northern Rhodesians united behind Kenneth Kaunda, and Nyasaland behind Hastings Banda. Both demanded black rule, secession from the CAF and independence. The British sent Commissions to investigate the affairs of the Federation, and first the Devlin Report and then the Monckton Report proved critical. Monckton recommended that states should be allowed to leave the CAF if that was their wish – what Welensky called the 'death-knell' of the Federation. It was dissolved in 1963. A year later Banda led Nyasaland to independence under its new name of Malawi, and Kaunda achieved independence for Northern Rhodesia, now called Zambia.

Southern Rhodesia remained a British colony. Having failed to retain control of the CAF, the whites were all the more determined to keep control of Southern Rhodesia (see Glossary). But the British had already been fiercely criticized for supporting the CAF for almost ten years and, by 1964, it no longer seemed possible for a British government to transfer power to a white minority, as had so unthinkingly been done in South Africa in 1910. Indeed, full independence had been withheld since 1923. The whites in Rhodesia comprised only about 5 per cent of the colony's population, and there would have been uproar in the Commonwealth and at the UN if the British had granted them the total authority of independence. The Rhodesian whites argued, with truth, that their country was one of the most economically advanced in Africa, and was thus equipped to be independent. But that was not the issue. Before independence, black Rhodesians would have to be admitted to government.

However, white Rhodesians were moving steadily to the right. Garfield Todd's government, from 1953 to 1958, had been comparatively liberal, but the Rhodesian National Front then came to power; and the Front, in search of ever stronger leaders to stand up to the blacks and the British, made Ian Smith Rhodesia's Prime Minister in April 1964. Smith, urged on by his white supporters, demanded immediate independence, visiting London to argue his case with Douglas-Home. Not only were black Rhodesian leaders such as Joshua Nkomo and Ndabaningi Sithole kept in detention, Garfield Todd was now detained too, for advocating a compromise. Douglas-Home insisted that there could be no independence without such compromise, but Smith's supporters had not elected him to make concessions. A confrontation seemed unavoidable, but matters had first to await the outcome of the British general election of 1964. Whatever government the British elected was sure to find Rhodesia high on its list of problems (see Unit 20.2).

Fig. 14.6 The Citizen, a right-wing newspaper in Rhodesia, proclaims its confidence in Ian Smith shortly before the confrontation between Rhodesian whites and the British government led to UDI: Salisbury, Rhodesia

14.5 Hovering Uncertainly

During the thirteen years from 1951 to 1964 the British had groped rather uncertainly to find a new role in the fast-changing world. By 1964 the decision had been taken to dismantle virtually the whole of the British Empire and much of that task had already been completed. There was greater understanding that the days of imperial glory had gone for ever, and yet there were lingering doubts in some quarters. Eden had had considerable public support during the Suez Crisis. There was a good deal of sympathy in British backwaters for South African and Rhodesian whites. The government had made a stand against conceding independence to Rhodesian whites, but it had no stomach for tackling the problem of dispossessing them of the authority they already had. The Conservatives had also begun to seem lukewarm about the Commonwealth in its new multi-racial phase, and there were misgivings about the development of a multi-racial society in Britain itself. When Britain tried to join the European Economic Community in the early 1960s, some observers saw it as an attempt to turn away from the Commonwealth to seek a new role in Europe. De Gaulle's veto had ruled that out, however, at least for the time being (see Unit 20.3).

Only the alliance with the USA seemed wholly secure in the mid 1960s. Otherwise, Britain still seemed to hover uncertainly between its imperial past and the world of the super powers, between the multi-racial Commonwealth and the narrower interests of western Europe and the EEC. The idea nevertheless persisted in Britain that the country ought to find a distinctive role to play in world affairs; and this was perhaps itself merely part of the nostalgia for past glories to which many in Britain seemed addicted.

Further Reading

Medlicott, W.N.: *British Foreign Policy since Versailles*. Methuen (London, 1968).
Northedge, F.S.: *Descent from Power, British Foreign Policy 1945–1973*. George Allen and Unwin (London, 1974).
Watson, J.B.: *Empire to Commonwealth, 1919–1970*. Dent (London, 1971).
Watson, J.B.: *Success in Twentieth Century World Affairs*. John Murray (London, 3rd edn. 1984).
Watson, J.B.: *The West Indian Heritage*. John Murray (London, 1979).
See also Unit 13.

Documentary

The Commonwealth Today. Commonwealth Institute Study Kit (London, 1980).
Windrich, E.: *The Rhodesian Problem, 1923–1973*. Routledge (London, 1975).

Exercises

1. (*a*) Making use of Fig. 12.7 and Unit 12.3, explain what interests Britain had in the Middle East in the years after 1945.
    (*b*) What were the 'events in Persia' which had 'already humiliated Britain' (page 239)?
2. Trace the development and explain the outcome of the Suez Crisis of 1956. Explain, and comment on the appropriateness of the cartoon concerning Eden's part in this Crisis (Fig. 14.2).
3. Draft two sets of notes suitable for speeches in November 1956 on the motion, 'This House supports the policy of the government in sending troops to Egypt', *one* speech in favour of the motion, *the other* against it.
4. Making use of the Index to this book, summarize the career of Anthony Eden to his resignation in 1957. What changes took place between 1935 and 1957 in his attitude towards appeasement?
5. Trace the part played by Britain in East–West relations in the years 1951–64. How true is it that Britain now had 'comparatively little influence' (page 245) on the policies of the super powers?
6. Explain in your own words the extracts from the speeches of (*a*) Selwyn Lloyd, quoted on page 247 and (*b*) Macmillan, quoted on page 252. In what ways were the ideas expressed in these speeches important for the development of the Commonwealth?
7. Why was there considerable international interest in British attitudes towards developments in southern Africa during the twenty years after the end of the Second World War? Why was Britain's policy towards South Africa 'a matter for political controversy in Britain' (page 253), and how far was there similar controversy about policy towards Rhodesia?
8. Making use of Table 14.1, explain how the British Commonwealth of Nations in the years 1945 to 1964 (*a*) grew and (*b*) developed new characteristics.

9. In what ways by 1964 was Britain's policy towards overseas problems (*a*) similar to, and (*b*) different from, the policy at the beginning of the 1950s?

10. Making use of the Index to this book, outline the career of Harold Macmillan up to 1963, and identify his main achievements both within Britain and overseas. (Compare what you have written with a biography of Macmillan in Alan Palmer's *Dictionary of Twentieth-Century History*, or a good encyclopaedia.) Suggest reasons why Vicky dubbed him *Supermac* (Fig. 13.3).

Unit Fifteen

Economic Struggle and Political Compromise: Labour Government, 1964–70

15.1 Labour Aims and the General Elections of 1964 and 1966

The Labour Party had high hopes of winning the general election of 1964. The Conservative image had become tarnished in various ways and even if Douglas-Home had the ability, he had not had time to achieve a stature similar to Macmillan's. The Labour Party, on the other hand, seemed at last to be recovering from internal strife. Optimistically, the Labour Manifesto promised *The New Britain:*

> mobilizing the resources of technology under a national plan; harnessing our national wealth in brains, our genius for scientific invention and medical discovery; reversing the decline of thirteen wasted years; affording a new opportunity to equal, and if possible surpass, the roaring prosperity of other western powers while Tory Britain has moved sideways, backwards but seldom forward.

In *Prosperity with a Purpose* the Conservatives alleged that what Labour really offered was:

> not a 'New Britain', but a camouflaged return to the dreary doctrines which had already proved a failure when they were last dismissed from office.

A Conservative vote, on the other hand, would be one for:

> our philosophy . . . to use what is good from the past to create a future which is better.

The Labour Party expected to gain handsomely from the confident bustling leadership of Harold Wilson (see Unit 13.5). Wilson's trump card in the election was the impression he gave that he could manage the economy more effectively than the Conservatives appeared to have done; just how this feat would be performed was largely to be taken on trust. But the Labour Party in 1964 was more concerned with 'modernization' than with ideology and pursuing old objectives such as nationalization. The balance of payments was again heading for a deficit, the cost of living was rising, growth remained disappointing, and all this against the background of evils such as Rachmanism (see Unit 13.5). Labour promised a new Ministry of Economic Affairs to plan economic growth, and social reform to bring about a fairer society but, as Table 10.1

shows, there was no upsurge of support for *The New Britain*. Labour's success was due to the falling away of support for the Conservatives. Far from winning a sweeping victory, Wilson became the Prime Minister of a new Labour government with an overall majority of only four seats in the House of Commons. More than three million voters chose to support the Liberals, engagingly led in this campaign by Grimond.

'THERE GO THREE MORE DON'T KNOWS'

Fig. 15.1 Opinion polls had become an established part of British life by the mid 1960s, not least in seeking to forecast the results of general elections. Emmwood in the Daily Mail *took an unflattering view of the party leaders at the general election of 1964: from left to right, Douglas-Home, Wilson and Grimond*

Such a small government majority made another election likely in the near future. The Conservatives quickly elected a new leader, and Edward Heath replaced Douglas-Home in 1965. The Labour government also needed to act quickly, to try to prove its competence to the voters. Its management of the economy would provide the most important test, and the main responsibility fell on Wilson, James Callaghan, the Chancellor of the Exchequer, and George Brown, at the Department of Economic Affairs (see Table 15.3). The balance of payments deficit turned out to be almost £400 million in 1964, and there was perhaps a case for devaluing the pound again, to produce results similar to those of 1949 (see Table 11.1). But devaluation would be controversial and could well damage Labour's re-election hopes, so other remedies were tried instead. A temporary surcharge was imposed on imports, to make them less attractive to British buyers. A Prices and Incomes Board was set up, with trade union co-operation, to try to check inflation and to hold down production costs. Bank Rate was raised again to 7 per cent. Certain taxes, including income tax, were also raised to reduce demand and to pay for higher pensions and the abolition of NHS prescription charges, both promised during the election.

There were various other social reforms but the Labour government was balancing on a tightrope. Its tiny majority could be lost at almost any moment on such delicate issues as non-white immigration into Britain, the Rhodesian problem and the renationalization of the iron and steel industry. Wilson had to tread very carefully, while at the same time seeking economic success. The balance of payments was likely to prove the vital issue. The deficit was reduced during 1965, and there was a small surplus in 1966. There was evidence that public opinion was moving in the government's favour at the beginning of 1966, and Wilson decided to appeal to the voters for a bigger majority. His slogan for the election of March 1966 was 'You Know Labour Government Works'. The Labour government had certainly worked hard, but whether it had worked more effectively than the Conservatives was not so clear – and inevitably the answer became obscured in a forest of statistics, claims and counter-claims.

Labour emphasized that planning was essential to overcome economic problems, and the Party's new Manifesto, *Time for Decision*, put forward an array of new plans. There were plans for the various regions of the United Kingdom, for a coherent transport policy, for an Industrial Reorganization Corporation to modernize British industry, and for numerous social reforms. The programme certainly supported Labour's claim to be the party of change, but it said little about the matters of ideology which had caused so much dispute during Gaitskell's leadership. Wilson's aim was to appeal to broadly progressive opinion in all classes, to avoid giving the impression that the Labour Party consisted only of convinced socialists or represented merely sectional interests, such as those of trade unionists. The Manifesto nevertheless showed some social concern, including an ambitious housing programme and a plan for cheap ('option') mortgages, so that house-owning could come within the reach of lower-paid workers.

The Conservatives attacked Labour's links with the trade unions, and pointed out that the Prices and Incomes Board had so far done more to hold down prices than wages. There had been no upsurge of industrial unrest since the 1964 election, but the Conservatives increasingly blamed the unions for weakening the British economy. *Action not Words* set out the Conservative policy, which included proposals for trade union reform. Under the new leadership of Edward Heath, the Conservatives hoped to persuade the voters that they were now ready to make a fresh start on tackling the country's problems.

The voters' verdict was decisive. Labour gained forty-six seats and almost a million votes, and Wilson now had a comfortable majority (see Table 10.1). As in all postwar elections, however, the winning party did not poll even half the votes cast. It seemed that the voters looked forward to the solving of Britain's problems with hope rather than with confidence. They preferred Labour to the Conservatives, but the Liberals attracted more than two million votes, this time

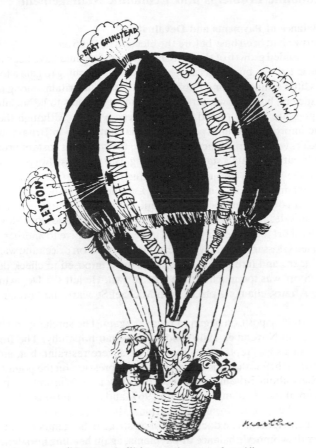

"Brothers! We're running out of gas!"

Fig. 15.2 Martin in the Sunday Express *(February 1965) noted the discomfort of the Labour government soon after the general election of 1964: Wilson, Callaghan and Brown already anxious that the Labour balloon was less easily kept airborne with the promise of '100 Dynamic Days' and reminders to the voters of the '13 Years' of the Conservatives. By-elections, such as that at Leyton where Gordon Walker was defeated, quickly showed the insecurity of Wilson's government*

winning twelve seats in the Commons, three more than in 1964. The Liberals still found it difficult to make real headway against the larger parties, however, and Grimond gave up the leadership soon after the election. His successor was Jeremy Thorpe.

15.2 Economic Problems and Economic Management

(a) The Balance of Payments and Devaluation

George Brown had been busy before the election of 1966 on Labour's National Plan for the guided growth of the British economy. It would have been a major innovation in Britain, but events moved too fast for planning to gain a foothold. There was little sympathy for a Labour government in Britain among international financiers, however weak that government's claims to be socialist, and renewed pressure on the pound soon produced a crisis. Although there had been some improvement in exports, overseas confidence in Britain was low. The financiers wanted drastic action to reduce the country's costs of production – in effect, a cut in Britain's standard of living. But this was always likely to be resisted by the workers and to lead to industrial unrest (see Unit 15.2(b)). Wilson complained that it seemed easy for Labour's economic management to be 'blown off course', but the government found itself under pressure from financiers outside, and squeezed by a seaman's strike at home from May to July 1966. In the short term, there appeared to be no alternative to another bout of deflation (see Glossary): there was a temporary freeze on prices and wages, and additional taxes and hire-purchase controls were imposed to check demand. This new 'Stop' was too much for George Brown. He left the Department of Economic Affairs, changing places with Michael Stewart, the Foreign Secretary.

Britain's trading position began to recover again. The surcharge on imports was removed in November 1966, and 1967 began hopefully. The freeze on prices and wages was replaced by a phase of 'severe restraint' but, almost at once, that brought another crisis. There was new pressure on the pound, giving rise to anxiety about Britain's gold and dollar reserves. Wilson took personal overlordship of the economy in August 1967, and made furious efforts to get support for the pound from international banks and the International Monetary Fund (IMF). The dockers went on strike in September, threatening still further the country's balance of payments, again heading into deficit. The devaluation of the pound began to seem likely, but it was resisted by James Callaghan, the Chancellor:

> Those who advocate devaluation are calling for a reduction in the wage levels and the real wage standards of every member of the working class in this country.

In fact, Callaghan could do little more than delay in the face of mounting pressures. Devaluation was the only obvious solution to the immediate crisis, though it seemed unlikely to provide any long-term answer to Britain's problems.

The pound was devalued on 18 October 1967. Its value was cut by a seventh, from the 2.80 dollars fixed in 1949 to 2.40 dollars – but the international bankers and the IMF, which offered Britain a new loan, also demanded further fierce deflation. Callaghan resigned as Chancellor, changing places with Roy

Jenkins, the Home Secretary. But 1968 brought yet more pressure on the pound and, for a time, there was even talk of further devaluation. In trying to curb inflationary pressures, Jenkins imposed further tax increases, brought back NHS prescription charges and took steps to reduce the government's own spending. Such a fierce and lengthy 'Stop' was hardly what the voters had expected in March 1966. The National Plan for long-term growth was an early casualty in the day-to-day battle to rescue the economy. George Brown was another: he resigned from the government in March 1968. Wilson was reminded that he himself had resigned in 1951 in circumstances which were in some ways similar (see page 194).

1968 was another bleak year for Britain, but other countries were now running into difficulties too. There was pressure on the French franc, which was devalued during 1969. About the same time, the West Germans revalued the mark upwards, a move which was helpful to their competitors in international markets. Table 15.1 shows that Britain's balance of payments improved, with a movement back into surplus, but Jenkins remained cautious. He insisted that the next priority must be investment for growth rather than a new boom in consumption. The government's wages policy was made only slightly less severe and Bank Rate, which reached 8 per cent in both 1967 and 1969, only fell to 7 per cent shortly before the general election of 1970.

Unit 15.2(c) will show that the Labour government by no means entirely neglected modernization and growth in the years after 1964, though much of its term of office was dominated by economic crises. Short-term measures had again taken priority over long-term planning, and economic growth stayed stubbornly at around an annual 2.5 per cent (see Table 13.1). The government had not achieved the breakthrough to increase that growth in the way envis-aged in Brown's abortive National Plan. The new calm at the end of the 1960s suggested there might be an opportunity to look further ahead and attack Britain's underlying economic problems more vigorously, but there was now another obstacle in the way – the general election of 1970.

(b) Incomes and Industrial Relations

Soon after taking office in 1964 Wilson's government had persuaded employers and trade unions to sign a Declaration of Intent on Productivity, Prices and Incomes. The intention was to boost productivity and, at the same time, to keep prices and incomes from running ahead of the growth in Gross National Product. If that could be achieved, it would be a major step towards a healthier economy, for inflation would be curbed and British exports kept competitive. It was therefore an important factor in the struggle for a healthy balance of payments. By restraining prices and all forms of income, the govern-ment hoped to persuade workers that the system was fair and that they should refrain from excessive wage claims.

The government also aimed to win goodwill by measures such as the Redun-dancy Payments Act of 1965, which provided compensation for workers who lost their jobs through no fault of their own, often as the result of technological

Table 15.1   Britain's balance of payments, 1966–81

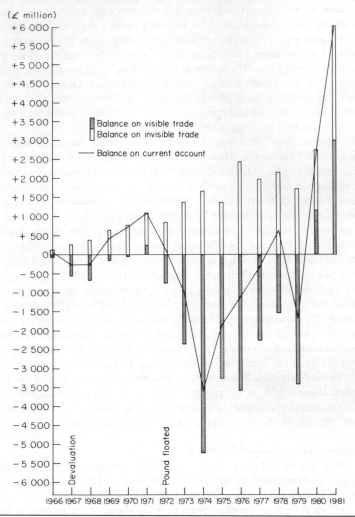

Source: adapted from *Economic Trends*, January 1979, with additions.

changes. The Prices and Incomes Board was set up in 1965 and achieved some modest success, though incomes in 1965–6 increased at around 9 per cent rather than the target figure of 3.5 per cent. The merchant seamen's strike over pay and conditions in the spring of 1966 worsened the country's trading and financial position. The seamen returned to work in July, but Wilson felt that the basically voluntary system of restraint had not been firm enough. The freeze

Fig. 15.3   George Brown (centre), triumphant with the Declaration of Intent on Productivity, Prices and Incomes, December 1964. George Woodcock (extreme right), General Secretary of the TUC, looks thoughtful

was now imposed, with a standstill on wages (see Unit 15.2(*a*)). There were further strikes, for example by the dockers in autumn 1966, but prices and incomes rose by only about 2 per cent during the following twelve months. The Prices and Incomes Act of 1967 allowed some small relaxation, with the government keeping the power to refer any apparently unreasonable increases to the Prices and Incomes Board. This permitted flexibility in dealing with cases where there might be good reason for 'extra' increases, perhaps resulting from greater productivity, or injustice because of the freeze and severe restraint.

Wilson's aim was to achieve 'voluntary restraint' and his government steadily reduced its own controlling role by 1970. But every intervention tended to create its own problems. It was easier to impose a freeze than to ensure restraint when that freeze was lifted. A system of voluntary restraint needed time in which to grow, and this was seldom available as the British economy staggered from crisis to crisis. At the heart of the problem lies the delicate question of the right balance in a free society between the authority of government and the liberties of individuals. Rigid and lengthy controls tend to breed resentment and to lead to disruption. Complete freedom almost certainly leads to the triumph of strong sectional interests over the weak. George Woodcock, the General Secretary of the TUC, and many other trade union leaders tried hard to co-operate with Wilson's government in matters of incomes policy, recognizing its importance to the health of the country's economy. Nevertheless, strikes occurred and, indeed, increased during the late 1960s (see

Tables 13.4 and 15.2). The vast majority were again unofficial (see Unit 13.4). About half were mainly about wages, and many others were about working conditions and allegedly unfair dismissals. Their effect on output was slight: the loss of production was little more than 0.1 per cent of any annual total, and was much less than losses due to sickness. The nation was nevertheless worried about strikes and the turbulent industrial relations to which some industries seemed especially prone. There had been no thorough inquiry into Britain's industrial relations for almost a hundred years and, in 1965, the government thought such an investigation might be helpful. The task was entrusted to a Commission led by Lord Donovan.

Before the Donovan Report was published in 1968, another problem involving trade unions developed from a dispute about a closed shop (see Glossary). Union pressure forced BOAC to dismiss an employee, Rookes, who was no longer a member of the union at his workplace. Rookes sued for damages and was successful in the Rookes v. Barnard Case. The government promptly introduced the Trade Disputes Act of 1965 to give fuller protection to union leaders in such cases. The Act tended to increase the feeling in the country that unions were in some cases above the law and that, while it might be argued that a worker had a duty to join a union from whose activities he might well benefit, union pressure on individuals might itself be a form of intimidation. The Donovan Report did not recommend any further legislation, however, taking the view that new laws would not improve the existing system. On the other hand, it did recommend ways in which employers and unions could make improvements themselves, urging a reduction in the number of small trade unions, a clearer definition of the duties of shop stewards and better training for union officials. The Report also suggested that procedures for settling disputes and dealing with redundancies should be more clearly defined. It further proposed a Commission on Industrial Relations to have general oversight and provide an advisory service. The government quickly set up this Commission, appointing Woodcock as its first Chairman while Vic Feather succeeded him as the General Secretary of the TUC.

Some members of Wilson's government still felt that there was room for new law and the job of preparing it was given to Barbara Castle, the Employment Secretary. The plans were outlined in *In Place of Strife* at the beginning of 1969. They included provision for a 'cooling-off period' before a strike could begin, for voting on workers' attitudes towards a strike, and for legal penalties against those who broke the new rules. But the cabinet was itself divided on the proposals. Callaghan was against them, and so too was Crosland at the Board of Trade. The TUC resisted strongly and a revolt of Labour MPs began to take shape. There were genuine fears that legislation might simply make matters worse. In June 1969 Wilson and Castle had no choice but to bury *In Place of Strife*, since legislation seemed unlikely to be carried through the House of Commons. The TUC, on the other hand, undertook to do its best to check unofficial strikes and to prevent strikes which resulted from inter-union disputes. It set up its own 'fire-fighting' machinery for this purpose. Wilson claimed this as a victory, but there was still disquiet about the limited nature of legal restrictions on trade unions. The Conservatives, at the general election of 1970, insisted that new laws were essential.

Table 15.2 Working days lost annually in Britain through industrial disputes, 1964–81 (millions)

Year	Days	Year	Days
1964	2.0	1973	7.1
1965	2.9	1974	14.8
1966	2.4	1975	5.9
1967	2.8	1976	3.5
1968	4.7	1977	10.1
1969	6.9	1978	9.4
1970	10.9	1979	29.5
1971	13.6	1980	12.0
1972	23.9	1981	4.3

(c) **Modernization**
Labour had come to power in 1964 with a keen awareness of changing technology, and convinced of the need to try to direct it. In 1963 Wilson had declared:

> It is a choice between the blind imposition of technological advance, with all that means in terms of unemployment, and the conscious, planned purposive use of scientific progress to provide undreamed of living standards and the possibility of (unbelievable) leisure.

The Labour government intended to be active in shaping industrial development. Wilson promptly set up a new Ministry of Technology (Mintech) and, three years later in 1967, created the Industrial Reorganization Corporation (IRC). Frank Cousins was the first Minister of Technology, but he resigned in protest at the government's policy on wage restraint. He thus failed to fulfil hopes that he might become another Bevin, a trade union leader successfully brought into government. Mintech in 1966 passed to Wedgwood Benn who proved both vigorous and competent, supervising a steady shift of resources from areas such as defence to Britain's export industries. Mintech undertook useful research work too, and it directed government money into the development of industries such as power-supply, vehicle-building and engineering.

Conventional thinking in the 1960s was that size was important and that successful industries needed to be both large and streamlined. The government encouraged the closure of small and uneconomic plant, though trying to take account of social problems and keep down unemployment at the same time. The IRC and bodies such as the Shipbuilding Industry Board encouraged private undertakings to merge and modernize. The IRC fostered the merger between Leyland Motors and the British Motor Corporation to create British Leyland, for example, trusting that the vast resources of the new organization would enable it to compete more effectively with giant companies overseas. But British Leyland inherited problems as well as resources: it had to marry together a bewildering collection of vehicles, factories and local working practices, which it would take many years to harmonize. In the 1970s, there-fore, the performance of British Leyland continued to be disappointing in the face of foreign competition in the family-car market. GEC (General Electric) similarly absorbed other electrical engineering companies, to create another giant.

In 1967 the Labour government took the thirteen largest iron and steel firms back into public ownership (see Unit 11.2(b)), forming the British Steel Corporation. This promptly found itself faced with enormous problems. Expensive modernization was urgently needed, and there was also the problem of a labour force which was larger and, partly because of old-fashioned plant, less productive than those of many foreign competitors. This was the only major act of nationalization in the years 1964–70, although the Post Office also became a public corporation instead of a government department. Here too it was hoped that management might make it more efficient and improve its commercial performance, but there were soon further problems, though with mail rather than telecommunications. In 1969 Mintech itself grew bigger and took on new responsibilities, including power. The Department of Economic Affairs was wound up at that time. By 1970 the Conservatives especially were demanding less interference and greater freedom for private enterprise, arguing that the government had busied itself too much with the affairs of industry.

Meanwhile, Wilson's government looked for other ways in which to lay foundations for a better economic performance. Another attempt was made to join the European Economic Community, though the Labour Party as a whole was not enthusiastic. Once more, however, de Gaulle blocked Britain's mem-bership (see Unit 20.3(a)). The Labour government reassessed Britain's defence commitments overseas and, as early as 1965, cut back government spending on costly new weapons such as military aircraft and Polaris nuclear submarines. Denis Healey was Defence Secretary throughout the years 1964–70 and his policy was to achieve a reduction in the real costs of the armed services. Neither West Germany nor Japan spent anything like as much of its GNP on defence as Britain did. Britain's overseas possessions were now shrinking fast, and the Labour government recognized that there were limits to how far the country could go on behaving as a world power. The most dramatic decision was to withdraw British forces from all bases 'east of Suez', except those in the Persian Gulf and Hong Kong, by 1971. It was hoped that reduced spending on defence would make more money available for Britain's economic development, and some shift of emphasis certainly took place. The aircraft industry, for example, successfully turned its attention to winning more export orders when the government cut back on military aircraft. On the other hand, still pursuing the fashionable gigantism of the 1960s, Wilson's government went on with the building of Concorde. The Conservatives had begun this project for a supersonic passenger aircraft in 1962 in partnership with the French. Development costs at that time were estimated at not more than £170 million. By 1965 the estimate had doubled. The French were eager to continue with it and the Labour government was reluctant to offend them by withdrawing. When Concorde was completed in 1973, however, it had cost over £1 000 million, half of which was paid by British taxpayers. The British and French aircraft industries gained prestige from their technological achievement, but Concorde's cost was out of proportion to its usefulness and it was widely believed that continuing with it had been an extravagant blunder.

Fig. 15.4 A British stamp of 1969: Concorde can fly its passengers ten miles high at twice the speed of sound but there has been fierce controversy about the costs of building and operating these supersonic aircraft

No progress was made in the building of a third airport for London. The existing airports at Heathrow and Gatwick would soon be inadequate for the growing volume of traffic but there was fierce local resistance to any new site which was proposed. Stansted, in Essex, was favoured by the planners but a decision was deferred, and went on being deferred throughout the 1970s. The Transport Act of 1968 meanwhile moved back towards the national planning of Britain's transport system after its partial return to independent ownership by the Conservatives (see Unit 13.2). Road passenger services for which the government was still responsible were to be run by the National Bus Company. The Act also set up the National Freight Corporation to co-ordinate goods traffic by road and rail. Container traffic and Freightliner Services were improving the business of the railways, but British Rail continued to lose traffic to road transport. In the five years from 1966 to 1971 annual rail passenger journeys fell from 835 million to 816 million, and the annual freight carried from 217 million tons to 198 million. The government supported the railways by financing uneconomic lines, keeping them open where there was a social need for such services in spite of operating losses.

Table 15.3 Labour and Conservative ministries, 1964–79

Date	Prime Minister	Chancellor of the Exchequer	Minister of Economic Affairs	Minister of Technology	Foreign Secretary	Home Secretary
1964–70 (Labour)	Wilson	Callaghan (1964–7) Jenkins (1967–70)	Brown (1964–6) Stewart (1966–7) Shore (1967–9) *Ministry wound up*	Cousins [from TGWU] (1964–6) Wedgwood Benn (1966–70)	Gordon Walker (1964–5) Stewart (1965–6) Brown (1966–8) Stewart (1968–70)	Soskice (1964–5) Jenkins (1965–7) Callaghan (1967–70)
1970–4 (Conservative)	Heath	Macleod (1970) Barber (1970–4)		*[Mintech merged in new Department of Trade and Industry]* Davies [from CBI] (1970–2) Walker (1972–4)	Douglas-Home	Maudling (1970–2) Carr (1972–4)

1974-6 (Labour)	Wilson	Healey	*Minister for Energy* Wedgwood Benn (1975-6)	[*now Department of Industry*] Wedgwood Benn (1974-5) Varley (1975-6)	Callaghan	Jenkins
1976-9 (Labour)	Callaghan	Healey	Wedgwood Benn	Varley	Crosland (1976-8) Owen (1978-9)	Rees

15.3 Social and Administrative Reform

In spite of the country's economic problems, the years 1964–70 brought increasing ownership of such material possessions as cars, television sets and washing machines to a wide section of the population. Government spending on social security had overtaken spending on defence in the early 1960s, and the gap now widened steadily. The Labour government also increased its spending on the Health Service, on education and, until the economic crisis of 1967, on housing. It worked busily on social and administrative improvements without making fundamental changes of the sort Attlee's government made after 1945. Pensions and family allowances were raised, though this was partly to keep up with increases in the cost of living. Family allowances were raised twice during 1968. There was then a 'claw-back' in the form of taxation from those families with no desperate need for the allowances, but the Labour Party believed in the principle of universal benefit in the first instance to ensure assistance to all in real need. The government was nevertheless criticized for its failure to take radical action to relieve the poverty of a still substantial section of the British people. The Child Poverty Action Group was founded in 1965 to bring pressure on the authorities and on society as a whole; and many trade union leaders regularly drew attention to the problems of the millions of low-paid workers in a society which was beginning to take prosperity for granted.

The government was not unconcerned. Apart from increasing benefits, a new Rent Act was passed in 1965, repealing that of 1957 and setting up tribunals to fix 'fair rents', though the new Act so discouraged private landlords that some rented accommodation disappeared. And the problem remained. *The Circumstances of Families*, an official survey in 1967, showed that over three-quarters of a million British people lived below the minimum level laid down for supplementary benefits, the term now used for national assistance. The problem was not just one of priorities among the limited sums the government had available to spend: the welfare state itself grew ever more complicated. Many of the poor failed to claim benefits to which they were entitled, lost in the maze of regulations. The regulations also required armies of administrators, adding fuel to the criticism that Britain was over-governed and had too many officials. Administrative change sometimes seemed only to add to the confusion. The Ministry of Social Security was set up in 1966. In 1968 it was merged into the Department of Health and Social Security (DHSS), with the aim of unifying responsibilities which had earlier been divided. But that the DHSS had still so often to meet needs with supplementary benefits suggested that the welfare state still had serious shortcomings (see Unit 11.3(*a*)).

The modernization of the country's institutions was of almost as much concern to the government as its attempts to modernize the economy. Government as a whole grew more complicated, with the number of civil servants increasing to 700 000 by 1971. Wilson set up the Fulton Commission to review the operations of the civil service, the first such study for well over a century.

The office of Ombudsman was created in 1967, to investigate injustice in the administration of certain government departments. The ordinary citizen was now entitled to appeal to the Ombudsman, though an appeal could only be made through a member of parliament. The government also implemented the recommendations of the Latey Commission, and reduced the age of majority from twenty-one to eighteen. Eighteen thus became the age at which young adults could take on financial commitments such as mortgages, marry without parental consent and vote, as they did for the first time in the parliamentary election of 1970. Nothing much came of the government's proposals to reform the House of Lords, however. The hereditary peerage and the delaying powers of the House survived proposals for their abolition, though the practice grew of creating life peers, entitled to sit in the House of Lords but not to pass on that right to their heirs. Other changes made by Wilson's government included the setting up of the Open University, to extend educational opportunity, and the introduction of the Murder Act of 1965 which suspended the death penalty (see Unit 13.2). The Docks and Harbours Act of 1966 combined administrative change with social reform, to secure greater efficiency and better working conditions. The Road Safety Act of 1967 introduced breath tests for suspected drunken drivers. Deaths in road accidents had now reached almost 8 000 a year and accidents, almost 300 000.

Housing continued to be a matter for concern. Like the Conservatives, the Labour government encouraged the trend towards home ownership, introducing the promised option mortgages (see Unit 15.1). By 1970 about half the nation's houses were owner-occupied, though the proportion was much lower in Scotland and the north of England. But the government did much more than encourage owner-occupiers. Richard Crossman was Wilson's first Minister for Housing and Local Government, and he was succeeded in 1966 by Anthony Greenwood. A Land Commission was set up, 'to acquire land for the community', and to ensure that it was wisely used after the property speculation which had flourished in the early 1960s. Tenants were protected against eviction. Rate rebates were introduced, to help those who could not afford their local rates. Leasehold reform also enabled the holders of long leases to buy the freeholds of their property, and escape from paying ground rent. Crossman also stepped up the pace of council building again, after it had fallen under the Conservatives. Of 400 000 dwellings completed in 1967, almost half were council homes; but the building programme was then cut back. Slums remained in many British cities, but there were not the resources for limitless improvements. In 1968 the government set aside some £20 million for 'urban renewal', mainly in decaying city centres, and further money was allocated to assist houseowners to modernize old properties. Disillusionment with postwar tower blocks began to increase at this time, especially when part of a block collapsed at Ronan Point.

Education was another area in which the Labour government aimed to make changes. Stewart was the Minister of Education in 1964, but he was quickly followed by Crosland and then, in 1968, by Edward Short. No major legislation was introduced, but the government strongly encouraged the movement towards comprehensive schools, instead of separate secondary schools for different levels of ability (see Unit 10.2). The Certificate of Secondary Education (CSE) was also introduced in 1965, to provide a less traditional public examination at the age of sixteen than the General Certificate of Education (GCE), which dated from 1951. The raising of the school-leaving age to sixteen continued to be postponed, however, though more children were encouraged to remain at school voluntarily. Higher education expanded rapidly after 1964, with a considerable increase in teacher-training. By 1970 spending on education reached almost £3 000 million each year and, like social security, education too was now costing more than defence.

15.4 Problems of Race and Role

Barbara Castle's first government appointment in 1964 was at the new Ministry of Overseas Development, set up to give new weight to Britain's aid programme to developing nations, especially those in the Commonwealth. By 1970 Britain was spending about £200 million a year on aid and technical assistance, although this still fell short of the target set by UNO. The United Nations had asked wealthy countries to give 1 per cent of their national incomes; Britain managed about 0.8 per cent, but only three wealthy countries did better.

Further indications of the sympathies of Wilson's government came when a ban was quickly imposed on the export of arms to South Africa, in protest against apartheid. The decolonization of the British Empire continued steadily, and most of the new nations joined the multi-racial Commonwealth (see Table 14.1). However, when Britain left Aden in 1967 after a savage confrontation, and after the failure of yet another Federation, the South Arabian, Aden stayed outside the Commonwealth. The British government's aim, nevertheless, was to preserve the Commonwealth and to foster good race relations, though the task was complicated by two issues which will be considered more fully in later units. One was the problem of Rhodesia, which came to a head in 1965 with the illegal declaration of independence by the white minority there (see Units 14.4(b) and 20.2). The other involved Britain itself, for some people found it difficult to accept a non-white minority in British society. Questions of race and colour were now burning issues in Britain and in the world as a whole. The Labour government made some effort to travel in a liberal direction introducing Race Relations Acts in 1965 and 1968 (see Unit 17.3), but the results were not always impressive.

Another controversial issue was Wilson's attempt to secure Britain's entry to the European Economic Community. After Britain's withdrawal from bases 'east of Suez' and frustration over the Rhodesian problem, some observers suggested that the Labour government might after all prefer Europe to the Commonwealth. There was less controversy about the continuing alliance with the USA and NATO. Even so, the left wing of the Labour Party still protested about Britain's nuclear weapons and some Party members pressed the government (unsuccessfully) to change to a policy of non-alignment, taking the side of neither the USA nor the USSR in the East–West rivalry. American policy in Vietnam, and Britain's attitude to it, were always likely to produce fierce debates within the Labour Party, and it was not enough for some that Britain played no part in the war. Outright condemnation of the USA was demanded, but the British government stopped well short of that.

The government did, on the other hand, condemn the USSR for suppressing dissent in Czechoslovakia in 1968. Diplomatic pressure was as far as Britain could now go: the lessons of the Suez Crisis had been learned. Brown, when Foreign Secretary, and Stewart, who returned to the Foreign Office as Brown's successor in 1968, both recognized the limits of Britain's influence. Some efforts were made to act as peacemakers, but these failed in Vietnam, and only succeeded in the new Arab-Israeli war in 1967 in concert with international pressures through UNO. When civil war broke out in Nigeria in 1966 Britain could give little but moral support to the Nigerian government. The latter crushed the Biafrans, who attempted to break away from Nigeria, and the savage conflict went on for several years. Critics alleged that Stewart was concerned less with the merits of the case than with his fears of the USSR, and that Britain supported the Nigerian government mainly in an effort to outbid the Russians for Nigerian goodwill. Nigeria, however, had been created as a single state by the British, and it was believed that its future would best be served by remaining as one country. There was also civil war in Cyprus, where British troops undertook peacekeeping duties as part of the United Nations forces. But diplomatic efforts to restore harmony made little headway, and peacekeeping in Cyprus turned out to be a long vigil. Peacekeeping troops also had to be rushed to Northern Ireland in 1969. This too was the beginning of a long vigil (see Unit 19.2).

15.5 The General Election of 1970

There was a widespread feeling among voters in 1970 that there was little to choose between Labour and Conservatives, and the turnout in the general election was the lowest since 1935. There had certainly been much common ground between the two main parties during the 1960s, and it was fashionable to speak of 'consensus politics', meaning that governments had pursued policies about which the parties were not in deep disagreement. The problems Britain faced both at home and abroad were complicated and often rather technical, and government seemed to have become a matter of management rather than of great conflicts of principle. Television added to the impression that the election mainly involved a choice between Wilson and Heath, and that voters were required to choose the better manager, especially of the British economy. It is unlikely that many voters expected either to solve the economic problems, but they hoped for as few crises as possible.

Interest focused on certain aspects of the economy. The Conservatives

THE FICKLE FINGER OF FATE

Fig. 15.5 In January 1970, Emmwood speculated about the influence of the US economy on the outcome of British general elections, Harold Wilson precariously balanced on the finger of President Nixon (Daily Mail)

attacked the rising cost of living. In the twelve months before June 1970, the month of the election, prices had risen by about 8 per cent, and Heath gave the impression that this rise could be much reduced – 'at a stroke' – by the Conservatives. Labour stressed the success of Wilson's government in returning to surplus on the balance of payments (see Table 15.1). The alarm bells rang again when the monthly trade figures, issued during the election campaign, showed a sudden short-term deficit but Wilson hastened to assert that this was due to the unusual purchase that month of 'two Jumbo Jets' from the USA.

Passions were roused most of all by the issue of strikes. In spite of the Donovan Report it was widely believed that Wilson and Castle had failed the nation by not carrying through laws about industrial relations. Heath promised a Conservative Industrial Relations Act, which appealed all the more to those who believed that laws could stop strikes when a newspaper strike occurred in the middle of the election campaign. Labour, on the other hand, claimed a special understanding of trade unions and workers, and ridiculed 'Selsdon Man'. Shortly before the election, Conservative leaders had met at the Selsdon Park Hotel, Croydon, to plan their strategy. 'Selsdon Man', Labour alleged, showed that the Conservatives had moved to the right, away from consensus politics, and were likely to provoke even more conflict in British society. The Selsdon programme called for less government interference, more police to combat growing crime and violence, the curbing of trade unions and greater reliance on market forces.

The parties remained close on many other issues, such as the Rhodesian problem, however, and both sought to play down the emotional issue of coloured immigration into Britain. No party wanted to unleash unhealthy prejudices, but the issue did surface in some areas. A section of the voters resented non-white immigration and wanted safeguards, though both Conservative and Labour governments had already introduced immigration controls (see Unit 17.2). The general feeling among those who thought it was important, was that the Conservatives would better 'protect' the white British against non-whites than would Labour.

Opinion polls suggested that a Labour victory was highly likely, not least because Wilson enjoyed more popularity than Heath. Wilson himself traded on this popularity, while Heath stuck determinedly to the Conservative campaign of a 'Better Tomorrow', repeatedly attacking rising prices. Table 10.1 shows that this strategy appeared to work. Contrary to expectations the Conservatives won a clear majority in the new House of Commons. Critics alleged that Wilson and the Labour Party had been complacent, made over-confident by the opinion polls. George Brown was among the defeated Labour candidates, losing his seat at Belper. The Liberals suffered too, partly because of a shortage of money and of candidates: their vote fell, and their seats in the Commons were reduced to six.

Wilson claimed that:

> No incoming Prime Minister . . . in living memory has taken over a stronger economic situation.

In fact, more clearly even than the 1950s, the 1960s had shown that Britain's economy was dogged by persisting problems for which governments could produce only short-term solutions. Economic growth went on lagging behind that of other developed countries. After the upheavals of the 1960s, the voters in 1970 merely hoped that 'Tomorrow' might indeed be 'Better'.

Further Reading

Sked, A. and Cook, C.: *Post-War Britain, a Political History*. Penguin (Harmondsworth, 1979), chapters 8–9.

James, R.R.: *Ambitions and Realities, British Politics 1964–1970*. Weidenfeld and Nicolson (London, 1973).

Lapping, B.: *The Labour Government, 1964–1970*. Penguin (Harmondsworth, 1970).

McKie, D. and Cook, C.: *The Decade of Disillusion; the 1960s*. Macmillan (London, 1972).

Wilson, H.: *The Labour Government, 1964–1970*. Penguin (Harmondsworth, 1974).

Exercises

1. Making use of Table 10.1, describe and account for the results of the general elections of (*a*) 1964 and (*b*) 1966.

2. Explain what the cartoonists suggest in Figs 15.1, 15.2 and 15.5. Of what characteristics of British elections do the cartoonists make use? State with reasons

which of the three cartoons you find the most perceptive comment on British political affairs.

3. Explain what Table 15.1 shows of Britain's balance of payments in the late 1960s. How do you account for the annual changes up to and including 1970?

4. Show what you understand by *devaluation*. Compare the reasons for, and the effects of, the devaluation of the pound in 1949 and 1967.

5. Explain what you understand by *each* of the following terms: 'Declaration of Intent' (page 263); 'voluntary restraint' (page 265); 'a closed shop' (page 266); 'redundancies' (page 266). What did the Donovan Report recommend concerning industrial relations in Britain?

6. Write *two* letters for publication in a newspaper at the beginning of 1969 on the subject of *In Place of Strife, the first* an emotional outburst either for or against trade unions, *the second* an informed and reasoned statement expressing your support for or against the government's proposals.

7. What were the main economic and social policies of the Labour governments from 1964 to 1970? Which of these policies do you consider were (*a*) the most needed and (*b*) the most successful?

8. Two views of *The New Britain* are quoted in small print on page 258. How true is it that by 1970 neither had proved an accurate forecast of what Labour government would achieve?

9. What issues had British voters to consider at the general election of 1970? Design *two* posters for display during the election campaign, *one* seeking support for Wilson and the Labour Party, *the other* seeking support for Heath and the Conservatives. Include in *each* poster some selected statistics about the British economy which might create the desired impression on the voters.

The 1970s: Political Swings and Economic Roundabouts

16.1 Political and Economic Patterns

Britain's pattern of government in the 1970s was at first sight remarkably similar to that of the 1960s. The Conservatives ruled for the first four years of the decade. Then Labour came to power in 1974, but again needed a quick second election to secure a firmer grip on the House of Commons. At the end of the decade, the pendulum swung again and the Conservatives returned to power. But this apparent similarity masked important differences between the 1970s and 1960s. For one thing, there was now a deeper rift between the parties. Both Edward Heath and Margaret Thatcher, the Conservative Prime Ministers in 1970 and 1979 respectively, were accused of practising the politics of confrontation rather than consensus. In both cases the original Conservative intention was to give greater freedom to market forces, to kill off rather than support economic 'lame ducks', and to shake the British people out of their alleged lethargy. Labour argued that such attitudes were likely to produce both chaos and conflict, but the Labour Party itself was accused of shifting to the left or, alternatively, of losing its sense of direction altogether. Moreover, since government intervention failed to produce economic cures, there was growing exasperation with government generally, and growing scepticism about the extent to which any government could achieve its objectives. Public support for the two main parties seemed to be falling away during the 1970s. Heath came to power in 1970 with an overall majority of only thirty, on a low turnout of voters. Labour had no overall majority at all in the first election of 1974, and one of only three seats in the second. In neither election did Labour win even 40 per cent of the total votes cast. More voters – as many as one in four – turned to the minority parties, including the various Nationalist groups (see Unit 19.1), and there was persistent muttering that what Britain really needed was some sort of coalition government. Yet in 1979 the vote for the Conservatives was as high as at any time since the Second World War, and the minority parties suffered marked setbacks (see Table 10.1).

Economic problems, of course, accounted for a large part of the erratic behaviour of both politicians and voters. Table 15.1 shows the difficulties with the balance of payments in the 1970s. Tables 16.1 and 16.2 show high levels of both unemployment and inflation, hitherto considered a contradictory combination in the age of Keynesian economics. And Table 15.2 shows the fluctuating effects of strikes in terms of working days lost. Strikes and the unions were dominant political issues, influencing all four general elections from 1970 to 1979. Indeed, the turbulence of industrial relations was almost certainly the decisive factor in the Conservatives losing the 1974 election and Labour that of 1979. There seemed to be a new sourness in British society and escalating confrontation stemming, at least in part, from the complexities and frustrations of the country's economic disappointments.

Britain was not alone in experiencing severe economic problems. The whole world, including the USA, staggered under a variety of difficulties. Sharp increases in the price of commodities, especially oil, pushed most countries into recession in the mid 1970s. The extent of unemployment recalled the 1930s; and yet again there were currency problems. The US dollar was devalued in 1971 so that, for a time, the pound was worth 2.60 dollars. In the following year, however, the pound was allowed to 'float', that is, its value was no longer fixed in relation to other currencies. The dollar followed suit in 1973, and rigidly fixed exchange rates were generally abandoned. The international value of the pound was now flexible. When the pound was weak, it could depreciate: its value would fall to a more realistic level, which might be helpful to British exports while avoiding the sudden shock of a single act of devaluation such as that of 1967. But such depreciation could hardly be avoided when international confidence in Britain's economy was low, and it was hoped this might provide a stimulus to British industry to rouse itself. At the beginning of the 1980s, however, an opposite and unexpected trend set in. The development of British North Sea oil, coupled with the high interest rates set by the Conservative government attracted foreign money, and brought a temporary confidence in a British economy which still had major weaknesses. The pound floated upwards, creating grave problems for British exporters whose goods were now even more expensive in overseas markets (see Unit 21.2(a)).

The British economy still suffered from serious underlying problems. The rate of growth remained low, stopping altogether at the end of the 1970s; and investment in up-to-date technology was still limited (see Tables 13.1 and 13.3(b)). There were two important aspects to the problem of industrial modernization. One was that governments still found difficulty in channelling the country's wealth into new plant and equipment. The other was that modernization often resulted in a threat to jobs which aroused fear and anger in the workers and their unions. Something of this problem can be seen in Fig. 16.1. Though some work forces had already been much reduced, demands for new plant and equipment, for automation and fewer workers, became incessant during the 1970s and 1980s. It was vital for British industry to reduce its costs in order to compete with foreign suppliers, but workers and unions had a natural inclination to try to protect existing jobs, especially when there could be no guarantee that others could be found. They were therefore accused of restrictive practices, of holding back ˙progress and even of themselves destroying jobs by handicapping industries with poorly productive labour forces. But the problem was a social as well as an economic one, and there were no easy solutions.

Two men were watching a mechanical excavator on a building site.

There are two ways to regard technological development. As a threat. Or as a promise. Every invention from the wheel to the steam engine created the same dilemma.

"If it wasn't for that machine," said one,

But it's only by exploiting the promise of each that man has managed to improve his lot.

Computer technology has given man more time to create, and released him from the day-to-day tasks that limit his self-fulfilment.

"twelve men with shovels could be doing that job."

We ourselves are very heavy users of this technology, ranging from golf-ball typewriters to ink-jet printers to small and large computers, so we're more aware than most of that age-old dilemma: threat or promise.

"Yes," replied the other, "and if it wasn't for your twelve shovels, two hundred men with teaspoons could be doing that job."

Yet during 27 years in the UK our work-force has increased from six to 15,000. And during those 27 years not a single person has been laid off, not a single day has been lost through strikes.

Throughout Britain, electronic technology has shortened queues. Streamlined efficiency. Boosted exports. And kept British products competitive in an international market.

To treat technology as a threat would halt progress. As a promise, it makes tomorrow look a lot brighter.

IBM

IBM United Kingdom Limited, P.O. Box 41, North Harbour, Portsmouth PO6 3AU.

Fig. 16.1 A comment, and opinion, on the relationship between technology and jobs in an advertisement by IBM, 1980

The British Steel Corporation (BSC) provides an example of the difficulties. In 1979, under some pressure from the new Conservative government, BSC demanded increased productivity from a smaller labour force. Reduced demand for steel and increasing foreign competition produced a grim picture of financial loss. Yet in the years 1966–76 the number of steel furnaces had

Fig. 16.2 The onward march of technology and automation: the blast-furnace control room at the Redcar, Teesside, plant of the British Steel Corporation, the end of the 1970s

already been cut from 724 to 534, and along with the furnaces went jobs. In 1974 there had been some 230 000 workers in the industry. In 1979 there were 150 000, and the shedding of some 50 000 more was demanded and by 1982 achieved. This savage pruning had severe social consequences for communities like Corby and Consett, which depended almost totally on the steel industry for jobs, and in South Wales. Yet in 1982 new plans were launched to cut the labour force to less than 80 000. Many industries found themselves in a similar position, struggling to compete in tight markets. Shipbuilding was again in deep trouble, and vehicle-building firms including British Leyland (BL) entered the 1980s with the desperate problem of making any profit at all on their annual operations. For British Rail it was a problem that had long been familiar.

Conservative and Labour philosophies for dealing with these economic and social problems were markedly different in the 1970s, though each was consistent with its own traditions. The Conservatives put their faith in freedom and market forces, trusting that economic pressures would lead to Britain's recovery through private enterprise and initiative. Labour continued to argue that government intervention and planning were needed, and that little could be achieved without the workers' consent. In practice, both parties found they had little room to manoeuvre once in office. Like Wilson in the 1960s, prime ministers were often 'blown off course' and U-turns became a feature of British government, with politicians being forced to change direction at an almost bewildering speed.

16.2 Conservative Government, 1970–4

(a) The Management of the Economy and of Industrial Relations

Edward Heath became Prime Minister in 1970 with fixed ideas of what his government intended to do. Heath declared that he would 'change the course of history of this nation, nothing less'. No time was wasted in abolishing the Industrial Reorganization Corporation and the Prices and Incomes Board. Industries were expected to become profitable through their own efforts and, in doing so, to resist excessive wage claims. If the competitive system allowed prices to rise, that would produce more profits which could be used by businessmen for investment and modernization. Reduced taxation would increase the incentive of individuals to work harder. The emphasis was to be on competition and self-help. As an example of the new climate Margaret Thatcher, the Minister of Education, withdrew official encouragement for comprehensive schools; and she went on to withdraw school milk from primary school children, as a tiny part of the government policy of cutting official spending. New law on industrial relations, meanwhile, was expected to curb the disruption caused by strikes; and entry to the EEC would give Britain access to European markets and boost exports (see Unit 20.3). Britain, at last, did gain admission to the European Community – but the government achieved few of its other ambitions.

The sudden death of Iain Macleod robbed Heath of his Chancellor of the Exchequer, and the post was given to Antony Barber (see Table 15.3). Before long, Barber was in trouble. Unemployment and inflation both rose significantly (see Tables 16.1 and 16.2). Although exports improved, the balance of payments was heading back into deficit by 1972, and the British economy yet again stubbornly failed to increase its rate of growth. Tax concessions merely led to more spending on imported goods. Nor was the government able to stick to its policy of letting industrial 'lame ducks' perish. Some, at least, had to receive government aid and rescue in view of the unemployment, social problems and other complications which would have resulted from their collapse. Rolls Royce and Upper Clyde Shipbuilders, in both of which the government already had a holding, had to be helped. In 1972

Table 16.1 Unemployment in Britain, 1960–81

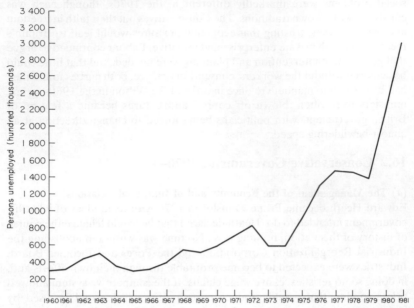

Source: based on *Annual Abstract of Statistics* and Department of Employment *Gazettes*.

Heath also found it necessary to set up the Industrial Development Executive, with functions similar to those of Labour's Industrial Reorganization Corporation. Another U-turn followed on incomes policy. A financial crisis led to a near-freeze on prices and wages in 1972, and the setting up of the Price Commission and the Pay Board. Heath then searched desperately for ways of implementing a continuing incomes policy, though he had earlier argued against one. Another policy was reversed too. In 1971 Bank Rate had been lowered to 5 per cent, to make borrowing easier. By the end of 1973 Bank Rate, known as Minimum Lending Rate from 1972, had climbed to a new height of 13 per cent, to the dismay of borrowers generally, including those with mortgages.

The Industrial Relations Act of 1971 created storms, both inside and outside parliament. Its aim was to make contracts and wage settlements legally binding, and it set up the National Industrial Relations Court to enforce them. Unions had to register in order to qualify for legal protection and tax concessions, and the new Registrar of Trade Unions had the power to insist on changes in union rules. A long list of 'unfair practices' set out a code of conduct for industrial relations, and the NIR Court could order a sixty-day 'cooling off' period and a ballot of members when the government thought a strike

Table 16.2 Index of retail prices in Britain, 1962–81

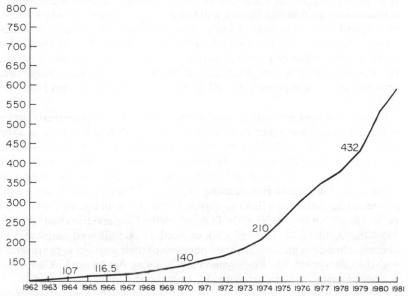

Source: based on *Economic Trends*.

particularly damaging. The existing Commission on Industrial Relations was fitted into the new system. Far from bringing industrial peace, the Act created greater bitterness (see Table 15.2), and there were strikes in protest against the Act, against incomes policy, and against dismissals and unemployment.

Independent arbitration went against the government's wishes on several occasions. The National Union of Mineworkers (NUM) had been founded in 1945, to replace the forty or so separate unions of the MFGB, and it called its first national coal strike in 1972. Arbitration resulted in a wage award in excess of what the government wanted, and Heath found that he had to give financial help to the National Coal Board, though this too was part of another change of policy. For years governments had been allowing Britain's coal industry to run down. Now, with new thinking about future supplies of energy, it was realized how vitally important the country's coal reserves were. Meanwhile, a dock strike in 1972 led to a legal judgment against the NIR Court, a further blow to the government.

(b) **Other Legislation and Policy**
The problems of Northern Ireland and Rhodesia continued to defy solution, but Britain's main parties had few major differences on these issues (see Units 19.2 and 20.2). Another storm blew up, however, over the government's policy on matters of race. Heath had deliberately excluded Enoch Powell from

his government in 1970. Powell might well have expected an official appointment, but he had made himself the spokesman for those who resented coloured immigration into Britain, and had expressed views with which Heath had no wish to be associated. Even so, the government's immigration policy provoked criticism from those who thought it racist (see Unit 17.2). Heath also created uproar when he proposed to renew the sale of arms to South Africa. He was forced to give way at the Commonwealth Conference in Singapore, however, and to compromise by selling only certain types of arms (see Unit 20.1).

Several new laws met with general acceptance or merely provoked flurries of protest. Heath had a particular interest in the rights of consumers, and the Fair Trading Act of 1973 gave some protection against unfair trading practices. In the previous year, the Housing Finance Act had provided fair rents for the tenants of local authorities, and had helped the poor with rent allowances. The Sound Broadcasting Act of 1972 set up the Independent Broadcasting Authority (IBA) to supervise the development of commercial radio – an authority parallel to the ITA, which the Conservatives had set up in 1954 (see Unit 13.2). The 1973 Social Security Act allowed employers to operate schemes to increase the state pensions of their workers in conjunction with the state system. The Employment and Training Act set up the Manpower Services Commission, to promote the training of workers in new skills. A Criminal Justice Act attempted to reduce the overcrowding in prisons, now fuller than ever before as crime went on increasing, and made it possible for criminals' victims to seek compensation from those who committed the crimes.

Many of the changes made by Heath's government were administrative. The National Health Service was reorganized, and new arrangements for regional development included the introduction of Regional Development Grants. But the most comprehensive administrative reform was the Local Government Act of 1972, which set up a new system of county, metropolitan and non-metropolitan authorities, replacing the Victorian county and borough authorities. The Water Act of 1973 also created ten new regional authorities in England and Wales, to administer supply and tackle the problem of river pollution.

Many people were bewildered by the scale and pace of change, and the extension of the Ombudsman system to local government provided little consolation. Even the familiar old pennies and shillings were abandoned when, on the eve of entry into the EEC, Britain's coinage was decimalized in 1971. Such changes added to the general uneasiness and suspicion of government; and pessimists, contemplating the disruption caused by strikes and the fierce conflict in Northern Ireland, with bomb outrages in England spilling over from that, speculated on whether Britain was perhaps becoming ungovernable.

(c) **The State of Emergency**
The Organization of Petroleum Exporting Countries (OPEC) had been

founded in 1961 with the aim of ensuring that a fair price was paid to the producing nations for their oil, which was being consumed at an ever-increasing rate, especially by wealthy countries. In 1973 another Arab–Israeli war triggered off an international oil crisis when Arab members of OPEC reduced their output and raised their prices, angered by the support which the USA and many western nations were giving to Israel. The cost of oil to Britain almost quadrupled, and the deficit on the balance of payments mounted alarmingly (see Table 15.1). There was even the threat of petrol rationing.

The oil crisis coincided with the NUM's rebellion against the Conservatives' pay policy. Electricity workers and railwaymen joined in and, like the miners, banned overtime. The government declared a state of emergency on 13 November 1973, and imposed restrictions on the use of fuel. It also had to deal urgently with the financial crisis, which was now worsened by losses in industrial output. From the beginning of 1974 electricity was only supplied to industry for three days of the week. The crisis deepened. But the government seemed determined not to give way to the miners' demand for higher wages, and brushed aside promises made by the TUC and other unions that they would not regard a settlement with the miners as the new 'going rate' for pay increases in general. The NUM leadership went on to recommend an all-out strike to its members and, when the miners voted on the issue, 81 per cent supported the strike call. The date fixed for the strike was 9 February, but on 7 February Heath decided to appeal to the nation in a general election. With a national vote of confidence in his government, he could perhaps bring the NUM to heel.

16.3 The General Elections of 1974

The election of February 1974 was fought against the unique background of the state of emergency and the three-day working week. For the Conservatives the main electoral issue was authority, and Heath told the people:

The challenge is to the will of Parliament and a democratically elected government.

The Conservative Manifesto, *Firm Action for a Fair Britain*, asserted that voters had a choice 'between moderation and extremism', and it asked for support for Heath's incomes policy as a key weapon against inflation. The Labour Party argued that Conservative government had led to confrontation, with Wilson claiming:

We know the trade unions. . . . We can talk with them and work with them. We can get their co-operation.

He promised a 'social contract' with the trade union movement – a better recipe for industrial peace and economic development, he argued, than a rigid incomes policy. The first Labour moves would be to repeal the Industrial Relations Act of 1971, and to reconsider the terms on which Britain had entered the EEC. The Labour Manifesto also proposed setting up a National Enterprise Board, to manage and develop the accumulating state interests in various industries, and suggested that there should be more positive help for the country's poor. This was a Liberal theme too, there being a particular need to increase pensions, but the Liberals argued that an incomes policy was essential. They blamed many of Britain's ills on a political system which led to party warfare and to too many short-term policies, all too quickly reversed.

The opinion polls of 1974 at first suggested a likely victory for the Conservatives, but a shift then took place. Enoch Powell probably exerted some influence, denouncing both the election and his former Conservative colleagues, and attacking Britain's membership of the EEC. He went on to announce not only that he was no longer a Conservative candidate but that he himself would vote Labour, though the Labour Party was wary of being linked with his anti-immigrant views. Heath suffered another blow when the leader of the Confederation of British Industries (CBI) spoke out against the Industrial Relations Act, declaring that it had:

> sullied every relationship at every level between unions and employers and ought to be repealed rather than amended.

It was one thing for the TUC to attack the Act; but the CBI was an employers' organization, usually sympathetic to the Conservatives. The Labour Party too had its troubles, however. It had to live down a series of resignations and the criticisms of former members, including Ray Gunter, Minister of Labour in Wilson's government of 1964. Dick Taverne, one of the most recent MPs to resign from the Party, won Lincoln as an Independent Labour candidate before he joined the Social Democrats in the early 1980s.

Neither of the two main parties gained much comfort from the results of the February election of 1974. Both lost votes compared with 1970, while the Liberals and various Nationalist parties made gains (see Table 10.1 and Unit 19.1(a)). No party won an overall majority. Though Labour was the largest single party in the new House of Commons, the Conservatives had won more votes. Heath delayed his resignation, consulting Thorpe, the Liberal leader, to see whether some kind of collaboration could be agreed. This proved impossible, and Wilson became Prime Minister on 4 March, four days after the election. He led a minority government similar to those led by MacDonald in the 1920s, and a further early election seemed certain.

As in 1964, however, Wilson first intended to try to demonstrate his government's ability to rule. The coal dispute was settled quickly, but at a price. Miners' wages were raised and the government undertook to provide more financial help for the National Coal Board. It took only a week, therefore, to restore the normal working week and to end the state of emergency; but coal prices to industry were increased, again raising costs. The

Industrial Relations Act was repealed and the Pay Board abolished, though something of an incomes policy nevertheless remained. But the 'social contract' was now one of the central planks of the government's strategy. This required a new climate of goodwill and Denis Healey, Wilson's Chancellor of the Exchequer, aimed to create this in his first budget. The budget, Healey said:

> must help restore the sense of national unity which has been so lacking in the past few
> years. It must be an essential instrument in establishing that social contract on which
> the solution of all our problems must depend.

The TUC supported 'that social contract' and Len Murray, the TUC General Secretary, worked at persuading the unions to accept it. It was agreed that all wage settlements should last for at least twelve months, and that wage bargaining should centre on the level of price increases and on compensating for them. But ambiguities remained as to whether these price increases were those past or in the year to come, and unions were generally reluctant to accept Murray's definition that future inflation should not be considered. The social contract did not, therefore, bring instant industrial peace. Nor could Wilson find an instant cure for Britain's many other problems. Nevertheless, he decided to hold a second general election in October 1974.

The election produced no great changes in support for the minority parties, but there was a marked fall in the Conservative vote, so Wilson remained in power with a tiny overall majority (see Table 10.1). The Labour government was less weak than it appeared, however, since there was little likelihood of the other parties uniting to overthrow it, and it had more urgent problems than that of its parliamentary majority. Heath too had problems. The Conservatives were quick to turn on him after two election defeats, and they voted on their leadership early in 1975. The first ballot was indecisive, but Heath came second to Mrs Thatcher and promptly stood down. Thatcher won an easy victory over William Whitelaw on the second ballot and, for the first time, a major British political party was led by a woman. The Liberals too changed their leader. Thorpe stood down in 1976, plagued by scandals and poor by-election results. New elections led to his replacement by David Steel after Grimond had acted as caretaker leader. Enoch Powell had meanwhile returned to the House of Commons in October 1974 as the Official Unionist MP for Down South, Northern Ireland.

16.4 Labour Government, 1974–9

(a) Ministers and Problems

A major achievement of the Labour government was actually to remain in office for five years, for by-election defeats soon ate away its tiny overall majority. In later years, however, it was kept in power by a pact with the Liberals, the aim of which, it was said, was to allow a sustained attack on the country's economic problems. The economy was chiefly the responsibility of Denis Healey, the Chancellor of the Exchequer throughout the five-year period (see Table 15.3). Wilson resigned as Prime Minister in April 1976 preferring, he said, to retire from office while still comparatively young and in good health. Three ballots were needed for Labour MPs to choose his successor, James Callaghan, who finally defeated Michael Foot. Callaghan's victory was generally regarded as a success for the right wing of the Labour Party over the left, though the issue was hardly so simple. Many members of Wilson's and Callaghan's administrations were survivors from the Wilson governments of the 1960s including, in addition to Healey, Barbara Castle, Edward Short, Anthony Wedgwood Benn, Roy Jenkins and Anthony Crosland. Jenkins was Home Secretary until he resigned in 1976 to become the President of the European Commission. The untimely death of Crosland in 1977 caused Callaghan to appoint a new Foreign Secretary. He chose David Owen, not yet forty, comparatively young for such high office.

Healey was known to have ambitions to be the Foreign Secretary, but duty and the need for a continuing attack on the country's economic problems kept him in the office of Chancellor. The Tables in this Unit and in Unit 15 show that there were no easy successes to be won. The world as a whole had plunged into recession, partly because of difficulties over the price and supply of oil, and only a limited recovery had taken place by 1979. In spite of its many problems, Britain again managed to improve its export performance, and helped by North Sea oil, the balance of payments was once more dragged back

Table 16.3 Britain's National Debt

	The National Debt as a percentage of the Gross Domestic Product
1920	150
1946	290
1969	86
1972	68
1979	61

Source: based on *Annual Abstract of Statistics*.

	The National Debt (£million)
1969	33 984
1979	86 974

Of the Debt in 1979, £4 283 million payable in external currencies

Source: *Lloyds Bank Economic Profile*.

into surplus. The rate of inflation was slowed, the rise in unemployment eventually checked and real incomes began to rise again after the cutback in the mid 1970s. It was widely believed that Healey, like earlier chancellors, achieved this mainly by extensive government borrowing. But since the end of the Second World War Britain's National Debt had in fact shown a steady fall as a percentage of the GDP (see Table 16.3). Nor was borrowing unique to Britain. West Germany's borrowing record was very similar to Britain's in the mid 1970s, while other countries, such as Italy, borrowed more heavily.

Economic problems were not, of course, the only ones in the years 1974–9. Later Units will consider the continuing difficulties in Northern Ireland and Rhodesia, the efforts to improve race relations in the United Kingdom and the issue of the devolution of power to Scotland and Wales.

(b) Wilson's Administration, 1974–6

The main task in the mid 1970s was to ride out the economic storm, and the government was forced to take measures which Healey called 'rough and tough'. Real incomes were cut back, after their sharp rise in the early 1970s. The social contract meant less industrial disruption in 1975–6 but it worked imperfectly, and the government was soon forced into a wages policy in the struggle against inflation. It also tried to curb price rises – part of the contract with the unions. There was a general freeze on rents during 1974, for example, and a Price Code required approval for most price increases. The price of basic foodstuffs was held down with the help of government subsidies. These were holding measures, however. As with earlier governments, the main aim was higher output, the surest defence against inflation. But growth remained elusive, and the international recession added to the difficulties of finding markets and generating funds for investment and modernization.

The government rested its hopes for the future on two new organizations, the National Enterprise Board (NEB) and the British National Oil Corporation (BNOC). The NEB's job was to stimulate and assist technological change and development in industries which, though not nationalized, needed government help. Rolls Royce, British Leyland, Triang and Ferranti were among those aided by the NEB. The Conservatives argued that this was a sort of nationalization and continued to protest against interference with private enterprise.

Important oil reserves had by now been discovered under the North Sea, and Britain had laid a successful claim to a substantial share of these. The Labour government wanted to make sure that the likely large profits from the oilfields went to the British people rather than to international companies and speculators. The BNOC was set up to take part in exploiting the oil reserves and, like the NEB, to work in partnership with private enterprise to promote development while protecting the national interest. The aim of the Oil Taxation Act, introduced in 1975, was to obtain for the British government a share of the profits made by the private oil companies. Meanwhile, economic anxieties were linked with anxieties about the effects of Britain's membership

Fig. 16.3 A North Sea oil rig on a British stamp of 1977

of the EEC and Wilson tried to improve the terms on which Britain had taken up its membership (see Unit 20.3(*b*)).

The social contract with the trade unions required the government to repeal the Industrial Relations Act of 1971. The Trade Union and Labour Relations Act of 1974 repealed most of it, and the remainder was repealed two years later. The Health and Safety at Work Act of 1974 set up a Commission to protect the workers' interests, and the Employment Protection Act of 1975 tightened control over dismissals. Government also made further changes in the details of the welfare state. The Social Security Pensions Act of 1975 amended the recent Conservative legislation, introducing a more ambitious scheme for earnings-related pensions, to become fully effective over the next twenty years. Children were given added protection in the Children Act. The Child Benefit Act of 1975 replaced the earlier family allowances and income tax relief to parents with a new system of benefits, normally payable to mothers. There were further controls on rents for houses and other accommodation, giving further security to tenants. Housing associations were encouraged, and the Community Land Act extended public control over development land. Women's rights were also protected in the Sex Discrimination Act of 1975, which aimed to promote equality between the sexes. The Employment Protection Act of 1975 also sought to improve the machinery for settling industrial disputes, setting up the Advisory Conciliation and Arbitration Service (ACAS).

The economic struggle was far from being over when Wilson retired in 1976. The value of the pound was sinking and he handed over a good many difficulties to his successor. Callaghan, however, made few changes either in basic policy or in the membership of government.

(c) Callaghan's Administration, 1976–9

The turning-point for the British economy came in 1977. It resulted from a variety of factors, including borrowing from the International Monetary Fund (IMF), expenditure cuts, stern taxation and North Sea oil, which began to arrive in significant quantities during 1976. The Price Commission played its part in restraining price rises, and the rate of inflation dropped below 10 per cent in 1978. Incomes policy also played an important part. The social contract faded into the background: the unions had been only partly successful in delivering their side of the bargain, and the government now concentrated on issuing guidelines for pay increases in successive Stages. Heath's pay policy had been similar, but that had run into grave problems during Phase Three, at the end of 1973. The Labour policy reached Stage Four towards the end of 1978. The unions had given Callaghan and Healey considerable support up to that point, but the ministers were now over-ambitious. Further to strengthen Britain's recovery, they demanded a 'norm' for wage increases of around 5 per cent, close to the increased output of the economy during 1978 but below the rate of inflation. The result was another 'winter of discontent', with renewed industrial strife, particularly among the low-paid workers whose incomes had suffered severely from the effects of inflation. The Labour–Liberal pact had meanwhile come to an end and, ominously for the government, the turbulent winter of 1978–9 was the prelude to Britain's next general election.

Apart from industrial unrest, itself interlinked with other economic problems, there was now growing anxiety about Britain's 'deindustrialization'. British industry seemed to be withering under the impact of foreign competition. Indeed, output in the late 1970s was much the same as during the three-day week in 1974, though the growth of output of North Sea oil tended to mask the fall in other industries. When living standards began to rise again after 1977 the country once more sucked in imports, among which foreign cars were prominent. Britain's motor-cycle industry had already been overwhelmed by foreign competition; now the British car industry was in severe difficulties. Except for British Leyland (BL) which had to rely on help from the NEB, vehicle-building firms in Britain had passed mainly to foreign owners. The aircraft and shipbuilding industries also faced financial and structural problems, and the Aircraft and Shipbuilding Act of 1977 attempted to rescue them by nationalization. The Dock Work Regulation Act aimed to bring about further reorganization, and was also intended to resolve the difficulties resulting from the rivalries of different groups of workers fearful of the loss of jobs.

Unemployment remained well above a million and continued to alarm Britain's labour force. Technological change might well bring greater output and increased prosperity. Along with oil from the North Sea, for example, came natural gas from which the nation as a whole benefited. On the other

Fig. 16.4 Freightliner terminal at Stratford, East London, at the end of the 1970s; again progress demanded that the equation be balanced in favour of technology rather than the labour-intensive methods which provided jobs

hand, gas-manufacturing virtually came to an end in most parts of the United Kingdom during the 1970s and this meant job losses. Government tried hard to put people into new jobs, making use of the Manpower Services Commission and retraining schemes, but loss of work had again become the social evil it had been in the 1930s. One industry after another – vehicle-building, shipbuilding, textiles, steel and electronics – complained bitterly of the difficulties it faced in competing with foreign producers.

The construction industry was also unable to make full use of its existing manpower. Housebuilding had slumped: only 276 000 dwellings were completed during 1974 and, though the total rose to 310 000 in 1975, it hardly increased in later years.

The government's resources were strained to the limit, though some argued that it was trying to do far too much. Pensions were raised whenever money was available, and the government also increased Family Income Supplements, introduced by the Conservatives to help the poor in the earlier 1970s. An attempt was made to link social security benefits to the rate of inflation, to protect the sick and unemployed. The movement towards comprehensive schooling was speeded up, and a new Race Relations Act in 1976 aimed to encourage racial harmony and extend equality in ways similar to those intended in the Sex Discrimination Act (see Unit 17.3(*b*)). A Police Complaints Board was also set up, since disquiet concerning the police force seemed to be growing in some areas of the country. More controversially, the Health Services Act of 1976 attacked private medicine within NHS hospitals, aiming to get rid of 'pay beds' and to reduce the waiting lists for hospital treatment under the National Health Service. But strikes and disruption during the winter of 1978–9 again focused the nation's attention on the highly charged issue of industrial relations. When the general election of May 1979 took place, trade unionism was again the subject which gave rise to disquiet and an almost universal sense of frustration.

16.5 The General Election of 1979

Callaghan and Healey had made some headway with Britain's economic problems by 1979. On the other hand, the old claim that the Labour Party had special expertise in handling industrial relations had received a fierce blow. The public had been much inconvenienced by the winter of strikes in the public services, and passions had not had time to cool. People were still bitter about the recent disruptions to hospitals and the ambulance service, seeming to believe that the many ill-paid workers in these jobs had a duty to accept lower standards of living than others in the community because of the vital nature of their work. Many strikers were now more militant and unruly than in the comparatively good-natured confrontations of earlier times, for example the General Strike of 1926. Workers picketed more vigorously, some of them organized in flying pickets, moving around the country. There were complaints about intimidation and violence.

The two main parties again offered the voters clearly differing philosophies. The Conservatives supported private and individual enterprise, and Labour adhered to state enterprise. Mrs Thatcher constantly emphasized her belief that state activity, direct taxation and government spending ought to be reduced. She claimed that many of the ideas of Keynes were now discredited. The new economic high priest of the Conservatives was Milton Friedman. Government intervention, Friedman argued, stifled initiative, while direct taxation reduced incentives and government spending fuelled inflation. Like Heath in 1970, Thatcher wanted to allow market forces to work freely. She saw the cure for inflation in tight control of the money supply, a policy which Healey had applied with some success but only, the Conservatives claimed, under pressure from the IMF and then not tightly enough. A Conservative government would cease to interfere and to distort the economy, so that competitive pressures and incentives would bring about modernization and, eventually, economic well being. This would also bring a healthier society, since the Conservatives believed that too many people relied on state benefits and made too little effort to help themselves. Thatcher would therefore abandon the machinery for controlling prices and incomes, including the Price Commission which had survived from Heath's government. On the other hand, new laws on industrial relations would be a Conservative priority.

The Labour Party rejected this philosophy almost totally. It rested its case on the Labour government's record and relied a good deal on Callaghan's

Fig. 16.5 *The two-party system was still strong in the general election of 1979, a choice for most voters – as Gibbard suggested in the* Guardian *– between Callaghan and the Labour Party and Mrs Thatcher and the Conservatives, in spite of the efforts of Steel and the Liberals to attract support. At the same time, Callaghan and Thatcher had party dogs they would rather keep in the background*

personal popularity. In spite of the recent difficult winter, and though many of the country's underlying problems persisted, Labour's argument was that the government's mixture of policies held out the best hope of long-term solutions. But doubts had been raised about Labour's ability to work with the unions and there were suspicions that the Party was not wholly united behind Callaghan. It was a favourite theme of the other parties that hot-blooded socialists, known as the Militant Tendency, were poised to wrest control of the Party from staid men such as the Prime Minister and his Chancellor. Former Labour MPs like Reginald Prentice, now standing as a Conservative candidate though once a Labour minister, added fuel to these flickering flames.

David Steel and the Liberals were forced to defend their policy of keeping the Callaghan government in office from 1977 onwards. Steel argued that this had been statesmanlike, in the national interest. The Liberals again offered distinctive policies but their main hope lay in holding the balance of power between Conservatives and Labour. That, they hoped, would enable them not only to curb the 'extremism' they alleged lurked in both the main parties, but perhaps also to insist on Liberal reforms such as changes in the electoral system. In Scotland and Wales, speculation centred on the likely effects of the recent failures to secure the devolution of power on the Nationalist vote (see Unit 19.1).

A close result was expected. In fact, the voters acted much as they had in 1970 (see Table 10.1). There was a marked swing to the Conservatives, making Margaret Thatcher Prime Minister with a comfortable Commons majority. Though there had been confident newspaper comment that people were tired of both main parties, the Conservative vote was as high as in any postwar election. But it was still less than 44 per cent of the total votes cast, while Labour, keeping as many votes as in 1974, nevertheless won its lowest postwar share of the poll. The result not only disappointed Callaghan, fighting his only election as his Party's leader. It disappointed the minority parties: the Liberals lost a million votes compared with 1974 and the Scottish Nationalists suffered a serious setback.

A feature of the general election of 1979 was the difference in voting behaviour in various parts of the United Kingdom. Conservative victories piled up in the areas of greater prosperity, especially the south of England. These were also the areas which had shown the most enthusiasm for EEC membership in the referendum of 1975 (see Unit 20.3). The north of England and Scotland showed more hostility both to the EEC and to the Conservatives. Meanwhile, those who liked to gaze into the future speculated on whether the 1980s would repeat the political patterns of the 1960s and 1970s – and perhaps the frustrating economic patterns too.

Further Reading

Sked, A. and Cook, C.: *Post-War Britain, A Political History*. Penguin (Harmondsworth, 1979), chapters 10–12.

Taylor, R.: *The Fifth Estate*. Pan (London, 1978).

Exercises

1. 'Conservative and Labour philosophies for dealing with . . . economic and social problems were markedly different in the 1970s, though each was consistent with its own traditions' (page 283). Explain and illustrate the truth of this statement.

2. In what ways did developing problems force governments 'to change direction' (page 283) (a) during the period of Conservative rule, 1970–4 and (b) during the period of Labour rule, 1974–9?

3. What problems concerning industrial relations confronted governments during the 1970s? Did any government during this period show that it had solutions to these problems?

4. What economic and social reforms were made by governments during the 1970s, and which of these reforms do you consider were in the best interests of the country?

5. (a) Explain the issue which is the subject of Fig. 16.1. Develop your answer with reference to the problems modernization brought in specific British industries.
   (b) What do other illustrations in this Unit (Figs 16.2, 16.3 and 16.4) show of developments in British technology?

6. Explain what Tables 15.1, 15.2 and the Tables in this Unit show of Britain's problems during the 1970s. Which of these problems were (a) comparatively new and (b) becoming more severe?

7. Summarize the appeal made by *each* of the major parties in the general election of February 1974. Making use of Table 10.1, explain how far each party had reason to be satisfied with the outcome of the election. Repeat this exercise for each of the general elections of October 1974 and 1979.

8. Explain the particular issues *each of five* of the following would be likely to have considered before deciding how to vote in the general election of February 1974, and how this might have influenced the vote cast: a coalminer; a housewife; a council house tenant; a would-be housebuyer; an eager supporter of law and order; the owner of a small manufacturing plant; an enthusiastic supporter of the EEC; a vigorous opponent of South African apartheid.

9. Show what you understand by each of the following terms: 'lame ducks' (page 279); 'allowed to "float" ' (page 280); 'inflation' (page 283); 'incomes policy' (page 284); 'social contract' (page 287).

10. Making use of Table 15.3 and of the Index to this book, write short paragraphs to summarize the careers (to 1979) and political views of *five* of the following: Anthony Wedgwood Benn; George Brown; James Callaghan; Alec Douglas-Home; Denis Healey; Edward Heath; Roy Jenkins; Reginald Maudling.

Unit Seventeen

Multi-racial Britain

17.1 The Multi-cultural Society

At the beginning of the 1980s Britain's population of about fifty-six million included about two million 'non-whites'. Despite the fact that some 40 per cent of these people had been born in Britain they were widely regarded as 'immigrants'. Public officials, preferring to avoid any mention of colour, referred to them as of 'New Commonwealth' origin, a term which conveniently distinguished those Commonwealth countries whose independence was comparatively recent (see Table 14.1) from the White Dominions. Some of the most accurate information about non-white immigration was contained in the 1971 census (see Table 17.1). It showed that Britain's population included more than a million people who had been born in the New Commonwealth, but this total did not include their children, who had been born in Britain. It also showed that the largest groups of these newcomers were from the West

Table 17.1 British citizens born in the New Commonwealth

Total	1 157 170
Born in:	
West Indies	302 970
Indian subcontinent:	
India	322 670
Pakistan and Bangladesh	139 455
Africa	176 060
Cyprus	72 665
Other New Commonwealth ,countries	143 350

Source: British census, 1971.

Indies, the Indian subcontinent and Africa (although many of the east African immigrants were of Asian origin, having moved in earlier times). Concern about the numbers of 'New Commonwealth' immigrants had become acute in Britain from the late 1950s onwards. It can hardly be denied that the roots of this 'problem' lay in colour prejudice and an unhealthy racism which lurked below the surface in many western societies. Less concern was expressed about the millions of other immigrants into Britain, from the Irish Republic, the Dominions, the USA and the European continent (from which many Jews and east Europeans had come in the first half of the century). Since their skins were white, such people were less noticeable. By the 1960s, therefore, two issues occupied the British public and the politicians: 'immigration' and 'race relations'.

Very few non-whites lived in Britain before the Second World War, although there were small communities in places such as Cardiff and Liverpool. The war brought many changes, however, especially in attitudes (see Unit 12.1), and non-white immigration into Britain was very much part of the changing postwar world and the winding-down of colonial empires. There was a new interest in some Commonwealth countries in migration to the mother country, the land which Britain's colonial subjects had been taught to admire and which they looked on as a land of opportunity and almost as a natural homeland. The relative wealth of Britain, compared with the poverty of the colonies, provided a strong incentive for the more adventurous to make the long journey, and developments in transport had made it easier to travel. Moreover, postwar Britain needed labour, whereas unemployment was high and persistent in many colonial territories. London Transport actively recruited workers in the West Indies, and the textile industries of Lancashire and Yorkshire welcomed Asian workers to man the night shifts, which were needed to make expensive new machinery profitable. By 1955 more than 100 000 non-whites had arrived in Britain, and many services such as transport and hospitals had already begun to rely on their labour.

By no means all the newcomers intended to settle in Britain. Many came simply to work and to earn, as was their right as citizens of the Empire and Commonwealth. Indeed, the British Nationality Act of 1948 had confirmed that 'British subjects' and 'Commonwealth citizens' had similar status, and that the latter could enter the United Kingdom freely. At first the authorities gave little thought to the influx. Statistics were not collected, and there were no arrangements of the sort made in some other European countries for housing the newcomers and for fitting them into British society. The availability of work mainly determined where the newcomers settled and, since many chose to stay in Britain, immigrant communities began to develop as the early arrivals were joined by their families and other new immigrants. In the English Midlands, north-west England and certain parts of London the newcomers began to make changes to the familiar environment – and their colour made their communities distinctive. Sections of British society began to feel uneasy.

The Asian immigrants included both Moslems and Hindus, who opened mosques and Hindu centres and, unlike the West Indians, many did not speak English, a factor which made it difficult for them to understand and be understood. Many Asian women wore eastern dress. Most of the newcomers were hard-working and law-abiding, and they diversified British society with new foods, recreations, entertainments, art forms and costumes. The West

Fig. 17.1 West Indians at Lord's cricket ground, London, 1950: early and optimistic immigrants into Britain, jubilant at the test-match victory of the West Indies over England

Indians, for example, brought Carnival to London's Notting Hill, and Indian restaurants opened in many towns and were patronized increasingly by the British who appreciated a style of cooking that had previously only been available on a small scale. Many people, however, found it difficult to accept that British citizens could be anything but white, and although few expressed active hostility, the suspicion lingered that the immigrants threatened traditional British values in various ways. Fears grew when racial clashes broke out in Nottingham and Notting Hill in 1958. There were exaggerations about the number of non-whites in Britain, and the non-whites were themselves said to constitute a 'problem'.

In fact, the newcomers shared the problems of all British people – of finding adequate housing, and work when unemployment rose again. There was a tendency for those who were competing for decent houses and jobs to see non-whites as people who made the difficulties worse in regions where there were big immigrant settlements. The problems actually created by the immigrants were few and specialized – their educational needs, for example, mainly in language – and it was a myth that immigration created strains by inflating Britain's population. In the twenty years from 1955 Britain actually had a substantial outflow of population, and in only six of these years (1958–63) did migration produce a net increase in the total number of British citizens. The real 'problem' lay with those whites in Britain who insisted on regarding the newcomers as aliens, and discriminating against them. Non-whites often found themselves in the poorest housing and worst-paid jobs, with little opportunity for promotion or advancement. In the late 1970s young blacks often found it very difficult to obtain any employment at all, though many were now British by birth. Race relations laws did something to smooth the path to racial harmony and equality, but a truly multi-cultural society needed time in which to grow. For all their imperial history and claims to be tolerant and liberal, the British were once again slow to adapt themselves to changing circumstances.

17.2 Immigration Laws

(a) The First Restrictions
Questions of race seemed to grow increasingly urgent towards the end of the 1950s. At that time the Commonwealth became more of a multi-racial association, leading Macmillan to show interest in the 'wind of change' in Africa in 1960 and South Africa to leave the Commonwealth a year later (see Unit 14.4(a)). Meanwhile, there was tension in some of the multi-racial communities in Britain, and fears were expressed about the number of non-whites who were entering the country. About 30 000 a year had been arriving since the mid 1950s, but the number doubled in 1960. In 1961, amid fierce debate about impending restrictions, and in an effort to get ahead of them, the number of New Commonwealth immigrants rose above 100 000. Macmillan's government had already decided to introduce controls, sensing public disquiet, and the Commonwealth Immigrants Act was passed in 1962. Gaitskell and the Opposition denounced the new law as an affront to the multi-racial Commonwealth. It was one thing to control immigration – unlimited population growth would add to Britain's social problems – but the fierce criticism of the Commonwealth Immigrants Act, both at home and abroad, centred on the argument that it was directed against immigration from the New Commonwealth and not against immigration in general.

The Act did not apply to immigrants from the Republic of Ireland, nor even to those from countries such as Spain and the USA. Instead, it abolished the right of entry into Britain of the citizens of the Commonwealth. In future, entry would be open to such citizens only if they possessed work vouchers or were near relatives of those already settled in the United Kingdom. Work vouchers would be issued to those who already had a job in Britain, or who could offer the special skills Britain needed. The detailed terms of the Act provided less of a barrier to would-be immigrants from the White Dominions than to those from the New Commonwealth. The provision for dependents nevertheless meant that immigration actually increased for a time in the mid 1960s, though West Indian immigration began to decline after 1964 and that from the Indian subcontinent after 1968. There was no similar downturn, however, in immigration from Canada and the other Dominions.

The Labour Party changed its attitude to immigration law after Gaitskell's death. When Wilson became Prime Minister, the screw was tightened further. In 1965, a ceiling was fixed on the annual issue of work vouchers: they were not to exceed 8 500 throughout the Commonwealth. In fact, the actual issues of vouchers regularly fell far short of that figure. On the other hand, no ceiling was fixed for immigrants from outside the Commonwealth. To soften the blow, the first of Britain's Race Relations Acts was introduced in 1965 (see Unit 17.3(a)), and Wilson strongly asserted the principle that:

> Once immigrants are here, they should be treated for all purposes as citizens of the United Kingdom, without discrimination.

This was a constructive policy, and Britain's political parties were hardly in dispute about it.

Labour's conversion to immigration controls seemed to smack of electioneering, however. Wilson's parliamentary majority was slender, and an early general election seemed likely (see Unit 15.1). Labour had suffered a surprising setback at Smethwick in the 1964 general election. The parties had been careful not to make immigration an election issue, for fear of unleashing dangerous prejudices. But it became an issue at Smethwick where Gordon Walker, an ardent supporter of the Commonwealth, became the victim of an anti-immigrant campaign, and of slogans such as 'If you want a nigger neighbour, vote Labour'. Against the general voting trend he lost what was thought a 'safe' Labour seat to Peter Griffiths, the Conservative candidate. Wilson called the campaign 'utterly squalid', and, when Griffiths arrived in the House of Commons, demanded that he be treated as a 'parliamentary leper'. No result in 1966 gave Labour greater satisfaction than to regain Smethwick, but Gordon Walker's defeat had shown how public emotions about non-white immigration could be exploited. Responsible politicians handled the issue with caution, but there was a further sinister development in 1966, when the National Front was formed (see Unit 17.3(b)).

(b) Further Restrictions

Two years later, in 1968, Wilson faced a new crisis over immigration. When the Conservatives had granted independence to Kenya in 1963 the Asian minorities there had been allowed to retain their British passports and claims to British citizenship. They were not, therefore, subject to the terms of the Commonwealth Immigrants Act of 1962. Since many refused to take up Kenyan citizenship, they became less acceptable to the Kenyan government and, by 1968, some 50 000 had arrived in Britain – and as many more were still in Kenya. Moreover, in places as far apart as Uganda and Malaysia, several hundred thousand held similar rights of citizenship and might one day wish to enter Britain. There was something like panic in London as the implications of this were realized. Callaghan, the Home Secretary, hastily produced the Commonwealth Immigration Act of 1968 which restricted entry into Britain for passport holders without 'substantial connection' with the country. An annual quota of 1 500 was fixed, though others could still compete for work vouchers. Many Asians, having left Kenya, found themselves stateless. At one time in 1970 a hundred were in prison in Britain for arriving 'illegally', almost as many were protesting outside the British Embassy in Belgrade and yet more were scattered throughout Europe, seeking ways of entering Britain. Another Race Relations Act in 1968 did nothing to rescue Britain's tarnished reputation or to shield Wilson's government from accusations of breach of faith, and Britain was condemned by the European Human Rights Commission.

Yet another crisis erupted in 1972. Asians holding British passports were expelled from Uganda and this time Heath's government looked for ways to keep them out of the United Kingdom. The government's main achievement was to persuade friendly nations such as Sweden to take on Britain's responsibilities, while some 20 000 were accepted in Britain as 'refugees'.

Meanwhile the question of non-white immigration came more into the open in Britain. The Nazi-like rantings of the National Front drew attention to it, but it was Enoch Powell, at that time a senior Conservative MP, who captured the headlines in April 1968 with a highly charged warning about the consequences of non-white settlement:

> As I look ahead, I am filled with foreboding. Like the Roman, I seem to see the River Tiber foaming with much blood.

Powell seemed to have forgotten that, as Minister of Health, he had seen the value of non-white labour in Britain's hospitals, and his apparent prophecy of something like civil war cost him the place he might have had in Heath's government in 1970. There was a strong following for Powell in the country as a whole, however. For a time, wild 'repatriation' schemes were suggested, to persuade Britain's coloured citizens to leave the country, even those British by birth who had known no other nationality. Few responsible politicians sided with Powell, but the Conservatives paid him some heed, continuing to talk of limiting immigration by yet further laws. In fact, except for the dependents of earlier settlers, non-white immigration was little more than a trickle by the 1970s. All the main political parties had long since pledged themselves to admit dependents, as an act of humanity and to provide balance in the immigrant communities.

Nevertheless, further legislation was passed. The Immigration Act of 1971 created a unified system of controls for Commonwealth and foreign immigrants, continuing work-voucher admissions but adding a four-year probationary period before permanent settlement was allowed. There were

Fig. 17.2   Enoch Powell, an impression by Richard Cole: Powell's hostility to non-white immigration and his forecasts of racial conflict in Britain cost him a place in Heath's government in 1970. Powell parted company with the Conservative Party during the 1970s though he had held ministerial office in the 1950s and was Minister of Health from 1960 to 1963

some special concessions, including the right of 'patriality', for those, mainly from the White Dominions, who could show descent from a parent or grandparent born in the United Kingdom. Further amendments followed in 1973 when Britain had to adopt the European Community's regulations about the movement of peoples.

The next Labour government responded to the persistent idea that regulations were still not tight enough by setting up the Franks Commission, to make inquiries about dependents awaiting entry to Britain. In 1977 the Franks Report rejected the idea of a register of such dependents and of further changes in immigration law. Nevertheless, it entered into the sterile debate about the numbers of non-whites in Britain, calculating that there were likely to be about 3.8 million by the end of the century. The issue came up again during the general election of 1979 when the Conservatives accused Labour of inertia and Thatcher and Whitelaw promised to give further study to ways of limiting non-white immigration, by defining more closely the categories of acceptable dependents. Minor legislation followed in 1980, with a more weighty Nationality Act later.

This history of concern about non-white numbers brought great discredit to Britain's political leaders and to at least a section of British society. A West Indian leader posed the question, as non-whites saw it in the 1960s:

> Can a coloured population of less than one per cent destroy this great country (of Britain)?

By 1980, the percentage was a little more than three, but non-whites were still a tiny minority who, in any case, contributed in full to the country's well-being. Anxiety about precise figures was disturbing evidence of prejudice, which seemed curious when set against Britain's imperial history and international interests. It was also foolish since the debate about past, present and future non-white numbers repeatedly suggested that such citizens were unwanted, creating bitterness and resentment, and undermining the many attempts being made to achieve racial goodwill. Moreover, the debate added to foreign suspicions that Britain still nursed old-fashioned ideas of white superiority, and that part of the 'British disease' was sluggishness in coming to terms with the changing world of the twentieth century.

17.3 Race Relations in Britain

(a) The Challenge and Legislation
The debate about numbers was, in any case, rather misleading. Relations between the races in Britain, though hardly close, were almost always cordial. Few serious clashes occurred. Those there were, were on a small scale and seldom bloody; the conflicts in Northern Ireland were far more extensive and ferocious. What was more remarkable than the clashes was the ease with which adjustment took place in the areas of immigrant settlement. It was unfortunate that the authorities did almost nothing from the outset to prevent uneven patterns of settlement, so that towns such as Bradford, Rochdale, Leicester and Wolverhampton came to have comparatively large non-white communities. It was usually the poorer classes in these towns who shared with the newcomers the dingy streets and sub-standard housing which was all many of them could afford. The host communities who found their lives changed often showed outstanding tolerance and goodwill, and most of these places of settlement could rightly claim a record of harmonious race relations. There were nevertheless disquieting examples in various parts of the country of acts of discrimination against non-whites – treating them as second-class citizens and denying them opportunities – and it was these which prodded government into race relations legislation.

With some hesitation, Wilson's government introduced the first of Britain's

Table 17.2 Places of immigrant settlement in Britain: examples (population (thousands) born outside the United Kingdom)

	Total population	Total born in New Commonwealth	Born in New Commonwealth (selected areas)				Born in Irish Republic	Born in Germany
			East Africa	West Indies	India	Pakistan Bangla-desh		
Greater London	7 452	476	37.5	168.7	106.4	30.1	197.9	34.3
Birmingham	1 098	69	3.9	25.5	18.2	17.6	40.5	1.8
Bradford	462	23	1.3	2.1	6.2	12.2	4.0	0.9
Glasgow	897	8	0.5	0.3	2.9	2.3	12.7	1.0
Leeds	739	15	1.3	4.7	4.1	2.6	7.6	1.7
Leicester	284	23	6.9	2.9	11.5	0.8	4.4	0.7
Liverpool	610	5	0.2	1.1	1.1	0.3	7.6	0.7
Manchester	544	17	0.7	7.1	3.0	3.4	20.2	1.2
Rochdale	91	4	0.3	0.1	1.0	2.8	1.8	0.2
Rugby	84	2	0.4	0.7	0.7	0.1	1.4	0.2
Sheffield	573	8	0.2	3.5	1.1	2.6	2.9	0.9
Wolverhampton	269	20	1.0	6.4	11.4	0.7	2.7	0.4

Source: British census, 1971.

More comprehensive details can be found in *Ethnic Minorities in Britain, Statistical Data* published by the Community Relations Commission, 1976.

Race Relations Acts in 1965. The ministers were aware that law itself can do little to remove prejudice, but they hoped that law could encourage a healthy climate in which equality could grow. Laws on public order already existed; the Act of 1965 merely extended them slightly, making incitement to discrimination an offence, the better to deal with those who preached racial hatred. What was essentially new in the Act was the condemnation of acts of discrimination with particular reference to hotels and public houses. This was a cautious beginning, as was the machinery the Act created for dealing with discrimination. The Race Relations Board (RRB) was set up and, rather like the Ombudsman system, individuals could make their complaints only to this Board. The RRB would then investigate and try to conciliate by, for example, trying to persuade a prejudiced hotel manager to change his ways. If that failed, the RRB could prosecute him at law. The Act set up signposts, pointing the way towards desirable behaviour.

The Labour government extended this law with a second Race Relations Act in 1968, based on similar principles. An official summary explained the new law:

> The Act defines discrimination as treating a person less favourably than another person on grounds of colour, race, or ethnic or national origins, in the provision to the public of goods, facilities and services, and in employment and housing. Discrimination includes segregating people on grounds of colour, race, or ethnic or national origins.

The scope of the new Act was therefore wider, but the RRB was again central to the system. In the early 1970s the Board was handling about a thousand complaints a year, but only found it necessary to take a small number of them to court. The government also gave an annual grant to a new Community Relations Commission (CRC) in 1968, whose job it was to encourage improved race relations, for example, by education and publicity. Many local authorities took similar positive steps, mainly through Community Relations Councils, whose members gave their services voluntarily to a cause they considered important.

(b) The Continuing Struggle

The Acts of 1965 and 1968 were never expected to produce changes overnight, but they did speed up moves towards equal treatment in many areas, and encouraged thinking about the needs of a multi-cultural society, for example in education. Numerous surveys and reports, however, bore witness to the continuing difficulties of British non-whites, many of whom suffered from higher-than-average unemployment, worse-than-average housing and lower-than-average wages. From 1973 to 1976, for example, unemployment among Britain's coloured minorities rose by 302 per cent, compared with an average rise of 135 per cent, while studies of housing in London, Bradford, Leicester, Manchester and Wolverhampton in 1975 all commented on the

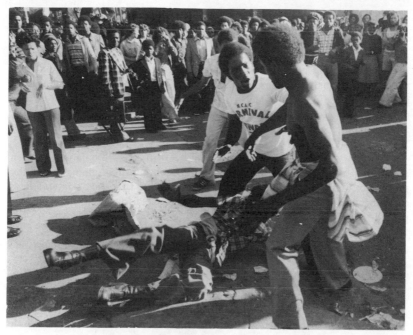

Fig. 17.3 The Notting Hill Carnival in London marred by violence among black youths, August 1977. By that time, many of the hopes of Britain's non-white communities remained unfulfilled, and this photograph captures many tense and worried faces

poor accommodation occupied by non-whites. *The Facts of Racial Disadvantage* (Political and Economic Planning) reported in 1976 that racial discrimination in employment seemed actually to be increasing in Britain. It was seldom easy to prove racial discrimination, for example in allocating jobs and awarding promotion, but it undoubtedly remained widespread. In the late 1970s there was a marked increase in the anger of young British blacks against what they regarded as white obstruction of their prospects and the hostility of white policemen. Rather belatedly, in 1975, the police launched a campaign to recruit more non-whites, especially in London, which had only forty-one coloured policemen at that time. Three years later, a new police station with a Bengali interpreter was opened in Brick Lane in east London, after ugly incidents and violence towards the Asian communities in that area.

The situation was inflamed by bigots, many of whom came together in the late 1960s and 1970s in the National Front (NF). This movement claimed to 'Put Britain and the British People First', reviving memories of the British Union of Fascists of the 1930s. But even Mosley ridiculed the NF for adopting its:

John Bull posture in order to get votes on the immigration question.

The NF had similar delusions to those of the German Nazis, and it thrived on the exploitation of prejudice – against Jews, trade unionists and the democratic system, but above all against non-whites. It was markedly unsuccessful in winning elections, although membership and votes for the movement both grew during the 1970s. Its acts of provocation inevitably embittered race relations, but also produced a counter-movement, the Anti-Nazi League, among people concerned enough to regard the NF as a dangerous poison in British society.

Part of government's difficulty was the need to strike a balance between preserving freedoms, such as freedom of speech, and restraining unhealthy prejudices. The Labour Party continued to believe that race relations laws could be useful, if not decisive. A third Race Relations Act was therefore passed in 1976:

> An Act to make fresh provision with respect to discrimination on racial grounds and relations between people of different racial groups.

Fig. 17.4 A British stamp of 1979 on the theme of the police: a constable and children white and coloured. Though many policemen worked hard to promote harmonious race relations, black youths often complained of harassment in the late 1970s and early 1980s

This Act dealt with education, trade unions and the police, in addition to the areas covered in earlier laws. It also tightened the laws against inciting racial hatred, but most of all, it overhauled the machinery for improving race relations. The RRB and CRC were replaced by a new Commission for Racial Equality (CRE), and individuals were now given the right to take to court cases of alleged discrimination. Community relations began to rely more on professionals than on well-meaning amateurs, with paid full-time Community Relations Officers and staff appointed at local level to tackle disputes and

Fig. 17.5 A classroom in a primary school in Enoch Powell's constituency (part of Wolverhampton) at the beginning of the 1970s. Powell was concerned that white children were outnumbered; others saw hope for the future in the easy mixing of races in this multi-racial class. Yet others feared that the school provided only an artificial protection for the non-white children who would continue to find Britain a harsher place when they came to compete for jobs, status and housing

promote goodwill and understanding. There was growing realization of the need for long-term educational effort, and the Department of Education encouraged schools to re-examine old textbooks, syllabuses and attitudes, to consider how best they could contribute to a society which now included a wider variety of cultures. The television authorities, and others in a position to set examples, were encouraged to give greater prominence to non-white British, and the TUC launched a campaign to lead trade unionists towards racial harmony.

Such efforts had the advantage of being built on the foundations of the good sense of most of the British people. Forebodings of racial confrontation, occasionally revived by Powell, seldom seemed realistic in the 1970s while the National Front, in spite of its passion for displaying the Union Jack and shouting its self-declared patriotism, remained no more than a freak in British politics. The NF put forward some 300 candidates at the general election of 1979, all of whom lost their deposits. The Front as a whole won less than 200 000 votes and David Lane, the Chairman of the Commission for Racial Equality, did not disguise his satisfaction:

> Overwhelmingly, the British people have treated them with the contempt they deserve.

The British Movement mushroomed at the beginning of the 1980s, however, rivalling the NF and competing with it for recruits, especially among the young who were frustrated and embittered by unemployment. Economic crisis also brought added strains and tension in the inner cities, many of them areas of high non-white settlement. Ugly new conflicts occurred, the violence of which sent tremors through British society (see Unit 21.4). These were by no means simple black–white confrontations and there was argument as to the causes of the rioting. It seemed clear, nevertheless, that Britain was still some distance away from total racial equality in the 1980s, and forebodings of racial confrontation began ominously to appear less absurd.

Further Reading

Cashmore, E.: *Rastaman, the Rastafarian Movement in England.* George Allen and Unwin (London, 1979).

Ethnic Minorities in Britain, Statistical Data. Community Relations Commission (London, 1976).

File, N. and Power, C.: *Black Settlers in Britain, 1555 to 1958.* Heinemann (London, 1981).

Griffiths, J.: *Asian Links.* Commission for Racial Equality (London, 1982).

Hiro, D.: *Black British, White British.* Penguin (Harmondsworth, 1973).

Jones, C.: *Immigration and Social Policy in Britain.* Tavistock (London, 1977).

Mullard, C.: *Black Britain.* George Allen and Unwin (London, 1973).

Rose, E.G.B.: *Colour and Citizenship, British Race Relations.* Oxford University Press (London, 1969).

Runnymede Trust: *A Review of the Race Relations Act of 1976.* (London, 1979).

Runnymede Trust: *Britain's Black Population.* Heinemann (London, 1980).

Exercises

1. Explain the term 'New Commonwealth' (page 299). Making reference to Tables 17.1 and 17.2, explain from which parts of the New Commonwealth immigrants came to Britain in the years before 1971 and how their settlement in Britain was 'uneven' (page 306).

2. Why did substantial migration to Britain occur in the years after 1945, and why did immigrant communities develop in places such as London, Birmingham and Bradford?

3. Why was it thought necessary to restrict immigration into Britain at the beginning of the 1960s? List the various immigration laws which have been introduced, alongside each writing the year of enactment, the party then in power and the main terms of the legislation.

4. How would you use the illustrations in this Unit in describing and assessing Britain's progress towards the development of a multi-cultural society?

5. In what years have Race Relations Acts been passed in Britain? Summarize the terms of each such Act. How true is it that these Acts 'set up signposts, pointing the way towards desirable behaviour' (page 308), but that the Acts alone could not be 'decisive' (page 310) in creating harmonious race relations?

6. Explain the different views of race relations in Britain and of British society that might have been expressed at the end of the 1970s by thoughtful representatives of *each* of the following groups: white Londoners of English descent; immigrants from

the Indian subcontinent resident in Britain since about 1960; Asians who came to Britain from Kenya about 1968; black teenagers born in Britain of parents who had migrated to Britain during the 1950s.

7. How far does your own experience of Britain's multi-cultural society suggest that 'total racial equality' (page 312) has or has not been achieved in Britain today?

Unit Eighteen

Life in Postwar Britain

18.1 An Age of Contradictions

The British celebrated Queen Elizabeth II's Silver Jubilee in 1977 with much the same enthusiasm as they had greeted her coronation in 1953. By 1977, however, it was clear that the new Elizabethan era had become an age of contradictions rather than of glorious achievements. Real incomes had almost doubled since the beginning of the 1950s, increasing steadily, except for a pause in 1962 and a small setback in 1976. The British were more prosperous, therefore, than ever before. Yet there were frequent warnings that the country was walking along the edge of an economic precipice, and living beyond its means. Units 13, 15 and 16 have shown something of the mounting frenzy of concern about the British economy, and the frequent crises could hardly fail to create a general sense of uneasiness, even of anxiety, in the country as a whole. In the late 1970s unemployment and inflation were the chief worries. Welfare legislation had lessened the hardships of unemployment, compared with the 1930s, but its impact was still considerable, not least psychologically; and unemployment was again spread unevenly, producing distressed areas and regional divisions in the United Kingdom. At the same time inflation ate away savings, created fears for the future and increased social tensions. Some sections of society, for example those organized in the more effective trade unions, could keep ahead of inflation with increased incomes, but other sections fell behind and grew bitter. Behind unemployment and inflation, moreover, lay continuous and rapid change in many aspects of life, so that the overall increase in prosperity did little to banish the general sense of unease and widespread confusion about the direction in which British society was moving.

Experts and politicians alleged that unemployment and inflation were evidence of a British 'malaise', and of deep-rooted economic problems about which people remained poorly educated, no matter how often they were admonished. By 1980 Britain's industrial output was actually falling, with North Sea oil production only thinly disguising a still unhealthy balance of payments position. The British people were criticized, at various times, for not working hard enough, for spending their increased wealth on imported consumer goods, and for their readiness to go on strike, sometimes in pursuit of greedy wage claims. The country's economic performance was contrasted regularly with rival nations, and that the comparison was often unfavourable seemed to be due to uniquely British problems and shortcomings. People were told that Britain was 'in decline': from being the world's richest country in the nineteenth century, it had slipped steadily down the league table of rich nations to become one of the poorest members of the EEC in the 1970s (see Table 18.1). The suggestion that Britain's 'decline' was the result of some defect in the national character led many to undervalue their own society and its achievements.

In the second half of the twentieth century Britain had not been shaken to its foundations either by revolution or by defeat in war, like so many other countries. Britain's problem was that of bringing about the gradual evolution of a modernized society and a matching economy. By 1980 higher standards of living and greater equality provided evidence of extensive social change, though the welfare state had by no means done away with poverty and under-privilege. There had been widespread economic change too, though science and technology, embraced so eagerly in the 1960s, had hardly proved to be the saviours they had seemed. Indeed, Britain appeared generally to

Fig. 18.1 It was alleged that the British public often blamed the politicians for their country's ills. Gibbard expressed a different view in the Guardian *in April 1979, commenting on the lethargy (or healthy indifference?) of British voters while Callaghan and Thatcher bawled in their ears and Steel pulled at their eyelids. The alarm clock was already set for the imminent general election*

Table 18.1   International league tables, annual Gross Domestic Product*

1961 Britain in 9th position		1966 Britain in 13th position		1971 Britain in 15th position		1976 Britain in 18th position	
USA	2 851	USA	3 827	USA	5 125	Sweden	9 030
Canada	2 167	Iceland	3 045	Sweden	4 439	Switzerland	8 871
Sweden	2 021	Sweden	3 043	Canada	4 373	Canada	8 409
Switzerland	1 773	Canada	2 898	Switzerland	3 958	USA	7 972
New Zealand	1 591	Switzerland	2 522	†West Germany	3 537	Norway	7 774
†Luxemburg	1 585	Denmark	2 309	Denmark	3 494	†Denmark	7 594
Australia	1 544	†France	2 148	†Luxemburg	3 251	†West Germany	7 247
†West Germany	1 477	†Luxemburg	2 103	Norway	3 241	Australia	6 763
Britain	1 439	New Zealand	2 083	†France	3 089	†Belgium	6 713
		†West Germany	2 081	Australia	3 081	Iceland	6 611
		Australia	2 049	Iceland	3 028	†France	6 552
		Norway	2 036	†Belgium	2 983	†Netherlands	6 501
		Britain	1 931	†Netherlands	2 812	†Luxemburg	6 276
				New Zealand	2 596	Finland	5 951
				Britain	2 497	Austria	5 407
						Japan	4 922
						New Zealand	4 126
						†Britain	3 914

* GDP per head of population, at current prices and calculated at prevailing exchange rates in US dollars. The countries listed are those which are members of the Organization for Economic Co-operation and Development (OECD) – *OECD calculations*
† members of the European Economic Community

move forward only slowly and clumsily. It was true that the British still clung
tenaciously to their traditions, but many were not unworthy. A stubborn belief
in freedom persisted, for example. Government regulation was now accepted
but suspicion of too much government intervention in society and the economy
still lingered. As Wilson was fond of declaring, the British people had to be led:
they could not be driven. Sometimes the result seemed like lethargy, but it
helped to preserve a society which was neither inhumane nor uncivilized. The
British simply refused to discard their past overnight, and they went on
persevering to adapt the past to the present, and to strike the right, delicate
balance between freedom and authority. The task was far from easy, and the
slowness with which results were achieved inevitably led to impatience.

Trade union freedoms, for example, had only been won through long struggle.
The structures of the unions, and of industrial relations, like those of British
industry itself, were rooted deep in history. To adapt them to modern needs
was more difficult than in most other countries, provoking passionate
argument especially when powerful groups of workers, in pursuit of their own
sectional interests, seemed to show little concern for the national interest.
From the 1960s successive governments tried to work out a new balance
between union freedoms and the interests of the people at large, but progress
was painfully slow. Beyond some general awareness that there needed to be a
balance between wages, prices and output, the country had little clear idea
about the right way forward. Nevertheless, the British people showed
sufficient maturity to recognize the impossibility of quick, fascist solutions.
Their attachment to freedom and fair play remained strong. Except for the
special problems of Northern Ireland, Britain suffered little of the various sorts
of extremism not uncommon elsewhere.

Uncertainty about goals in the 1960s and 1970s left the country a prey to
contradictions, however. Poverty and affluence still co-existed with a general
lessening of prosperity relative to distance from London. High technology in
industries such as aeronautics and electronics contrasted with growing
complaints of shoddy workmanship elsewhere. In an age of self-service,
service itself seemed to have become a casualty. Observers commented on a
trend towards 'private affluence and public squalor', recognizing the
contradiction that at a time of increased wealth there was marked
deterioration in services once taken for granted. Though Clean Air Acts were
very successful in ridding much of the country of the smoky atmosphere of its
industrial past, and many public buildings were transformed by scraping away
the grime of earlier years, there was concern about vandalism and litter in
Britain's streets and public places. Malicious damage and the growing fashion
for daubing on walls disfigured many an urban environment, but 'public
squalor' implied more than that. It meant the decline of services to the
community, for example of local transport services. The British postal service,
once universally admired for its high standards, seemed in the 1970s to
become less reliable the more its charges increased. The Post Office's public
telephones attracted special venom from society's vandals, creating problems

in London and elsewhere in making even a simple phone call.

Vandalism and hooliganism generally reached new levels in the 1960s and 1970s. Football hooligans became a special menace to more law-abiding citizens and to British Rail, whose trains they vandalized with a sometimes demented thoroughness. Football followers fought one another and the police, until almost military measures were employed to control crowds at some football matches: in the 1970s the larger football clubs fenced off rival spectators both from other groups and from the field of play. By no means all vandals and hooligans came from the under-privileged sections of the community, but the majority were youngsters. Indeed, there were periods in the 1960s and 1970s when Britain's youth threatened to become dangerously alienated from a society whose values they seemed unable to accept. The problem was not confined to Britain, however: it was common throughout the western world. It seemed a contradiction that youth should be so resentful, for Britain's schools were now paying much more attention than in earlier times to the social needs of their children, devoting time to their pastoral care and to individual counselling. Educational opportunity in the post-school years, moreover, had never before been so extensive.

Sociologists offered various explanations for youthful disaffection, not the least of which concerned the defects of a society far from at ease with itself. Prosperity had not brought contentment; the pace of change and uncertainties about the future bred confusion and tension. Advertising, moreover, fuelled the wants of individuals and their discontent until it sometimes appeared that all the system produced was a competitive 'rat-race', with people motivated by simple greed for yet more material possessions. British society seemed to have lost its idealism. Earlier collective outlets for it, such as trade unionism, friendly societies and co-operative movements themselves seemed to have lost their sense of direction in an age of money-making. Nevertheless, prosperity enabled people to contribute in time and money, and on an unprecedented scale, to innumerable charities, both national and international – Voluntary Service Overseas, Oxfam, War on Want, Help the Aged, the Samaritans, Shelter and the Spastics Society were just some of the better known agencies. Youth was in error if it assumed that society was entirely without vision and ideals. Britain had become more complex and puzzling, like the world as a whole, but that did not mean that it had grown heartless and callous.

Two world wars and other bloody conflicts had undoubtedly disillusioned and brutalized the twentieth century. Violence seemed on the increase almost everywhere – and Britain could not escape its share. But it was not easy to see this violence in perspective. The media, especially television, created greater awareness of it than had existed before, but there were no easy solutions to be found, and society could only grapple with such problems as the increase in crime, including crimes of violence, while avoiding merely vengeful responses. People's behaviour, on the other hand, was not always logical. In the late 1970s, when inflation steadily reduced the value of savings, the British practised thrift and saved with added vigour. They demanded tax cuts, yet

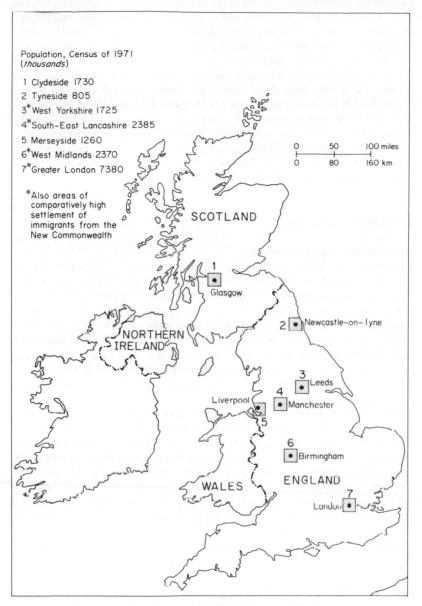

Fig. 18.2 The main conurbations, 1971

expected at the same time the full range of public services for which their taxes paid. They complained of strikes and wage claims but hoped for even greater pay increases for themselves. They bought imported goods and belittled British products, while complaining of unemployment in the United Kingdom.

Above all, however, the British people withstood their almost endless bombardment by radio, television and newspaper with news of 'gloom and doom', and got on with their daily lives. They were confused and it was impossible for them to be confident, but they could still see plenty of evidence that life in Britain was a good deal more than merely tolerable. Frustrations and problems had become very much a part of daily life, as people struggled with rising prices, fluctuating mortgages, redundancy, redeployment, reorganization and upheaval. But few would seriously have wished to change places with earlier generations in Britain.

18.2 Social Change

(a) Population and Convention
From 1940 to 1970 Britain's population grew from about forty-seven million to rather more than fifty-five million. It changed little during the 1970s, standing at about fifty-six million in 1980. Rising standards of living and further advances in medicine and health care much increased average life expectancy in the postwar years, until men could expect to live to almost seventy, and women to seventy-five. The birth rate, on the other hand, was only slightly higher than in the inter-war years (see Unit 7.1(a)). There was a boom immediately after the Second World War, and there was an upward trend from 1955 to 1964, but by the late 1970s Britain's schools had a declining population.

Postwar British society experienced a good deal of change. Teenage marriages increased markedly, though a disturbing number of them ended in divorce; and divorces generally rose substantially in the late 1960s and 1970s. Teenage marriages resulted partly from the lower age of majority and partly from greater prosperity, but they were also related to a general movement towards permissiveness and greater social freedom. People lost some of their inhibitions in the 1950s, and in the following decades sexuality was flaunted more openly, with displays of pornography, in print and on film, which would have scandalized earlier generations.

Female fashion again challenged convention, as it had done in the 1920s, arriving in the 1960s at hemlines which achieved a new brevity, when the mini-skirt seemed hardly more than a sort of pelmet. The fashion did not last, of course, any more than the adventurous new fashions sported by young British males. The latter adopted wide padded shoulders in the late 1940s and Edwardian styles in the 1950s, when 'Teddy boys' had their moment of glory. The 1960s saw 'mods' and 'rockers', contrasting elegance on the one hand with a deliberate flouting of convention on the other. Fashions in dress were often

Fig. 18.3 The Beatles, four young men from Liverpool whose distinctive sound in the 1960s produced Beatlemania, with a massive following in Britain, the USA and elsewhere. The Beatles popularized electronic effects and gave impetus to the age of pop groups. At the instigation of Harold Wilson they were later awarded MBEs, partly for their services to Britain's exports. Photographed in 1963, from left to right, Paul McCartney, George Harrison, Ringo Starr and John Lennon

linked with the forms of transport which came within the reach of Britain's youngsters at this time. The 'mods' had a liking for scooters while the 'rockers' with their leather jackets, studded with metal slogans and even Nazi emblems, favoured motor-bikes. But dress was associated even more with fashions in music, running to seed with the 'punk' movement in the late 1970s.

For the young generally, affluence, the almost universal availability of transistor radios, record and then cassette-players, and the rapid development of electronics and amplification, brought about a new age of 'pop' music, with groups achieving massive cult followings. Dancing now bore little resemblance to the more formal styles of the earlier twentieth century; and, with apparently interchangeable clothing and hair styles, even the distinctiveness of girls and boys began to disappear. Unisex clothes shops and hairdressing salons mushroomed in the 1970s and, though boutiques kept alive a wide variety of feminine fashions, and sometimes a fashion in male clothing, the most evident result was a widespread casualness in dress and appearance. Jeans, loose sweaters and the general acceptability of almost any style liberated many from the dictates of changing fashions and, for girls, marked a further stride along the road to complete emancipation. The young were, however, particularly vulnerable to the commercialization which held a general grip on British society, and more staid British opinion worried not only about the unconventional behaviour of youth, with a period of anxiety in the late 1960s and early 1970s about drug-taking, but about the skilful packaging and exploitation of their trends in music and dress. Unlike their predecessors, postwar teenagers had money to spend, and there were big financial profits to be made in manipulating the teenage market.

There were profits, too, in the adult market. After the shortages of the 1940s, Britain entered an age of unprecedented consumer spending, in which the potential buyer was bombarded on all sides by advertising. Prewar luxuries became conventional postwar possessions, often bought on hire purchase. Almost every British home had a television set by the end of the 1960s and, ten years later, that set was becoming more versatile with the beginning of an explosive new vogue for video-recorders, electronic games and information systems. By that time, of every hundred households, about ninety possessed a refrigerator, almost eighty a washing-machine, more than fifty at least one motor car and a telephone, and almost as many some sort of central heating. By 1976 the British were spending almost £6 000 million a year on durable goods, getting on for half as much as they spent on food. They also spent almost £6 000 million a year on clothing and footwear, and a similar amount on alcohol, more than £4 000 million on running their motor-vehicles, and about £3 000 million on tobacco. Even allowing for inflation, the trend was steadily upwards. As one want was satisfied, another took its place, carefully cultivated by the country's advertising agencies. Supermarkets, which had spread in the 1950s and 1960s, began to give way to hypermarkets in the 1970s. Woolworth, which had once offered 'Nothing over Sixpence', now sold furniture, and accepted credit cards. Buying on credit, in fact, was another habit which had expanded greatly in postwar Britain to become one of the new conventions of a large section of society.

(b) Social Divisions

Prosperity, and to some extent education, meanwhile, began to blur Britain's class structure, drawing together the country's two nations (see Unit 7.1(b)). Postwar Britain had a growing army of white-collar workers, many of them of working-class origin, who were now enabled, by widening educational opportunity, to join the professional classes. At the same time, many manual workers now had incomes that equalled or even exceeded those of some salaried workers. The number of owner-occupiers increased steadily, and changing habits in dress, mobility and the use of leisure blurred many of the old class differences. But the divisions were not wholly removed, and British class structures crumbled more slowly than those in other western societies. Regional differences persisted too. The south of England was more affluent than the north, and England more affluent than Scotland, Wales and Northern Ireland.

Incomes remained uneven everywhere, however. Postwar taxation policies did not radically undermine the favourable position of the most well-to-do in British society, as some believed (see Table 18.2). People dependent on state support, on the other hand, especially the old and one-parent families, received only a meagre share of the generally increasing prosperity. An observer wrote of National Assistance in 1964:

> This provides only the barest essentials to enable you to stay alive, not the extras which make you glad to be alive. Between five million and six million people are at present living about this level, at a time when the majority are more prosperous than ever before.

Later years hardly lessened the inequalities, partly because the British devoted a good deal of effort to maintaining differential incomes. They commonly grumbled that the gap between social security benefits and the wages of the poorly paid was too narrow, but they also made sure that preserving wage differentials played a prominent part in wage-bargaining.

The idea persisted in British society of a division between 'us' and 'them'.

Table 18.2 The distribution of income and wealth in Britain

Income	1949	1972		1976	
		Before tax	After tax	Before tax	After tax
Percentage of total incomes received by the richest 10 per cent in British society	33	27	23	26	23
Percentage of total incomes received by the poorer 50 per cent in British society	—	24	27	24	27

Wealth	1966	1976
Percentage of total wealth owned by the richest 1 per cent in British society	31	25

Source: Report of the Royal Commission on the Distribution of Income and Wealth: *An A to Z of Income and Wealth*. HMSO (London, 1980).

Nor was it merely a matter of incomes. It was part of the problem of industrial relations in Britain that a still considerable gap existed between those who worked in management, the professions and even clerical jobs, with their salaries and superannuation schemes, and those on the shop floor of industry. Even with helpful legislation, the latter generally had less job security, and their working conditions were less hospitable. Sharp divisions also remained between those who lived in private houses and those who were council tenants. There were divisions in schooling, not only between private and state schools but, among the latter, between grammar and secondary modern schools. A new division also threatened to take root, between white and non-white (see Unit 17). The divisions were generally less deep in 1980 than they had been in the 1930s, but attitudes would have to change further if Britain were to arrive at the classless society which some social reformers advocated.

Nevertheless, society was changing. There was less respect for those in authority, and shifts occurred in the status of a variety of occupations. Teachers, for example, and civil servants, of whom there were three-quarters of a million by the late 1970s, commanded less respect than in the 1930s. Sociologists and social workers, after achieving prestige in the 1960s, lost much of it in the 1970s. Coalminers, on the other hand, became a new elite among manual workers when the energy crises of the 1970s suddenly raised the status of what had seemed to be a dying industry. The reputation of transport workers declined with the general decline in public transport services, in the face of competition from private cars. Transport workers were now often poorly paid, along with the manual workers of public authorities generally; and there was also a good deal of low pay among white-collar workers, since rising numbers tended to debase their status in comparison with the coveted 'office jobs' of the inter-war years. Others were comparatively ill paid because of the fierce competition their industries faced, in areas such as textiles and some branches of engineering. Yet other jobs became so much less attractive than in the past that it became difficult to recruit sufficient labour, even in times of rising unemployment. There was a shortage of policemen and postmen in the 1970s, for example. Some jobs, meanwhile, almost ceased to exist at all, particularly those in domestic service, though there was still a demand for people to assist with cleaning and gardening, and the authorities organized Home Helps for some of those in acute need. The demand for female clerks and secretaries, especially in London, seemed insatiable, however, and there were almost limitless openings here for legions of young women. There was also more extensive employment of married women in postwar Britain, a trend which accelerated sharply in the 1970s. Working wives augmented household incomes, the better to cope with inflation, but the trend was also an expression of their growing interest in their own careers, and of their increasing confidence in their role as emancipated women. The relatively high proportion of married women who went out to work became, in fact, a distinctive feature of British society, in contrast to the rest of the European Economic Community.

Developing technology and the need to be competitive brought the most marked changes in status, however. Industry increasingly demanded skills, many of them new, and there were ever fewer openings for the unskilled. The country required scientists, technologists, researchers, managers and ideas men, and these were among the new elites. Computers produced new opportunities for those who could design, build and operate them. North Sea oil led to the development of a new industry in producing and operating the drilling platforms and their equipment. There was steady and rapid development in a variety of fields from electronics to the building of nuclear power stations.

Britain's educational system again came under criticism for its failure to produce the necessary numbers trained in science, mathematics and engineering. The British as a whole were being warned ever more stridently in the 1970s that no longer could a man expect his job to last a lifetime. Retraining schemes multiplied. Workers were 'shaken out' of declining employment, 'redeployed' into rising industries and, by 1980, threatened almost universally with redundancy. It sometimes seemed that Britain had become a land of academics and media men, public relations and advertising executives, experts and 'whiz kids', forever exhorting and admonishing the masses to adapt and modernize. Underlying all this ferment was the relatively low productivity of British industry: it was argued that, prosperous though the British might be, they were not as prosperous as they ought to be. One result of this was that the British worked longer hours, though less productively, than many of their fellow-Europeans. In fact, the normal working week for male workers in Britain fell to forty hours in the mid 1960s, though overtime meant that the average hours worked were around forty-seven, and still around forty-four in the late 1970s. Paid holidays were also gradually extended, until almost all workers had at least three weeks by the mid 1970s. This represented considerable social progress, compared with the inter-war years. But most of the comparisons made now were with European rivals, and alongside them the British record was again less impressive.

18.3 The Changing Environment

(a) Towns and Housing

The development of new towns was one aspect of the rehousing of British society in the years after 1945 (see Unit 11.3(a)). By 1972 more than thirty new towns had been planned, and the number of people living in those already built was nearing two million. Earlier Units have also shown the concern of successive governments to promote new house-building generally, both by local authorities and for private sale. No trend was more marked in postwar Britain than that towards owner-occupation, and one result was that the price of houses rocketed. In the mid 1960s the average price of a new house was ten times higher than in the 1930s; and house prices generally increased by around 60 per cent in 1978–9 alone. This was partly because new building often fell short of what was hoped for and because there were more households; but it was also because large numbers of people had become convinced of the attractiveness of owning one's own home.

By 1980 more than half the country's dwellings had been bought by owner-occupiers, or were in the process of being bought by the five million or so families who held mortgages with building societies. Neither the sharp rise in prices nor rising interest payments could damp the enthusiasm of would-be purchasers. Mortgage 'famines' occurred from time to time, when building societies simply could not meet the demand for loans. Interest rates on mortgages climbed with the end of cheap money in the 1950s (see Unit 13.2). They rose in the 1960s from around 6 to more than 8 per cent a year, in the 1970s to around 11 per cent, though with many movements upwards and downwards, and in 1980 and again in 1981 to a staggering 15 per cent. Yet there was still a queue of would-be buyers, whom the building societies for a time could not satisfy. At the beginning of the 1980s, the banks vigorously joined in the business of lending to house-buyers. Tax relief reduced the impact of interest rates for most of those who held mortgages, and the home was by now generally regarded as the most important of all investments. Having bought their homes, people worked busily to improve them. Postwar Britain saw a great boom in the do-it-yourself industry, with the rapid spread of shops and stores to supply it. Old properties were modernized, often with help from the authorities, with indoor lavatories, bathrooms and improved systems of heating. New houses were often enlarged, with a lively demand for home extensions, rooms in the loft and additional space in which to house the multiplying household durables. A home was not only an investment. For many people, it also became a hobby.

Except in London, little more than 10 per cent of British people at the end of the 1970s lived in homes rented from private landlords. The many Rent Acts, it was claimed, made it unprofitable to be a private landlord. Those who were not owner-occupiers were mainly the tenants of public authorities. The new private housing was largely built on the outskirts of urban communities and in surrounding villages but, apart from the new towns, much public building was in areas cleared of earlier slums. In the postwar years there was a fashion for tower blocks, not infrequently of a fortress-like ugliness, where the poor might be herded together, though not always within convenient reach of their work. So many social problems resulted, not least extensive vandalism, that such building had virtually ceased by the 1970s and a start had even been made on the demolition of some of the most disastrous of these ventures, for example in Liverpool.

The problem remained of providing acceptable housing for those too poor to buy their own. This was itself part of a general urban problem, in that there was marked decay in many inner-city areas, still inhabited by the less well-to-do, compared with the more affluent outer areas of Britain's towns and cities. It was noticeable that these inner-city areas were often inhabited by Britain's coloured people, whose housing problems were still acute. Areas such as Moss

Fig. 18.4 The Crossways Estate, Bow, London: by the time this development took place in 1970, the planners were having second thoughts about the suitability of tower blocks for housing Britain's urban population

Side in Manchester were in danger not only of becoming hideous slums but ghettos of 'second class citizens'. The Labour Party made more attempts than the Conservatives to solve the problem by increased council building, but the Liberals condemned both parties for their limited achievements in this field. Government argued that no more public money could be spared, but it remained a blot on society as a whole that the housing problems of the poor did not have greater priority. With what seemed a strange disregard for the basic housing needs of those people totally unable to buy their own homes, the Conservatives in the 1970s adopted a policy of selling council homes to their tenants, to add to the numbers of owner-occupiers, evidence of how housing policy in Britain tended to become something of a political football.

The majority of British people were undoubtedly better housed by 1980 than ever before, though pockets of real need were still easy to identify. However, much of the new building from the 1950s onwards was proving

*Fig. 18.5 The changing face of Britain: (a) Piccadilly Circus, London,
photographed in 1900*

shoddy. All too often, the nation's housing provided graphic illustration of
Britain's 'private affluence and public squalor', and the situation was not
helped by the disastrous failure of many local planning authorities in this field
of social policy in the 1950s and 1960s.

(b) Transport

The demand for private cars in postwar Britain was similar to the demand for
private houses, and nothing did more to change the face of the country than the
revolution in transport. In 1950 there were still fewer than three million
private cars on British roads. Buses and trams carried the bulk of passenger
traffic on short journeys; railways and motor coaches carried the bulk on
longer journeys. Thirty years later, however, Britain had more than fifteen
million private cars. Road traffic carried more than 90 per cent of the country's
travellers, and the private car had not only much reduced rail travel but had
seriously undermined the profitability of buses and coaches and defeated the
tram everywhere save in Blackpool. The railways had also lost heavily to road
transport in the carriage of freight: at the end of the 1970s some 90 per cent of
freight, in terms of weight, was carried by goods vehicles and almost two
million such vehicles helped to make Britain's roads the most congested in the
world. The bustle, noise and fumes of road traffic created a new tense and ugly
environment. In the 1960s road accidents claimed something over 7 000 lives
a year, and the demand for petrol and oil contributed to the world's energy

(b) Piccadilly Circus, London, photographed in 1952. Half a century of technological development had revolutionized Britain's urban transport and street furniture. In 1952, moreover, Britain stood on the threshold of another revolution in which the number of privately owned vehicles multiplied fivefold and threatened the profitability of almost all forms of public transport

crisis. For large numbers of people, however, the motor car had become an essential part of their lives, its purchase and maintenance a major item in the family budget.

Public spending on roads also rose steeply in Britain, especially after 1955. The authorities embarked on motorway building later than many European countries, beginning with the M1 between London, the Midlands and West Yorkshire in the late 1950s. By 1971 over 1 200 miles of motorway had been completed, and the mileage doubled in the following decade. Motorways and other road developments, with their elaborate tunnels, flyovers and 'spaghetti junctions', dramatically changed the face of Britain. At first speeds were unrestricted on motorways, but frightening new accidents, on a scale never seen before, soon led to a limit of 70 mph being imposed. By 1975, the annual toll of life on Britain's roads had fallen below 6 400. The new roads much reduced journey times and, as the network developed, intensified the competition faced by British Rail. One hundred mph Inter-City rail services gave trains a competitive edge on many key long-distance routes, however, and the Inter-City 125 train, coming into use at the end of the 1970s with even higher speeds, further aided the survival of the railways. When technical difficulties had been overcome, British Rail hoped to introduce an even faster

Advanced Passenger Train in the 1980s, on its electrified lines between London and Glasgow. Electrification, moreover, helped to shield the railways from the imminent oil shortages which threatened to cut short the motor revolution, but the road-vehicle industry itself began research into the possibilities of using electric power.

Air travel overseas expanded enormously. In 1976 almost forty-five million passengers passed through British airports, and Britain's airlines alone carried over eleven million passengers on scheduled flights. Many were businessmen, but they also included holidaymakers, millions more of whom travelled on charter flights. The taking of foreign holidays was another feature of postwar British society: in 1976 more than seven million people took holidays abroad, the vast majority of them in Spain and Majorca.

(c) The Media

It was still a minority who took overseas holidays, but watching television rapidly became an almost universal habit in Britain. In 1950 there were few licensed television sets. Ten years later there were ten million, and the growth continued until few homes were without a set. It was calculated that the average Briton watched television for some fourteen hours a week. Aside from entertainment, television was able to provide unique news coverage and background stories which, like radio before, threatened to undermine the popularity of newspapers.

Increasing costs also created problems for newspapers. The *News Chronicle* was swallowed up in the *Daily Mail* in 1960, while the *Daily Herald* perished in 1964, though reborn in a quite different form as the *Sun*. Other papers ceased publication too, like *Reynolds News*, and for a time it seemed that the country was likely to have many further reductions in its choice of daily reading. The smaller and independent newspapers, many of them evening papers, found survival difficult, though provincial weeklies fared better. Most of the national daily and Sunday papers weathered the storm, however, becoming more dependent on revenue from advertising and raising their prices time and again. Some also relied on support from their owners' other interests. Extensive changes took place in the ownership of the British press and new press barons emerged like the Canadian Lord Thomson who added *The Times* to his empire and also collected handsome profits from his interests in commercial television. Demand for the 'serious' or 'quality' papers actually grew, however, in the 1960s, perhaps a result of the expansion in education; and the popular press maintained its sales by increasingly emphasizing what was entertaining rather than what was merely news. Some papers nevertheless suffered a marked decline in circulation; the *Daily Express* was one which struggled to counter this by adopting the popular 'tabloid' format of smaller pages.

The political sympathies of the papers changed little (see Unit 7.2(c)). But the *Sun*, and to a lesser extent the *Daily Mirror*, believed bare bosoms were of greater interest to their readers than a daily diet of political commentary. The magazine world made similar discoveries. In the 1960s and 1970s British newsagents increasingly stocked a great variety of magazines – a variety which changed frequently as publications collapsed and others were launched. But in the 1960s and 1970s they increasingly stocked a range of publications which seemed to exist chiefly for the display of provocative and unclothed young ladies, to the fury of the growing number of feminists. They argued that women should have a more positive and dignified role in life than that of merely entertaining men. But the 1970s brought other problems for the publishers of newspapers and magazines. New technology in production collided with outdated union structures in the industry, and interruptions in printing brought renewed struggles for survival. *The Times* was not printed at all for most of 1979 and, a year later, Lord Thomson declared his intention either to sell it or close it. In fact Thomson sold, and Times Newspapers joined the many others which by this time belonged to vast, impersonal and sometimes international organizations: the press barons had had their day. Nevertheless, it was clear by 1980 that television had not inflicted the mortal wound on the printed word which some had forecast. Allowing for inflation, the British continued to spend as much as before on newspapers, magazines and books.

Television did not put radio out of business either. On the other hand, the BBC had to learn to face commercial competition, first from commercial television after 1954 (see Unit 13.2), and then from commercial radio, such as Capital Radio in the London area from 1973. BBC radio had to experiment vigorously in pursuit of audiences, and innovations included local radio. Though most of the BBC's traditions were preserved, reorganization gave birth to Radio One, providing almost non-stop 'pop' music, while other services catered for a wide variety of tastes. In the late 1970s Radio Four came to pour out an almost incessant torrent of words, ranging from international news and comment to earnest advice on how to cope with the complexities and mysteries of the welfare state. There was no doubt that television replaced radio as the centre of evening interest in the home, but the relentless spread of transistors and car radios enabled sound broadcasting to do far more than merely survive.

(d) The Nation at Play

Cinema competed less well with television than did the printed word and radio. It had been enormously popular until 1950 (see Unit 7.2(d)), but by 1970 attendances were only about a tenth of those twenty years earlier. The number of cinemas had similarly declined. Some cinemas survived by being divided into three or more smaller cinemas with differing programmes. A few stayed alive by presenting Asian films to Britain's minority groups. In London and provincial cities, others survived in the 1960s and 1970s on a repetitive diet of sex films. Many were simply boarded up and left to decay, further disfiguring the environment.

But cinemas, some theatres and even disused churches and chapels found other uses. Many cinemas were converted for playing 'Bingo'. The British public found a new priest in the Bingo-caller whose ritual cries echoed through

Fig. 18.6   'Eyes down': concentration on Bingo in what had formerly been a cinema in south-east London, the early 1960s. Bingo halls later catered for their customers with specially designed desks and other paraphernalia; here, they simply used the rows of seats where audiences once watched films

innumerable halls where Bingo 'sessions' took the place of 'houses' and 'performances'. Where once they had been transported into the make-believe world of screen and stage, the audiences now intently marked off the numbers called. The passion of Britain's new society seemed to be to win something rather than simply to escape to a world of drama and romance. At the same time, Bingo preserved an attractive simplicity in a highly complicated society. At the beginning of the 1980s it had the further merit of providing a comparatively inexpensive recreation for those of the working classes who suffered acutely from the new recession. In more than one sense, therefore, Bingo by the 1980s had taken the place of the cinema of the 1930s.

Television also struck at some spectator sports, especially football matches. Saturday afternoon matches had attracted a regular million and more spectators after the Second World War but 'gates' had dropped to around half a million in the 1970s, the casualty of television, do-it-yourself activities in the home and the antics of hooligans on the terraces. In the early 1980s they fell even further. England's football team won the World Cup in 1966, but subsequent results were often disappointing. Here too, it seemed, the British had lost their competitive edge.

Sport in general, however, began to come to terms with television, and with the changing times. Television was able to stimulate interest and thus attract new audiences, sometimes popularizing previously little known sports. In 1982, for example, independent television launched Britain's fourth television

Fig. 18.7 A British stamp of 1966 to commemorate a national triumph: England won the World Cup, the finals that year being held in Britain

channel which quickly set itself to stimulate interest in basketball. Meanwhile, popular sport adapted itself. With the help of sponsors, professional cricket organized competitions based on one-day matches. The rules of the game were amended and streamlined to present a new image of speed and excitement; and Sunday matches developed a new following. Society was indeed changing when, in the late 1970s, the captain of the English cricket team went in to bat wearing a crash helmet. Test matches, especially between England and Australia, nevertheless remained matters of grave importance – and a good many of the changes in British society were little more than superficial.

British seaside holidays were still far more popular than holidays abroad, though they became the second holiday in the year for many families. The slot machines and 'rides' grew more elaborate, the Bingo 'parlours' and discotheques outnumbered the skating-rinks and ballrooms, but Blackpool, for example, remained much the same as in the inter war years. Fewer visitors arrived by rail but millions came by road, and with much the same expectations as before. They had more money to spend, however, and holiday resorts in general had to keep up with the age of affluence. Boarding-houses became guest-houses, with bars and television sets, while the do-it-yourself movement also extended to holiday-making, and self-catering apartments, chalets, caravans and holiday-villages mushroomed. The motor revolution brought a great interest in touring. Tourist authorities quickly grew up, to attract not only British holidaymakers to their regions but also visitors from abroad, whose importance to the economy grew steadily. Scotland, Wales, and Northern Ireland too, until its troubles all but killed off its tourist trade, became better known to Englishmen, and tourism brought to these regions some of the greater prosperity which England normally enjoyed. Almost everywhere, it seemed, now had attractions to offer, and visitors were even solemnly invited to spend their holidays in such unlikely resorts as Manchester and Sheffield.

18.4 Education and Religion

The Education Act of 1944 long remained the basis of the schools system in England and Wales (see Unit 10.2), but the educational service expanded markedly in postwar Britain (see Unit 15.3). In 1972 the school-leaving age was raised to sixteen, but children were also encouraged to stay on in education beyond the compulsory years. In 1976 about one in five did so, though there were quite wide regional variations in the pattern, with significantly fewer remaining in schools and colleges in the north-west of England and East Anglia than in south-east England and Wales. Thousands of new primary and secondary schools were built in the years after 1945, and considerable progress was made in reducing the size of classes. Yet it was still often argued that a relatively rich country should achieve more, and that too many British children remained under-educated.

By the end of the 1970s the great majority of secondary schools were comprehensives, and the number of grammar schools had sharply declined. However, private education remained. Rather than become state comprehensive schools, as the Labour government required, many direct grant schools had chosen to become independent, and argument continued about the extent to which a division between state and independent schools helped to preserve the class distinctions which lingered in Britain. There were arguments, too, about teaching methods and what was taught, and about the costs of the educational system. In 1976 government spending on education was higher than on any other single item except social security benefits, and was thus rather more than on such items as the National Health Service, defence, and servicing the nation's debt. Nevertheless, the demand for more was incessant and nursery schools, in particular, were regularly the victim of economies.

Perhaps the most remarkable expansion was in the field of higher education. In 1945 Britain had seventeen universities; in 1972 there were forty-four, with Essex, Lancaster, York and Strathclyde among the most recent. Further opportunities came with the opening of some thirty polytechnics and, in the 1970s, many colleges of higher education. Some of the latter were established because of the cutback in teacher training colleges, itself a result of the decline in the nation's birth rate after 1964. The number of students in higher education soared, compared with the inter-war years. In 1950 Britain had about 80 000 full-time students reading for first degrees; by 1970 the total had doubled, although it still fell short of the 390 000 which had been forecast for the early 1970s in the Robbins Report of 1963. The 1970s saw big advances, however. In 1976 the universities alone had some 220 000 undergraduate students, with a further 50 000 engaged in postgraduate study. Yet the expansion still fell short of expectations, and it was also disappointing that the proportion of women students in higher education grew only slowly. In 1950 about one student in four was female; by the end of the 1970s, about one in three. This represented a great step forward in the education of young women, but not yet equality between the sexes. There was also concern about the subjects studied, with the arts and social sciences expanding more than science, engineering and technology, thus reviving a debate first begun over a century before. The concern tended to become alarm in the later 1970s, when Britain's schools found serious problems in recruiting mathematics and science teachers and anxiety grew lest interest in these subjects should perhaps decline even further. Britain had no tradition of government interference in the content of education or in teaching methods, but the 1980s opened with debate as to whether the educational system was in fact meeting the country's needs and whether, indeed, it needed to be so expensive.

The pursuit of material gains was undoubtedly strong in postwar Britain, so it was hardly surprising that there also seemed to be some decline in religious observance. There was a sharp fall in Church of England baptisms in the 1950s, and in the members coming forward for confirmation in the 1960s. Church of England marriages had declined throughout the twentieth century and, by the 1970s, almost as many couples were married in registry offices as in Anglican ceremonies. But one person in five remained a confirmed member of the Church of England in 1968, and the Church of Scotland claimed a further membership of well over a million. The Methodist Church, after an upsurge in the 1930s, suffered a drop in membership in the postwar years, and only Roman Catholicism could claim a growing support. The number of British Jews showed a small increase in the postwar years, and more Jewish children were educated in Jewish schools. The new ethnic minorities in postwar Britain also added to the religious diversity, firmly planting Islam, Hinduism and Buddhism in particular, while among Britain's Afro-Caribbean communities there was a lively interest in Rastafarianism. The British were still far from being atheistic in the 1980s. Indeed, the Church of England with some justification claimed a revival of religious observance at the beginning of the decade.

Soaring building costs made it difficult to maintain the many churches and chapels inherited from the past, however, and it was a further sign of the times that resources for such maintenance were often elusive. But the Church Buildings Act of 1969 made possible the sharing of premises between different religious denominations, and this was only one aspect of the coming together of the Christian Churches. New life was breathed into the ecumenical movement as the Churches sought greater Christian unity. The Church of England welcomed closer relations with the Catholic Church, and Geoffrey Fisher, Archbishop of Canterbury until 1961, visited Pope John XXIII, the first such meeting since before the Reformation. Joint marriage services began to be held, and the Catholic mass was sometimes celebrated in Anglican churches. The Churches generally relaxed their previously rigid attitudes towards those of different denominations, and there was revision and some simplification of worship and ceremonies, easing the way towards co-operation. A proposal to unite the Church of England and the Methodists ran into opposition, however. Conservative opinion was not ready yet for so radical a change. Change and 'modernization' proceeded nevertheless, one result being the completion in 1970 of the New English Bible in 'modern' English. Not everyone welcomed it, departing as it did from much that was traditional, just as not all Christians were enthusiastic about the ecumenical movement. But it was only in Northern Ireland, where religious hatred still festered, that the developing friendship between the Protestant and Catholic Churches encountered bitter hostility. It was a historic development and one which created great interest when Pope John Paul II visited England, Scotland and Wales in 1982.

Further Reading
Britain, Official Handbook. HMSO (London, annual).
Calvocoressi, P.: *The British Experience, 1945–1975.* Penguin (Harmondsworth, 1979).
Central Statistical Office: *Facts in Focus.* Penguin (Harmondsworth, 1978).
Clutterbuck, R.L.: *Britain in Agony, The Growth of Political Violence.* Penguin (Harmondsworth, 1980).
Davies, C.: *Permissive Britain.* Pitman (London, 1975).
Marwick, A.: *British Society since 1945.* Penguin (Harmondsworth, 1981).
Meadows, D.: *Living Like This, Great Britain in the 1970s.* Arrow Books (London, 1975).
Sillitoe, A.F.: *Britain in Figures, Handbook of Social Statistics.* Penguin (Harmondsworth, 1971).

Exercises
1. Show what you understand by *Gross Domestic Product.* What does Table 18.1 show of the growth of Britain's GDP from 1961 to 1976? Suggest reasons for the record you have identified.
2. Making use of the Index to this book, outline the main changes which have taken place since the end of the First World War in (*a*) the housing of the British people, and (*b*) Britain's educational system.
3. What weaknesses in the British public are suggested by Figs 16.5 and 18.1? Why has it often been alleged that 'a British "malaise" ' (page 314) has existed in recent years, and how true do you consider this generalization to be?
4. In what ways has Britain's welfare state since the 1940s provided assistance for those in need? What evidence can you find in Units 17 and 18 that some sections of Britain's population still live in want?
5. Making use of Tables 1.2 and 21.3 as well as of this Unit, show what changes have taken place during the twentieth century in the occupations of the British people.
6. Referring to your answer to Question 3, Unit 7, consider how the status of women in Britain has changed further since 1939.
7. What differing influences affected the lives of Britain's young people during (*a*) the 1950s, (*b*) the 1960s and (*c*) the 1970s?
8. Suggest in the form of daily entries in a diary how you might have spent a week free from work in the 1970s with sufficient money to afford the various recreations and entertainments then popular. Compare your answer with that you wrote in answer to Question 7, Unit 7.

9. 'The pursuit of material gains was undoubtedly strong in postwar Britain' (page 335). List the likely possessions of a family of average means in the 1970s, marking with an asterisk those a similar family would be unlikely to have possessed in the 1920s.

10. What differences are suggested in this Unit between the social policies of Conservative and Labour governments?

Unit Nineteen

The Disunited Kingdom

19.1 Scottish and Welsh Nationalism

(a) National Identity and Regional Policy

The United Kingdom of Great Britain and Northern Ireland was the formal title for Britain in the years after 1921, when the Irish Free State ceased to be a part of the Kingdom. Great Britain included England, Scotland and Wales as well as a variety of offshore islands, some of which, such as the Isle of Man,

Fig. 19.1 Isle of Man stamp of 1973, commemorating the island's postal independence. At the beginning of the 1980s, the island was intent on seeking even more political independence from the United Kingdom

preserved a distinct identity and a measure of Home Rule, underlined by the Isle of Man in the 1970s when it set up its own independent postal service and issued its own postage stamps. A Scottish Office had been set up as part of British government in 1885, and cabinets regularly included a Secretary of State for Scotland. In 1964, Wilson created a similar Office and Secretaryship for Wales. Nevertheless, British general elections from 1970 onwards saw the return to Westminster of Nationalist MPs, the first in 1970 from Scotland, but others, soon afterwards, from Wales too (see Table 10.1). Growing dissatisfaction among the Scots and the Welsh had produced such election results, and there was widespread criticism of a British system of government which seemed to be essentially English. Scotland and Wales, it was argued, were 'neglected', and their specific interests received too little attention from British governments and from MPs whose concerns were predominantly English.

The populations of Scotland and Wales were small compared with England. In the 1970s Scotland's population was rather more than five million and that of Wales about two-and-a-half million. Scotland had long kept certain distinctive Scottish institutions, such as the Church of Scotland, and its legal and educational systems differed from the English. Wales, on the other hand, had been more thoroughly anglicized in spite of the spirited survival of the Welsh language in parts of the principality. Both Scots and Welsh nevertheless struggled to keep alive their traditional cultures, and a national consciousness did survive in both countries, though it often seemed that its preservation was only of real concern to small, predominantly intellectual, minorities. However, there was growing awareness that Scotland and Wales were usually less prosperous than England. Both were hard hit by the Depression in the 1930s, and the British government embarked somewhat half-heartedly on regional policies, the first of which were contained in the Special Areas Acts (see Unit 6.1(b)).

All postwar governments paid at least some attention to regional policy. In 1945 the Distribution of Industry Act extended the Special Areas, renaming them Development Areas. In 1970 Intermediate Areas were also identified, and these too received government help, though their problems were less acute. Various methods were used to attract new industry, to create work and to raise the level of prosperity nearer to that of other parts of the United Kingdom. The results were often disappointing. Such policy was not, of course, confined merely to Scotland and Wales, nor did it extend to the whole of these 'countries'. Prosperity was distributed unevenly throughout the whole of the United Kingdom and, while Scotland and Wales had their pockets of affluence, England also had its distressed areas. Tyneside, for example, had many similarities to the Glasgow area, and Merseyside and south Lancashire shared some of the problems of south Wales. Yet innumerable economic and social indicators persistently showed that, as a whole, England ran ahead of Scotland, Wales and Northern Ireland. On the other hand, government spending per head of population was usually higher in these areas than in England. In 1978–9 the authorities spent, per head of population, £1 460 in Northern Ireland, £1 138 in Scotland, £1 079 in Wales and £919 in England. Moreover Scots, Welsh and Irish worked and settled in England in considerable numbers.

It could perhaps seem rather artificial to make distinctions between England and the other 'countries' of the United Kingdom, yet distinctions remained.

Separate national football teams were preserved, and nothing gave the Scots in particular greater satisfaction than to defeat England in these 'home internationals'. When they did so at Wembley in 1977 they celebrated by tearing up parts of the pitch and breaking down the goalposts, before carrying their nationalist fervour to the streets of London. Rather more seriously, some Scots were then claiming that North Sea oil rightly belonged to Scotland, and not to England nor even to the United Kingdom.

Fig. 19.2 British stamps of 1976 marking some of the differing cultural heritages of the 'nations' which made up Great Britain: respectively English, Scottish and Welsh

National differences, indeed, had become a heated political issue. It was one thing to preserve national cultures and to encourage national pride by setting up institutions such as the separate Scottish, Welsh (and English) National Opera Companies, but in the 1960s clamour grew for some political reorganization of the United Kingdom. Scots and Welsh demanded more control over their own affairs, and tiny minorities in Scotland and Wales even demanded secession from the United Kingdom and total independence. Protest against the alleged dominance of the English was channelled into political parties. Nationalist parties were not, in fact, new. Plaid Cymru, the political voice of Welsh nationalism, had been founded in 1925; and what became known as the Scottish Nationalist Party (SNP) dated from 1928. For many years neither won significant support, but interest quickened in the 1960s. They won no seats in the general elections of 1964 and 1966, but Plaid Cymru collected 60 000 votes in 1966 and the SNP gained twice that number. Nationalist support really took off when Winifred Ewing won a by-election for the SNP in 1967, gaining the apparently 'safe' seat at Hamilton from Labour. Wilson's government set up a Royal Commission, to examine and report on desirable political changes for Scotland and Wales, and it produced its findings in the Kilbrandon Report of 1973. The commission also produced a minority report, however, and the problem hardly seemed capable of any simple and quick solution. But the elections of 1974 added a new sense of urgency, for the

Fig. 19.3 Members of the Scottish Nationalist Party discussing plans for Scotland's future in July 1939. Some thirty years later the question of Scotland's relationship with the rest of the United Kingdom became much more urgent

SNP, and Plaid Cymru too, though to a lesser degree, enjoyed an upsurge of support (see Table 10.1), and the new Labour government seemed more willing than the Conservatives had been to introduce changes.

(b) Devolution

The main recommendation in the Kilbrandon Report was that there should be separate elected assemblies both for Scotland and Wales. These assemblies would have law-making powers, subject to a right of veto from London. The Scots and Welsh would continue to be represented at Westminster, and the government of the United Kingdom would retain overall authority. What was proposed, therefore, was a measure of Home Rule – of the 'devolution' of only a limited amount of authority to Edinburgh and Cardiff. The details of devolution would differ as between Scotland and Wales.

The Kilbrandon Commission also raised the question of whether there should be some limited devolution of power to the various regions of England. There had been general criticism of the pre-eminence of London in British affairs, and of the way in which prosperity seemed, in consequence, to be spread unevenly. On the other hand, many people had had quite enough administrative reorganization with the changes in local government made by Heath's government in 1972 (see Unit 16.2(b)). Englishmen in general, moreover, had little interest in devolution, and considered Plaid Cymru and the SNP somewhat eccentric. Labour governments after 1974 felt that they could safely postpone the question of regional assemblies in England, but they felt unable to neglect Scottish and Welsh devolution. Nationalism had already proved itself a threat to the Labour vote in Scotland and Wales and, in the House of Commons, the government was not strong enough to ignore the ambitions of the SNP and Plaid Cymru.

It took time to work out the points of detail, even when the general principle had been accepted that Scottish and Welsh assemblies should be set up. Such details involved decisions about the extent of regional powers, about finance and about voting procedures. When these were eventually incorporated in 1977 in a Scotland Bill and a Wales Bill, there was still no real confidence that the proposals actually met the desires of the Scottish and Welsh people. The Bills therefore provided for the holding of referenda, to allow the Scots and Welsh to vote for or against the new arrangements. Some argued that the votes for the SNP and Plaid Cymru had been only general protest votes, to show dissatisfaction with the other political parties; and that assemblies were not really wanted at all, especially since it was alleged they would increase administrative costs and perhaps lead to higher taxes. Others argued that the Bills were too weak, and that they fell too far short of any real independence. There was much opposition to them, moreover, in the House of Commons, and it took skilful parliamentary management to get them passed at all. That obstacle was overcome in 1978, but the Commons had by then inserted an important amendment concerning the referenda. The Bills would only take effect if the Scots and Welsh supported the new arrangements with a 'Yes' vote by 40 per cent of the whole electorate. And that was to be tested in March 1979.

The voting was an anti-climax. The Welsh in particular expressed a decisive opinion: the 'Yes' vote in Wales was less than 12 per cent of the electorate. The Scots showed rather more enthusiasm, but even in Scotland the 'Yes' vote was below 33 per cent. Both Bills had therefore failed, since neither won the required 40 per cent support. Why that was so was not clear. Some voters wanted no assemblies at all, while others doubtless considered that what was offered was too little. Yet the question of devolution suddenly seemed to lose its urgency. After frantic endeavours to solve the problem especially in the House of Commons, it almost appeared after all that there was no problem to be solved.

At the general election later in 1979 the Labour Party expressed its intention to consider the matter further. The Conservatives also gave it a mention, albeit a lukewarm one. The election results showed remarkably little concern on the part of the voters. The SNP lost nine of its eleven seats, and its vote fell from around 840 000 in October 1974 to just over 504 000. Plaid Cymru lost one of its three seats and over 30 000 of its previous 166 000 votes. Winifred Ewing was among the defeated SNP candidates and, though several such candidates lost by only very small margins, the SNP bandwagon seemed suddenly to have shuddered to a halt. The Party's chairman declared:

> We were not seen as relevant. But there is still a Scottish dimension in terms of votes, although . . . Labour, not the SNP, will (now) represent that mood.

The SNP also explained its setback as the product of working-class fears of Margaret Thatcher, producing a swing to Labour to try to keep the Conservatives out. Scotland did in fact move towards Labour in 1979, unlike the rest of Great Britain. Regional differences had not disappeared, however. British general elections show a history of setbacks to minority parties, when the voters seek the protection of one major party against the other; and the SNP, indeed, also lost votes to the Conservatives among Scots who wanted to bring down Callaghan's government. By-elections, on the other hand, often show a swing not only against any government in power but also against both major parties, with new enthusiasm for smaller groups. It seemed not impossible that the SNP would recover in the 1980s, and that the question of devolution would return to British politics.

That the question had arisen at all showed that the United Kingdom was less united than had usually been assumed. The politicians, at least, had been worried enough in the 1970s to take the SNP and Plaid Cymru seriously. Another source of disunity in British society could also be detected in a study of voting habits. There was no cause for satisfaction to be found in the tendency of Britain's coloured citizens in the late 1970s to vote Labour, from some fear of Conservative policies. The non-white minorities in Britain so far stopped short of founding their own 'nationalist' parties, but they too, like the Scots and Welsh, suspected that the United Kingdom was not a Kingdom of equals.

19.2 Northern Ireland

(a) The Roots of the Problem

Devolution of power to the people of Northern Ireland had occurred when they were granted Home Rule by the Government of Ireland Act of 1920. Northern Ireland's parliament at Stormont, Belfast, was first opened in 1921. Although the rest of Ireland became a Dominion in 1922, effectively independent of the United Kingdom, the majority of people in the six counties of Northern Ireland seemed well satisfied to remain a part of the UK. They had their own parliament, their own administration for the affairs of their province, and the right to continue to send twelve MPs to the UK parliament in London (see Unit 4.4). The system lasted for half a century, during which time the politics of Northern Ireland were dominated by the Unionists. Unionists formed the administrations in Belfast, where James Craig (Viscount Craigavon) was the first Prime Minister of Northern Ireland from 1921 to 1940; and Ulster Unionists regularly won almost all Northern Ireland's seats in the House of Commons at Westminster. There they joined hands with the Conservatives whose traditional policy was to preserve the 'Union' with Ireland. The system collapsed in 1972, however, when direct rule from London was imposed on Northern Ireland in the wake of spreading unrest, violence and sectarian murders.

At the census of 1971 the population of Northern Ireland was just over one-and-a-half million. The majority of people were Protestant, a mixture of Presbyterians, Methodists and supporters of the Church of Ireland. Many of them, especially the Presbyterians, were the descendants of Scottish immigrants into Ireland in the distant past. Few Protestants felt any close kinship with the peoples of the Irish Republic (formerly, the Irish Free State), and they scarcely doubted that their destiny was to remain within the United Kingdom. But Northern Ireland had a substantial minority of Roman Catholics – about 35 per cent of the population in 1971. These were almost all of native Irish descent and some, at least, were drawn more towards the idea of a united Ireland than towards the permanent preservation of the United Kingdom. The Catholic minority, moreover, grew restless, since Northern Ireland's affairs seemed permanently to be divided on sectarian lines. The Protestant majority dominated. The Catholic minority had little influence, and Catholics complained increasingly that they were the victims of discrimination.

Unionists remained complacent. As late as 1964 William Craig, Northern Ireland's Minister of Home Affairs, declared:

> Our opponents must never be allowed to succeed in their objectives of merging Ulster within an Irish Republic, nor . . . must their efforts be allowed to poison the community climate, setting neighbour against neighbour. . . . Freedom must be enjoyed with consideration for the rights of others.

The words were fine, but it was hardly enough to suggest that criticism of Unionist government was always the work of extremists and that Unionist government was a model of liberalism. At much the same time that Craig spoke, Northern Ireland's Prime Minister, Terence O'Neill, addressed a meeting of Orangemen:

> No smoke screen can hide the fact that under our Unionist Government there is more prosperity in Ulster and it is more widely shared than ever in the past.

But the Lodges of the Orangemen themselves existed to preserve Protestant supremacy, vigorously keeping alive memories of the seventeenth-century victory of the Protestant William of Orange over the Catholic James II. Their supporters ornamented walls with romantic pictures of 'King Billy' and with sectarian advice to 'Kick the Pope'; and other orators ranted at frequent intervals that there must be 'No Surrender' to Popery, the Irish Republic and the IRA.

The IRA had waged campaigns against the alleged injustice of dividing Ireland in 1922 and there were numerous terrorist outrages during the 1950s. But Orangemen and the IRA were both extremist minorities. What many of the people of Northern Ireland wanted from their leaders was even-handed government. What Unionist government provided, however, fell far short of that in the eyes of many Catholics. The Royal Ulster Constabulary (RUC) was the only armed police force in the United Kingdom, and it was supported by an almost military force of B-Specials who, to many Catholics, seemed to exist mainly to preserve Protestant supremacy. Catholics found problems in securing desirable jobs and housing, and equal treatment generally. Northern Ireland suffered from a deep social division which was mainly religious and which official policies did little to heal. Children were often educated in separate Protestant and Catholic schools. The religions lived apart, on different housing estates, for example, in cities such as Belfast and Londonderry. While the rest of the United Kingdom had almost ceased to notice religious differences in society, they remained fundamental in Northern Ireland. O'Neill and Craig made some movement towards reform in the 1960s but time was now running out.

(b) From Home Rule to Direct Rule

A new phase in Northern Ireland's history began quietly enough with moderate protest movements. The Campaign for Democracy in Ulster was launched, to protest against inequalities in the laws concerning local government elections. It was followed in 1968 by the Civil Rights Association, a mainly Catholic movement. The Protestants meanwhile had set up the Ulster Volunteer Force in 1966, for the defence of existing privilege. By the summer of 1969 civil rights demonstrations had been broken up, and riots and sabotage were occurring. The situation then worsened. On the one hand, the interest of the IRA was rekindled. A new 'Provisional' wing of the IRA was born (the 'Provos'), who were soon to develop a fanatical programme of urban terrorism with the aim of bringing about the reunification of Ireland. On the other hand, the B-Specials and Protestant extremists in general seemed almost to welcome opportunities to humiliate the Catholics. In August 1969 the Protestant Apprentice Boys again swaggered through the streets of Londonderry in their annual revival of yet more ancient history; and serious riots followed. There were petrol bombs in Londonderry and gunfire in the streets of Belfast. Blazing buildings disfigured the province, buses were hi-jacked for use as barricades and the police and the B-Specials used tear gas and even machine-guns. Ireland's 'Troubles' were obviously erupting yet again. The British government sent troops to Northern Ireland in August 1969, the start of what was to prove a lengthy vigil. The violence continued spasmodically, and the first British soldier was killed in Northern Ireland in February 1971

British politicians hoped that the troops would calm the situation in the turbulent province while the politicians at Belfast might be persuaded to make urgent reforms. O'Neill retired, quickly followed by his successor, Chichester-Clark, and Brian Faulkner became Northern Ireland's Prime Minister. Meanwhile, the British general election took place in 1970, and the problem of Northern Ireland was passed on from Callaghan to Maudling, the successive Home Secretaries. Neither could make much headway against the bigoted refusal of many Ulster Unionists to accept real change. The Protestants found a new hero in the Reverend Ian Paisley, an honorary doctor of divinity of the American Bob Jones University. Paisley's strenuous anti-Catholic bellowings seemed regrettably closer to the true voice of Ulster Protestantism than did Faulkner's mild advocacy of reform. Paisley was reported to have claimed that 'What we need is another Cromwell', resurrecting yet more history, with its memories of Oliver Cromwell's massacres of Irish Catholics in the seventeenth century. The Provos could feed on such memories but hardly needed to go so far back in time. Unionist rule had a sorry history of its own, with censorship, floggings, imprisonment without trial, and Special Powers to exempt Northern Ireland from some of the law of the United Kingdom.

The environment of the province favoured bitter confrontation rather than reconciliation, and moderate politicians, both in London and Belfast, fought a losing battle. The RUC was disarmed and the B-Specials disbanded; but the Protestants set up a new Ulster Defence Association, to continue the war against the IRA. The killings multiplied in 1971, and Maudling lost a good deal of Catholic goodwill when he gave British approval to a new phase of internment, and of detention without trial. Catholics were interned, but not Protestants; and the idea took hold that British troops were in Northern Ireland less as peacemakers than as custodians of the Unionist system. 'Bloody Sunday' reinforced that idea: on 30 January 1972 British soldiers killed thirteen civilians in Londonderry when there were protest demonstrations against internment, in defiance of an official ban. In the following month a bomb attack destroyed the British Embassy in Dublin, and another IRA bomb claimed seven lives in an attack on army property at Aldershot in southern England. Northern Ireland's troubles were escalating and spreading.

Though Faulkner protested, Heath's government decided to suspend Northern Ireland's system of Home Rule in March 1972. Direct rule was imposed on the province, and Whitelaw was appointed Secretary of State for Northern Ireland in Heath's cabinet. The new arrangement was intended to last for twelve months, to provide time in which to find solutions to the problems. As well as taking a toll of lives and property, the disruption in Northern Ireland was damaging the province's economy, discouraging not just tourists but also investment. The people of Northern Ireland already lagged well behind all other regions of the United Kingdom in terms of GDP per head of population, and the continuing disturbances made certain that the gap would not be closed during the 1970s. By 1976, for example, Northern Ireland was the only region where male unemployment had already risen above 10 per cent of the work force: at that time it was almost 12 per cent, compared with a UK average of just over 7 per cent.

(c) **The Experiment in Power-sharing**
A referendum in Northern Ireland in 1973 showed that almost 58 per cent of the total electorate supported remaining part of the United Kingdom. Heath's government therefore concentrated on devising a new administrative system in the province, to restore a measure of Home Rule and, at the same time, to satisfy both Protestants and Catholics. The background to these efforts

Fig. 19.4 William Craig at a Protestant rally outside Belfast's City Hall, March 1972. The rally was part of a protest against direct rule of Northern Ireland from London. The banner, with its historical recollection of the doings of William of Orange (King Billy) in 1690, helped the Protestants to keep alive their hostility to Catholics

remained turbulent. By the end of 1973 more than 900 people had been killed in Northern Ireland since the violence had begun in the late 1960s, and 241 of the dead were British soldiers. The politics of Northern Ireland also had grown more complicated. To satisfy both Protestants and Catholics was difficult enough, but the Unionists were dividing into factions, each of which also had to be pacified. Reforms in local government, with proportional representation in local elections to increase Catholic influence, won some goodwill, but Heath and Whitelaw rested their hopes on a system of power-sharing in Belfast. There was to be a new assembly for Northern Ireland: its seventy-eight members would again be elected by a system of proportional representation, and there would then be an executive made up of representatives of the various parties in the assembly. This would ensure the sharing of power in a sort of coalition government. The government would remain under supervision from London, however, and the British hoped, optimistically, that Protestants and Catholics would learn to co-operate in the executive's day-to-day business. Round-table conferences were held at Darlington and then at Sunningdale, where the government of the Irish Republic also agreed to support a Council of Ireland, to consider certain problems which were common to the whole of Ireland.

Craig and Paisley would have nothing to do with a Council of Ireland. Before the new executive came into being, they condemned that too. Elections to the new assembly in June 1973 had returned twenty-three Unionists, led by Faulkner, who were willing at least to try power-sharing. But they also returned twenty-seven Protestant Loyalists whose slogan was still 'No Surrender', and who included separate factions led by Craig and Paisley. Catholic opinion was represented mainly by the Social Democratic and Labour Party (SDLP), which won nineteen seats. Gerard Fitt, the leader of the SDLP, thought power-sharing a genuine step towards peace and hoped to help make it work. The Alliance Party, with eight seats, also supported the experiment, which promised to fulfil the Party's aims of politics freed from religious strife. But it was doubtful whether Faulkner's Unionists, the SDLP and the Alliance Party could be strong enough to overcome both Loyalist opposition and widespread intolerance in Northern Ireland. The experiment began with hope rather than faith on 1 January 1974, when the direct rule of the province from London came to an end.

Power-sharing lasted less than five months. The executive had to struggle against terror by the Provos and disruption by the Loyalists. In May 1974 the latter organized a general strike among Protestant trade unionists, and the executive was almost paralysed. A Labour government had meanwhile returned to power, after the British general election in February, and Merlyn Rees took over responsibility for Northern Ireland from Whitelaw. Rees had little alternative: almost his first act was to disband the executive and restore direct rule. Wilson, the incoming British Prime Minister, bitterly denounced the strike which had dealt power-sharing its death blow. It was, he said:

> a deliberate and calculated attempt to use every undemocratic and unparliamentary means for the purpose of bringing down the whole constitution of Northern Ireland, so as to set up there a sectarian and undemocratic state.

Though with the best of intentions, power-sharing had, of course, interfered with the principle of majority rule in Northern Ireland. The two British general elections of 1974, in February and October, merely confirmed the support of the majority of Northern Ireland for Unionism and Loyalism, which seemed inseparable from Protestantism. Fitt held Belfast West for the SDLP, but the first-past-the-post system of voting in British general elections again gave the

Catholics little comfort elsewhere. Unionists and Loyalists closed ranks again as United Ulster Unionists (UUU). The UUU won eleven of the twelve Northern Irish seats in February 1974, and held ten of them in October, losing only Fermanagh and South Tyrone to an Independent. Craig and Paisley were both returned to Westminster as UUU MPs, but there was no likelihood that Wilson's government would agree to their demand for the restoration of Unionist rule in Belfast. Meantime Faulkner retired, giving up the unequal struggle to make Ulster Unionism more tolerant.

(d) Violence and Stalemate

Rees launched another initiative in 1975. Elections were held for a new assembly in Northern Ireland, to work on the constitutional problems of the province. The UUU won forty-six seats, heavily outnumbering the SDLP and the Alliance Party. The UUU would not share power with the minority groups and, for good measure, they expelled Craig from their membership for suggesting an interim coalition administration. The new experiment was therefore stillborn. Rees could do little more than concentrate on maintaining whatever was possible of law and order. He made some progress in restoring the authority and fairness of Northern Irish courts and in reducing the extent of detention without trial, but the problem he handed on to Roy Mason in 1976 was as far from solution as ever. Mason remained the Secretary of State for Northern Ireland until the general election of 1979, when he too had to hand on the unsolved problem. The level of violence fluctuated in the late 1970s, but it was always a cause for grave concern. Mason stepped up internment again, and he infuriated the IRA by refusing to regard terrorists as 'political' prisoners and thus add to their status as freedom-fighters. The British troops in Northern Ireland seemed increasingly to be regarded as an army of occupation, and their casualties mounted.

It was often argued that the people of Northern Ireland were sick of the murders and outrages, and wanted nothing more than reconciliation and peace. In 1976 a women's Peace Movement was set up, with both Catholic and Protestant membership. Hope also grew when, in 1977, there was only a lukewarm response to Paisley's call for another widespread strike, this time to demand even tougher measures against the IRA. Against this, however, must be set the results of the British general election of 1979, when Unionists of one sort or another again took ten of Northern Ireland's twelve seats. By this time the Unionists had become divided again. The election seemed to show substantial support for Paisley and his Democratic Unionists, who now outmatched the Official Unionists in their extremism. Paisley himself won Antrim North with a majority of some 18 500 over an Official Unionist, and a Democratic Unionist defeated Craig at Belfast East. Craig himself had once been considered a hardliner, but his Official Unionists were not apparently now hard enough for much Protestant opinion in the province. Fitt held Belfast West for the SDLP, however. But the tensions and frustrations of Northern Irish politics showed yet again, when Fitt soon afterwards resigned the leadership of his Party. Humphrey Atkins, the new Conservative Secretary for Northern Ireland, once more explored the possibilities of some political solution to the problems, but renewed bitterness developed in 1980–1 over the treatment of IRA men detained in the Maze Prison, Belfast. Ten prisoners died during 1981, starving themselves to death in protest at the British government's refusal to regard them as political prisoners rather than criminals. When Atkins handed over his office to Jim Prior late in 1981, there was little reason for confidence that a solution to Northern Ireland's many problems was imminent, though Prior at once began to prepare for yet another experimental Northern Ireland assembly. Elections were held in autumn 1982, but the results held out little promise for co-operation and further progress towards self-government.

The Catholics of Northern Ireland continued to argue that the authorities were often biased against them. The RUC had been overhauled, and after 1970 the B-Specials had been replaced by the Ulster Defence Regiment. The RUC and the Defence Regiment remained targets for the Provos, however, as did the British army. The 1970s were violent and brutal, and outrages were by no means confined to Ireland. Bombs took a toll of lives in England. In 1974 twelve people died when a coach was blown up on an English motorway, and twenty-one more died later that year in an explosion in a public house in Birmingham. Terrorism was then extended to the European continent, with attacks on British government representatives. Letter bombs were posted, and bombs were planted at railway stations and in parked cars. The authorities were forced to take precautions, and these also caused disruption. Mail was delayed when bombs went off in sorting offices, and letter boxes were sometimes sealed. Suspicious cars were isolated and sometimes destroyed. Air passengers were searched for explosives.

In Northern Ireland itself people were searched before being allowed to enter city centres, where bombs frequently caused deaths, injuries and damage. Bombs were planted on trains, and further disruption was caused to public transport when buses were hi-jacked, many of them to be set on fire and used for makeshift barricades. The explosions and the spectacular acts of terrorism were only part of the story, however. They took place against a background of innumerable acts of personal viciousness and brutality. Kidnappings and murders became almost commonplace, and the savage 'punishment' of 'knee-capping' provided a regular undercurrent of horror. Knees were destroyed by gunshots, to maim those who had in some way offended the terrorists and to warn others of the price they too might pay for offending. The Provos were the main terrorists, but they had no monopoly of extremism and violence. The Protestant Ulster Defence Association had played its part in wrecking power-sharing, and Protestants too committed outrages. Savagery bred more savagery. And it did no credit to the British government that the European Court of Human Rights ruled that it too was guilty of brutality, in its treatment of those in internment.

There were occasional periods of comparative calm in Northern Ireland

Fig. 19.5 Firemen search the ruins of a Birmingham public-house, November 1974, after the explosion of a bomb, assumed to have been planted by the IRA. The 1970s were violent in many parts of the world, and much of the violence which plagued Britain stemmed from the problems of Northern Ireland

during the late 1970s. It was also true that many people in the province had little personal experience of the violence and brutality. But there was tension and uncertainty, and tragedy could strike at any moment. It was from such a tragedy that the Peace Movement of 1976 grew, when IRA gunmen in a stolen car ploughed into a family group and killed three young children. The women who started the Movement received the Nobel Peace Prize, but such voices of moderation and compassion seemed constantly to be out-shouted by the strident claims and counter-claims of the extremists. It was a harsh climate for any growth of goodwill, and it was far from promising that the hardliners continued to receive such widespread support from the Northern Irish at the polls. Like other British politicians, Callaghan reasserted in the late 1970s that, while the Northern Irish wanted it, their province would remain within the United Kingdom; and it followed from that that British troops would remain in Northern Ireland as long as they were needed. But the 1970s ended with the death toll reaching 2 000, of which some 300 were British soldiers.

    With Irish divisions as deep and bitter as ever, the rest of the United

Kingdom counted the cost in lives and money with widespread dismay. Northern Ireland was a burden on the UK which not everyone was willing to carry, though it was argued that such 'defeatism' merely played into the hands of the IRA. Against this, it was also argued that the removal of British troops might help to bring Northern Irish Protestants to their senses, and force them to make genuine concessions to the minorities in the province. It was only the British troops, in fact, which seemed to protect Northern Ireland from civil war, and it was these soldiers who were daily exposed to injury and death, part of the price of British patience with the Northern Irish question – a patience which was itself quite remarkable.

When the 1980s began, the United Kingdom was still intact and, for one reason or another, there was no Home Rule in any of the restless regions of Northern Ireland, Scotland and Wales.

Further Reading

Sked, A. and Cook, C.: *Post-War Britain, A Political History*. Penguin (Harmondsworth, 1979), chapters 10–12
Calvocoressi, P.: *The British Experience, 1945–1975*. Penguin (Harmondsworth, 1979).
Cook, C. and Ramsden, J.: *Trends in British Politics since 1945*. Macmillan (London, 1978).

Documentary

Dures, A.: *Modern Ireland*. Wayland (Hove, 1973).
Hepburn, A.C.: *The Conflict of Nationality in Modern Ireland*. Arnold (London, 1980).
Magee, J.: *Northern Ireland, Crisis and Conflict*. Routledge (London, 1974).

Exercises

1. What evidence can you find in this book that Scotland, Wales and Northern Ireland have been persistently 'less prosperous than England' (page 339)? How would you wish to modify this generalization?
2. Show what you understand by each of the following terms: 'national consciousness' (page 339); 'regional policies' (page 339); 'devolution' (page 341); 'home rule' (page 343).
3. Making use of Table 10.1, trace and account for the electoral fortunes of (*a*) Plaid Cymru and (*b*) the Scottish Nationalist Party.
4. Why was there still neither a Scottish nor Welsh Assembly at the end of the 1970s?
5. Why, and how, did Northern Ireland first achieve Home Rule? Why, and in what circumstances, was Home Rule suspended in 1972?
6. In the history of Northern Ireland, explain the interests of *each* of the following: Unionists; Loyalists; the RUC; the SDLP; the Alliance Party; the IRA; the Provos.
7. How would you use Fig. 19.4 to explain aspects of the problems of Northern Ireland in the 1960s and 1970s?
8. 'Power-sharing lasted less than five months' (page 348). Explain what is meant by 'power-sharing', and why it was short-lived.
9. Why has it proved so difficult to solve the problems of Northern Ireland in the years since 1970, and in what sense are the problems 'sectarian' (page 348)?

Unit Twenty

Britain and the Outside World

20.1 The Emerging Role

By the end of the 1960s, there was still no confident answer to the question as to what Britain's place in the fast-changing world should be. An answer of sorts was taking shape nevertheless. To some extent it followed the guidelines laid down in the late 1940s by Attlee and Bevin, and in the 1950s and 1960s British policy continued to be based on alliance with the USA, on decolonizing the Empire and on close association with the developing Commonwealth (see Units 12, 14 and 15.4). But a new strand was added in the 1960s, when the decision was taken to seek membership of the European Economic Community. When this was achieved, in 1973, it seemed that Britain had at last come near to finding its place in the postwar world. It was not untypical of the confusion which often surrounded British affairs, however, that uncertainty remained as to whether it was, in fact, the right place.

Half-heartedness seemed to be one of the chief characteristics of British overseas policy, and its effect was frequently to raise doubts about British sincerity. The principle of racial equality was a cornerstone of the developing Commonwealth, yet the Conservatives showed some reluctance to accept the full implications of such equality at the Commonwealth Conference of 1961, when South Africa sought renewed membership of the association (see Unit 14.4(a)). Britain's immigration policy also raised doubts about the country's enthusiasm for racial equality (see Unit 17.2). There were further doubts, at the beginning of the 1970s, when Heath's government headed straight into conflict with many fellow-members of the Commonwealth by proposing to renew the sale of arms to South Africa. There were heated exchanges at the Commonwealth Conference in Singapore in 1971, and Heath subsequently modified his policy. He also accepted the Declaration of Commonwealth Principles, which was drawn up at the Conference, part of which read:

> We recognize racial prejudice as a dangerous sickness threatening the healthy development of the human race and racial discrimination as an unmitigated evil of society. Each of us will vigorously combat this evil within our own nation.

The Declaration continued:

> We oppose all forms of colonial domination and racial oppression. . . . We will

therefore use all our efforts to foster human equality and dignity everywhere, and to further the principles of self-determination and non-racialism.

Not all those who signed this idealistic Declaration could do so with wholly clear consciences, but there was a particularly embarrassing skeleton in Britain's cupboard at this time. Since 1965 British governments had conspicuously dealt less than 'vigorously' with the problem of the illegal seizure of independence by the white-minority regime in Rhodesia (see Unit 20.2).

Britain's entry into the EEC sometimes seemed similarly half-hearted. The Conservatives made the first application for membership in the early 1960s. The Labour government renewed the bid, though Wilson in 1966 left no doubt that the application was:

> with the clear intention and determination to enter . . . if . . . our essential British and Commonwealth interests can be safeguarded.

Admission was finally secured in 1973, but arguments about the terms and costs of membership rumbled on into the 1980s. The sincerity of Britain's commitment to Europe was also in doubt therefore (see Unit 20.3). It seemed to have become a British habit to hover between enthusiasm and disenchantment, and the country brought uncertainty to its dealings with both the Commonwealth and the EEC. The Conservatives often gave the impression of preferring Europe to the Commonwealth, while Labour took the opposite stance, the Party's leaders being well aware of the strong anti-European feeling in the ranks of their supporters. But Britain's admission to the EEC showed that the European Community and the Commonwealth were not necessarily mutually exclusive. It was the British themselves who seemed to keep alive the idea that the two organizations might offer alternatives for Britain to embrace. By 1980 Britain still seemed less than whole-hearted in its commitment to either, more because of a general lack of decisiveness in British policy than because of divisions between political parties.

20.2 The Rhodesian Problem

(a) UDI and Sanctions

Douglas-Home had denied independence to the government of Ian Smith and the Rhodesian Front before the British general election of 1964, and Wilson continued to deny it afterwards (see Unit 14.4(b)). Like Douglas-Home, Wilson tried vainly to persuade Smith to accept black participation in the government of Rhodesia. Wilson himself visited Rhodesia, and confirmed that British policy was based on NIBMAR (No Independence Before Majority African Rule). There could be no grant of independence until there was a constitution which guaranteed black Rhodesians at least the right eventually to rule the country in which they were the overwhelming majority. That was precisely what Smith intended to prevent. On 11 November 1965, therefore, the Rhodesian Front issued a Unilateral Declaration of Independence (UDI). Smith broadcast to his supporters, rejecting what he called 'appeasement', and proclaiming that white Rhodesians would not 'sell their birthright':

> If we were to surrender, does anyone believe that Rhodesia would be the last target of the communists in the Afro-Asian bloc? We have struck a blow for the preservation of justice, civilization and Christianity.

The outside world was not impressed by Smith's rhetoric, though there was fellow-feeling for the Rhodesian whites in South Africa and among the rulers of the neighbouring Portuguese territories of Mozambique and Angola. The British promptly declared that the UDI was an act of rebellion and that Rhodesia's seized independence was illegal. Even with the sympathy of the South Africans and Portuguese it seemed unlikely that less than a quarter of a million white Rhodesians could successfully defy, not only Britain, but a world generally hostile to such a blatant attempt to perpetuate white supremacy.

Fig. 20.1 Rhodesia's UDI stamp, 1965

Yet Wilson had perhaps already given the game away by renouncing the use of troops against the Rhodesians, unless law and order broke down in the colony. Smith's security forces were strong enough to prevent such a breakdown, at least in the short term. The British argued that Rhodesia's geographical position made military action very difficult but that, anyway, economic sanctions would quickly bring the rebel colony to heel. An international trade boycott was implemented with the support of the United Nations Organization, and British warships patrolled off Beira, in Mozambique, to prevent the landing of oil for the Rhodesian pipeline. Sanctions damaged Rhodesia's economy, hurting the tobacco growers for example, but they fell far short of bringing Smith's defiance to an end. South Africa, and for a time the Portuguese, helped to ensure that Rhodesia received vital supplies, and Rhodesia continued to export much of its own produce. The sanctions were too weakly enforced and too widely evaded to undermine the rebel regime. The weakness of Britain's response to the UDI brought quarrels with outraged Commonwealth nations, and Tanzania and Ghana were among those who were quick to break off diplomatic relations with Britain, albeit only temporarily. The British parliament solemnly renewed the sanctions against Rhodesia at yearly intervals until 1979, and the patrol off Beira was maintained. But the Bingham Report at the end of the 1970s only added to Britain's humiliation, revealing something of the sorry history of how arrangements had been made during these years to ensure that Rhodesia nevertheless obtained fuel.

(b) **Talks and Constitutions**
British governments meanwhile made regular efforts to negotiate a settlement with Ian Smith, so that a legal grant of independence might be made to resolve the problem. Wilson met Smith twice in the late 1960s. They talked for three days on HMS *Tiger*, off Malta, and produced a 'working document' as the basis of a new constitution, but Smith's colleagues instantly rejected it. After they met on HMS *Fearless*, at Gibraltar, in October 1968, Smith again took home proposals for a new constitution. Wilson thought this would make African rule in Rhodesia possible in some fifteen years, though many who examined the proposals considered it very unlikely. In any case that was too soon for the Rhodesian Front, and the proposals were again rejected in Salisbury, the Rhodesian capital. Wilson was fiercely criticized for his concessions, but as yet the Rhodesian whites saw little reason to compromise at all. They consolidated their grip on the colony, adopting some of the measures of a police state, and seemingly drawing nearer to South Africa's system of apartheid. The colony was declared a republic in 1970, with a new constitution of the Rhodesian Front's own making and with the almost universal support of the white minority. Roy Welensky observed that:

> few men, with the exception of Hitler and Mussolini, have had greater internal power than now rests on Mr Smith's shoulders.

Heath's government also tried to come to terms with Smith. New 'Proposals for a Settlement' were discussed in 1971. Douglas-Home was sent to Rhodesia and Smith seemed conciliatory. But the British insisted that the blacks too must be consulted about their country's future, and the Pearce Commission of 1972 found that the Proposals were totally unacceptable to a black population whose suspicion and resentment of white rule now ran deep. It seemed that the British could neither bring down the rebel regime by economic pressures nor conjure up a successful compromise.

There were changes in the 1970s, however, though at first they had little to do with Britain. Black resistance groups began to organize guerilla action against Smith's government in about 1973, and two years later they grew more threatening. Changes within Portugal led to the granting of independence to Mozambique, and the setting up there of a black government under Samora

Fig. 20.2 Ian Smith, troubled by the sun when he arrived in Gibraltar for the Fearless *talks, 1968. Smith again took home to Rhodesia proposals for a constitutional settlement but, back in Rhodesia, he again rejected them*

Machel. Machel not only imposed tighter economic sanctions on Rhodesia: he provided bases in Mozambique for Rhodesian guerillas. Attacks could now be launched against the white minority both from Zambia in the north, and from Mozambique in the east. The forces from Zambia were under the command of Joshua Nkomo, a veteran of the long struggle for black rights in Rhodesia. Those based in Mozambique were organized by Robert Mugabe, whose politics were Marxist. Nkomo and Mugabe, however, came together in the Patriotic Front, agreeing that their first priorities were to destroy the white-minority regime in Rhodesia and establish the African state of Zimbabwe there. They had widespread support from fellow-Africans, and from outside Africa; but they could get no support in London for their war of liberation. Wilson summarized what was still British policy, writing of his meeting in 1975 with Nkomo and the leaders of neighbouring African states:

> They knew they had no hope of persuading us to use military force through the newly opened Mozambique to bring down Ian Smith's Rhodesian regime. But they pressed us to supply arms and money for the guerillas based in Mozambique and elsewhere, and operating or seeking to operate across the Rhodesian borders. This we flatly – and I am sure courteously – refused to do, and all their arguments and blandishments

failed to change our minds. We did however agree, if the matter was pressed, to convene an early constitutional Conference, whenever the auspices looked right for political change in Rhodesia.

The guerillas had to carry on without British help, but they succeeded nevertheless in steadily weakening the confidence of the rebel regime, and it was they who finally brought the Rhodesian problem to a head.

(c) The Liberation of Zimbabwe

Smith's first concession was to talk with some of Rhodesia's black leaders – a step forward from his earlier practice of simply imprisoning them. The USA now increased the pressure on Smith, and in 1976 he was persuaded to declare his intent to consider ways of transferring power to the black majority. He nevertheless played for time. A conference met at Geneva towards the end of 1976 but achieved little. A new initiative by David Owen, Callaghan's new Foreign Secretary, also made little headway. Smith took every opportunity to exploit the divisions between Rhodesia's black leaders, and to cling to power for as long as possible. But he could not ignore the mounting guerilla pressure and, though the Rhodesian security forces, especially the Selous Scouts, were still able to contain the freedom fighters, the days of white rule were now clearly limited.

In 1978 Smith made a last bid to outwit his enemies. He decided to conjure up an 'internal settlement', in defiance of joint British and American proposals for a new constitution and the transfer of power. Nkomo and Mugabe were organizing the liberation struggle of the Front from outside Rhodesia, but there were other black leaders in Salisbury whom Rhodesian whites believed to be more moderate. It was to these men that Smith turned, to work out a system of power-sharing and a new constitution which might preserve at least something of white influence and privilege. Bishop Muzorewa and Ndabaningi Sithole co-operated with him. Blacks were admitted to government office, and elections were held on the basis of universal adult suffrage early in 1979. Muzorewa thus became Rhodesia's Prime Minister, and the demand was made that Britain should give approval and grant independence since Rhodesia now had a black government. The internal settlement had been condemned by the Patriotic Front from the outset, however, and world opinion in general was deeply suspicious. The guerilla war went on, in 1978 alone claiming 5 500 lives, both black and white. Britain still withheld independence, insisting that the Patriotic Front must be consulted, and that more solid evidence was needed of black support for the Rhodesian system of government.

Britain's change of government in 1979 brought Lord Carrington to the Foreign Office. One of his first duties was to attend the Commonwealth Conference in Lusaka, Zambia. Margaret Thatcher went too, and the Rhodesian question was uppermost on the agenda. There were meetings with the 'Front-Line Presidents', the rulers of the African states which were

Fig. 20.3 The device that failed: the signing of the 'internal settlement' in March 1978. From left to right, Muzorewa, Smith, Chief Chirau and Sithole. But there was little support for the settlement outside Rhodesia and the Patriotic Front denounced it

Rhodesia's neighbours. It was these Presidents, men like Kaunda, Nyerere and Machel who had supported the Patriotic Front, and their states had suffered far more than Britain had from the economic disruption in southern Africa which had followed the UDI. The Commonwealth Conference therefore prepared the way for a new conference on the Rhodesian question, and this met later in 1979 under Carrington's chairmanship at Lancaster House, in London.

The negotiations were long and difficult, but there seemed at last to be a general readiness to reach a settlement. The guerilla war by this time had taken some 22 000 lives. Agreement was eventually reached on a new Rhodesian constitution with universal adult suffrage, a parliament of one hundred seats, of which whites would occupy twenty, and a government genuinely representative of the wishes of the majority. The Patriotic Front agreed to stop the war. Muzorewa agreed to resign, with power in the colony temporarily restored to a British governor. All parties agreed to accept the result of a 'free and fair' election, and elaborate arrangements were made to hold and supervise this election as soon as possible. In December 1979 Lord Soames arrived in Salisbury as Governor, to re-establish Britain's authority and to conduct the general election. His task was hardly an easy one: the UDI and white rule had embittered race relations, and both the security forces and the revolutionary armies would have to be curbed. Soames was supported by units of men from a variety of Commonwealth countries, as well as by officials, soldiers and policemen sent from Britain. But this manpower was thinly spread, and much would depend on the co-operation of the Rhodesians themselves, both black and white. The vast majority co-operated with a will. The election which took place was remarkably 'free and fair' coming, as it did, after the years of disruption and bitter conflict.

Smith's Rhodesian Front had no difficulty in winning all the twenty parliamentary seats reserved for the whites. The main question to be resolved, however, was the division of the black vote. In the event, Muzorewa and his supporters won only three of the eighty black seats. Nkomo's party won twenty seats, securing massive support from the Ndebele people in western Rhodesia, but Mugabe scored the real success in the election. With fifty-seven seats, Mugabe had an overall majority in the new parliament and a clear title to form the new government. The guerillas of the Patriotic Front had forced the white minority to surrender power, but British organization did in the end do something to rescue the mother country's reputation, after almost fifteen years of fumbling with the problems posed by the UDI.

'Majority African Rule' had now been won in Zimbabwe, the new African

'Now wasn't that a dainty dish to set before the king?'

Fig. 20.4 Robert Mugabe's success in the elections was beyond dispute, but Gibbard was among those who suggested it was a not altogether welcome result for Lord Soames. Mugabe's political rivals, Joshua Nkomo and Bishop Muzorewa (top right), were also surprised and disappointed. Ian Smith (left) and the Rhodesian Front already had the twenty seats reserved for whites in the new Zimbabwean parliament (the Guardian, *March 1980)*

name for Rhodesia. Mugabe formed his government in March 1980, finding places in it not only for Nkomo, in charge of Home Affairs, but for two white ministers, though neither was a member of Smith's Rhodesian Front. The legal granting of independence was now only a formality. Zimbabwe became independent on 18 April 1980, freeing Britain's last large colony. It was alleged that the outcome of the election had not been what Britain had wanted, and there were certainly white Zimbabweans who had grave misgivings about the new Prime Minister's political inclinations and who feared the 'communists' Smith had spoken about in his UDI speech. Perhaps a more serious problem for Zimbabwe was the way in which the voting of the Ndebele and Shona peoples had been divided between Nkomo and Mugabe. Tribal rivalry was deep-rooted: like many other African leaders, Mugabe would need to bridge such divisions in building the new nation. There were also pressing economic problems and the goodwill grant which Britain made to aid the new Zimbabwe was far from lavish. The new Prime Minister was a man of considerable intellectual stature, however; and though he had personally suffered a great deal at the hands of white-minority rule in Rhodesia, he presented himself in 1980 as a man of wisdom and moderation. To repair the damage of the years of struggle was likely to require not only these qualities of the Prime Minister but good sense and tolerance among the Zimbabwean people as a whole.

The country was under considerable strain in the early 1980s. In February 1982 Mugabe dismissed Nkomo from his cabinet, arguing that – eventually – Zimbabwe's political difficulties would best be solved by a one-party state of the sort common in much of Africa.

20.3 The European Community

(a) Britain's Delayed Membership

Britain's early lack of interest when the European Coal and Steel Community (ECSC) was set up in 1952 continued when the same founder-members (France, West Germany, Italy, the Netherlands, Belgium and Luxemburg) created the European Economic Community (EEC) and the European Atomic Energy Community (Euratom) in January 1958 (see Unit 12.2(b)). These Communities were undoubtedly useful in healing old wounds between the French and the West Germans and in restoring western European economies. But British interests ranged far wider than western Europe. Britain claimed a 'special relationship' with the English-speaking peoples of the USA, and still enjoyed substantial trade in the 1950s with its Empire and the Commonwealth, with the advantage of comparatively cheap supplies of food and raw materials. Except for purposes of defence, the British felt no need to forge close relationships with western Europe. Joining the Communities – they were merged in 1967 into one European Community – would also involve the surrender of a degree of national sovereignty and some limitations on each member's freedom to make its own decisions. It was thought that such limitations would be unacceptable in Britain, and few voices were raised among Britain's leaders in favour of entry into the Communities. Neither the immediate prospect of favourable tariff arrangements, enabling British exports to be sold in Europe without duties, nor the more distant prospect of co-operation which might one day lead to a United States of Europe, persuaded the British that membership was worthwhile.

Britain preferred a looser trading system. A committee of the Organization for European Economic Co-operation (OEEC, see Glossary) explored possibilities with the result that Britain became a founder-member of the European Free Trade Association (EFTA) in 1959. The seven members of EFTA (Britain, Austria, Denmark, Norway, Portugal, Sweden and Switzerland) agreed to reduce tariffs between themselves without the more ambitious rules and regulations of the EEC for economic integration. EFTA markets, on the other hand, offered British exporters narrower opportunities than might have been available in the EEC.

Fig. 20.5 British stamp of 1967 with the flags of the then members of the European Free Trade Association. The eighth flag (second from the left) was that of Finland, an associate member of EFTA

The Liberals urged that Britain should join the EEC, show commitment from the outset and help in framing the Community's agreements, but the first official British approach was not made until 1961. It was in that year that the Commonwealth readily accepted South Africa's resignation and more whole-heartedly embraced a commitment to multi-racialism. Clearly the Commonwealth was no longer a white man's club. At the same time, the British economy was giving cause for concern. The growth rate lagged behind that of the members of the EEC, and there was a balance of payments deficit of over £260 million in 1960 (see Unit 13.1). Macmillan therefore applied for EEC membership but the negotiations, enthusiastically conducted by Edward Heath, came to nothing when de Gaulle, the French President, vetoed Britain's application in 1963. EEC regulations allowed any member to veto new admissions, and de Gaulle saw no reason to admit a country he considered too closely linked with the USA, too much bound up with the Commonwealth, burdened with a variety of economic problems, and likely to be a rival to France for influence within the Community. Wilson's attempt to join the Community met a similar response in 1967.

Fig. 20.6 President de Gaulle rejects another British application to join the EEC, and Wilson shares the fate of Macmillan: a comment by Cummings in the Daily Express, *November 1967*

De Gaulle's resignation from the French Presidency in 1969 led to the almost immediate renewal of Britain's application for Community membership, this time with the encouragement of all the existing members. The negotiations began within weeks of the British general election of 1970, which had returned a Conservative government under Edward Heath, whose enthusiasm for Europe had grown steadily in recent years. The Community nevertheless insisted that there could be no changes in its rules to suit new members:

> The solution to any problems of adjustment which may arise must be sought in the establishment of transitional measures and not in changes in the existing rules.

Thus Britain was able to negotiate a transitional period of just over four years in which to adjust its tariffs, in favour of the Community and to the disadvantage of outsiders. Other transitional arrangements provided safeguards for Britain's trade with members of the Commonwealth, for Britain's fishing industry, and for limitations on Britain's contributions to the Community's budget. But all such arrangements were transitional and, by the end of the 1970s, Britain might expect to have come fully into line with the other members of the Community. It was on this basis that Britain joined the Community (the EEC, the ECSC and Euratom) on 1 January 1973. Denmark and the Republic of Ireland also joined, though Norway chose at the last moment to remain outside, after testing public opinion in a referendum.

Many British people also had misgivings. The government nevertheless presented an attractive picture of the future in a white paper, *The United Kingdom and the European Communities:*

> Provided we seize the opportunities of the far wider home market now open to us . . . we shall obtain, as the Six have done since the Communities were founded, a substantial increase in our trade, a stimulus to growth and investment, and a greater rise in real wages and standards of living than we have known in recent years or would be possible if we remained outside the Communities.

With the exception of Italy, every member of 'the Six' in 1970 had a higher GDP per head of population than had Britain (see Table 18.1); and this, it seemed, was Britain's main reason for securing membership. It could hardly be said that Britain joined the Community with much popular enthusiasm for the European ideal. Real enthusiasm for Europe lay with pressure groups and with individuals such as Edward Heath. The Labour Party, especially, was still divided on the issue, though Roy Jenkins resigned as Labour's Home Secretary in 1976 to become the President of the European Commission, the powerful bureacracy in Brussels which manages the Community's affairs.

(b) Britain's Hesitant Membership

The Labour Party, indeed, questioned whether the transitional terms on which Britain joined the Community were good enough. When Wilson became Prime Minister in 1974 he insisted on further negotiations, and won some small additional concessions. The government then took the unprecedented step of holding a national referendum on the question, 'Do you think the

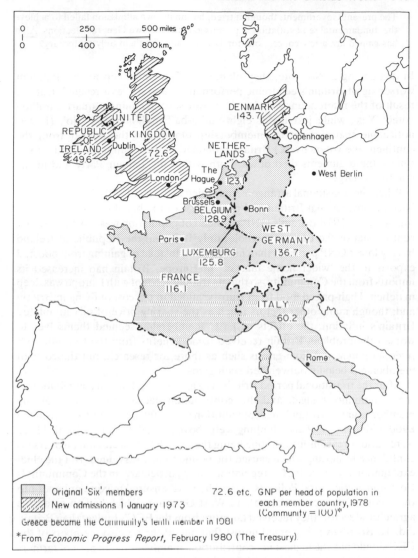

Fig. 20.7 The European Community

United Kingdom should stay in the European Community?'. The government itself recommended a 'Yes' vote, though opposed by Benn, Castle, Foot and four other members of Wilson's cabinet. Some observers argued that the debate was heavily weighted in favour of 'Yes', with Jenkins leading the vigorous *Britain in Europe* lobby. Opponents of Community membership asserted that:

The present Government, though it tried, has on its own admission failed to achieve the 'fundamental re-negotiation' it promised at the last two General Elections. All it has gained are a few concessions for Britain, some of them only temporary.

In demanding a 'No' vote, they blamed EEC membership for an apparent worsening of Britain's economic performance, and for 'evil results'. But the result of the referendum was decisive: over seventeen-and-a-quarter million voted 'Yes', while just under eight-and-a-half million voted 'No'. (It was noticeable that support for membership diminished the further from the continent the voters lived.) Britain remained in the Community, and – for a time – the arguments died down, both within the Labour Party and in the country at large.

When the transitional arrangements ended in the late 1970s, however, it had become obvious that Britain had reaped few of the benefits which had been predicted. In 1978 Britain's GNP per head of population was less than 73 per cent of that of the EEC as a whole, only Italy and the Republic of Ireland having lower GNP per head than had Britain. Instead of gaining from boosted exports to the 'wider home market' in Europe, Britain had increased its imports from the Community, so that its trading account with Europe was deep in deficit. High-priced food from Europe added to the cost of living in Britain and, though many other factors (such as the soaring price of oil) stimulated Britain's inflation, the effects of EEC membership seemed themselves to worsen the problem. Britain received some benefits from the Community's regional policy and from grants such as those for research, but the costs of membership heavily outweighed such gains.

After the transitional period Britain had to pay its full rate of contribution to the Community budget, and this contribution became the highest of any member country. Britain's net contribution was £800 million in 1978, rising to £900 million in 1979 and climbing well above £1 000 million in 1980. There were various reasons for this, one being that North Sea oil created an overseas confidence in sterling which caused the pound to be overvalued. But the chief explanation lay in the EEC's regulations, and particularly in the Community's Common Agricultural Policy (CAP). The CAP ensured maximum benefit to those countries, such as France and West Germany, which had an extensive agricultural sector; they received far more from the EEC's budget than Britain did. To British eyes it seemed unjust that one of the poorest members of the EEC should pay the highest net contribution, mainly for the benefit of farmers in richer member-states. The budget contribution and the deficit on trade with Europe again called into question whether the decision to join the Community had been a wise one. Thatcher's government, elected in Britain in 1979, loudly demanded some reduction in Britain's financial obligations and, eventually, won some concessions.

Controversies about the financing of the Community were not the only reasons for British disquiet. When the first elections to the European Parliament of the Community were held in 1979, British voters showed

'Ah yes, madame, a most unfavourable position . . . and yet, are you not fortunate to have such a wonderful umbrella?'

Fig. 20.8 A comment on Britain's membership of the European Community in March 1980: Howe (Chancellor of the Exchequer), Carrington (Foreign Secretary) and Mrs Thatcher (Prime Minister) struggle with the costs of membership, while the French President, Giscard d'Estaing, admires the British stake in North Sea oil. (Gibbard, the Guardian)

widespread apathy. The great majority did not bother to vote, though the best hopes of eventually curbing the powers of the European Commission rested on successfully establishing the democratically elected Parliament. In general, the Community aroused little enthusiasm. Indeed, it seemed to become something of a scapegoat for many of Britain's problems. Imports from the EEC were beginning to fill Britain's shops, adding to the threat to British jobs. Even the traditional supplies of English and Commonwealth apples seemed to be almost submerged by imports from France of 'Golden Delicious' apples, which many British consumers found neither 'Golden' nor 'Delicious'.

Membership of the EEC, moreover, seemed only to have added to the troubles of Britain's fishing industry. Declining fish stocks led to 'cod wars' with Iceland in the 1970s, when that country began to drive foreign fishing fleets from Icelandic waters. At the height of the conflict, the government sent gunboats to protect British trawlers, but Iceland effectively established its claim to a 200-mile zone around its shores, gravely damaging the fishing industries of Fleetwood and Britain's east-coast ports. Britain's fishermen then found themselves insecure even nearer home, competing for dwindling fish stocks with EEC trawlers. There were charges and counter-charges – that continental fishermen, for example, used nets with an illegally small mesh through which young fish were unable to escape – and there was grave anxiety not only about the fishing industry but about future fish supplies. Certain fish, such as cod, once a staple food in Britain, became almost a luxury. The Community merely delayed the settlement of the problem which was desperately urgent. Over-fishing was allowed to continue until, by the end of the 1970s, fishing ports such as Fleetwood, Hull and Grimsby were in deep depression, and Britain's fishing industry was in general decline. No common EEC policy was worked out until 1982, and even then the agreement was opposed by Denmark, eager for more advantages in 'British' waters.

Membership of the Community made possible a new mobility both of capital and people. By 1979, however, Britain seemed conspicuously to have failed to attract investment from Europe. British investment in Europe seemed to be some five times higher than EEC investment in Britain. There was evidence of increased American investment in Britain, though, since this gave American firms a foothold within the Community. British people, on the other hand, now found opportunities to obtain work in Europe, and tens of thousands seized this chance in the late 1970s. Holidaymakers could also profit from relaxed travel regulations within the Community, while an influx of tourists from Europe brought some benefit to Britain's hard-pressed balance of payments problem. In the eyes of many British people, such advantages did little to offset what seemed to be the major disadvantages of Community membership. It could be argued, though scarcely proved, that Britain's economy might have been in even worse trouble had the country not entered Europe in 1973, but this was small consolation. Meanwhile, Britain's suspicious attitude towards the EEC did not make for harmonious relations with the other members of the Community. Britain delayed joining the European Monetary System, a significant step towards a common European currency, and this too seemed to confirm that the British were hardly yet zealous Europeans.

 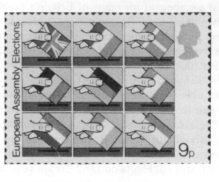

Fig. 20.9(a) and (b) Britain finally became a member of the European Communities in 1973. In 1979 voters in the nine member-states voted in direct elections to the European Parliament for the first time. Two British stamps commemorate these events and incidentally show the escalating cost of postage in Britain in the 1970s

20.4 Britain and the Major Powers, 1964–79

(a) The Balance of Power

Douglas-Home summarized something of his own attitude towards international affairs in 1963:

> I believe that Britain has a fine part to play on the world stage. Not as a 'trimmer' in international politics but as a country standing for true values. But to carry weight we must be in the First XI and not only that but one of the opening batsmen.

Writing in the same year, Malcolm Muggeridge complained of the impressions England made on him each time he returned from abroad:

> . . . the editorial pretensions of its newspapers a little emptier, and the vainglorious rhetoric of its politicians a little more fatuous. On one such occasion I happened to turn on the television, and there on the screen was Harold Macmillan blowing through his moustache to the effect that 'Britain has been great, is great, will be great'.

The 1960s and 1970s merely confirmed, however, that Britain had neither the wealth nor the manpower to continue to demand a place as 'one of the opening batsmen'. The armed forces of the USA and the USSR each totalled more than three million in 1970, while British forces, well below 400 000, were smaller even than those of France and West Germany. But armed might, though an indication of power, was not necessarily a good indicator of influence; Britain could still exert influence through associations such as the Commonwealth, the United Nations Organization and the North Atlantic Treaty Organization, and perhaps in this sense remained an important and respected power, if no longer a 'great' one. The USA, the USSR and, perhaps increasingly, China now dominated world affairs in a way that Britain could no longer hope to do.

At about the time that Wilson became Britain's Prime Minister in 1964, Leonid Brezhnev began to emerge as the leader of the USSR, in succession to Khrushchev. Brezhnev remained in power throughout the 1970s, until his death in 1982. The USA had a succession of Presidents in this period: Johnson to 1969, Nixon to 1974, briefly Ford, Carter from 1977 and Reagan from 1981. Mao Tse-tung continued to influence affairs in China until his death in 1976. In the years after 1960 the relations of the major powers were complicated by the widening rift between China and the USSR. The West continued, cautiously and erratically, to improve relationships with the USSR during the 1960s (see Unit 14.2). In the eyes of the USA it seemed that China perhaps represented the greater threat now, while the Russians too saw advantages in some thaw in the East–West Cold War, to counterbalance tense Sino–Soviet relationships. China exploded its first atomic bomb in 1964, registering its claim to be regarded as a major power. The British had never fully shared American fears of China since the Chinese Communist Party had come to power in 1949, but it was not until Nixon changed US policy towards China that close West–Chinese relationships began to develop. Nixon withdrew America's opposition to Communist China's membership of the United Nations Organization, and China gained admission in 1971. With the Chinese themselves showing a greater interest in cordial relations with the West after Mao's death, the late 1970s saw a tendency for the West to begin to prefer China to the USSR. The Russian invasion of Afghanistan towards the end of 1979 confirmed this trend.

It was against this background that British foreign policy was conducted in the 1960s and 1970s, and in this period it seemed that it was the world which changed rather than British policy. There was American–Soviet confrontation over the Cuban Missiles Crisis of 1962; the Americans were defeated and forced to withdraw from Vietnam in the mid 1970s; the international financial system collapsed; a severe energy crisis developed; and in the late 1970s there was reconciliation between Egypt and Israel. In none of these developments was Britain able to play a leading role 'on the world stage'. On the other hand, the British made no attempt to seize for themselves a leading role of the sort so foolishly assumed in the Suez Crisis of 1956 (see Unit 14.1(b)). British troops were now used for peacekeeping duties, for example in Cyprus, in safeguarding Belize from the ambitions of neighbouring Guatemala, and in policing the ceasefire and elections in Rhodesia at the beginning of 1980. Above all, however, British troops remained in West Germany, honouring Britain's obligations to NATO, the alliance from which Britain had never wavered since it was set up in 1949 to defend western Europe. British influence, meanwhile, was exerted wherever possible in support of the 'true values' Douglas-Home had spoken of in 1963. These values meant first and foremost British interests as the politicians saw them, but beyond that Britain gave a general support to peace, and to upholding its own traditional liberalism – the liberalism of a land in which the people were not in the habit of killing one another.

(b) **British Policy and Influence**
Wilson's government after 1964 broadly associated itself with United States policy though attempting with little success to mediate in the struggle in Vietnam. Even the USA, however, could do no more than protest when the Russians invaded Czechoslovakia in 1968 to suppress dissent. That invasion again checked the movement towards detente and, meanwhile, Wilson's own efforts to improve East–West relations by substantially increasing Anglo–Russian trade came to little. Yet East–West agreements were signed. In 1967 Britain joined the USA and USSR in banning nuclear weapons in outer space and the next year, with many other powers, in the Non-Proliferation Treaty, aiming to prevent the spread of nuclear weapons to powers not already possessing them. Neither France nor China signed the Treaty, however, and there were the usual criticisms on the left that Britain should have gone further and surrendered its own nuclear armoury.

The USA and the USSR took a further step towards curbing the arms race in 1969, beginning the Strategic Arms Limitation Talks (SALT) and reaching a first agreement in 1972. Willy Brandt, the West German Chancellor, also launched a new initiative, working vigorously to improve West Germany's relations with eastern Europe in his *Ostpolitik*. Conditions were now more favourable for expanding East–West trade, and Wilson seized the opportunity on his return to power in 1974. With a policy similar to that of MacDonald in 1924, he made credits available to the Russians, pursuing detente through trade. There was another similarity to 1924, however: like Baldwin, Margaret Thatcher rejected these agreements favourable to the USSR soon after she took office in 1979.

Meanwhile, a European Security Conference opened at Helsinki in 1975, with the earnest co-operation of Britain further reducing international tension. Agreements were reached on Europe's existing frontiers, on methods for avoiding conflict, on East–West economic co-operation and on human rights. The Conference was resumed in later years at Belgrade, but President Carter now expressed the West's strong feelings about the extent to which earlier agreements on human rights were being ignored in eastern Europe. Callaghan's government supported him, but the talks at Belgrade proved less than fruitful. Before the Conference met again at Madrid, towards the end of 1980, Thatcher had brought a new fury to Britain's government in denouncing Soviet totalitarianism as alien to British values. The Kremlin had already dubbed her the 'Iron Lady' for her anti-Russian stance, a title in which she seemed to take some pride. Along with the West generally, Britain therefore bitterly condemned the Russian invasion of Afghanistan in 1979 and intended to debate it at Madrid. East–West detente seemed near collapse at the end of the 1970s. Hostile to the USSR, Britain's new Conservative government confirmed the country's commitment to the USA and busily cultivated Chinese friendship.

China now appeared considerably less unfriendly to the USA than in the days when Mao Tse-tung had persistently denounced 'American imperialism'. It took the USA more than twenty years longer than Britain to give diplomatic recognition to the Communist government in Peking (see Unit 12.2(*c*)), but in the 1970s the Americans conceded that the British had perhaps been right all along, and that China need not be feared. British politicians like Heath were quick to take advantage of the new West–Chinese goodwill, hastening to Peking to foster diplomatic ties and to explore the prospects for British exports in Chinese markets. Other politicians and trade missions followed, especially after Mao's death. Mrs Thatcher, in particular, seemed to consider the 'China card' a useful one in the poker game with the Kremlin, though observers were not without misgivings about the extent to which it might be unwise to try to exploit divisions between China and the USSR.

The fact remained, however, that Britain had little history of conflict with the Chinese. Hong Kong, Britain's colony on the coast of China, was tolerated by the Communist government in Peking, and the authorities in Hong Kong

'er . . . don't phone us – we'll phone you'

*Fig. 20.10 Two views of the Anglo-American alliance in the late 1960s.
(a) Willson the cartoonist remembers the close co-operation between Churchill
and Roosevelt and between Macmillan and Kennedy, but thinks it hard going for
Prime Minister Wilson to win much enthusiasm for the Anglo-American alliance
from President Nixon. In fact, instead of Wilson visiting Washington, Nixon
visited London (the* Observer, *February 1969)
(b) (opposite) It was the Soviet view anyway that all the steering in the Anglo-
American alliance was done by the USA: the British only helped to paddle
(*Krokodil, *1967)*

remained on generally amicable terms with the Communists. Even so, the
future of the colony was in doubt. Britain had seized the offshore island by
force in 1842, and the mainland New Territories of the colony were held by a
later lease, which was due to expire in 1997. Though China seemed willing
enough for the present to honour the terms of the lease, it seemed unlikely that
it would be renewed. Meanwhile Hong Kong throbbed with vitality. It
remained a colourful and not unprosperous survival from Britain's imperial
past, and its population of some five million seemed well content with British
rule. Hong Kong's relations with China, and Britain's too, were also a
reminder that other nations still had a role to play in the world of the super
powers. British influence might be limited in the affairs of the much larger
states, but it was not negligible and was sometimes constructive.

It was also constructive in the 1970s in promoting the growing recognition
that there was another, perhaps more important issue in international affairs,
beyond that of East–West relationships. A North–South dialogue began,
though it quickly faltered. A vast wealth gap existed between the rich, mainly
white nations of the northern hemisphere and the poor, mainly non-white
nations of the southern hemisphere; and the gap was growing wider. By 1980
not much had been done effectively to narrow this gap, and most of the

demands for a 'new world economic order' had gone unheeded. Britain's record on aid to the poor nations was hardly more outstanding than that of most of the wealthier nations, and British aid programmes consistently lagged below even 1 per cent of the country's GNP. But the problem needed far more radical solutions than the aid programmes of individual nations, and British voices were often raised in the growing efforts to arouse international awareness and action. An initiative was taken in 1975 by Wilson, along with other Commonwealth leaders. Their intention was to draw attention to the fact that:

> the relationship, the balance, between rich and poor countries of the world is wrong and must be remedied . . . that the wealth of the world must be redistributed in favour of the poverty-stricken and starving. (That) this means a new deal in world economics, in trade between nations and the terms of trade.

1975 was also the year in which Britain helped to promote in the EEC the Lomé Convention, to assist almost fifty poor countries to sell their produce in Europe, and to provide them with aid and investment. Britain supported similar schemes within the Commonwealth, and through the specialized agencies of the United Nations Organization. But such schemes were piecemeal, and little more than palliatives. The real problem was to develop the collective will-power of the North to make the radical changes in the economic order which would enable the poor to earn a decent income for their output, and to contribute more effectively to the economic health of all. No one country could hope to tackle this problem alone, and certainly not Britain with its own tottering economy. But Healey, by his efforts, earned for himself the name of 'the Oliver Twist of the Commonwealth Poor'.

Heath too committed himself to the struggle, working with Willy Brandt and others to produce in 1980 the Brandt Report, 'A Programme for Survival'. This emphasized not only humanitarian considerations, but also those of self-interest, comparing the miserable lot of '800 million absolute poor' with the erratic economies of the richer nations:

> The industrial capacity in the North is under-used, causing unemployment unprecedented in recent years, while the South is in urgent need of the goods that the North could produce. Rapid inflation, erratic exchange rates, and the unpredictable interventions by Governments are seriously disrupting the trade and investment on which an immediate return to world prosperity depends.

In short, the Programme argued, the interests of the rich themselves would best be served by collective action, to increase the prosperity of the poor. The North desperately needed customers, but the South remained too poor to buy. Here lay one of the most urgent problems of the late twentieth century, and one towards whose solution Britain, with its international interests and expertise, was well qualified to work. Here, indeed, was a role in the world for Britain. As the 1980s began, however, the new Conservative government promptly reduced Britain's already limited aid to poor nations, again giving priority to efforts to solve Britain's own economic problems.

Further Reading

Calvocoressi, P.: *The British Experience, 1945–1975*. Penguin (Harmondsworth, 1979).

Loney, M.: *Rhodesia, White Racism and Imperial Response*. Penguin (Harmondsworth, 1975).

Mowat, R.C.: *Creating the European Community*. Blandford (Poole, 1973).

North–South, A Programme for Survival (The Brandt Report). Pan (London, 1980).

Taylor, N. and Richardson, R.: *Change and Choice: Britain in an Interdependent World*. World Development Education Centre (London, 1980).

Watson, J.B.: *Success in Twentieth Century World Affairs*. John Murray (London, 3rd edn. 1984).

Exercises

1. Set down arguments on behalf of the Rhodesian Front to support Ian Smith's demand for independence in 1964. Write a reply to these arguments on behalf of the British government, explaining why independence could not be granted at that time.

2. What do you understand by 'economic sanctions' (page 355)? What were they expected to achieve in relation to Rhodesia, and why did they not achieve it?

3. Trace the history of the efforts made by British governments and others after 1965 to solve the Rhodesian Problem, and explain why legal independence was eventually granted in 1980.

4. Why did Britain not seek to join the European Communities when they were founded? Why did Britain later decide to seek entry, and what does Fig. 20.6 show of the reasons why entry was not achieved until 1973?

5. What evidence in this Unit helps to explain why Britain retained a 'suspicious attitude towards the EEC' (page 368) even after being admitted to membership of it?

6. Explain the importance of *each* of the events commemorated in the stamps reproduced in this Unit (Figs 20.1, 20.5 and 20.9(*a*) and (*b*)).

7. Explain the two views of the Atlantic Alliance put forward by the cartoonists in Figs 20.10(*a*) and (*b*).

8. Making use of the Index to this book, write a review of the career of Harold Wilson to the time of his resignation in 1976. Which of his achievements would an admirer be likely to emphasize? Which of his failures would a political opponent be likely to emphasize?

9. How true is that 'it was the world which changed' rather than 'British foreign policy' (page 370) during the 1960s and 1970s? To what extent had this policy been established by Bevin during the years after the Second World War?

10. What 'role "on the world stage" ' (page 370) had Britain found for itself by the end of the 1970s?

Unit Twenty-one

A Sea of Troubles

21.1 The New Strategy for the 1980s

The government which came to power in Britain at the general election of 1979 was determined to adopt a new strategy for solving the country's problems (see Unit 16.5). Margaret Thatcher, the Prime Minister, and Geoffrey Howe, Chancellor of the Exchequer, believed that postwar governments had interfered too much – supporting the economy, helping 'lame ducks' and shielding people from economic realities – and they argued that previous attempts at regulation by government, based upon Keynesian economic doctrines, had singularly failed to produce a healthy economy or even a healthy society. Conservative policy still had similarities to Heath's, ten years earlier, but in 1979 the 'Iron Lady' set out to try to make sure her regime was much more thorough.

The new government shaped its strategy round several key policies, largely based on the monetarist advice of the economist Milton Friedman and his disciples. Controlling inflation was the priority, and the government hoped to achieve this by tight control of the money supply and reductions in government spending. Cutting public spending would be part of a general reduction in government activity and intervention. All nationalized industries were to be scrutinized closely and, where possible, the government aimed to bring about 'privatization' – transferring assets and work to private enterprise. Ministers expected such changes, combined with a reduction in direct taxation, to unleash the initiative and drive which they considered Keynesian policies had stunted, perhaps even crippled. The British people would now be forced to 'face the consequences of their own actions'. The government would no longer concern itself with prices and incomes, for example: their future levels would simply result automatically from the expected new, highly competitive economy. On the other hand, the government intended to tighten discipline in industrial relations, by introducing new legislation.

Introducing his budget in 1980 Howe declared:

> In the year before the election (of 1979), consumer spending rose by more than 5 per cent. That was much too good to last.

The Conservatives intended to create a new climate of responsibility, where demand would be matched more closely with production. Howe believed that persistently rising consumer demand in the past, unmatched by a similar growth in output, had led to problems that were 'so deep-seated and serious as to make tough policies inescapable'. In the long term, however, increased production would provide a much healthier basis for demand. The goal was hardly new. Twenty years earlier a Report on the British Economy had complained similarly of 'the pressures of demand' and had asserted:

> Increased production would be the most satisfactory way of solving Britain's economic problems.

The Report had also spelled out the consequences of the fact that the country's production failed to keep pace with spending:

> The Government has available a whole armoury of monetary and fiscal measures for the regulation of demand . . . (but these) have not succeeded in . . . preventing strain on resources and consequent price increases and balance of payments crises.

This was even more true in 1980 than it had been in 1960. Table 21.1 shows that output grew only slowly during the 1970s and, although there was some improvement in 'output per person employed' (productivity) – partly because of shrinking 'employment' (fewer employed workers) – 'labour costs' rose sharply.

Table 21.1 Index of British manufacturing industries

	1966	1970	1971	1976
Total output	89.2	100	99.2	103.2
Employment	102.6	100	96.8	87.8
Output per person employed	86.9	100	102.5	117.4
Labour costs per unit of output	83.5	100	109.6	232.0

Source: from *Facts in Focus*, Central Statistical Office.

In Howe's view, and Thatcher's, it was time that the British people felt the cold wind of reality which blew through these and similar statistics. The Chancellor therefore insisted:

> There is need for a much greater public awareness of the link between pay increases, price inflation and unemployment.

In effect, the government would reduce the 'armoury of monetary and fiscal measures' to just one monetarist super-weapon: there would be tight control of the money supply to squeeze inflation out of the economy. At the same time, however, the 'tough policies' would mean less support for businesses in difficulty, especially such nationalized industries as British Rail, less government support for local authority services such as education and council-house building, and less government spending generally. The hoped-for transition to a more competitive Britain coincided, however, with a worldwide recession and the British people were now likely to feel the stick of rising unemployment and a perhaps severe cutback in living standards. The carrot of some reduction in income tax – to make people eager to earn more and thus work more energetically – was another part of the government's

'Good luck, kid – and by the way, there don't seem to be any brakes!'

Fig. 21.1 A greeting from Gibbard in the Guardian to a new year (1980) and a new decade with just some of the problems the world then faced. An assortment of international passengers on the upper deck, and British politicians downstairs – Thatcher and Howe on the front seat; Healey to Thatcher's right and Callaghan behind Howe; Steel, and Anthony Wedgwood Benn, now more commonly known as Tony Benn

strategy, though it was soon undermined by substantial increases in other forms of taxation. These, in turn, again fuelled inflation.

Les Gibbard's cartoon, drawn at the end of 1979 (Fig. 21.1), suggested that the world generally was entering the 1980s without confidence and even without optimism. Mrs Thatcher and Howe, like the other British politicians on the lower deck, faced formidable struggles with Britain's economy. The upper-deck passengers represented something of the uncertain international outlook – Carter seeking re-election to the United States presidency but soon to be defeated, as it turned out; the ageing Brezhnev, whose health was deteriorating; and a host of others, some of whom symbolized the turbulence of the Middle East. Early in 1980 a public opinion poll suggested that about half the British people thought a nuclear war likely during the 1980s, though Britain's erratic economic course yet again provided the most urgent and widespread reason for gloom. Britain faced worsening unemployment against a background of 'World Recession', inflation was again rising and the balance of payments was unstable. On the other hand, at a time of 'Energy Crunch', Britain was now getting the benefit of North Sea oil, which seemed likely to be at the peak of production during the 1980s. Yet that too brought complications. North Sea oil boosted overseas confidence in sterling, pushing up the value of the pound; but this made it harder to sell Britain's exports, all the more so since the Prime Minister's policy was to remove controls on exchange rates, in pursuit of the goal of reduced government involvement.

21.2 Destination Unknown? Conservative Government from 1979

(a) The Economy
The Thatcher government claimed to know where it was taking Britain, but others were less sure. One result of British industry's comparatively low productivity, high costs and dulled competitiveness was the alarming penetration of imported goods into the domestic market. Table 21.2 shows something of the extent of import penetration by 1979 and of how the position had worsened during the 1970s; and John Kent's satirical handstamp (Fig. 21.2) provides telling comment. Only North Sea oil fended off what would otherwise have been enormous balance of payments difficulties. It was not hard to recognize that British industry needed to become more efficient. The Conservatives wanted industry to achieve this goal by pruning surplus labour, resisting inflationary wage settlements, trimming prices in the fight for markets and, at the same time, investing in new technology for the future. The immediate effect of government policy, however, was to raise fears that the Prime Minister's 'cure' might be even worse than Britain's 'disease'. At the beginning of the 1980s the British recession seemed deeper and more severe than recession elsewhere in the world; and there were many critics (some within the Conservative Party) who laid the blame for this at the door of the government, with its insistence on 'tough policies'.

Table 21.2 Import penetration into the United Kingdom, 1979

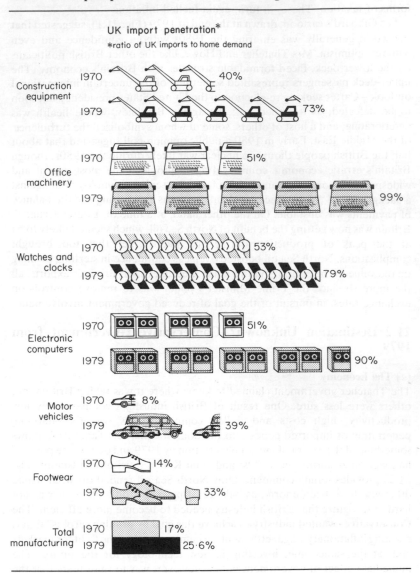

UK import penetration*
*ratio of UK imports to home demand

	1970	1979
Construction equipment	40%	73%
Office machinery	51%	99%
Watches and clocks	53%	79%
Electronic computers	51%	90%
Motor vehicles	8%	39%
Footwear	14%	33%
Total manufacturing	17%	25·6%

Source: the *Guardian*, 21 January 1980.

Inflation soared after the general election of 1979 and the squeeze on the money supply brought unprecedentedly high interest rates even before the end of the year. The Minimum Lending Rate (MLR), soon to be abolished by the

Fig. 21.2

government as smacking too much of official direction, rose to 17 per cent and remained at that level for much of 1980, similar rates returning for a time towards the end of 1981. All borrowing was therefore expensive: mortgage-holders were saddled with an annual interest rate of 15 per cent and businesses suffered far higher rates. Thousands of businesses were driven into bankruptcy, and hundreds of thousands of jobs were lost. Not until summer 1982 was inflation brought down to an annual single-figure increase, then falling sharply towards the end of the year by which time interest rates were tumbling too.

Fig. 21.3 An early result of the government's pursuit of monetarism: Gibbard's cartoon in the Guardian, *November 1979, made unflattering comment on the policies of Mrs Thatcher and her ministers when the Minimum Lending Rate soared to 17 per cent. Howe, the Chancellor, with whip; Whitelaw and Joseph assisting Thatcher in policy-making*

But unemployment rose steadily, climbing above two million in autumn 1980, nearing three million twelve months later (see Table 16.1) and three-and-a-half million by autumn 1982. As usual, it bit most deeply in Northern Ireland and the other poorer areas of the United Kingdom. In July 1982 Northern Ireland's unemployment reached 21 per cent of the labour force, while more than 16 per cent of the workers were without jobs in Scotland, Wales, North-West England and the West Midlands. These 'averages' hid even worse blackspots where, locally, unemployment was well above 30 per cent. The crisis brought acute anxiety about the job prospects for Britain's young people. Many observers argued that the official figures actually underestimated real unemployment, with another half million or more absent from the unemployed register because of factors such as involvement in the Youth Opportunities Programme (YOP). This Programme provided work experience for school leavers who had had no success in finding a job. The government found itself forced to make this provision along with the retraining of older workers, in spite of its preference for being uninvolved.

During 1981 the government also began to set up Enterprise Zones in areas of decay and special need, extending the scheme in 1982. These Zones were much smaller than the Development Areas, carefully pinpointed to try to create jobs by encouraging small businesses. The earlier enthusiasm for massive undertakings was now evaporating and it became a Conservative priority to help small businessmen. Bankruptcies nevertheless multiplied, 6 814 businesses being declared insolvent during 1980 alone – a record number and 50 per cent more than in 1979. About 450 of the failed businesses were in building and construction, with a similar number in engineering and metals; over 370 failed in textiles and clothing, and over 270 in furniture and upholstery.

A major part of the government's strategy, however, was to cut down its own spending and that of other public authorities. This would help to reduce demand and inflationary pressures, but it also tended to deepen the recession. Strict 'cash limits' were introduced and tightened several times, with effects which were felt particularly in the nationalized industries and elsewhere in the public sector. Crisis hit the steel industry first. BSC claimed that it could pay no more than a tiny wage increase, well below the rate of the inflation, without financial help from the government, while plans for modernization threatened thousands more jobs (see Unit 16.1). A prolonged and bitter strike by steelworkers followed during 1980 at the end of which both sides, and the government too, had to compromise. By the end of 1980 BSC had cut its labour force to below 130 000 men. It then produced new plans to axe thousands more jobs. Thatcher and Howe made it clear that this new harsh climate had to be expected; any assistance must be earned by vigorous modernization. But even the 'Iron Lady' could not cut off aid overnight to ailing industries of vital national importance. The National Enterprise Board was allowed to continue for the time being, though a spate of resignations from it suggested that its relations with the new administration were uneasy. In 1981 government subsidies helped to keep alive not only BSC but also British Leyland and British Rail, though they too were forced into new programmes in pursuit of efficiency, BR having to make savage reductions in some of its services and enduring a lengthy strike in 1982 by members of ASLEF. Meanwhile, the nationalized electricity and gas industries were forced to raise their prices to make more profit, and a government plan to sell off gas showrooms to private enterprise led to a new storm of protest among those who worked in the gas industry and some of their customers.

Though protesting that she would not deviate from her policy Mrs Thatcher, like earlier prime ministers, was forced to trim her sails on occasions. Ambitious plans for closing coal pits were hastily toned down in February 1981 when confrontation with the miners seemed imminent. Keith Waite in the *Daily Mirror* promptly marked the occasion with a cartoon called 'The Coal Hole', reminding the Prime Minister, if she needed it, that 'Ted Heath disappeared here'. There seemed, in fact, to be more flexibility in applying 'cash limits' than Thatcher admitted. Nevertheless they brought cuts, economies and some loss of jobs to the public sector. By the end of 1980, while denying it was a wages policy, the government was also trying to reduce pay increases for public-sector workers to a level much below the rate of inflation. This brought confrontation in 1981 with the civil service, whose members bitterly accused the government of breaking agreements. Conflict with some local authorities also developed when the government put pressure on them to cut their spending, partly to try to slow down the rise in local rates, and there were angry denunciations of central government interference in local democracy. Cutbacks in almost all public spending, except that on the police and on defence – a cutback in real terms, given the continuing inflation – brought a deterioration in many public services, adding to the country's 'public squalor' (see Unit 18.1). The National Health Service was forced into stringent economies and assistance to those in need, such as through the provision of Home Helps, was pared down. In 1982 there was bitter conflict between the government and workers in the NHS. Housebuilding by the authorities came near to standstill. Road maintenance declined, grass verges went uncut and public amenities were forced into economies, perhaps by shortening hours as libraries did. Local transport services deteriorated further and there were severe cuts in most sections of the educational services.

Even so, and in spite of persistent cuts in the numbers of civil servants, teachers and other public employees, there were loud complaints that it was the private sector which felt the worst effects of government policy. Industrial production fell alarmingly. In autumn 1980 it had dropped more than 16 per cent compared with 1979 levels and was well below that of the three-day week of 1974. In 1982 production comparisons were with the 1960s, not the 1970s. The GDP also fell, though less markedly (six per cent after two years of Conservative government). Labour forces were reduced and factories closed. Even ICI began to suffer and, with profits slumping, indeed often turning into losses, few businesses could find investment capital for the future. There was new urgency about fears of Britain's deindustrialization – fears that the new realism might well do such irreparable damage to industry, especially manufacturing industry, that it would become too weak ever to recover (see Table 21.3). By the end of 1982, there was still little evidence that Britain would return to achieving even a tiny growth rate.

Not for the first time Britain seemed to have a government of contradictions – not always apparently practising what it preached, not entirely achieving what it expected to achieve from the policies it did practise. Thatcher maintained that there had been too much government in the past and ought to be less, but her government proved meddlesome, affecting the lives of the British people at almost every turn. The government vigorously changed regulations affecting tax and benefits, making the country's social security system even more complicated; it interfered with the financing and functions of local government, with wage negotiations and with arbitration; and with its policy of 'cash limits' it limited opportunities as well as threatening jobs.

Privatization went on apace, the government lining up state-owned assets for sale to private shareholders – particularly the state enterprises which were profitable. The government, for example, sold enough of its shares in British Petroleum (BP) deliberately to wipe out its own controlling interest, half of Cable and Wireless and rather more than that of British Aerospace. The list lengthened: to the National Freight Corporation were added British Shipbuilders, British Airways and, in 1982, Britoil, the country's stake in North Sea oil production about whose sale the Opposition protested fiercely. The Opposition and many people in the country at large were also angered when the idea was floated of abolishing the National Health Service in favour of a system based on private insurance. On this issue the government retreated, at least for the time being, but privatization elsewhere was continued vigorously.

The emphasis was on competition and 'radical restructuring'. The Post Office was divided, one part for posts and another for telecommunications, each losing its monopoly. Private organizations could now compete for postal business, and were expected to do so in areas which were compact and likely to be profitable, while the Post Office was still obliged to handle mail for the nation as a whole, including the remote and unprofitable areas. Private enterprise could also now compete with British Telecom in supplying telecommunications equipment; but, in any case, the government already had plans for selling at least parts of British Telecom, yet another state industry listed for privatization. Bus and coach routes were meanwhile thrown open to private firms, leading to more competition and a price-cutting war in which British Rail too was forced to take part. This benefited the consumer and seemed to demonstrate the virtues of private enterprise but again it ignored the problem of financing the transport services which could never be made profitable and could go unprovided, for example in rural areas. Private firms could choose not to run such services. British Rail and other public authorities had to struggle to operate them for the benefit of society.

Consistently, however, the government hammered away at a central message: that public spending must be cut and that Britain must become more efficient. The Prime Minister repeated over and over again that there was no alternative, but there were many who disagreed, including former Conservative Prime Ministers, Macmillan and Heath. Heath spoke out in the Commons shortly before the end of 1980, urging a less rigid application of government theories. About the same time the CBI grew critical, though some businessmen applauded Mrs Thatcher and resigned from the Confederation. There were also right-wing Conservative MPs who felt that the government ought to go further, noting that for all the upheaval the government had not managed effectively to control the money supply either in 1980 or 1981. Even Friedman was critical, suggesting that this was because the attack on the money supply had been made from the wrong direction – less on the supply of money than on the demand for it. Towards the end of 1981 other monetarist theorists who had advised the government speculated about the errors which their experiment had revealed – the over-hasty abandonment of exchange controls, for example, which had seriously handicapped British industry.

At least Thatcher and Howe remained outwardly confident that all would come right. The Prime Minister derided her critics, including those in her own Party, as 'wets', lacking faith or strong nerves and too ready to abandon the struggle. But it was not clear, in the middle of the government's term of office, what the outcome of Thatcherism would be. The Prime Minister claimed that industry was now 'leaner and fitter', better able to compete with foreign businesses. Exports had indeed fared better than many had expected, and the fall in imports resulting from the recession had helped, with North Sea oil, to avoid balance of payments crises since 1979. On the other hand, the exchange rate fluctuated bewilderingly and exporters often complained that sterling was overvalued. There was little hard evidence to support those who claimed that the recession was ending and that output was about to expand. However, it did seem that 1981–2 had brought marked increases in productivity in many of Britain's industries. It remained to be seen whether this was more than temporary, perhaps brought about by the fear of unemployment. Ian Gilmour, a 'wet' whom the Prime Minister had dismissed from government office, summed up the country's confusion over the economy and the government's strategy, writing in a newspaper article towards the end of 1981 of:

> the results of the Treasury policy, under which everything that should be going up is going down and everything that should be going down is going up.

(b) Industrial Relations

Mrs Thatcher matched her assertion that British industry was becoming

Table 21.3   Some of the main occupations of British workers, 1975 (thousands)

Total labour force	22 707
Male workers	13 533
Female workers	9 174
Total in manufacturing industry	7 488
Metal manufacturing, engineering*	3 883
Textiles, clothing	931
Food, drink, tobacco	726
Chemicals	430
Transport, communications	1 518
Agriculture, forestry, fishing	401
Mining, quarrying	352
Building, construction	1 312
Distributive trades	2 763
Professional services, banking, insurance	4 659
National and local-government services	1 654

* including ship- and vehicle-building

In 1975 manufacturing employed only about a third of Britain's labour force. In the early 1980s there was fear of further decline, with far fewer employed in the manufacturing sector, and the weakening of Britain's industrial base (deindustrialization). The last three entries in this Table show how other sectors of the economy had already grown in relation to manufacturing. (Compare with Table 1.2.)

Source: from *Facts in Focus*, Central Statistical Office.

'leaner and fitter' as a result of her policies with the claim that there were signs of a new realism in industrial relations. Industrial relations were a little less turbulent after the steel strike, the number of days lost through disputes falling in 1980 and again in 1981 (see Table 15.2). Some put this down simply to the widespread fear of unemployment. The figure rose again in 1982, in any case. It remained to be seen whether the change of attitude among workers that the Prime Minister detected was substantial and, if so, whether it would prove durable. Thatcher herself had little use for agreements with the trade unions such as Wilson's 'social contract' of 1974 (see Unit 16.3), and the TUC found itself with less influence on government than at any time since 1945. Meanwhile James Prior, the Employment Secretary, had the job of drafting new industrial relations law, promised at the election of 1979. Prior's inclination was to proceed cautiously and to steer a middle course between cabinet colleagues more hostile to trade unions than he himself was and the unions themselves, who still opposed all new legislation. Howe and Keith Joseph, the Secretary of State for Trade and Industry until he was moved to Education, were reported to be among ministers who wanted more forceful action. Len Murray, General Secretary of the TUC, repeated the union view that 'legalistic intervention in the conduct of industrial relations' could only be 'harmful'. While Prior prepared his Employment Bill, Howe withdrew certain social security benefits from the families of strikers, seeking to transfer such payments to the unions as a way of discouraging strikes.

Prior's Bill had several purposes: to encourage the balloting of union members on issues such as strike action; to give greater protection to individuals in matters connected with closed shops; to weaken existing law on employment protection lest such law discourage employers from taking on workers for fear of being unable to dismiss them; and, above all, to restrict picketing in support of strikes. It was this last which aroused the fiercest controversy. The government aimed to stop 'secondary picketing', that is, picketing of places not involved directly in an industrial dispute. The steelworkers in 1980, for example, tried to stop work at non-BSC plants and to halt the movement of steel (see Fig. 21.4). They also had support from workers outside the steel industry who joined their picket lines. Prior found it difficult to draft law which would make these practices illegal without leading to further confrontation or endangering the basic right of a dissatisfied worker to withhold his labour. When the Employment Act became law, therefore, it remained less precise about picketing and closed shops than hardliners wished. Later in 1980 Codes of Practice were added to try to define further ground rules. Eric Varley, for the Labour Opposition, pronounced them 'provocative', likely to 'worsen good industrial relations', but it was something of a tribute to Prior's moderation that these changes produced no immediate explosion of active resistance. Yet many questions remained unanswered; for example, Prior laid down no maximum number for the pickets on any one site – as Conservative right-wingers often demanded – leaving that to the discretion of the police. When Prior was moved from Employment to take on

Fig. 21.4 Steelworkers picketing the Ford car plant at Dagenham, March 1980, seeking to strengthen the effects of their strike in the steel industry by stopping the distribution of steel to industry. Picketing at factories not directly involved in the original dispute was just one area of industrial relations about which bitter controversy raged

responsibility for Northern Ireland, in autumn 1981, the government had made only limited steps towards changing industrial relations law. Though it made no secret of its hostility to the trade union movement, it had disappointed many of its supporters by relative mildness in this area. Opinion polls went on showing a good deal of popular support for legislation to 'curb' the unions, and the hopes of the right-wing rose again when the Prime Minister chose to replace Prior with Norman Tebbit, a man with an appropriate record of anti-union rhetoric.

Tebbit during 1982 brought in further legislation, for which he inherited preparations bearing the imprint of Prior's moderation. Now the intention was to place further restrictions on the closed shop and to remove some of the 'immunities' which protected trade unions from legal action in connection with industrial disputes. In certain defined areas the government planned to allow employers to sue for damages, for example where losses were sustained as the result of a dispute arising from inter-union squabbling. This was again something less than a violent assault on trade unionism, though more uncompromising ideas went on lurking in the background. Threats to reopen the question of the political levy stirred memories of the Trade Disputes Act of 1927 (see Unit 3.4(*b*)).

(c) **Society**

Although the Conservatives had promised tax cuts at the general election of 1979, the logic of Thatcherism was always that living standards must fall since the British people were living beyond their means. By 1982 small cuts in direct taxation, which mainly benefited the well-to-do, had been more than offset by rises in other taxes and levies, such as Value Added Tax (VAT) and National Insurance contributions. With inflation now generally running ahead of increases in incomes, most people had begun to feel the squeeze; and unemployment had returned to the level of the 1930s. Not surprisingly, the government's popularity at first fell steeply. While placing traditional Conservative emphasis on the Party's ambition of creating One Nation, the government seemed in effect to be presiding over a country whose confusion, bitterness and divisions ran deeper than ever. Whatever the long-term results of Thatcherism, the immediate results were uncomfortable and dispiriting. The government came into conflict with one section of society after another in pursuit of the transformation of Britain in which the Prime Minister and her colleagues believed. Apart from the conflicts already mentioned in this Unit, there was frequent wrangling about issues such as the use of public funds to assist education in private schools, the sale of council houses, the increasing size of lorries and the decreasing size of the nation's fishing fleet. There was also some questioning of the favoured status the government reserved for the armed forces and for the police.

Disquiet and distress attached to the Nationality Act the government brought in in 1981, which created three new categories of citizenship. The first was British citizenship, covering most of those born in the United Kingdom but with certain exclusions which meant that some children born in the UK would not qualify and could be stateless. The other two categories were British Overseas citizenship and British Dependent Territories citizenship. Neither carried any right to settle in Britain, striking a further blow at those who held British passports but whose right of entry had been severely restricted since 1968 (see Unit 17.2(b)). This went much further than the government's first minor amendments to the immigration regulations and it prolonged the unease of Britain's ethnic minorities. It was widely believed that the Act discriminated against non-whites, all the more so when it was amended to give concessions to the people of Gibraltar but not those of Hong Kong, and to extend British citizenship to those born abroad of white descent. Ethnic minorities, most of Britain's churches, political opponents of the Conservatives, Commonwealth governments and even the European Community expressed distaste for the Act – but it became law in the autumn of 1981, further hampering the development of harmonious race relations in Britain (see Unit 21.4(a)).

The 1970s had seen considerable strides towards social equality in Britain in other respects. At the beginning of the 1980s almost all homes had a television set, a refrigerator, a vacuum cleaner and an inside lavatory. Telephones and central heating had also become much more common. The spread of household durables and improvements in housing had benefited women and lightened the burden of housework but, though the admission of women to the Stock Exchange was another milestone, it was too soon to say that the sexes yet shared true equality of opportunity. Moreover, *Inequalities in Health* (the Black Report, 1980), which received comparatively little publicity, pointed to the wide differences which still remained between the classes in Britain in terms of health, life expectancy and infant mortality.

21.3 Destination Unknown? 'Breaking the Mould'

(a) Labour in Opposition

Electoral defeat in 1979 again brought ferment in the Labour Party. Old arguments were reopened; and the left launched a new and determined assault on leadership it thought too conservative and policy it thought too cautious. While Margaret Thatcher seemingly dragged the Conservative Party to the right, Tony Benn (he now preferred to drop Wedgwood) and others tried to drag Labour to the left, towards radicalism and more full-blooded socialism. Something of this had been forecast at the time of the election (see Unit 16.5), though perhaps few would have foreseen the vigour of the assault which the left mounted at the 1980 Labour Party Conference in Blackpool. Conference approved more radical policies – for nuclear disarmament and withdrawing from the European Community, for example – and cheered Benn's war-cry for the abolition of the House of Lords. It also voted to alter the rules for electing the Party's leader and to change the practice of automatically reselecting sitting MPs to fight new elections. There was still personal affection for Callaghan but he emerged much bruised from the Blackpool Conference: there had been heated debate about how the Party's election manifesto was drafted, with thinly veiled criticism that the 1979 manifesto had not been radical enough.

Even Labour's hatred of Thatcherism and Friedmanism was almost submerged in internal wrangling. One group, around David Owen, made a stand to preserve right-wing traditions while another, around Benn, fought to implement left-wing policies. MPs, union leaders and Party members in general seemed deeply divided. Division was not, of course, new in the Labour Party's history, for the Party had always been a rather 'broad church', a coalition of various interests. Now, however, further resignations seemed imminent and there was renewed speculation about the Party's future.

It was no surprise when Callaghan resigned the leadership in autumn 1980. He was nearing seventy and age was against his prospects of successfully leading the Labour Party at the next general election. Healey seemed his most likely successor, but divisions in the Party complicated the issue. There was strong support for the idea that the new leader must be a peacemaker. Healey was broadly on the right of the Party, a formidable parliamentarian, known and quite popular in the country. But he was less popular with the Party's National Executive Committee (NEC), traditionally left-wing and even more influential after the Blackpool Conference. Moreover, the new rules for choosing the leader had not yet been worked out and there was the embarrassing possibility that the choice of Labour MPs could be rejected under whatever new system was adopted in due course. Labour MPs therefore voted for Michael Foot, formerly the deputy leader, a man with a radical past and perhaps fewer personal enemies than the sometimes caustic Healey, whom he narrowly defeated. A veteran of the Campaign for Nuclear Disarmament from its founding in 1958, the biographer and political heir of Aneurin Bevan, Foot seemed an adventurous choice. There was no doubting his hostility to Thatcherism and his passionate loathing of unemployment, the blight of which had often struck his constituency of Ebbw Vale. On the other hand, Foot was only a year younger than Callaghan and seemed sure to be sorely tested in his efforts to control the turbulent Labour Party and reunite it as Wilson had done twenty years earlier.

The turbulence continued in 1981. Benn contested Healey's bid for the deputy leadership, and the right–left struggle again dominated the Party's affairs and the annual conference. Healey won a wafer-thin majority, the voting under Labour's new rules being shared by MPs, trade unions and constituency parties. Many Labour MPs were uneasy with these new arrangements, resenting them as an attempt by the left to weaken the traditional influence of MPs and of the leadership. There was disquiet, too, that union leaders cast votes on behalf of millions of union members with too little certainty as to what those members actually wanted. The left remained critical of the extent to which the Party's rank and file were properly represented by their leaders and spokesmen, while the right continued anxious about the extent to which various sorts of militants and Marxists, such as those in the Militant Tendency, were threatening to take over the Labour Party in the name of 'democracy'. The traditional divisions of the Party were once again on public display.

This time, however, there were serious defections from the Party. Throughout 1981 right-wingers and self-declared 'moderates', MPs and local councillors among them, asserted that they could no longer stomach the activities of left-wing 'extremists'. These people argued that, with Thatcher dragging the Conservatives to the 'extreme' right and Benn and his followers trying to drag the Labour Party to the 'extreme' left, the middle ground of British politics was being left vacant; that this traditional area of Butskellism appealed to the majority of voters; and that there was therefore an opportunity 'to break the mould' of the party system which had existed since the First World War. The Liberals embraced these arguments eagerly. More spectacular was the birth of the Council for Social Democracy, from which grew the Social Democratic Party (SDP).

(b) The Social Democrats
Four dissident members of the Labour Party launched the SDP. One was Roy Jenkins, returning to British politics from the Presidency of the European

Commission. The others were David Owen, Shirley Williams and William Rodgers. At the beginning of 1981 they issued the Limehouse Declaration:

> We propose to set up a Council for Social Democracy. Our intention is to rally all those who are committed to the values, principles and policies of social democracy. We seek to reverse Britain's economic decline. We want to create an open, classless and more equal society, one which rejects ugly prejudices based upon sex, race or religion.

The Declaration outlined the philosophy of the new grouping but details of policy were deliberately left vague, and the question of a Party leader was similarly deferred. Nevertheless, 1981 was a good year for the Social Democrats. They attracted supporters, including a number of sitting MPs. They made an alliance with the Liberals. And they began to win votes, finally winning a parliamentary seat at Crosby, near Liverpool, towards the end of the year, when Shirley Williams (who had lost her Labour seat at the general election of 1979) overturned a Conservative majority of nearly 20 000 to secure a Social Democratic victory in a by-election. Earlier in the year Jenkins had narrowly failed in an attempt to unseat Labour in a by-election at Warrington. Naturally there was controversy about what the votes for the SDP represented. Protest votes against governments between general elections were nothing new in British politics. But some significance perhaps attached to the fact that the Social Democrats were not only winning votes from the Conservatives but also winning recruits from the Labour Party.

By the end of 1981 the composition of the House of Commons had changed somewhat from that resulting from the general election of 1979 (see Table 10.1). There were now 334 Conservatives, 243 Labour MPs, 12 Liberals and 25 SDP MPs, one Independent Labour MP being among the remaining members. There had been remarkably few by-elections since 1979 and only Williams, among the SDP MPs, had got into the House of Commons by that route. Of the rest, twenty-three were deserters from the Labour Party and one a deserter from the Conservatives. Precise details of SDP policy were still elusive, though to change Britain's first-past-the-post system of voting seemed to be part of it. What the SDP principally offered, however, was something different from the simple choice between Conservative and Labour.

Dissatisfaction with the Conservatives and Labour undoubtedly helped the SDP. It was a feature of the early 1980s that there were deep divisions in both the major parties, and there was a ferment of speculation about what new SDP recruits might yet be won. Criticism of Thatcherism was outspoken among the Conservatives, with Edward Heath especially restless. Before the end of 1981 he sharply asserted:

> It must now be obvious that monetarism no longer has any intellectual justification whatever.

He also contradicted the Prime Minister and her Chancellor by denying that the end of the recession was in sight. Heath showed no inclination to leave the Conservative Party, but seemed to encourage the idea that one day he might be willing to work with the SDP in a coalition government. Meanwhile, when the Liberals won the by-election in October 1981 at Croydon North-West, taking the seat from the Conservatives, Jenkins gleefully commented:

> It opens up the prospect of a complete reorientation of British politics with a Social Democrat–Liberal majority government a real possibility, even a probability, after the next general election.

When Williams won Crosby a month later SDP–Liberal euphoria was all the greater, blossoming yet again when Jenkins himself took Glasgow Hillhead in a by-election in March 1982. A few months later, Jenkins was elected leader of the SDP.

In fact, the 'Destination' of British politics was still 'Unknown'. The SDP–Liberal Alliance seemed to grow stronger in preparation for the next general election, but public support showed signs of fading during 1982. Only when the general election came would it be seen whether 'the mould' of the two-party system had been broken by the upsurge of the SDP. But both Conservatives and Labour faced formidable problems in the meantime. For the Conservatives, much would depend on the fortunes of the Thatcher government – fortunes which were dramatically boosted when Britain came into conflict with Argentina over the Falkland Islands in 1982 (see Unit 21.4(b)). In the Labour Party, the outcome of the in-fighting had still to be determined. The Party had already suffered many losses to the SDP, among them former ministers such as Owen and Brown (now Lord George-Brown), and earlier dissidents such as Taverne. It would not be easy for Foot to bring about reconciliation among those – still the great majority – who remained; and it was at least possible that the 'broad church' which had been the Labour Party throughout the twentieth century might not survive another general election, though the Party's right wing rallied during 1982. Politics, like much else in British society in the early 1980s, were in confusion.

21.4 An Age of Strife

(a) Civil Unrest
The United Kingdom did not escape the 'Civil Unrest' Gibbard had forecast at the end of the 1970s (see Fig. 21.1). In Northern Ireland the killings and maimings went on, with little to suggest that solutions to the province's problems were at hand (see Unit 19.2). The tension was heightened, during the first years of Mrs Thatcher's government, by hunger strikes and deaths among IRA and nationalist prisoners in the Maze Prison, Belfast. They demanded political status, to differentiate themselves from 'common criminals', and complained about prison conditions. The government refused

to yield. Starting with Bobby Sands, ten hunger strikers died by the autumn of 1981. Each was a new martyr. Before his death, the electors of Fermanagh and South Tyrone chose Sands to be their MP in a by-election. Another factor which provoked unrest was that Thatcher had talks with the Prime Minister of the Republic of Ireland and the authorities in Dublin. It was not clear what had been discussed, and Protestant suspicions flared. Towards the end of 1981 Enoch Powell alleged that there were secret plans afoot, with the connivance of the USA, to unite Ireland and to betray Northern Ireland's Protestants. Paisley was already protesting loudly, threatening to inflict on Northern Ireland a Third Force which was likely to add still further to the turbulence. Both Catholics and Protestants, therefore, continued restless and resentful.

Atkins made little headway and handed over the Secretaryship of Northern Ireland to Prior in autumn 1981. By that time the 345th British soldier, a Sikh, had died on duty in the province. Late 1981 was a particularly bitter period, made worse when Robert Bradford was murdered by the IRA. Bradford was one of Northern Ireland's Westminster MPs, a hardliner with fiercely Unionist loyalties and a colleague of Ian Paisley. Hardly surprisingly, Bradford's death injected new energy into Paisley's campaigning. It also put extra steam behind the cruelties of the IRA, explosions in summer 1982 causing horrific casualties to cavalrymen and their horses in London. Though there were still many in Northern Ireland who longed for compromise and peace, both seemed distant. Every new atrocity helped to rally support behind the hard men. Northern Ireland was still under direct rule at the end of 1982 while Prior went on struggling to find the key to reconciliation which had eluded his Conservative and Labour predecessors (see Unit 19.2(d)).

'Civil Unrest' had also erupted in England, though not yet with the viciousness that plagued Northern Ireland, except where the latter's problems spilled over, bringing terrorism to other parts of the UK. Early in 1980 there was a sudden upsurge of violence in Bristol. Residents of the poor district of St Paul's, an area of immigrant settlement with absolutely no history of conflict, fought a pitched battle with the police. Arson and looting followed. The country had hardly recovered from this shock when Easter 1980 brought violence in many English seaside resorts, with teenage gangs leaving a trail of wanton damage after outbursts of thuggery. At much the same time football hooligans practised more of their own brand of nihilist confrontation. But there was worse to come in 1981. In April, similar events to those at Bristol occurred on a far larger scale at Brixton, London. For the first time petrol bombs were used on the capital's streets, and there was an almost total breakdown of law and order in the area for a couple of days. Brixton's example triggered off violence and destruction elsewhere. Dozens of cities and towns experienced disorders, the most serious being at Toxteth, Liverpool.

One element common to most of the riots was often very violent hostility to the police. Another was that most of the outbreaks were in areas of deprivation and high unemployment. The Prime Minister, somewhat prematurely, tended to dismiss unemployment as of any relevance, preferring to emphasize

Fig. 21.5 Brixton, April 1981: street violence flares with cars set on fire and, out of picture, confrontations with the police

criminal elements; and it was true that vandalism and theft went hand-in-hand with the riots, and that areas such as Brixton had a history of an above-average level of street crime. Brixton and other disturbed areas also had substantial non-white populations, especially people of West Indian origin. There was little evidence to suggest, however, that the disturbances were race riots in the sense of being confrontations between black and white. Black and white shared common frustrations and miseries in depressed areas like Brixton. The rioters were mixed in race and so too were their victims, though the mainly white police always attracted a special venom in the settlement of old scores, real and imagined.

Public concern about the upheavals led to an inquiry by Lord Scarman. The Scarman Report about Brixton's riots was published in November 1981, and stressed that:

> The failures of the police and of the community leaders neither justify nor excuse the disorder or the terrifying lawlessness of the crowds.

But Scarman had a great deal to say about the police and their relations with ethnic minorities, and made constructive suggestions for future improvement. He also dwelt on the social problems of Brixton and similar inner-city areas, where poor housing, decaying facilities and corrosive unemployment destroyed hope. In particular, he paid attention to racial disadvantage, the disproportionate share of the country's misfortunes borne by the country's non-whites. One controversial recommendation Scarman made was that there should be 'positive discrimination' in favour of Britain's non-whites, to boost their opportunities and to wage war on the disadvantages from which they suffered:

> A policy of direct co-ordinated attack on racial disadvantage inevitably means that the ethnic minorities will enjoy for a time positive discrimination in their favour. But it is a price worth paying if it accelerates the elimination of the unsettling factor of racial disadvantage from the social fabric of the United Kingdom.

It was mainly the responsibility of William Whitelaw, the Home Secretary, to decide what action should follow the Scarman Report.

Whitelaw had other evidence before him. Summer 1981 brought him *Ethnic Minorities in Britain*, a Home Office study of the continuing discrimination against non-whites, especially in employment, which documented extensive racial disadvantage. Another report drew attention to the escalating level of violence of the growing number of racialist attacks on ethnic minorities. There seemed, too, to be a revival of anti-semitism in Britain, causing the Jewish Board of Deputies to express anxiety. The National Front and the British Movement it spawned continued their sinister activities, with the BM seemingly making a special effort to recruit the young for a course of indoctrination in a sort of Nazism. There were, therefore, dark corners in British society in the early 1980s. Enoch Powell did little to encourage harmony when he renewed his prophecies of doom and racial conflict 'on a scale which can only be adequately described as civil war'. The Nationality Act of 1981 added to the anxiety. It was therefore a sad comment on Britain's traditionally tolerant and fair-minded society that Caribbean House, a West Indian organization of which Whitelaw himself was a patron, felt it necessary to begin helping to finance the emigration from Britain of those non-whites despairing of the future the country could, or would, offer them.

(b) External Storms

The deepening 'World Recession' was not the only worldwide problem at the beginning of the 1980s. Those British people who feared a nuclear war were clearly influenced by worsening relationships between the West and the USSR. There had been bitter arguments between President Carter and the Russians in the late 1970s, mainly about Human Rights, and there were problems and delays on the American side over the ratification of the latest US–Soviet agreements on arms limitations. The tension increased late in 1979 when the Russians invaded Afghanistan in response, they claimed, to a request from the Afghan government for help against Western-provoked sedition. Carter angrily denounced the Russian move – and the West went on protesting, while the USSR became entangled in a lengthy struggle to subdue Afghan resistance. It seemed that detente was coming to an end, and the West at least suspected that a new Cold War was beginning.

Mrs Thatcher staunchly supported the USA, claiming confirmation of the suspicions she had already voiced about the USSR (see Unit 20.4(b)). Like Carter she persistently demanded a boycott of the 1980 Olympic Games, held in Moscow. Many British athletes took part nevertheless, though boycotting the official ceremonies.

Carter, meanwhile, faced another problem in Iran, next door to Afghanistan, and Britain again gave him cautious support. A Moslem resurgence in Iran brought to power the Ayatollah Khomeini (seated behind Brezhnev in Fig. 21.1); the Shah was deposed and anti-Western passions unleashed, with the expulsion of foreign oil companies (see Unit 12.2(c)) and revolutionary students seizing the US embassy in Tehran and taking more than fifty Americans hostage. Four British subjects also disappeared into Iranian captivity. Carter tried diplomatic and economic sanctions but the US hostages were not freed until he had lost the presidential election of 1980. Their release coincided with the installation of the new President, the staunchly conservative Ronald Reagan. Three of the four Britons were freed a month later. The Iranian revolution disturbed settled trade patterns and the area became even more disturbed when war broke out between Iran and Iraq. Even the USA could exert little influence over these events, and the USA and Britain together were driven simply to strengthening ties with those countries like Pakistan which were still receptive to their approaches.

President Reagan shared many of Thatcher's views, both about economics and world problems generally. Their personal friendship for a time strengthened the Anglo-American alliance but, at the same time, their sabre-rattling infuriated their critics. Thatcher shielded defence spending from many of the cuts her government was making in Britain, and her readiness to welcome yet more US nuclear weapons on British soil caused controversy. There were storms, too, when she and Reagan came up with the idea of a rapid deployment force for the Middle East, a sort of Anglo-American fire brigade to deal with crises, especially those which might affect the oilfields. There were strong protests by the Arab states and from the Opposition in Britain. Steel, the Liberal leader, accused the government of aspiring to the role of 'uninvited world policeman'. The force was dropped. There was far more support when Thatcher and Carrington, her Foreign Secretary, proposed late in 1981 to take part in peace-keeping operations in Sinai, which the Israelis were evacuating as part of their agreements with Egypt. So far, Britain had had little to do with the moves towards Israeli–Egyptian reconciliation, the spadework having been done by Sadat of Egypt, Begin of Israel and President Carter. But when Sadat was assassinated in 1981, Britain and other European states rallied to keep up the momentum of the peace process he had started.

In 1982, however, Britain became involved in an undeclared war against Argentina. The Argentines had long laid claim to the Falkland Islands, a British dependency in the South Atlantic some eight thousand miles from the UK. About 1 800 people inhabited the Falklands, the descendants of British settlers who much preferred English-speaking British government with its civil liberties to Spanish-speaking Argentine government which some dubbed fascist. Argentina claimed, however, that the Falklands (the Malvinas, their Spanish name) should be under Argentine sovereignty, and that Britain's title to the islands by conquest and occupation a hundred and fifty years ago was invalid. Tiring of diplomatic exchanges which had gone on for many years, the Argentines seized possession of the Falklands early in 1982, finding them only weakly protected. Carrington promptly resigned from the British Foreign Office, accepting responsibility for what appeared to have been negligence on the part of Thatcher's government.

Britain's response to the Argentine invasion was furious. Armed with condemnation of Argentina's use of force by the UN Security Council, the British government dispatched a huge task force to liberate the Falklands, not only in the interests of the inhabitants, but, it claimed, to uphold the rule of law, deter aggression and preserve democracy. The military junta ruling Argentina was denounced as a brutal dictatorship, though Britain was among those who had recently sold weaponry to this same government as valued customers and anti-communists. Critics questioned the likely costs of the British operation in terms of lives and money, and some uneasy memories stirred of Britain's part in the Suez War of 1956. The financial costs of the task force seemed certain far to exceed what would have been needed to resettle the Falkland islanders in comfort elsewhere under British government. But the expedition stirred deep emotions among the British people. Much of the country was swept by a wave of patriotism. Resolute in her determination to regain the Falklands, Mrs Thatcher's popularity and that of her government soared.

On the whole, Britain was well supported in the crisis by its allies. The early international support nevertheless began to evaporate before victory was won. The USA, while expressing great sympathy with Britain, was torn between its American and European alliances so that Reagan acted cautiously. The European Community helped with economic sanctions against Argentina, but there was uneasiness as the military operations went on, and sanctions were rejected by Italy and the Irish Republic. The Spanish-speaking world generally upheld the Argentine cause, and there was lingering suspicion in the world as a whole that the war was about colonialism and old-fashioned prestige as well as about justice and right. By the time Britain had regained possession of all its islands in the South Atlantic, almost 1 800 Argentines, 255 British and three Falkland islanders had been killed. The British government now stationed in the area a garrison much larger than the population of the Falklands, to deter Argentina from further aggression. But the long-term future of the Islands seemed no more settled than during the years of negotiation which had preceded the Anglo-Argentinian conflict. British fighters had shown heroism and a lot of military skill in conducting operations in a hostile environment far from Europe, and during the following months were welcomed back home with great enthusiasm. But an inquiry was set up to find out just how the Argentine invasion and the crisis had come about and, though it seemed that the government's policy was popular in Britain, a substantial minority of the British people was troubled that such a way of settling colonial disputes could still occur in the 1980s.

Lord Carrington and Mrs Thatcher had hoped that the states of the European Community might move closer to a common foreign policy. In spite of the general backing for Britain against Argentina progress was, at best, hesitant. Towards the end of 1982 Europe closed ranks, however, resisting pressure from the USA to withhold supplies from the Soviet Union in connection with a massive pipeline which would bring natural gas from Siberia to western Europe. There was now strain in the relations between Thatcher and Reagan, though Britain continued at the same time to have differences with members of the Community about budget contributions and agricultural policy. The Labour Party, meanwhile, seemed to harden in determination to withdraw from the Community when next in power; and this was one issue on which the SDP and Labour were sharply divided.

Despite the strong lobby which existed on behalf of the poor nations of the world, in the wake of the Brandt Report, the Thatcher government had cut and cut again Britain's programme of overseas aid. In 1979 Britain devoted 0.5 per cent of its GNP to such aid, coming around the middle of the league table of donor countries. There was much external as well as internal criticism when the Conservatives reduced this. On the other hand, in 1981 a further £25 million were found to assist the development of Zimbabwe, where Mugabe was still grappling with the problems of nationhood. Around the same time, independence was at last granted to Belize, with guarantees of British support in case the new country was attacked by neighbouring Guatemala. In other respects, the British government seemed to take the view that national interests should over-ride all other considerations. The selling of arms to Chile was resumed, for example, though the brutal military regime which had seized power in 1973 still ruled there and the Opposition at least thought the ban should continue. The government's encouragement of expanding arms sales as a way of helping the British economy caused unease even before the conflict with Argentina. The world was much over-stocked with weapons, and anxiety about armaments seemed to be increasing again.

A rash of television programmes about nuclear warfare and fallout shelters generated yet more gloom among the British people, some of whom noted that in this area too Britain seemed less well prepared than certain continentals, such as the Swiss. The fears and confusion which beset the world in the early 1980s created a difficult background against which to pursue the Conservative strategy for Britain's survival, and added to the difficulties of the British people in carrying on their daily lives and planning for the future. It was a time of stress, and the tension in society was reflected in various ways, among them increasing deaths from heart disease and rising divorce statistics, the highest in western Europe. Yet there were still many more successful marriages than marriages which failed, and most British people went on absorbing change, adapting and keeping their balance. They were also capable of taking a traditionally humanitarian view of those in need, responding readily and generously, for example, to a terrible famine in east Africa, another in Kampuchea, and earthquakes which devastated much of Algeria and southern Italy.

In many ways the Britain of the 1980s was greatly changed from that of the 1920s and, in an age of seemingly accelerating upheaval, it was likely to change still further by the end of the century. Yet a good deal remained that was distinctively British and, for all the transformation that had taken place, the history of twentieth-century Britain had been of evolution rather than of revolution.

Glossary

ABCA Army Bureau of Current Affairs. ABCA's educational activities, by informing members of the forces about the Beveridge Report, for example, probably influenced the armed forces vote in the general election of 1945.

Abdication The act of resigning office, usually of a king or queen.

Apartheid South African system for separating the races and for separate development of the races.

Arbitration The settlement of disputes through the verdict of a third party.

Authoritarian Not liberal; usually applied to a government or ruler and to the practice of strict discipline and repression.

Balance of payments The relationship between a country's international earning and spending in a given period, usually a year. If more is earned than spent, the country has a *surplus*. If the reverse, a *deficit*.

Bank Rate The rate at which the Bank of England will lend money (technically, at which it will discount bills of exchange). The authorities can raise it to attract foreign money or to discourage a run on the pound, or lower it if the aim is *cheap money* (see below). Bank Rate was renamed Minimum Lending Rate (MLR) in 1972. MLR was abandoned in 1981.

By-election An election to fill a vacancy in the House of Commons or on a local council. Parliamentary by-elections occur between *general elections*.

Cabinet The council of senior ministers which directs government affairs.

Cheap money Money which can be borrowed at low rates of interest.

Closed shop A closed (work)shop is one where all the workers are required to belong to an appropriate and perhaps specified trade union.

Cold War A war fought with propaganda, diplomatic and economic weapons, stopping short of military confrontation: as between the West and the USSR after the Second World War.

Collective security Mutual support to achieve a common system of protection and defence. Each member of an alliance, for example, may undertake to assist the fellow-members of the alliance when under threat.

Comintern The Communist International, 1919–43: a Marxist agency for propaganda and subversion, based in Moscow.

Conscription The compulsory enlistment of individuals for military service.

Constituencies Areas in which elections are held. Each member of the House of Commons is elected in a specific constituency: Lloyd George, for example, was elected at Caernarvon. Slightly different electoral laws distinguish borough constituencies (towns) from county constituencies (larger, often rural areas).

Deflation   The policy of reducing demand, for example by increasing taxation, raising interest rates, reducing government spending. Also a period of falling demand is one of deflation.

Demagogue   A popular leader, usually with powers of oratory, and sometimes one who stirs up dissent.

Democracy   Rule by the people: a system of government which permits the masses some effective influence.

Detente   The easing of strained relations between states; perhaps a thaw after a period of *Cold War*.

Devaluation   A reduction of the value of a currency in terms of other currencies.

Devolution   The handing down of power, usually to a regional authority (see *Home Rule*).

Dominion   Term used to describe the first independent members of the British Commonwealth of Nations, e.g. Canada.

Enosis   A movement for the union of Greece and Cyprus, alarming to Turkish Cypriots.

Federation   A union of states with a central authority, for example, the short-lived West Indies Federation of 1958.

First-Past-The-Post-System   See *Voting*.

Franchise   The right to vote.

Free trade   Trade which is free from *tariffs* and restrictions. The opposite of *Protection*.

GDP   Gross Domestic Product. See *GNP*.

General election   An election to choose new members of the House of Commons in all *constituencies*. Since 1911 British general elections have been required at intervals of not more than five years, though this rule has been suspended in wartime.

Gestapo   Secret state police in Nazi Germany.

GNP   Gross National Product: the money value of the total output of all the units of production, wherever situated, of any one country. GDP (Gross Domestic Product): the money value of the total output within the country.

Gold standard   A country is on the gold standard (for example, Britain from 1925 to 1931) if its central bank will exchange its national currency for gold on demand.

Home Rule   Self-government for a region which nevertheless remains part of a larger political unit. For example, Northern Ireland had Home Rule from 1921 to 1972 while remaining part of the United Kingdom.

Imperial Conferences   Meetings of Prime Ministers of the Dominions and Britain. Imperial Conferences were the forerunners of modern Commonwealth Conferences.

Imperial Preference   Part of a system of *tariffs* whereby preference is given to imperial goods, that is, goods from within a country's empire. Such goods are free of tariffs or are taxed less heavily than foreign goods.

Independence   Freedom. The freedom won by former colonies when the mother country ceases to control them.

Index   A table showing by numbers the relationships between variables. For example, the spending of Country A on education may be expressed as 100 and that of Country

B, spending twice as much, as 200. If Country *C* spends half as much as Country *A*, the spending of Country *C* may be expressed as 50.

Inflation   Rising prices. A period of rising demand. Economists do *not* apply the term to the policy of increasing demand. See *Deflation*.

International Monetary Fund (IMF)   A specialized agency of the United Nations Organization set up in 1945. The IMF provides loans to assist countries in difficulty, especially those faced with serious balance of payments deficits. Much of the funds available to the IMF come from the USA, and the IMF is often alleged to be an instrument for the defence of capitalism.

Invisible (as of exports, trade)   Payments for services which do not include the transfer of goods are said to be for *invisibles*, and include payments such as those connected with insurance, loans, carrying services, tourism. See *Visible*.

Mandates   Mandated territories. Areas placed under the control of selected powers by the League of Nations. Palestine was a mandated territory placed under British rule.

Minimum Lending Rate   See *Bank Rate*.

Multi-cultural   With several cultures, as in a multi-cultural society.

Multinational   Involving several nationalities or countries. Multinational companies have interests in several countries other than that in which they may be based, for example, multinational oil companies.

Multi-racial   Involving several races, as in a multi-racial association such as the Commonwealth.

Nationalism   Pride in one's country or nation; enthusiasm for the country's success. Nationalism may take various forms, for example a campaign to free one's country from foreign rule or a movement to make one's country supreme over others.

Nationalization   Converting into national property; placing under state ownership and supervision. For example, the nationalization of the coal industry in Britain transferred the industry from private owners to the state, to be administered by the National Coal Board.

National Income   Similar to *GNP*, with a reduction for depreciation.

Organization for European Economic Co-operation (OEEC)   Founded in 1948 with Britain as a founder-member. It was extended in 1961 to become the Organization for Economic Co-operation and Development (OECD).

Productivity   A measure of output. Rising productivity means that there is increasing output in relation to a unit of input, such as a worker.

Proportional Representation   See *Voting*.

Protection   A system of *tariffs* to protect home industries against foreign competition. The opposite to *Free trade*. See also *Imperial preference*.

Protocol   A diplomatic statement, perhaps of an agreement.

Radar   Radio Detection and Ranging: a system of locating and identifying by using radio waves.

Radical   Enthusiastic for major change, for reform; generally the opposite to *reactionary*.

Reactionary   Backward-looking, opposed to change.

Real (as of wages, growth)   The measure after allowance has been made for distorting factors due to inflation. The price of an article may rise in a given period from, say,

£100 to £200, an apparent rise of 100 per cent. But purchasing power may also rise in the same period by 100 per cent, making the *real* rise in price nil.

Referendum (plural, referenda) A vote by people in a given area on a particular question.

Reparations Compensation for injury, damage; payment to make good a loss for which the one paying is responsible.

Reserves (of gold or foreign currency) The gold or foreign currency available within a country to meet foreign debts. There is often a relationship between a country's reserves and the confidence in that country of foreign financiers.

Rhodesia After 1964 it became usual to refer to Southern Rhodesia simply as Rhodesia since Northern Rhodesia at that time took the African name, Zambia. At independence in 1980, Rhodesia took the African name, Zimbabwe.

Sanctions Penalties. Methods with which to put pressure on those guilty of unpopular acts. Economic sanctions involve restrictions on trade and financial dealings. Military sanctions involve the use of armed forces.

Sectarian Relating to groups identifiable on mainly religious grounds.

Sinn Fein A fiercely nationalist Irish political movement founded in 1902.

Sterling area A group of states whose members tied their currencies to the pound (sterling) rather than to gold or the dollar, and who kept their reserves with the Bank of England.

Suffrage The right to vote. For example, adult suffrage – the right of all adults to vote.

Syndicalism A movement for securing power by trade union action. (French *syndicat*: trade union.)

Tariffs Duties (taxes) on imports. See *Protection.*

Visible (as of exports, trade) Trade in merchandise is said to be *visible* trade. See *Invisible.*

Voting Voting in British elections is by secret ballot. The *First-Past-The-Post-System* (simple majority system) means that victory goes to the candidate with most votes, no regard being paid to whether his vote reaches any required minimum. The claim has often been made that this is 'unfair' and that, in a variety of ways, the system could be changed to relate victory to the real wishes of the voters – for example, elected MPs could be 'in proportion' to the votes cast for their parties. *Proportional Representation* is a general term for various such systems, all of which are more sophisticated than the *First-Past-The-Post-System.*

War Loan Stock in exchange for loans to the government during the war of 1914–18. No date was fixed for the repayment of these loans and so the stock is held indefinitely.

Welfare State A state with comprehensive social services and social security system – services in health and education, for example, and a system (often by national insurance) to provide benefits in sickness, old age and times of unemployment.

Zionist Supporting the colonization of Palestine by the Jews and the re-establishing of a Jewish nation there.

Bibliography

Further Reading has been suggested at the end of each Unit. The following books will be found useful on the period as a whole.

General Histories
Bartlett, C.J.: *A History of Postwar Britain, 1945–1974*. Longman (Harlow, 1977).
Gayler, J.L., Richards, I. and Morris, J.A.: *A Sketch-map Economic History of Britain, 1880–1939*. Harrap (London, 1957).
Havighurst, A.F.: *Modern England, 1901–1970*. Cambridge University Press (Cambridge, 1976).
James, R.R.: *The British Revolution, British Politics from Asquith to Chamberlain, 1914–1939*. Methuen (London, 1978).
Marwick, A.: *Britain in the Century of Total War – War, Peace and Social Change, 1900–1967*. Penguin (Harmondsworth, 1970).
Mowat, C.L.: *Britain Between the Wars, 1918–1940*. Methuen (London, 1968).
Seaman, L.C.B.: *Post-Victorian Britain, 1902–1951*. Methuen (London, 1966).
Sked, A. and Cook, C.: *Post-War Britain, A Political History*. Penguin (Harmondsworth, 1979).
Taylor, A.J.P.: *English History, 1914–1945*. Oxford University Press (London, 1965).

Documentary Collections
Bettey, J.H.: *English Historical Documents, 1906–1939*. Routledge (London, 1967).
Evans, L. and Pledger, P.J.: *Contemporary Sources and Opinions in Modern British History*. Warne (London, 1967).
Hay, J.R.: *The Development of the British Welfare State, 1880–1975*. Arnold (London, 1978).
Lane, P.: *Documents on British Economic and Social History, 1870–1939* and *1945 1967*. Macmillan (London, 1968)
Lane, P.: *British History 1914–1980*. Documents and Questions 3. John Murray (London, 1981).
Watkin, B.: *Documents on Health and Social Services, 1834 to Present Day*. Methuen (London, 1975).
Wroughton, J.: *Documents on British Political History, 1914–1970*. Macmillan (London, 1973).

Thematic and Miscellaneous
Adelman, P.: *The Rise of the Labour Party, 1880–1945*. Longman (Harlow, 1972).
Adelman, P.: *The Decline of the Liberal Party, 1910–31*. Longman (Harlow, 1982).
Aldcroft, D.H.: *The Inter-War Economy, Britain 1919–1939*. Batsford (London, 1971).

406   Success in British History since 1914

Breach, R.W. and Hartwell, R.M.: *British Economy and Society, 1870–1970*. Oxford University Press (London, 1972).
Bruce, M.: *The Coming of the Welfare State*. Batsford (London, 1972).
Cook, C.: *A Short History of the Liberal Party, 1900–1976*. Macmillan (London, 1976).
Cook, C. and Ramsden, J.: *Trends in British Politics since 1945*. Macmillan (London, 1978).
Coogan, T.P.: *The I.R.A*. Fontana (London, 1980).
Craig, F.W.S.: *British Parliamentary Election Statistics, 1918–1970*. Political Reference Publications (London, 1971).
Craig, F.W.S.: *British Parliamentary Election Results, 1950–1970*. Political Reference Publications (London, 1972).
Cross, C.: *The Fall of the British Empire*. Hodder and Stoughton (London, 1968).
Douglas, R.: *The History of the Labour Party, 1895–1970*. Sidgwick and Jackson (London, 1971).
Fraser, D.: *The Evolution of the British Welfare State*. Macmillan (London, 1973).
Gilbert, B.B.: *British Social Policy, 1914–1939*. Batsford (London, 1973).
Harris, J.: *The Welfare State*. Batsford (London, 1973).
Hodder-Williams, R.: *Public Opinion Polls and British Politics*. Routledge (London, 1975).
Lewis, P.: *The Fifties*. Heinemann (London, 1978).
Lindsay, T.F. and Harrington, M.: *The Conservative Party, 1918–1979*. Macmillan (London, 1979).
Marwick, A.: *Class, Image and Reality*. Collins (London, 1980).
Northedge, F.S.: *Descent from Power, British Foreign Policy 1945–1973*. George Allen and Unwin (London, 1974).
Palmer, A.: *Dictionary of Twentieth-Century History*. Penguin (Harmondsworth, 1979).
Pelling, H.: *The British Communist Party*. Black (London, 1975).
Phillips, G.A. and Maddock, R.T.: *The Growth of the British Economy, 1918–1968*. George Allen and Unwin (London, 1974).
Pollard, S.: *The Development of the British Economy, 1914–1967*. Arnold (London, 1969).
Rayner, E.G., Stapley, R.F. and Watson, J.B.: *Evidence in Question – British Social and Economic History since 1760*. Oxford University Press (London, 1980).
Seabrook, J.: *Unemployment*. Quartet (London, 1982).
Shlaim, A., Jones, P. and Sainsbury, K.: *British Foreign Secretaries since 1945*. David and Charles (Newton Abbot, 1977).
Stapley, R.F., Rayner, E.G. and Watson, J.B.: *Evidence in Question – British History 1815–1951*. Oxford University Press (London, 1980).
Van Thal, H.: *The Prime Ministers, Russell to Heath*. George Allen and Unwin (London, 1975).
Watson, J.B.: *Success in European History 1815–1941*. John Murray (London, 1981).
Watson, J.B.: *Success in Twentieth Century World Affairs*. John Murray (London, 3rd edn. 1984).
Watson, J.B.: *The West Indian Heritage*. John Murray (London, 1979).
Wilson, E.: *Only Halfway to Paradise, Women in Britain, 1945–1968*. Tavistock (London, 1980).
Wood, S.: *The British Welfare State 1900–1950*. Cambridge University Press (Cambridge, 1982).
Woodcock, G.: *Who Killed the British Empire?* Cape (London, 1974).

Index

Note: Bold numbers indicate principal references. Italic numbers indicate illustrations and tables. Abbreviations used in this Index: d. = year of death; r. = years of reign; FWW = First World War; SWW = Second World War; PM = Prime Minister.